What Is Asian American Biblical Hermeneutics?

INTERSECTIONS

Asian and Pacific American
Transcultural Studies

Russell C. Leong
General Editor

What Is Asian American Biblical Hermeneutics?

● ● ● ● ● ● ● ● ● ● ● ● ● ● ● ● ● ● ●

Reading the New Testament

Tat-siong Benny Liew

University of Hawai'i Press
Honolulu
In association with UCLA
Asian American Studies Center
Los Angeles

Library of Congress Cataloging-in-Publication Data
Liew, Tat-Siong Benny
    What is Asian American biblical hermeneutics? : reading the
New Testament / Tat-Siong Benny Liew.
        p. cm.
    Includes bibliographical references and index.
    ISBN 978-0-8248-3162-2 (pbk. : alk. paper)
    1. Bible. N.T.—Criticism, interpretation, etc. 2. Asian Americans—
Religion. 3. Theology, Doctrinal. I. Title.
    BS2361.3.L54 2008
    220.6089'95073—dc22

                                           2007044637

Designed by University of Hawaiʻi Press production staff
Printed by Versa Press, Inc.

To my extended family in Hong Kong
for staying with me
despite the passing of time
and the separation in distance

Contents

Preface

As it is often the case in my experience, this research project on Asian American biblical hermeneutics has led me into seemingly endless searches. Searching and re-searching on this academic *and* social project for the last ten years have been rewarding for me. I can only hope that my readers will also find my end product at this point in time helpful and constructive.

Generally speaking, this book has three foci. The question of "methodology"—or more precisely, what constitutes the distinguishing characteristics or sensibilities of Asian American biblical hermeneutics—preoccupies the first two chapters. The next three chapters of the book focus on the issue of community, or the politics of inclusion and exclusion. Finally, the last three chapters will center on exploring agency. Since (1) the entire book is concerned with demonstrating what Asian American biblical hermeneutics will look like in practice, and (2) considerations of both community and agency are intricately intertwined with questions of identity, it should come as no surprise that these three foci of the book are, in a sense, present in every single chapter. Put differently, the way I have specified the divisions above functions more like a heuristic guide or orientation. As we all know, orientation, like generalization, is always helpful, but it is seldom accurate in every single detail. I myself tend to see Chapter 5 as a pivotal chapter; a shift is detectable in that chapter, not only from the issue of community to that of agency, but also from a discussion of ethnicity to one of racial relations in the Greco-Roman world.

This book on Asian American biblical hermeneutics has two more general characteristics. First, it covers all of the major genres found within the New Testament. While Chapters 2 and 3 deal with the Gospels of Mark and of John respectively, Chapter 4 has to do with Acts; after giving attention to Paul's (first) letter to the Corinthians in both Chapters 5 and 6, I will move onto Revelation, or the mode of apocalyptic writing and thinking, in Chapter 8. I should also point out that while Chapters 2 through 6 contain my own reading of specific biblical texts, Chapter 7 concerns my reading of another Asian American writer's reading of the Bible (mainly Matthew and John), and Chapter 8 broadens biblical hermeneutics to cover not only literary texts (biblical or otherwise), but also films and events like genome research and September 11.

Second, this book is intentional in affirming Asian America as a panethnic coalition and acknowledging the differences within that very same coalition. As a result, five of the chapters (Chapters 1, 3, 5, 6, and 8) talk about the broader Asian America in general (and in ways that go beyond East Asian America), but two (Chapters 2 and 4) discuss Chinese America and one (Chapter 7) deals with Korean America in particular. I do so not only because the dominant culture continues to dismiss the heterogeneity of Asian America, but also because I want to be sensitive to the charge of "ethnic monopolizing" that other Asian Americans have levelled against Chinese Americans (Ono 1995: 71). This question of Asian American pan-ethnicity *and* heterogeneity—or that of balancing identity politics and coalition building—is very important; readers who are interested in reading more might find a more positive prognosis in Espiritu 1992, a more negative evaluation in Ono 1995, and a challenge to balance the two in Koshy 2000.

Since my book will focus on the "whats" and the "hows" of Asian American biblical hermeneutics, let me address here the important question of "why." This question becomes even more pertinent since a recent and lengthy review by three scholars of Uriah Y. Kim's Asian American reading of the Deuteronomistic History within the Hebrew Bible (2005) has questioned several times why one should put the Bible and its interpretation alongside Asia America in the first place (Lipschits, Shavit, and Sergey 2006). In Chapter 2, I will talk about how, despite the disciplinary habit to ignore or dismiss religion within Asian American studies, religion in general and the Bible in particular have been used to racialize and colonize Chinese (as well as other Asians) as a race of "heathens," and are thus important to investigate. Since Uriah Kim's reviewers acknowledge that he has provided a related reason (the place and role of the Bible in the United States) but obviously consider it to be inadequate given their persistence in posing the question, I will provide some additional responses here to why the Bible and Asian America might or even should come together.

A simple but significant reason is that Asian American communities and Bible-reading communities, despite the "race-of-heathens" construction, are not only *not* mutually exclusive but also actively overlapping. To put it a little more aggressively, while those whose communities and/or contexts have been institutionally and/or socio-culturally legitimated to read the Bible might feel the "right" to patrol the boundaries and demand from others an explanation of their use of the Bible, there is no racial/ethnic and/or disciplinary monopoly over the Bible and its interpretation. In fact, the burden of the "why-the-Bible" question seems to deny the fact that persons may have multiple identities and belong to multiple communities. Instead of living in a hermetically sealed and sealed-off community (in racial/ethnic and/or disciplinary terms), Asian Americans and Asian Americanists may also be Christians and/or critics who read the Bible for faith and/or professional reasons. Despite the discomfort and/or disorientation on the part of those who have been "legitimated" to read the Bible, biblical interpretation does come from multiple, internally diverse, and externally traversing communities. Putting the Bible and Asian America together only becomes suspect if one erases or suppresses (1) how the two have been mixed in the past and in the present, and (2) how many recent monographs and anthologies have appeared to point, respond, and contribute to that long-standing and on-going liaison (see, for example, Yang 1999; Liew and Yee 2002; Matsuoka and Fernandez 2003; Jeung 2005; Foskett and Kuan 2006). Since the focus of my own constructive project within this book is less genealogical, I will suggest that as long as Asian Americans are reading the Bible—despite for how long and for what reasons—Asian American biblical hermeneutics becomes not only legitimate but also compelling. This is so because as soon as one is able to see that Asian American communities and Bible-reading communities are not mutually exclusive, one will need to deal with the mutually constitutive relations between reading and identity. As David L. Eng argues, questions of canon are important because what one reads help construct who one is (1998: 13–17). Of course, the relations between reading and being go both ways—so, to borrow from the title of a recent anthology on Asian American biblical interpretation (Foskett and Kuan 2006), different ways of being may lead to alternative ways of reading, and readers are never passive reflections of what they read—but the point here is that reading matters. One should, as Eng implores, never underestimate the interpellative or performative force that the subject matters of one's reading might have on the development of a reader's subjectivity and identity. If Asian Americans are reading the Bible, then we must talk about not only the implications of what they read, but also how they read.

There is a sense, therefore, in which Asian American biblical hermeneutics is but a symptom of the globalized world. At the same time, putting together the Bible and Asian America should also be understood as a deliberate move. At the end of Chapter 2, I will suggest that Asian American biblical hermeneutics is—again, in light of the "race-of-heathens" construction—a form of "talking back." Just as Asian American biblical hermeneutics should not be viewed as a mere symptom, this form of "talking back" is also not only reactive. Precisely by putting together what many might see as "disparate" elements, Asian American biblical hermeneutics has the positive potential and purpose to interrogate many assumed understandings and practices, whether they concern biblical hermeneutics or Asian America. Assembling the Bible and Asian America, in other words, is an intentional attempt to appropriate a cultural canon in order to re-create and transform multiple cultures through a form of multicultural critique. (In addition to understanding culture here as internally diverse and externally traversing, it should also be understood in ways that are other or more than racial/ ethnic.) The Bible is particularly good for this purpose not only because of its canonical status but also because it is a collection of texts that was first written by the colonized but then has become instrumental for colonization. Put differently, the Bible is—as I hope the pages of this book will help make evident—a fascinating library of texts that pose issues and raise questions concerning multiple and interlocking differential relations of power. Given its status and history, the Bible is therefore particularly good to "think with." "Thinking with" the Bible means not only that the Bible in no way determines or dictates one's thought, but also that the Bible itself remains open because of the points of departure that it provides for its readers. If I may adopt what Stuart Hall says about another text, the Bible in this sense becomes "an *open text*, and hence a text we are obliged to go on working *on*, working *with*" (1996: 34; emphasis in original).

Just as "Asian American" threatens the apparent divide between "Asia" and "America," Asian American biblical hermeneutics might put into crises more binary assumptions, purity obsessions, and unity illusions. I have in mind here not only questions surrounding the ownership of the Bible, but also those about origins. While it is standard to situate the Bible in Palestinian soil and within the Jewish heritage, the very word "Asian" uncannily brings back echoes that the so-called biblical land was often referred to—for instance, by Greeks and Romans between fifth century B.C.E. and fifth century C.E.—as "Asia" or "Asian" (Okihiro 1994: 7–12). Just as Egypt is often separated from its North African location, so "Asia" is now generally considered to be apart from rather than a part of the "biblical" landscape. Perhaps herein lies the heart or the threat of Asian America in general and Asian American biblical hermeneutics in particular: both gesture towards an "other" who might also be part of the self. It challenges "closure" by stirring up forgotten histories or stories, and/or by shaking up what has long been accepted as "self-evident." It is my hope, as I will further elaborate in Chapter 1, that the intellectual work of theorization or defamiliarization through one's reading of the New Testament *might* usher in a new political will, or perhaps even a different political vision and program.

(This critique of "closure" or intellectual defamiliarization is also particularly important in light of the context of Uriah Kim's three reviewers: they are all situated in Tel Aviv, Israel. The late Edward W. Said has suggested, through a reading of Sigmund Freud's reading of Moses as an *Egyptian* founder of the Jews, that troubling identity and purity might be key not only to diasporic existence but also to a future when Jews and Palestinians might peacefully co-exist [2003: 50–55; see also Bailey 1995]. Once again, I hope one can see how questions about the "whys" of Asian American biblical hermeneutics are—like its "whats" and "hows"—also inseparable from issues of identity, community, and agency. More immediately, I hope one can see that race/ethnicity is a significant factor in one's reading of the Bible, and what seems to be an illegitimate, impure, or improper mixing might actually herald and help bring about the coming of the imponderable or impossible.)

Are there other texts that Asian Americans and/or Asian Americanists can "work *on*" and "work *with*" to critique the unequal power dynamics of race/ethnicity and other interlocking power differentials and/or help construct a different vision? Of course there are; a quick glimpse of the numerous books that have been published under the rubric of "Asian American studies" will confirm that. In addition to the happenstance that I am a biblical critic by profession, I have suggested that the Bible's canonical status and contents in general, and its history within and crossings into Asian America in particular, make it one potentially provocative and productive site of intervention. There is, however, also an undeniable link between hermeneutics—ancient as well as contemporary—and the Bible (Bruns 1992; Jasper 2004). Reading and identity are, as I have pointed out, mutually constitutive, but the theory and practice of reading are also themselves deeply rooted in the reading of the Bible. Just as the Bible and Asian Americans are not necessarily strangers to each other, so the four words that make up "Asian American biblical hermeneutics" also belong together, even if the term—like Asian America—may look jarring at first glance.

Parts of this book have appeared elsewhere, although these "original" publications have all been revised, expanded, and/or adapted. Chapter 2 was first published in Brill's *Biblical Interpretation* 9 (2001): 309–335; Chapter

3, as "Ambiguous Admittance: Consent and Descent in John's Community of 'Upward Mobility,'" in *Postcolonialism and the Gospel of John: Travel, Space and Power,* ed. Musa W. Dube and Jeffrey L. Staley (New York: Sheffield Academic, 2002), 193–224; and Chapter 4, as "Acts" in *Global Bible Commentary,* ed. Daniel Patte, J. Severino Croatto, Nicole Wilkinson Duran, Teresa Okure, and Archie Chi Chung Lee (Nashville, TN: Abingdon, 2004), 419–28. A section of Chapter 7 has come from "Margins and (Cutting-)Edges: On the (Il)Legitimacy and Intersections of Race, Ethnicity, and (Post)Colonialism," in *Postcolonial Biblical Criticism: Interdisciplinary Intersections,* ed. Stephen D. Moore and Fernando F. Segovia (New York: Continuum, 2005), 114–65. I am grateful to these publishers for kindly granting me the permission to reprint.

Since a major portion of my writing and rewriting for this book was done when I spent my sabbatical as a Visiting Scholar at the Department of Cultural and Religious Studies and the Divinity School of the Chinese University of Hong Kong, I want and need to thank the administrators and trustees of Chicago Theological Seminary for that sabbatical leave, as well as many old and new friends in Hong Kong, especially Lung Kwong Lo and Archie Lee of CUHK. It so happened that a month before I assumed my role as a Visiting Scholar there, my mother passed away in Hong Kong. My semester-long return to Hong Kong after moving to the United States two decades ago thus turned out to be both nostalgic and melancholic. (It is perhaps little wonder that I ended up writing about Paul's melancholia over Jesus' death in Chapter 6.) In any case, I know full well that this new time that I spent in an old place has been invaluable not only to my grieving, but also to my belief that separation in time and space—because of life and/or death—does not necessarily sever relations. (I should have known this, given my continual interest and investment in an ancient book written in Koine Greek, which is a "dead" language for many who nevertheless keep on viewing this same book as "sacred" and "life-giving.") For this reason, I am dedicating this book to my extended family that has remained in Hong Kong *and* with me in spite of my relocation across the Pacific. I am blessed to be a part of such an international family.

As always, I owe almost everything to Pam and Aaron. Pam, I think or I hope, knows why; I trust that Aaron will also learn to know the reasons in due time . . . wherever he may be.

What Is Asian American
Biblical Hermeneutics?

CHAPTER I

What Is Asian American Biblical Hermeneutics?

● ●

Medi(t)ations on and for a Conversation

Henry Louis Gates, Jr., has related his puzzlement when he found out as a student that the Nobel laureate Wole Soyinka's appointment at the University of Cambridge had gone through a curious circuit. Originally Soyinka was supposed to have been appointed to the faculty of English, but since that faculty did not recognize African literature as a legitimate area of study, he was appointed to the faculty of social anthropology instead. Gates remembers asking his tutor about this development, at the same time expressing his own desire to one day write a doctoral dissertation on "black literature." According to Gates, his tutor, with "great disdain," responded to the inquiry with a telling question of his own, "'Tell me, sir, . . . what *is* black literature?'" (1992: 88; emphasis in original).

This kind of "what-is" question emerges not only out of ridicule and ignorance. I remember having lunch several years ago with a senior Asian American Bible scholar. As we were chewing and chatting, we began to talk about a recent attempt made by another Asian American scholar to construct an Asian American theology. Suddenly my lunch partner, whose work I greatly respect and admire, said in all seriousness, "I would like to know what is Asian American about that theology, and what is theological about that construction." Racial/ethnic minority scholarship often finds itself facing a crisis of legitimacy from both friends and foes.

My friend might not realize this, but his statement over the lunch table that day has been haunting me ever since. This chapter should be read amid the echo of his bipartite question.

1

Before My (Ad)Venture

Let me state, however, several caveats before I venture to consider what is "Asian American" and what is the "biblical hermeneutics" in Asian American biblical hermeneutics. First, I want to highlight the complicated negotiations that I face with the task ahead. On the one hand, Asian American biblical hermeneutics involves the convergence of different fields, of which the most obvious are, of course, Asian American studies and biblical studies. I am aware that, from the perspectives of these fields, I am liable to be regarded as an "insider" or "outsider," depending on the person making the evaluation. On the other hand, I also feel very keenly that in what I am about to do I may be viewed as an anthropologist and a native informant simultaneously. Later, I will have more to say about this view. Right now, let me focus on my own ambivalent feelings about my task. I am fashioning an account of an ongoing conversation, in which I am only one participant, so that afterwards a larger community can join in for another conversation. This larger community is made up of many people who are both the object and the subject of Asian American biblical hermeneutics. In other words—and this is my second caveat—my ideas do not represent the views of all Asian Americans; they are meant to stimulate multiple projects simultaneously rather than to suggest a single project of a monolithic dimension or direction. Or, in the vocabulary of Sharon K. Hom, what I offer are "prefigurative" rather than "prescriptive" (2001: 81, 97–98) remarks. "Prefigurative" is a term Hom borrows from Maureen Cain and Christine B. Harrington, for whom the adjective describes practices that are not about ordaining what "ought" to be followed, but about opening up other options and opportunities for the purpose of helping to level the playing field (1994: 8). My final caveat is that, following from this "prefigurative" emphasis, readers will not find in this book project anything like an "epilogue" or a "conclusion" at the end. Instead, the onus or demand will be on the reader to decide what he or she should do or pursue next.

Inventing a Tradition: Referencing without Referentiality

The fact that "prefigurative" has to do with power differentials is significant, because Asian American biblical hermeneutics is at least partly about giving a group of people recognition, rights, privileges, responsibilities, and obligations within the discipline of biblical studies as well as that of Asian American studies. The term "discipline" is, of course, suggestive of Michel Foucault's argument about knowledge and power (1980). Asian

American biblical hermeneutics, like Asian American studies, is coded as "(multi)cultural" or "racial/ethnic." As such, it is in need of explanation and justification. In contrast, longer-established biblical hermeneutics, though developed and practiced mainly by whites, have no need of any racial/ethnic label. This assumed legitimacy, when placed alongside the crisis of legitimacy confronting Asian American biblical hermeneutics, effects a different kind of "higher" and "lower" criticism that white-washes, baptizes, or sanctions "an institutionalization of racialization of intellectual labor . . . resulting in an aristocracy and a subordinate class in terms of the production and dissemination of 'knowledge'" (Chow 1998: xvi).[1] Put differently, the racial/ethnic label "Asian American" simultaneously facilitates and frustrates "visibility," "diversity," and "inclusivity" through an insidious ideologic of minoritization.

What, then, is "Asian American" about Asian American biblical hermeneutics, given its potential to define and delimit simultaneously? Conventionally, this has been a debate of "who" and "what," with "Asian American" as arguably a descriptive or demographic term that refers to bodies that have been racialized as Asian in the United States, and/or a political term that signifies Asian-raced bodies committed to opposing racialized oppression in the United States (Chuh 2003: 116; Radhakrishnan 2001: 253). Translating these two understandings for our purposes, one would be inclined to suggest that Asian American biblical hermeneutics is biblical hermeneutics done by Asian-raced persons from the United States, and/or biblical hermeneutics done with the explicitly political goal of helping to address issues confronting Asian American communities.

The simultaneous use of these two different, though overlapping, renditions of "Asian American" have, however, been a source of both confusion and conflict among Asian Americanists. With recent demographic and political changes within Asian America, both meanings have increasingly become targets of criticism.

There is no question that the "Asian American Movement" (Wei 1993) started as a politically progressive movement in the 1960s to resist the "Asiatic racialization" of the forever foreign and utterly unassimilable "Orientals" (Gotanda 2001), and to protest the imperialist advance of the United States against Asian countries like Vietnam. Since then, Asian America has not only become more diverse in terms of ethnicity,[2] but its internal politics have also become more diverse and contentious. Just one example is the controversy of the Asian American Studies Association's decision to award Lois-Ann Yamanaka's *Blu's Hanging* (1997) as "best fiction" at its 1998 annual conference. That decision resulted in an embarrassing rescinding of the award, as well as the resignation of the association's entire executive board. This incident has now—after the Frank Chin–Maxine Hong Kingston debate—become the *next* "most protracted and notorious" (Cheung 1997a: 10) controversy in the history of Asian American studies.

If the Chin-versus-Kingston debate had to do mainly if not entirely with the conflict between a masculinist heroism and feminism (Cheung 1990), the debacle involving Yamanaka centered on the Japanese American novelist's racist representations of Filipino Americans as being cruel to animals and sexually abusive of children.[3] The diversity question—in terms of not only gender and ethnicity but also class, generation, nativity, and sexuality—has thus helped to pinpoint the false differentiation between a "descriptive" and a "political" understanding of the term "Asian American." Who embodies or represents the description of an Asian American is itself always already a political question. This is particularly problematic for self-identifying Asian Americans who are bi- or multi-racial, and are thus capable of "passing" the disciplinary eye of Asiatic racialization or description. The same is true for those who practice "flexible citizenship" (Ong 1999), which has become more characteristic of Asian/Americans since the 1960s.[4] How does one categorize these Asian-raced bodies that shuttle across the Pacific consistently and insistently? Does the phrase "in the U.S.A." (dis)qualify them as Asians or Asian Americans?

In addition, the diversity question exposes the politics of Asian Americans as divergent rather than equally or even necessarily "progressive." Viet Thanh Nguyen has recently used the controversy surrounding Yamanaka to frame his argument that, alongside our recognition of ethnic heterogeneity within Asian America, there must also be an equally honest acknowledgment of its ideological or political heterogeneity (2002). Both the "descriptive" and "political(ly progressive)" renditions of "Asian American" are liable, indeed likely, to be exclusionary.

It should be clear how exclusionary politics also become a problem when one interprets the "Asian American" of Asian American biblical hermeneutics in terms of "who" and/or "what." The exclusionary problem of the "what" may be exposed by the—under certain circumstances, rather "reasonable"—response: "I am an Asian American, so *whatever* I do as a Bible scholar is Asian American biblical hermeneutics." Defining Asian American biblical hermeneutics on the basis of "who" is beleaguered by the extra and extremely unhealthy implication that only "Asian American persons" (however defined) can participate in the production and discussion of Asian American biblical hermeneutics. In addition to exclusionary politics, the "it-takes-one-to-know-one" assumption of this understanding further points to a different and more disturbing problem: that of representational or referential politics.[5]

This problem of representational or referential politics is, of course, also at play in both the Chin–Kingston debate and the Yamanaka affair.[6] Reading "Asian American" in terms of "who" and "what" often implies an implicit but indisputable assumption or expectation that Asian American intellectual labor—whether literature or biblical hermeneutics—is or should be, among other possible things, a form of ethnography or autobiography that reveals the "truth" of Asian Americans (S. C. Wong 1988: 4).[7] Conflicts over the meaning of "Asian American"—about who or what counts as Asian American—are symptomatic of the need and/or desire for authenticity and verifiability. Not to be (dis)missed here is the issue of power in anthropology and ethnography, in which a colonial audience demands the "truth" on and from subject people (R. G. Lee 1991: 55).[8] This particular "colonial desire" for representational or referential politics on the part of the (ex)colonized (R. J. C. Young 1995: 5) is perhaps most explicitly expressed by Gilles Deleuze and Félix Guattari when they claim that "minor literature" has three characteristics: "deterritorialization," "everything in it is political," and "everything takes on a collective value" (1990: 59–60). Similar totalizing, reifying, and referential dynamics are at work in Fredric Jameson's essentialization of all "third world literature" as national allegory (1986). Again, as the controversies involving Chin, Kingston, and Yamanaka show, the "colonial desire" for representational or referential politics is not limited to colonial masters.[9] Much racial/ethnic minority and/or postcolonial criticism has been "radically fractured" by an internalization of this referential politics (Slemon 1991: 5). This has led to contradictory impulses to deconstruct colonial representation on the one hand, and to "discover" or determine an authentic and representative identity on the other.

If the "Asian American" in Asian American biblical hermeneutics becomes solely a matter of "who" and/or "what," it will end up assuming and/or accentuating a referentiality that supposedly yields identity, authenticity, and legibility.[10] It will then become problematic, not only because of its exclusionary and ethnographical or colonial implication, but also because of its essentialist (mis)understanding of racial/ethnic identity. I have already alluded to how "Asian American" identity was first "patched together" in contexts of domination and discrimination (Clifford 1988: 338). Identity, however, has too often been read as a cause of interpretation when identity is in many ways also an interpretive effect (Liew 2002a: 10). To say that identity is also an aftereffect is to propose that it is contingent upon historical motivations as well as historical accidents.[11] Racial/ethnic minority culture and identity are, as Keya Ganguly's work on a South Asian American community in New Jersey argues, often coincidental creations of everyday practice that are recognizable only in hindsight (2001: 6, 18).[12] I will return to the importance of everyday practice in the last chapter of this book. For now, let me point out on the basis of Ganguly's work that racial/ethnic identity is not only unstable and subject to history but also more like a phantom that always eludes one's grasp. As soon as an identity is retrospectively recognized, it is already being reshaped by forces and practices both of and beyond human plans and wills. In the words of Jacques Derrida, "An identity is never given, received, or attained, only the interminable and indefinitely fantasmatic process of identification endures" (1998: 28; see also Appiah 2005: 17–21).[13]

Referentiality is thus ideologically undesirable as well as logically infeasible. A ghost-like phantom is, in contrast, actually more haunting precisely because one cannot arrest it, and hence cannot assess its reality, property, or authenticity. Racial/ethnic identity is not something that one can figure out, tidy up, authenticate, and then adopt as one's springboard for intellectual and interpretive endeavors.

I am not claiming here that identity is unimportant. However, I am contending that identity is not of the first or the greatest importance. As Traise Yamamoto rightly suggests by citing Trinh T. Minh-ha (1989: 96, 104), difference "both 'undermines the very idea of identity' and . . . 'does not annul identity. It is beyond and alongside identity'" (1999: 79). I reject the Gnostic view that knowing your identity—or *truly* knowing who you are—is the sole basis for salvation and liberation.[14] This is a case in which, as Theodor W. Adorno puts it, "[t]he injunction to practise [*sic*] intellectual honesty" might amount to "sabotage of thought" (1978: 80). I am therefore interested in how to make sense of "Asian American" in Asian American biblical hermeneutics, and how to make the whole enterprise legitimate without referentiality. One way to do so is to put the identity question on the back rather than the front burner.

According to Eric Hobsbawm, modern nation building is often tied up with the existence of a national tradition (1983). This tradition is for Hobsbawm something that is more founded than found. Tradition is for him often an invention, and this invention is a practice or a performance of repetition. Narrative, ritual, and/or symbolic performance, when repeated enough times, becomes shared history that brings about a sense of national belonging. If Benedict Anderson's "imagined communities" (1991), with its similar focus on nations, does not extend Hobsbawm's argument beyond national(ist) projects,[15] Timothy Brennan provides the link between modern nation-state and *natio*—as in pre- or sub-national—communities (1990: 45). I will return to this stream of scholarship in Chapter 3, but for our purposes here—whether or not cultural nationalism is still a priority for Asian America in this age of transnationalism—its significance lies in its connection with David L. Eng's proposition that canonicity is also a matter of citation and repetition (1998). Academic or intellectual capital accumulates and becomes recognizable through repeated references or citations (see also Inden 2000: 44).

By combining the above views we can construct an Asian American biblical hermeneutics by a different directionality. Rather than founding and floundering Asian American biblical hermeneutics *solely* on the basis of "who" and "what," I want to start *also* with the "how" of tradition invention. Against the demands and desires for a putative referentiality that reveals an "authentic" Asian American identity or culture, I want to explore a different way. I want to legitimize Asian American biblical hermeneutics through an inventive tradition of citation, or of reference without referentiality.

In this construction, what is "Asian American" about Asian American biblical hermeneutics hinges on its references to contemporary Asian American scholarship.[16] This scholarship includes those from Asian American studies for sure, but also notably those within biblical studies. If there is a consistent body of work that refers to the scholarship of a Frank Yamada or a Mary Foskett, if the interpretive work of a Devadasan Premnath or a Seung Ai Yang is cited time and again, if there is a recognizable trail of publications where we find a Bundang, an Iwamura, a Kim, a Kuan, a Sano, a Seow, a Yee, or a Yieh going back and forth in dialogue and exchange with each other, there will before long surface a tradition, even a canon, of Asian American biblical hermeneutics that is not so easily dismissible.[17] This is what I attempt to do most explicitly in Chapter 4, where I specifically reference, among others, David W. Pao's book on the intertextual link between the Isaianic Exodus and Acts (2002), Timothy Tseng's article on Acts 6:1–7 as an inter-racial/ethnic conflict (2002), and Khiok-khng Yeo's chapter on Acts 17:22–31 as a model for inter-religious dialogue (1998: 165–97).[18]

Some may question how one can decide whom to reference or cite if one is not even sure about "who" and "what" really counts as Asian American. My answer is: "Don't worry too much about it." That is why I call this practice "reference without referentiality." Asian American studies is now already a legitimate and recognized field, so there is no lack of reference possibilities there. In terms of Bible scholars, the number is admittedly and regrettably still more limited, but provocative and engaging choices are still available. More important, it does not matter if those being cited identify themselves as Bible scholars and/or Asian Americans. Identity, as I have argued, is often invented by chance or happenstance and becomes recognizable only in hindsight. What Laura Hyun Yi Kang writes about "Asian/American women" is also true of Asian Americans in general: such racial/ethnic grouping or category "is cast backward in historical time to point to and group together ethnically diverse bodies of women [and men], who likely did not recognize themselves and each other as part of this collectivity" (2002: 151).[19]

There are several distinct advantages in this citational invention of tradition. As we shall see in detail in Chapter 7, understanding originality in terms of citationality helps to downplay identity and bypass authenticity or referentiality. Not only does such reference acknowledge the scholarship of those being cited and thus "*recognize* agency in others" (Spivak 1997: 473; emphasis in original), but it also highlights the inventive agency of people in diaspora as it underscores the power of (discursive) construction. As one references other Asian American (Bible) scholars in agreement and/or disagreement, one further demonstrates the diversity of interpretations and ideologies among Asian Americans (and hence the differences within a culture as well as between cultures). In addition, one deconstructs the "canonical quota" of the dominant that one and only one racial/ethnic minority person can be a "representative" of his or her racial/ethnic group at any given time (Li 1998: 65).[20] In other words, citing effects a "speaking alongside" rather than a "speaking for" or "speaking on" others in one's racial/ethnic minority group. It therefore points to the impossibility of any single authentic or representative "voice."[21] The Asian American biblical hermeneutics that I envision has no individual center; instead, the sub-discipline is built upon the interaction, or the in-between-ness of multiple and mutual references or engagements.

This approach is akin to what Homi K. Bhabha has called a "performative" representation that functions under a "repetitious" and "recursive" temporality to create a horizontal citizenship (1990a: 297).[22] Bhabha is clear that there is another way to invent a national or communal tradition. He calls it a "pedagogical" representation, which legitimizes through an "accumulative" or a linear temporality that claims a fixed origin and thus a "continuous" history (1990a: 297). Put differently, "pedagogical" representation invents a tradition through historical or genealogical "archiving." This is, for example, what Gates has arguably attempted to do with his proposal that the "Signifyin(g) monkey" is an African American tradition of literary theory and practice traceable not only to the Middle Passage but all the way to Africa (1988).[23] Others may well be interested in this kind of historical or pedagogical representation, and it will be interesting to see what particular resources can be invent(ori)ed regarding how Asian Americans have read (the Bible) in the past.[24]

My comment on resources being invent(ori)ed, however, problematizes the singular "past" as something being dictated and limited by an extant archive that results from power and/or chance (Kang 2002: 147, 154), not to mention the colonial factor in reifying a certain partition out of the past(s) into the complete past (Bhalla 1993; Chakravarti 1990; Chakrabarty 1992).[25] Moreover, the inventive nature of this alternative tradition making or legitimation is often masked by the critic and/or mistaken by the reader as archaeological recovery rather than an artificial creation. Even if one can put aside the danger of essentialism (of both the past and the practice of reading), one still needs to confront or implicate the implicit ideolologic that the past—being privileged as more "authentic"?—should/could determine and delimit the present (Chow 2002: 120–21).[26]

I do not mean to deny that memory, history, and the "past" may be effectively used to establish tradition and identity. But, as I will argue particularly in Chapters 3, 4, and 7, this very efficiency often ends up—or even depends on—masking the essentializing implications of such a construction. One should carefully consider the political economy of this strategy before claiming the by now all too convenient course of "strategic essentialism" as an alibi, particularly if another effective strategy is available. Not only does the citational invention of tradition not essentialize history or identity, but referencing without referentiality or restoration further features how Asian American biblical hermeneutics can be legitimized with identity on the back burner, as well as how community can be understood in terms of exchange and engagement rather than authenticity and univocality.[27]

Reading with and as Theory: Biblical Hermeneutics as a Grammar of Ideologic

In addition to marking both the presence and agency of Asian Americans within the field of biblical hermeneutics, Asian American biblical hermeneutics should also open the field of biblical hermeneutics itself for interpretation (Liew 2002a: 3–7). If I may adapt Jonathan Culler's statement about literature, "To ask 'what is [Asian American biblical hermeneutics]?' is in effect a way of arguing about how [the Bible] should be studied" (2000: 276). Arjun Appadurai is even more explicit when he writes, "More [racial/ ethnic and curricular diversity] may be better, but it is not good enough. It is not good enough . . . unless the commitment to diversity transforms the way in which knowledge is sought and transmitted . . . let us invoke the minor and minority in the landscape of disciplines, not just as part of a program of distributive or affirmative reform, but as a way to destabilize the authority . . . of the 'major'" (1996: 26, 35). Asian American biblical hermeneutics is not merely about legitimating or "canonizing" a different group of people. If it is, it will only end up reinforcing the "universality" and the dominance of what has already been established as the "truth" or "true" practice of biblical hermeneutics. It is not only about "re-insertion," but also about "re-vision" (Ashcroft 2001: 98). Our discussion of Asian American biblical hermeneutics must therefore not focus only on what is "Asian American," it must proceed to *stress*—in the doubled sense of premiering and pressuring—the theory and the practice of biblical hermeneutics.[28]

Let me then venture on to "prefigure" one possible direction, although readers should remember that the suggestion of a citational invention of tradition to legitimize Asian American biblical hermeneutics does not itself dictate any particular theory or practice of biblical hermeneutics. Neither will my remarks—not only in the rest of this chapter but also the rest of this book—necessarily imply any rigid methodological steps to follow in one's reading of the Bible, since they are more a matter of sensibility than methodology.

Rather than reading the Bible for a different interpretation or meaning to "add onto" already existing interpretations, I would like to suggest a reading of the Bible "with and as theory" to help confound the traditional understandings of reading the Bible as history, theology, story, and/or a (re)search for original meaning.[29] By "theory," I have in mind attempts to understand conditions and consequences of making meaning, making sense, or making reality. Biblical hermeneutics in this sense is less about what meaning one can read in a biblical text, and more about how one can use the biblical text to understand the very making of meaning, or the working of power in the wor(l)d.[30] Put differently, biblical hermeneutics becomes a scrutiny of the construction and operation of power/knowledge in and through the Bible, keeping in mind at all times that power/knowledge is enacted within and enacting on a larger institutional and materialist field like social subjectivity and social subjection.[31] Or, in the words of Malini Johar Schueller, "the alternative to disempowerment . . . is not to create a 'true' voice or to define a singular . . . identity to celebrate, but to question the very political structures that make [identity desirable and] positions of power and powerlessness possible" (1992: 146). For the sake of emphasis, indulge me here for quoting a relatively long passage from Foucault:

The role of the intellectual is not to tell others what they have to do. By what right would he [*sic*] do so? . . . The work of an intellectual is not to shape others' political will; it is, through the analysis that he [*sic*] carries out in his [*sic*] field, to question over and over again what is postulated as self-evident, to disturb people's mental habits, the way they do and think things, to dissipate what is familiar and accepted, to reexamine rules and institutions and on the basis of this re-problematization (in which he [*sic*] carries out his [*sic*] specific task as an intellectual) to participate in the formation of a political will (in which he [*sic*] has his [*sic*] role as citizen to play). (1988: 265)

Reading the Bible—or, in my case, mainly its New Testament portion—this way is particularly timely, not only because "'religion' [has] return[ed] to center stage" in the twenty-first century (Castelli 2004: 9), but also because, as Michael Hardt and Antonio Negri have demonstrated over and over in their work (2000), many overlaps and associations exist between our "globalized" world and the Roman imperial world from which the New Testament came. It is important in this regard to point out also—particularly in our time of quick fix, or at least quick returns—that there is a consistent current among many revolutionary intellectuals that recommends slowing down, particularly slow reading of canonical texts, even or especially in times of great political urgency. While Spivak (2005) and Bhabha (2005), though writing separately, converge on identifying slow and careful reading as a major lesson or legacy we must learn from Derridean deconstruction, the most memorable model arguably belongs to Friedrich Wilhelm Nietzsche when he suggests that humans should learn how to read and ruminate from observing a cow that chews and rechews her cud (1967: 23). After all, the importance of slow and careful reading is not lost on the same Karl Marx who famously stated in his Eleventh Thesis on Feuerbach that "philosophers have only ever interpreted the world, the point however is to change it" (1977: 158). As Thomas Keenan explains in his commentary on *Capital*, "Against the eagerness of a reading that wants to skip over the interpretation to get to the change, that wants to know how to relate general principles to immediate questions, Marx advises that articulation takes patience" (1997: 102).

On the one hand, understanding biblical hermeneutics as reading "with and as theory" undoubtedly displaces the Bible's authority, since the Bible is no longer treasured for the particular meanings it "originates." Instead, biblical texts are historicized as both products and productions of specific historical moments. On the other hand, this understanding of biblical hermeneutics also ensures the Bible's ongoing significance, since its value is no longer dependent on the "acceptability" of its particular ideological positions (however defined), but rather on its delineation of an ideological grammar. Paying attention to how the machinery of discursive constructions has functioned in biblical texts of the past sensitizes and enables one to critique constructions of the present.

If this biblical hermeneutics disrupts and disappoints persons on both sides of the "biblical authority" question because it reads the Bible as neither total "trash" nor total "treasure," the same is true regarding its stance on theory. If reading "with" theory signals a positive use of existing theory, reading "as" theory implies a more critical view. The relevance of existing theory to one's reading of the Bible to scrutinize productions and products of ideologic can be seen in Spivak's statement that deconstruction "is constantly and persistently looking into how truths are produced" (1996: 27). The ways meaning or reality is made in a biblical text may, however, reveal a lacuna in or a challenge to existing theories (Liew 2001: 185–86). I will, for instance, read the ways in which John's Gospel constructs community with the help of Bhabha's abstraction or theorization on (national) community formation (Chapter 3), but I will also argue that the dynamics of colonial mimicry in Mark's Gospel are more accommodative and less transformative to colonial ideology than Bhabha's theory of mimicry might lead one to believe (Chapter 2). Similarly, I will read Paul's 1 Corinthians both with and against, among others, Frantz Fanon's exploration of resistance and Sigmund Freud's theory on mourning and melancholia (Chapter 5 and 6 respectively).

I hope the kind of mutual challenge implied in "reading the Bible with and as theory" is enough to alleviate any anxiety over its use of "Western" theory. The main *subject* of my inquiry in Chapter 7, Theresa Hak Kyung Cha, is an excellent example—or perhaps even model—of both use and ab-use of Western theory. Cha's statement that she will "take on" Western languages (1995: 4) has been interpreted in terms of both assumption and opposition (Kang 2002: 224), my reference to theory—Western or otherwise—should be seen simultaneously also as a resource for *and* a target of inquiry.[32]

This discussion of (Western) theory should show that what counts as theory must be argued or articulated rather than assumed. I take it as a given that "reading the Bible with and as theory" is an interdisciplinary endeavor. Interdisciplinarity allows a rather open-ended range of theoretical/methodological practices, as well as an array of understandings or emphases (Utset 1995; Klein 1996; Kang 2002: 18–21). One will notice in and from this book, particularly in Chapters 7 and 8, that Asian American biblical hermeneutics involves a lot more than reading the Bible. Wanting to open up rather than close off Asian American biblical hermeneutics to various possibilities, I will suggest or "prefigure" three more specific sites to help ground my reference to theory and interdisciplinarity.[33]

I want to highlight, first of all, the importance of Asian studies in general and Asian biblical hermeneutics in particular. Within Asian American studies, the emphasis on "claiming America" and the ensuing separation of "Asians in America" from "Asians in Asia" have become increasing problematic and untenable because of two main factors. The new immigration law of 1965 meant the continual arrival of first-generation immigrants with vivid memories and ties to their homelands (E. H. Kim and Lowe 1997: viii; Nguyen 2002: 27). Then there is the phenomenon of transnationalism effected by globalization and technology (S. C. Wong 1995a; Ong 1999), effects of which are not necessarily limited by nativity.[34] Kang, for instance, mentions several sites of transnational "interlocking formation" that are important for Asian/American women: industry or factory, the military, prostitution, and tourism (2002: 164–214). Chuh, referring to the hostility between the United States and Japan during World War II as well as Japan's colonization of Korea in the first half of the twentieth century, suggests that the perception of Asian Americans (by themselves and by others in the U.S.A.) did not, do not, cannot, and should not be limited by national boundaries (2003: 58–111). The need and/or desire of diasporic persons to be more transnational than national (Shukla 1997) is also visible in the number of Asian American scholars who focus on studying Asia and/or the way in which some Asian American scholars involve themselves in both "area" and "ethnic" studies (Kondo 2001: 35).[35]

If Asian America is always already entangled with multiply located histories and with multiple locations, it seems to make sense also for Asian American biblical hermeneutics to have more exchange and greater engagement with Asian studies in general and Asian biblical hermeneutics in particular. This is especially so if the line between Asian and Asian American is less than clear. Doing so—particularly if one manages to avoid falling into the trap of achieving "authenticity" through "root-finding" and the trap of colonial appropriation or absorption—may also help "decenter U.S. scholarship while challenging it with new formulations, new questions, and new critiques" (Desmond and Dominguez 1996: 486).[36] With the formation of the "Asian and Asian American Hermeneutics Group" within the Society of Biblical Literature, more and greater intentional "traffic" may be created for these two hermeneutics to have a substantial conversation.[37]

Second, I would like to suggest situating the theory and interdiscipli-

narity of Asian American biblical hermeneutics in postcolonial theory and
studies. One should note that trafficking between Asian and Asian American hermeneutics may help destabilize U.S. nationalism as well as disrupt
U.S. imperialism. If it is well known that "area" studies like Asian studies
had a colonial or orientalist beginning (Kondo 2001: 35), it may be less
known that Asian American studies have been complicit in as well as con-
testing against colonial dynamics. In addition to the Yamanaka affair and
how it points to inter-ethnic conflicts that are long-term and systemic within
Asian America, the location of Yamanaka's novel—Hawaii—further points
to the ways Asian Americans have been acting and abetting to silence and
colonize native Hawaiians (Chuh 2003: 117, 136–45). One can, of course,
also focus on colonial oppression committed by the United States beyond
its national boundary (something that Asian studies will help bring out).
What postcolonial theory and studies would help point to, then, is that
Asian American biblical hermeneutics should no longer be merely about
making Asian Americans visible or legible to enable a claim on "America"
(Liew 2002b: 44),[38] but about its need to interrogate the very makeup of
(colonial/imperial) power through and beyond discourse. W. E. B. Du Bois
actually made this connection between racial/ethnic minority struggle and
transnational anti-colonialism years ago (J. K.-J. Lee 2004: 183–84). Postcolonial theory and studies thus occupy a very significant role in a biblical
hermeneutics that reads the text as an ideo-grammar.

Finally, as my reference to Du Bois intimates, I would like to see Asian
American biblical hermeneutics situated in an alliance with other minority
communities and scholarships. As Asian and postcolonial studies help challenge both nationalism and imperialism, one should come to realize rather
quickly that one cannot afford to make Asian America one's entire world
of concerns. Not only are there Asian-raced persons in diaspora in various
other parts of the world, there are also other racial/ethnic minority groups
within the United States. Building coalitions with these other racial/ethnic
minority groups makes sense not only because there is a "convergence of
aims," like erasing racism (Chakrabarty 2001: 113), but also because Asian
American is itself already a "panethnic" (Espiritu 1992) or "coalitional
identity" (Visweswaran 1993: 305) that reaches across different ethnicities
and national origins. In addition, there are definite benefits in doing so,
and well beyond the sentimental view that racism against one group is racism against other groups. Not only will coalition building help cut down
on the need for all parties involved to relearn old lessons or reinvent old
wheels at points of convergence, but at places or points where divergence
occurs, coalition building will also help develop an understanding towards

comparative racializations or racisms (Goldberg 1993: 97–116; Gotanda 2001).[39] By turning "our" attention away from whites to each other, different racial/ethnic minority groups can work together to form new ways of reading, knowing, and be(com)ing that go beyond reversing, reinscribing, and resisting dominant, colonial, or orientalist ideologic (Radhakrishnan 2001: 261–62). One of these new ways is precisely how alliance or coalition may help displace identity-based politics (Pulido 2006).

It is important to emphasize that minoritization or oppression is not only based on race and ethnicity (Liew and Wimbush 2002).[40] Coalition building among minority groups should be understood in the broad context of marginality and alterity where various identity factors are imbricated with each other. What Kang calls "interlocking formation" (2002: 164–214) calls for what Sherene H. Razack calls "interlocking analysis" (1998: 14), and "interlocking analysis" can be greatly facilitated with the formation of alliances. I do not suggest that this kind of alliance politics will make things easier to categorize or contain. In fact, the opposite is true. These alliances will intensify awareness of rather than deflect attention from hegemonies, whether they are scattered transnationally, nationally, or even within one's own minority group. Yet, as Chow puts it, conflict can be a constructive "locus of reproduction and regeneration" (2002: 190), particularly if it can help move beyond single-issue and/or identity-based politics.

Conclusion

I have suggested that in addition to dealing with the "who" and/or "what," one can narrate Asian American biblical hermeneutics into legitimacy not through a narrative of identity or authenticity but through repeated references to existing (biblical) scholarship by Asian American scholars. If these repeated references help make biblical hermeneutics "Asian American," I have further suggested that the "biblical hermeneutics" of Asian Americans be geared towards the direction of reading the Bible with and as theory, and that we can do so by developing close contacts with Asian studies, postcolonial studies, and various kinds of minority or oppositional studies. These two steps are important to avoid becoming exotic on one hand and conforming to Eurocentrism on the other. Tools and theories can be shared and overlapping, but that does not mean that there is "the white way or the highway." Asian Americans need to be visible, but that does not mean we have to be transparent to the white gaze.

I must, however, reiterate my commitment to multiplicity and elasticity, or my emphasis on invention rather than preservation. No single strategy or suggestion will be sufficient for all situations, and as we have seen in the history of Asian America, situations also do not remain static. Asian American identities and Asian American biblical hermeneutics are both processes of "becoming-being," "being-becoming," or in a word, performance. As performance, these processes get repeated and remade simultaneously, responding creatively to contingent and/or changing situations. Asian American biblical hermeneutics is part of this historical and processional performance "through which identity or [identification] is constantly sought and 'found'" (Harrison 2003: 132; see also Lowe 1996: 65). In other words, what I said above about Asian American biblical hermeneutics is not only inadequate by itself for this moment, I will also need to change my views in a different moment. The Asian American Movement is literally a "movement"; it does and must keep moving and changing, since "[m]ore often than not, it is mobility that has been seen as radical and transformative" (Pile 1997: 29). Asian American biblical hermeneutics is important, but I refuse to "discipline" it once and for all. And I refuse the tyranny of authenticity, or to be trapped by the tenet or dictate to "tell the truth" (the singular is itself telling). What I envision for Asian American biblical hermeneutics is a movement that has "centers . . . everywhere and circumferences nowhere" (Pollock et al. 2000: 588).

Since I have been medi(t)ating on "method," let me close with two brief readings with and as theory. One reading is based on the New Testament, the other on Kingston's *Woman Warrior* (1976). A couple of Asian-raced scholars in the United States, Sze-kar Wan (2000b) and Eung Chun Park (2003), have followed up on Daniel Boyarin's theory-laden reading of Paul's letters in terms of universality and particularity (1994). Despite important differences between their assumptions and arguments, all three agree that Paul's theology, ideology, or construction of identity is related to the question of inter-ethnic relations.

At the end of Kingston's *Woman Warrior* is an episode about a Han princess and poetess, Ts'ai Yen, who was abducted and raped by "barbarians," or non-Hans (1976: 207–209). Ta'si Yen was eventually able to return to her father, but she created a song during her captivity that she sang to "barbarian" flute music. According to Kingston, this ended up being "a song that the Chinese sing to their own instruments. It translated well" (1976: 209). This amazing story shows that tradition and culture, like Paul's identity, are matters of in(ter)ventions. Unlike Wan's and Park's readings of Paul's letters, however, Kingston makes it explicit that such in(ter)ventions are not results of some kind of friendly inter-ethnic dialogue, benign disagreements, or "nice" attempts to overcome ethnic division. Instead, they are results of inter-ethnic warfare that involves abduction and rape. In other words, as Walter Benjamin suggests, the birth of culture is inseparable from deathly violence (1968: 256). More important to our purposes, however, is Anne Anlin Cheng's musing that "the creation of national culture, revealed by Ts'ai Yen's story, is always already itself a response to loss and exile" (2001: 91). The same is true of the desire and need to invent and legitimize Asian American biblical hermeneutics.

CHAPTER 2

Reading with Yin Yang Eyes

Negotiating the Ideological Dilemma of a Chinese American Biblical Hermeneutics

A s it is well known to all of us, one of the defining—if not *the* defining—characteristics of a Chinese person in mainstream U.S. culture is our eyes (Gilman 1999: 98–110).[1] This distinction has elicited such descriptions as "squinty" or "slanted" from those who do not possess it. In Ambrose Bierce's "The Haunted Valley," a short story published back in 1870, Chinese eyes had already become the difference marker. The main female character in this story is a dead—and thus passive and silent—Chinese woman in California, Ah Wee, whose physical description is reduced by her killer to a single line regarding her eyes, "I guess maybe they were the damn'dest eyes in this neck o' woods" (1946: 453). Likewise, when the dominant culture found it necessary after Pearl Harbor to distinguish "bad" Asians (Japanese) from "good" Asians (Chinese) instead of lumping all Asians together as the "Yellow Peril," the so-called distinguishing marks included the frequency of "epicanthic fold" (R. G. Lee 1999: 147). This fascination with the Chinese eyes, "borrowing" from Meyda Yeğenoğlu's study of the Arabic veil, can be seen as the "Lacanian 'triumph of the gaze over the eyes'" (1998: 42). For Jacques Lacan, all eyes are evil eyes with maleficent intent (1978: 114–19).[2] This maleficent gaze of the "Westerner" over the Chinese eyes also frequently ends up projecting onto the latter its own evil and haunting dynamics. In Bierce's short story, Ah Wee's killer becomes haunted by one of her "damn'dest eyes" peering at him through a knothole in the wall. This time, this single Chinese eye is described as "a full, black eye that glared . . . with an entire lack of expression more awful than the most devilish glitter" (Bierce 1946: 454). In another popular medium, a 1919 Hollywood film entitled *Broken Blossoms* featuring the well-known actress Lillian Gish actually has Gish being harassed by an unsavory denizen of an unsavory Chinatown named "Evil Eye."[3] Even Sax Rohmer's (in)famous stereotypical construction of Fu Manchu states that "the soul of the great Chinese doctor lay in his eyes. Never had I seen before, and never have I seen again, such power in a man's eyes as lay in those of Dr. Fu Manchu" (1939: 107).

Instead of the slanted and evil eyes that the dominant U.S. culture has popularized as a metonymy to reify a Chinese person, I want to talk about another kind of eyes that is popular within Chinese culture and its implications for my work of interpreting the Bible. Although the terminology is slightly different, it is the same concept that the Chinese American writer Amy Tan uses to construct her novel *The Hundred Secret Senses* (1995). She titles her first chapter "The Girl with Yin Eyes," and she opens that chapter with these words: "My sister Kwan believes she has yin eyes. She sees those who have died and now dwell in the World of Yin, ghosts who leave the mists just to visit her kitchen on Balboa Street in San Francisco" (1995: 3).

Chinese talk about people, generally women, who have yin yang eyes, eyes that can see persons and ghosts, and eyes that witness both the living and the dead.[4] Before I talk about what yin yang eyes mean to my reading of the Bible, I would like to spend some time scrutinizing the ideological dilemma that I face in this "business" called biblical hermeneutics.[5]

The Eye/I of the Dilemma

Since many revisionary studies have been done to highlight the marginalization of Chinese Americans within U.S. history through official legislation and popular representation, I do not need to repeat here the accounts of an already massive volume of literature (see, for example, S. Chan 1991; Takaki 1989; Cassel 2002; and Lai 2004).[6] What I want to do, however, is to identify two seemingly contradictory strategies that have been employed in various forms and disguises to turn Chinese Americans into an alien nation of what Mia Tuan calls "illegitimate Americans" (1998: 39).[7] Generally speaking, Chinese Americans are represented (in both the literary and the political sense of the term) as "foreign" and required to go through a whole process of "re-humanization" (a cultural clone, if you will), or as distinctively exotic display pieces that never adjust or change in any way. Given my interest in biblical hermeneutics, I will illustrate these two strategies as they are employed by people who have something to do with the Bible. One reads, for example, in Wallace Irwin's "Young Mr. Yan":

> Yu can take a Chink from 'is hop,
> 'Is lanterns an' gals an' pigs an' chop,

Yu can dress 'im up in yer Christian clo'es,
Put texts in 'is head an' hymns in 'is nose,
But yu'll find, when he's actin' a dead straight part,
He's a Chinaman still in 'is yellow heart. (1906: 13)

Just as this stanza betrays a sense of disgust and disappointment, so it reflects the attitude that Chinese Americans need to replace their culture and heritage with so-called Christian belief and practice if they are to integrate themselves into the mainstream of life. On the other hand, John J. Epsey, son of a missionary in China, reflects the strategy of "freeze and behold the exotic" in the following paragraph:

As we got to thinking about it, there were so many things in Oo-zong's nature that weren't a bit Chinese. So we began to remold him into a member of his own race. There was his grin, for example. We had to explain to Oo-zong that the Chinese are an inscrutable people who rarely show joy or sorrow in public. He was to make his face, we told him, blandly intelligent. The effect, we added, would be heightened if he were to droop his eyelids a little. Then, when he was addressed, he was to tighten the corners of his mouth ever so slightly, which was as far, he should know, as any Chinese ever went in showing amiability. . . . It took hours of patient work in front of a mirror, but the result was the most Orientally bland face in all China. . . . The more I think of it, the more I realize how essentially responsible my sister and I were for making Oo-zong conscious of the habits of his own race, for making him, indeed, really Chinese. (Cited in E. H. Kim 1982: 20–21)

As I have already mentioned, biblical hermeneutics, like all academic disciplines, is a business inseparable from economic and materialistic entanglements. In this light, it is important to realize that the twin strategies of "melt" or "freeze" are also at work within the academic and publishing industry of the United States. Works by Chinese Americans are seldom published, and thus are seldom taught. As a result, a cycle is created in which the voices of Chinese Americans may be silenced forever.[8] When a publisher is finally ready to publish something by a Chinese American, chances are good that the same twin strategies will be put into operation. In other words, the publisher is either working intently to strip manuscripts of any racial traces, or looking specifically for something exotically different (something unmistakably "Chinese") that can be frozen and beheld.[9] The severity of this problem is well illustrated in Sui Sin Far's "Leaves from the Mental Portfolio of an Eurasian":

I also meet some funny people who advise me to "trade" upon my nationality. They tell me that if I wish to succeed in literature in America I should dress in Chinese costume, carry a fan in my hand, wear a pair of scarlet beaded slippers, live in New York, and come of high birth. Instead of making myself familiar with the Chinese Americans around me, I should discourse on my spirit acquaintance with Chinese ancestors and quote in between the "Good mornings" and "How d'ye dos" of editors.

"Confucius, Confucius, how great is Confucius. Before Confucius, there never was Confucius. After Confucius, there never came Confucius," etc., etc., etc.,

or something like that, both illuminating and obscuring. . . . (1995: 230)

Underlying these two strategies is, of course, the same insistence, or the same desire to keep—borrowing Palumbo-Liu's nuanced designation (1999)—Chinese/Americans purely separate and separately pure.[10] It is, for example, actually arguable that what makes Rohmer's Fu Manchu so effective as a cultural threat is less his Chineseness than his hybrid appearance, abilities, and alliances that pronounce a mixing of what is supposedly "Eastern" and "Western" (T. Chen 2005: 43–52). It is this same fear of and prejudice against hybridity that underlie some criticisms that have been made about some better-known writings by Chinese Americans. For example, the characters in Adet Lin's *Flame from the Rock* (1943) have been criticized as overly "modern" (Ling 1990: 69), while those in Frank Chin's *The Chickencoop Chinaman* (1981) draw the complaint that "they did not speak, dress, or act 'like Orientals'" (cited in E. H. Kim 1982: xv). Likewise, the sometimes aggressive, sometimes docile women in Maxine Hong Kingston's *The Woman Warrior* (1976) become troubling to some critics. In other words, one finds exactly the same strategies of marginalization, which Rey Chow (1991: 90–92) has articulately described as the "King Kong" or the "Gorillas in the Mist" approach. The ugly foreign monster must be killed and gotten rid of, or the "natives" must always remain what they are and stay where they belong.

To be sure, this kind of oppression comes not only from without, but also from within the Chinese American community. Chinese emigration to the United States in the mid-1840s was a result of domestic corruption on the part of the Qing dynasty as much as of foreign imperialism. There are also plenty of Chinese Americans who desire to keep their race and culture "pure." According to this "idea(l)," the term "Chinese American" should signify nothing more than "Chinese who live in the United States," thus resulting in the alternative term *huaqiao* (overseas Chinese) and in the parodic terms *zhuoxing*, or the more current "bananas," in reference to second- or third-generation Chinese Americans.[11]

Being part of this wider society, I find myself confronted with the same "melt" or "freeze" dilemma as a Chinese American Bible scholar. Kwok Pui-lan, in her article "Jesus/the Native," talks about the Eurocentrism that pervades the field of biblical studies within the United States (1998: 69–75), but she also warns against the danger of overlooking the problem of what Marianna Torgovnick has called "gone primitive" (1990), or what Dorinne Kondo calls "self-Orientalizing" (1997: 10; see Kwok 1998: 81–82). For instance, it appears odd to me that during the brief existence of the Society of Biblical Literature's "Reading the Bible in Asia, Africa, Latin America and the Caribbean Group," its officers and presenters were consistently and primarily made up of minority scholars who reside in the United States rather than in Asia, Africa, Latin America, or the Caribbean. The stronghold of this "freeze and behold the exotic" mentality became even clearer to me when an officer of this group, having heard of me indirectly, called and asked me many years ago if I would be interested in writing a paper on "Reading the Bible in China." During our brief conversation, two of the first questions she asked me were: "Where were you originally from?" and "How long have you been in the States?" Such questions seem to suggest that her motive (unintentional, I am sure) was to locate some "pure" and "uncontaminated" Chinese to do this paper.[12] Yet, that begs the question: if you are looking for someone with a "pure" or "un-Americanized" Chinese viewpoint (whatever that may mean), why are you searching for a Chinese person within the United States? I am not denying the possibility that there are those who may choose to maintain a separateness from all things "American," but it should not be the suggestion or assumption that all racial and ethnic minorities fit into this category. Insisting on such an "exotic purity" is certainly not valid to many Chinese Americans like myself, who in addition to studying, working, and living in both the United States and Canada for over twenty years, have been married to an Anglo American woman. Many Chinese Americans have done much more than just "live" in the United States; while we have not been "melted," we have certainly "merged" (no pun intended).

If beneath the strategies to either "re-humanize" or "fossilize" is the rigid mentality that every culture should always be kept pure and separate, I must denounce the ideological dilemma thrust upon me as a "repressive" and "naive" practice that "betrays and falsifies the dialectic of real life" (Radhadkrishnan 1990: 60–62). While I oppose universalist claims of one white/right way, I also resist the culturalist position that may end up making my work a kind of intellectual tourist site where one may visit and "sight-see" now and then.[13] A rigid culturalism, and the kind of separatist "theoretical tourism" it implies, may create another situation in which exchange and engagement can both be avoided in the name of "imponderables, incomparables, and incommensurables" (Rosaldo 1989: 43)—a language that reminds me of the so-called separate but equal development emphasis of apartheid.[14] What Adrienne Rich wrote almost thirty years ago still rings true today: "What has stopped me short, what fuses my anger now, is that we were told we were utterly different, *that the difference between us must be everything, must be determinative, that from that difference we each must turn away; that we must also flee from our alikeness*" (1979: 310; emphasis in original).

A Contradictory Look

How may the concept of yin yang eyes help me negotiate the pressures to either "Eurocentralize" or "(self-)orientalize" my reading of the Bible?[15] I want to make four suggestions, and will use the Gospel of Mark for the purpose of illustration.[16]

First, the paradoxical doubling of yin yang eyes suggests the possibility that my interpretation of the Bible no longer needs to be done with a single, unified perspective. The insistence on "purity" that aims to put a slash between and separate Chinese from Americans is, in many ways, a desire to constitute unity, disavow mixings, and negate contradictions. If the term "Chinese American" (without a slash or hyphen) appears to be contradictory, the history of Chinese Americans is replete with more contradictions. What is it if not a contradiction that a "democratic" society championing "human rights" would continually racialize and ostracize certain members from that society? What is it if not a contradiction that the "greater" income generated by some Chinese Americans (and Japanese Americans) who decide to have more people bringing in a paycheck and living under one roof suddenly becomes a proof that all Asian Americans have reached a "model minority" status? What is it if not a contradiction that Chinese Americans have become a buffer to ward off the "black menace" since the 1950s when, only a century ago, Elihu Burritt was arguing that transforming African slaves into wage laborers was more sensible than importing "heathen" Chinese to work in the United States (R. G. Lee 1999: 58–59, 156–60)? What is it if not a contradiction that a Chinese American, John

Huang, was turned into the embodiment of the so-called campaign finance scandal as well as the threat of globalized capital when globalized capital is in many ways a U.S. product?

Reading with yin yang eyes alerts me to many contradictory aspects within the Gospel of Mark. My concern for both the "internal" and "external" colonization associated with the United States has certainly predisposed me to view Mark as a piece of colonial literature that challenges colonial authority and envisions a new, inclusive community through its apocalyptic emphasis. After all, Mark was written when the entire Palestinian area was under Roman colonization (see also Myers 1992; and Blount 1998). Various studies have also suggested that ancient Jewish apocalyptic rhetoric bears a relationship to colonial politics and that the writers, in the interest of self-preservation, tended to level their attacks at a more benign target than the imperialists themselves (see, for example, Cohn 1993; and J. J. Collins 1998). In this light, Mark's negative representations of the Jewish elites and his apocalyptic emphasis may take on an anti-colonial twist.

For Mark, Jewish elites are both weak and wicked. Unlike those of Jesus, their teachings are unimpressive (Mark 1:21–28) and their pronouncements unsubstantiated (1:9–11; 3:22–30). While Jesus operates in accordance with divine directives (1:35–39; 14:32–36), they cater to the moods and opinions of the crowd (11:27–33; 12:12; 14:1–2). Although they refer to the law constantly, they plan to murder Jesus on the Sabbath (3:1–6), send people to trap Jesus in a calculated manner (12:13–23), and rob God's people as well as warp God's design (11:15–17; see also 6:30–34). Given (1) the fact that Mark's Jesus is frequently casting out demons in the synagogues (1:21–28, 39); (2) the parallel vocabularies Mark uses to describe what Jesus says in parables about exorcisms (3:23–27) and what he does in cleansing the temple (11:15–17); as well as (3) how Mark equates the Jewish elites with the "hard ground" from which Satan feeds within the parable of the sower (4:1–20; see Tolbert 1989: 153–54), Mark seems to be implying that the wickedness of the Jewish elitist establishment is nothing less than demonic. As a result, Mark's Jesus makes a threefold promise in the parable of wicked tenants (12:1–12). He promises that God will come, God will destroy the Jewish authorities, and God will transfer their positions of leadership.

This apocalyptic message becomes more explicitly anti-colonial when one takes into consideration several subtle criticisms of Roman authorities in Mark. Mark's Jesus "predicts" that "Gentiles" will do several things to bring about his death (10:33e–34), and this "prediction" turns out to be fulfilled through the hands of the Romans (15:15–20). Correspondingly, one can read Jesus' definition and denouncement of an oppressive and authoritarian "Gentile" ruling style (10:42b–43a), as well as his "prediction" that "governors" and "kings" will participate in persecuting his followers (13:9), as references to the imperial power of Rome. More cogently, Mark's Jesus implies, immediately after the parable of the wicked tenants, that there are things (like the vineyard of the parable?) that belong to God rather than Caesar (12:13–17). In view of the many parallels that Mark also draws between Jewish and Roman authorities in the deaths of John the Baptizer and Jesus (6:14–29; 14:53–65; 15:1–24), I think one has good grounds to see Mark as more than a story of intra-Jewish conflicts, but one of (anti-)imperial struggles.

However, I have also come to see, in true yin yang fashion, that the Gospel is also a site of neocolonial domination, or—to problematize Homi K. Bhabha's positive use of the term—one of "colonial mimicry" (1994: 85–92).[17] For example, is Mark's sense of history, which is typified by an apocalyptic destruction of all the "wicked tenants" who oppose Jesus, not one of repetitive violence? Is Mark's "solution," the imminent second coming of Jesus (13:1–37), nothing more than a new cycle of imperial rule in which the roles of rulers and ruled are merely reversed? Note, for example, how Mark's Jesus describes his household in terms of a "lord" who authorizes his servants and commands his doorkeeper to perform various tasks before he goes on a trip (13:34). Since this parable both begins and concludes with the warning that one should stay alert and awake (13:32–33, 35–37), the imagery is that of an institution where vertical structure and the threat of punishment are all accepted modes of operation. What we have, then, is a Jesus sitting at the pinnacle of the hierarchy of his household, dishing out commands and punishments. How is that different from the Gentile or Roman rulers who also sit at the pinnacle of their hierarchy of power, lording over and exercising authority over those who rank below them (10:42)?

A Returned Gaze

I hope it is becoming clear by now that the contradictory look that I have in mind regarding yin yang eyes is not the aesthetic experimentation and indeterminate free play that became popular over a decade ago when some Bible scholars were "infatuated" with Derridean deconstruction in an obsolete and solipsist kind of way.[18] Instead of an ambiguity that proclaims "nothing means anything," I am referring to my double-edged attitude that the Bible and its interpretation are at once both sources of liberation and oppression.

Instead of passing through the contradictions within a biblical text play-
fully to celebrate bliss, this biblical hermeneutics pushes for messy debates
regarding biblical texts and contemporary power relations. To put it bluntly,
reading with yin yang eyes means a reading that never assumes the normative authority of the Bible.[19]

One must realize that yin yang eyes are always understood as posing a
threat to people's security. As Amy Tan relates it in her novel, yin yang eyes
are forbidden secrets; once known, people would try to submit Kwan to
various religious and scientific apparatuses in a desperate attempt to restore
order (1995: 14–17). Kwan, however, is defiant to the end. Toying with the
views of those who want to "cure" her of—or kill off—her yin yang vision,
Kwan says to her sister, in Chinese, "When the doctors and nurses ask me
questions, I treat them like American ghosts—I don't see them, don't hear
them, don't speak to them" (1995: 15).

In contrast to Chinese American Bible scholars who use yin yang as a
symbol of, and/or means to, harmony (A. Y. Lee 2006: 62–63; Yeo 1998:
51–105), my biblical hermeneutics refuses to see the Bible as only a field of
aesthetics, assent, and appreciation (see also Yee 2006). Reading with yin
yang eyes accents instead disruption, disagreement, and discord. The contradictory look I mentioned above functions as a refusal to "white-wash"
(in both the racial and the political sense of the term) the Bible. This, in
my opinion, is particularly important in light of the ways religion in general and the Bible in particular have been used to racialize, hierarchize, and
colonize people within the United States.[20] I agree with Robert Lee's thesis
that the basis of marginalization often slides seamlessly among race, culture, ethnicity, and sexuality, but his otherwise insightful analysis should
not have elided the Bible and religion within culture and ethnicity.[21] After
all, Lee himself quotes over and over again (though without any sustained
emphasis or analysis) how Chinese Americans have been portrayed as "bar-
baric heathens" (R. G. Lee 1999: 29, 37–38, 68–69, 79, 104), "idolatrous
foreigners" (1999: 59), "prostitute[s] from instinct, *religion*, education,
and interest" (1999: 62, emphasis mine), and "a race of ancestor worship-
pers" (1999: 117). Chinese Americans, in other words, are disenfranchised
because they are not Bible-believing Christians, but Buddhists (1999: 127,
130) or "the archetype of Lamaism" (1999: 117). The separation between
Chinese and Americans is then justified as a struggle between Chinese and
Christendom (1999: 114).[22] If I may refer once again to Ambrose Bierce's
"The Haunted Valley," the inter-racial relationship between Ah Wee and
her killer is understood by her killer as a religious transgression between a
"pagan" and a Christian, since "there was nothing about Chinamen in the

New Testament" (Bierce 1946: 451–52).[23] Reading with yin yang eyes, I will contend that the very book used to oppose racial and cultural hybridity is itself already highly hybridized with contradictions. If yin yang eyes enable us to see the dead, I must re-vision my biblical hermeneutics to re-member the ghost of Ah Wee and other Chinese Americans who have been victimized by the notion of "biblical authority" (see also A. Gordon 1997).[24] Because Chinese American communities continue to be extremely diverse in terms of religious traditions, and since Chinese Americans continue to be a minority within a so-called Christian nation, it is imperative that we do not overlook this issue of biblical authority.[25] Instead of effacing contradictions, my biblical hermeneutics features them to contest narratives of submission demanded by this powerful can(n)on.

There is yet another reason why my reading with yin yang eyes focuses on the oppressive as well as the liberating potential of the Bible. As I have already intimated, oppression comes from without as well as from within Chinese American communities. This realization should alert us to the danger of idealization or romanticism of any form. As there is no innocent history, there is no perfect culture; neither is there a book that is solely and squarely on the side of liberation. This awareness pertains to Chinese Americans in particular, because, being made representative of other Asian Americans and touted as the so-called model minority, we *often* "occupy a [middle] position in the social structure that makes [us] simultaneously oppressed and oppressor" (Bonacich 1988: 92).[26] Developing a double-edged attitude towards the Bible may help develop a habit of re-viewing and problematizing one's own arguments and positions. This habit may, in turn, do more than just negotiating the tendency for Chinese Americans to be pigeonholed; it may also complicate the binary oppositions of "Chinese" and "American," "colonizer" and "colonized," "powerful" and "powerless." Such a complication will, at least, expose our complicity in oppression, and, if we are lucky enough, prevent the production of a new form of totalizing discourse and totalitarian practice.

Returning to the Gospel of Mark, I find myself resisting what Stephen D. Moore has called "zealot" readings (2004)—namely, readings that see Mark as "liberating" on all counts and, I would add, at all costs (for instance, Myers 1992; Blount 1998; and Horsley 2001). I resist, for example, Mark's "scapegoating" of the Jewish elites, even if it is a tactic typical of ancient Jewish apocalyptic writings to get away with attacking imperial Rome. How can it be otherwise given the way U.S. society has "scapegoated" Chinese Americans during numerous times of anxiety, whether it is one of economic/moral uncertainy or so-called homeland security? I have

already mentioned Mark's promise of a scorched-earth destruction at Jesus'
parousia that, even as an anti-colonial rhetoric, merely reinscribes imperial
violence. Such a reinscription seems even less desirable in light of the controversial Truth and Reconciliation Commission in South Africa, which aims
to chart a future that would include all, even those who have participated
in the crimes and atrocities of apartheid.[27] I also find it difficult to accept
as normative Mark's politics of postponement and passivity. Mark's Jesus,
despite being God's last and best attempt to change the world, finds himself
constrained in his movements and limited in what he can do with his disciples as well as his opponents.[28] For Mark, colonial subjects like Jesus and
his disciples are limited in their choices as well as in their abilities to bring
about positive socio-political change. This can be seen, for example, in the
way the Gospel shifts its emphasis from God and Jesus sending people out
for mission (1:2, 12, 43; 3:14; 6:7) to God saving people from suffering and
destruction (8:35; 10:26, 52; 13:13, 20; 15:30–31) before and after Jesus'
first passion prediction (8:31). Short of God's direct intervention, their
lives will inevitably be filled with frustration, pain, and anguish (8:34–38;
10:29–30, 39; 13:9–23). Although such a politics might be understandable
in a desperate colonial situation, which was what the Jewish circumstance
seemed to be both before and between the two Jewish-Roman wars, different politics must be imagined for a different situation.

A Broad View

In addition to a biblical hermeneutics that fixates on contradictions and
contests scriptural authority, I want to suggest further that yin yang eyes
signify the importance of moving beyond readings that are tied to single-
issue politics. As Kwan tells her sister in Amy Tan's novel, yin yang eyes
enable her to see "[m]any, many good friends" (1995: 15). Reading the
Bible as a "zero-sum game of racial struggle" (cited in Lowe 1995: 49) will
lead to unacknowledged violence against other less-privileged subjects (see
also Lowe 1996: 71). In the case of Mark, for example, fixating on only the
issue of Roman colonization will leave unaddressed the question of whether
the Gospel sows seeds of anti-Judaism in its sowing of "the word" (4:14).[29]
Even if the Jewish leaders are only "straw figures" who are standing in
for the Roman colonizers, can Mark's own victimization palliate such an
oppressive act of scapegoating? One must remember Robert Lee's thesis
regarding the mutations or the shifts and slides of racism as well as the
ways in which the dominant U.S. society habitually divides and conquers

its racialized members. If the latter makes evident the need for alliance, the former demonstrates that allies are readily available. As Ling-chi Wang suggests, we have by now before us the positive example of the Third World Liberation Front in the 1960s as well as the negative example of the Los Angeles riot in 1992 (L. L. Wang 1995: 163–65; see also Pulido 2006). If Chinese Americans, as "model minority," have in fact become "middleman [sic] minorities" (Turner and Bonacich 1980), it is imperative that we strive to align with the oppressed below rather than the oppressors above.

Since yin yang eyes are traditionally related to the threat of women, feminism is a logical ally and an indispensable element within my Chinese American hermeneutics.[30] As I focus on the colonial dynamics within the Gospel of Mark, I must not overlook, for instance, what Gayle Rubin terms "traffic in women" (1975). According to Rubin, homosocial communities of men and male-dominant kinship networks are often formed and reinforced by means of women, like the giving of women (by men to men) in marriage. How should one see, in that light, Mark's pithy but particular account in the first chapter of the Gospel that Simon's mother-in-law proceeds to serve five grown men (Jesus, Simon, Andrew, James, and John) immediately after being healed by Jesus (1:16–21, 29–31)? Is she not "serving" only as a building block for the early establishment of Jesus' all-male entourage? What about Herod's daughter, whose dance—like the food served on Herod's birthday banquet table—is supposed to facilitate the bonding between Herod and his men ("his courtiers and officers and . . . the leaders of Israel," 6:21)? Her running in and out of the banquet hall to talk to each of her parents respectively (6:22–25) further indicates that Herodias is also not included in this "for-men-only" celebration. This commodification of women may also explain the discrepancy in Mark between the Baptizer's rejection of the "wife swapping" between Herod and his brother, Philip (6:17), and Jesus' (tacit) recognition of the levirate marriage custom when the Sadducees bring it to his attention (12:18–27). Through the passing of a "son-less" widow to her brother-in-law, the levirate marriage (see Deut. 25:5–10) ensures the continuity of family names; it also fortifies men as proper subjects and women as properties. If Herodias' "grudge" against John the Baptizer (6:19) indicates her personal preference for Herod over Philip as her marriage partner, she would be "guilty" of intervening in this male business of exchanging women. Furthermore, she is "guilty" of disrupting the female "conduit" that is supposed to solidify male relations and benefit male participants. With her behind-the-scenes manipulation, Herodias creates instead "discord" between Herod and John the Baptizer

(6:26–29). By getting her revenge, she also participates in reaping a share of the benefit. Has Herodias been given such "bad presses" by both Mark and Mark's interpreters precisely because of her refusal to stay in her place as a woman (caught) in traffic?

It is equally telling if one takes a careful look at what Mark does with Jesus' women followers, whom Mark suddenly and belatedly introduces after the (male) disciples have all failed at Jesus' passion through betrayal, denial, and desertion (14:10–11, 26–72; 15:40–41). Mark is clear that these women's role is limited to the restoration of the broken bond between Jesus and his (male) disciples. In Mark's first Easter morning, these women are never told what the resurrection has to do with them; they are only told to "go, tell his disciples and Peter" that a reunion is awaiting them at Galilee (16:7).[31] These women disciples, in other words, are called upon to be mere channels, so that they can help renew a brotherly bond to which they remain marginal. Mark incorporates these named women disciples in the end of his Gospel in such a way that he secures their subordinate status even while portending, or pretending, their importance.

I mention these three issues in Mark's Gospel (colonialism, anti-Judaism, and sexism) to emphasize that focusing on any one of these issues alone would be doing an injustice to the other two. To be effective, we must start building coalitions or communities of resistance that are based on several issues rather than one differentiating factor of identity.

A Transgressive Perspective

Finally, I want to suggest that reading with yin yang eyes means reading beyond disciplinary lines. Reading from the standpoints of Asian American studies, postcolonial inquiries, and feminist theory has enabled me to look deep into, and even look back at, the biblical text. I hope I have already demonstrated the practical benefits of an interdisciplinary approach to studying the Bible, but I have yet to articulate the theoretical underpinnings for advocating such an approach.

Kwok, with what she calls "parallel processing" (1998: 80), affirms the need to read the Bible inside and outside the framework of traditional biblical studies. Her rationale is the Foucauldian assertion that each discipline has its own disciplinary norms or regimes of truth; one must therefore resort to other critical theories to demystify the established framework and read against the grain. Building on Kwok's Foucauldian rationale, I want to provide another reason why transgressing disciplinary lines is particularly pertinent for my *Chinese American* hermeneutics of the Bible.

Palumbo-Liu (1995b) has suggested that rigid disciplinary boundaries are built upon an assumption of origin and purity. Such an assumption idealizes an "originator" who owns a certain intellectual space, which will only be sullied by trespasses and/or transplants. With the resulting "inside/outside" or "pure/impure" binarisms, a power differential is created to downplay and arrest "guerrilla action within more 'traditional' (i.e., institutionally sanctioned) fields" (Palumbo-Liu 1995b: 57). As Palumbo-Liu readily acknowledges, this problem becomes more acute for scholars pursuing ethnic studies, since such studies are already looked down upon as works of *bricolage,* and thus works of secondary importance.[32]

I hope the connection between interdisciplinary study and my Chinese American biblical hermeneutics is becoming evident by the "border-crossing" language I intentionally employ. Chinese Americans, despite their nativity, are racialized to become perennial border-crossers who do not really belong. The assumptions and arguments that Palumbo-Liu identifies are used to patrol not only disciplinary borders within the academy but also cultural borders within a nation. In both the academy and the nation, our physical presence is used to flaunt "democracy" and "inclusivity," yet our pursuits and movements are circumscribed by invisible but equally inhibiting barbed wire (DuttaAhmed 1996: 340–44). A cross-disciplinary study of the Bible is another important component in my attempt to break out of the one right/white way, and to resist the tyranny of purity.

Eyes for "I"s

Lacan has suggested that a close relationship exists between the eyes and the "I" (1978: 67–119). For him, one sees to be seen; it is by looking at others that self comes into being. In other words, the "I" is generated by what the eyes see, just as the subject is constituted by language. If that is true, I will proceed to argue that the "I" being generated by yin yang eyes is very different from Lacan's imaginary and unified self that initially results from the mirror stage, but the multiple self that Lacan ends up theorizing (1977: 1–7, 292–325). This other "I" doubles, multiplies, and disseminates before my eyes in a yin yang web of contradictions, infractions, coalitions, and transgressions. If I may return to the Gospel of Mark, this other "I" is comparable to the demon (or a ghost, if you will) that answers Jesus with the words, "My name is Legion: for we are many" (5:9). This multiplicity of self, in contrast to the biblical text, is no longer a demon to be exorcised but a strategy to be embraced.[33] Yin yang eyes signify permeability, flux, and an ongoing hybridity. They help me negotiate the slash or hyphen that attempts to separate Chinese from American. They make me aware of various alignments and alliances. They sensitize me to the contradictions between my own sites of pain as well as my own sites of privilege (Tolbert 1995: 263–68). By "re/signing"—to borrow Ono's term to mean both retiring and reconfiguring (1995: 67–68)—binarisms of all forms, yin yang eyes produce for me a Chinese American identity that does not preclude change and difference. They bespeak a phantom-like presence that can be seen, but cannot be sieged or fenced in. As such, it is as threatening as the yin yang eyes that see ghosts.[34]

Seeing More . . . and Talking Back

Since I began this chapter with how a couple of popular media representations of Chinese Americans reify "our" eyes and depict an inevitably troubling relation between Chinese and whites in the United States, I would like to close with two more recent Hollywood movies. The first is the 1982 film *Blade Runner* (starring Harrison Ford). Both Palumbo-Liu (1999: 326–33) and Robert Lee (1999: 191–96) have commented in great detail upon how this movie portrays a "Yellow Peril" of the twenty-first century, when Los Angeles will be largely deserted by whites and populated by Asians engaged in various service and manufacturing industries. To keep their distance from invading Asians, wealthy and healthy whites are living in the "off world," where they are also served by almost-white-but-not-quite "replicant humans." The plot of the movie is, of course, driven by the eventually futile attempt of several replicant humans to escape to Los Angeles to pass as lawful (white) residents. As Robert Lee insightfully points out, the anti-Asian ideology of this film is clearly implicated by its designation of the eyes as the difference marker between white (or right) humans and replicant humans (1999: 195). Blade runners or replicant cops interrogate and detect replicants with a special equipment that looks into the dilation of or reflection in a person's eyes. There is yet another parallel between these replicant humans and the cultural stereotypes of Asian Americans (1999: 11). The dominant culture may call us "model minority," but according to it, our efficiency is always undercut by our lack of emotions. We are "natural" for technologies and sciences but not arts or humanities. We are more like machines, robots, or cyborgs than human beings; in other words, we are replicant, not real, humans.

The other movie is the 1985 hit *Year of the Dragon* (starring Mickey Rourke), which depicts Chinese Americans as the originators of organized crime. Despite their outward appearance of business propriety and prosperity, their international crime ring threatens U.S. society and its white/right way of life. This victimization of white life is personified by the underappreciated and misunderstood anti-hero, whose last name seems like an intentional pun, Inspector White. Inspector White is accused of being a racist because, unlike others around him, he alone can see the "truth" about Chinese Americans. Like *Blade Runner,* this movie also has its share of emphasis on Chinese eyes.[35] As Inspector White becomes emotionally involved with a Chinese American reporter (after raping her), his wife asks sarcastically if he plans to have "slant-eyed" babies. When a Mafia boss hears about the young man who is heading up the Chinese American triad, the Italian comments: "I want to see his face, his eyes. I want to know if he is reckless; one look in his eyes, I will know." Likewise, when Inspector White demands that the Chinese American reporter tell him the truth about her love life, he says: "Tell me the truth. There is no Roger, is there? You know how I know? It's because when you talk about him . . . your eyes, they are not real. . . . I want you to look me in the eyes, and I want you to say it." "Our" eyes never fail to tell the sorry truths about "ourselves."

Yet in each of these two movies, I have managed to see a single line that has captured my argument that, in reading the Bible with yin yang eyes, Chinese Americans—occupying an "outsider within" location that is analogous to both Greco-Roman and African American slaves (P. H. Collins 2000: 10–11; Harrill 2006: 147–54)—can see more as well as talk back to the dominant culture that has racialized "us" by reifying "our" eyes.[36] In *Blade Runner,* one of the fugitive replicants says to the genetic engineer who specializes in making eyes, "If only you could see what I have seen with your eyes." In *Year of the Dragon,* an elderly Chinese American worker says to Inspector White, "I have been here a long time. I have seen many things. I see things a lot of people don't even think I see."

Reading with yin yang eyes is reading from—to borrow James S. Moy's wonderful pun (1993)—a marginal sight/site. Such a marginal sight/site features a contrary look that reads against itself, a returned gaze that reads without any assumption of biblical authority, a broad view that reads beyond single-issue politics, and a transgressive perspective that reads across disciplines. In my opinion, the negotiating power of this approach to biblical hermeneutics lies in its flexibility to "re/sign" the various forms of binarisms that have worked towards the alien-ation of Chinese Americans. It is a biblical hermeneutics that explores the complexity of power, encourages vigilant self-critique, and enables the building of alliances.

CHAPTER 3

Ambiguous Admittance

● ●

Consent and Descent in John's Community of "Upward" Mobility

The idea of a multiple self, which I put forth toward the end of the previous chapter, happens to be the theme of Hual-ing Nieh's *Mulberry and Peach: Two Women of China* (1988). The novel's protagonist, Mulberry, develops another personality known as Peach as she makes her way from China through Taiwan and finally to the United States. What causes the development of this schizophrenia or yin yang personality is a series of traumatic events that are too complicated to retell here. It is, however, important to point out that throughout her journey, Mulberry/Peach is haunted or hunted by various cultural and national authorities determined to construct a singular self to match an undivided body in both individual and communal terms.[1]

While the novel begins with a U.S. immigration officer visiting Peach and, in the process, attempting to control Peach's bodily appearance and, by implication, her sexual behavior (1988: 3–7), it also details Mulberry's need to hide her "undocumented" daughter in an attic in Taiwan (1988: 116–54). Trying to comfort her daughter, Mulberry explains: "The earth is a huge attic. The huge attic is divided into millions of little attics, just like ours" (1988: 129). The immigration apparatus of the United States encountered by Peach is, like the Taiwanese government authority, another "green eye" (1988: 118) that polices a national "attic" with its gaze to determine whether a body is acceptable for inclusion. In fact, one can say that the entire journey of Mulberry/Peach is about traversing bodies or boundaries, and hence deconstructing singularity or unity.[2] Just as patriarchy demands purity or chastity in a female body, so communities and nations require regulated and homogeneous bodies within their borders.

Since the threat of a shared body or non-singular self has much to do with divided allegiance and betrayal, it is not surprising that Asian American bodies—as the internment of Japanese Americans during World War II as well as the more recent cases involving Wen Ho Lee and James Yee show—often become suspects of espionage.[3] Chang-Rae Lee's *Native Speaker* (1995) also deals with this issue of belonging and betrayal, but he complicates the related ideas of identity, community, and nation by casting the main character, Henry Park, in the role of a double agent who spies *on* rather than *for* his fellow Korean American, a politician named John Kwang. If Asian American difference makes assimilation into mainstream white society problematic, Chang-Rae Lee ironically suggests that their marginalization also makes them particularly suitable to play the role of an unnoticeable spy or—to continue the flow from last chapter—a secretly observing private eye. This irony is doubled as Park's race, face, and accented English actually facilitate his double agency or double crossing in yet another way: they make him readily embraceable by Kwang as one of his own.

The politics of inclusion and exclusion is central to this chapter on the Gospel of John. However, I do not begin by assuming that John's Gospel is a product, and thus a reflection, of a so-called community of the beloved disciple. Instead, I see John as a site of struggle for community.[4] As Homi K. Bhabha states, "Community has to be created and negotiated; it isn't just there because you are black or gay" (Bhabha, Gilroy, and Hall 1991: 19). In other words, this chapter will not provide a view of what John's community "was actually like" through the "window" of the Fourth Gospel, but will focus rather on how John's Gospel constructs community. It takes as its point of departure what Anthony P. Cohen calls "the symbolic construction of community" (1985),[5] or what Benedict Anderson calls "imagined communities" (1991).[6] Both Cohen and Anderson emphasize the formation of community through a myriad of symbols, including language or literary texts. Or, to adapt the alliteration of Bhabha (1990b), they claim a close relation between neighbor(liness) and narration. In contrast to Craig R. Koester's attempt to demonstrate how specific symbols *within* John's Gospel bring together "apparently contradictory ideas" (given the root meaning of "symbol" as "putting together," 1995: 27), this chapter will explore how John's Gospel functions *as* a symbol to put people together in a community.[7] More particularly, it will give attention to John's construction of consent, descent, and ascent. As many readers will recognize, the phrase "consent and descent" has been used by Werner Sollors to identify a powerful cultural code in the United States (1986). I borrow his phrase, along with another powerful cultural code (that of "upward mobility") in the chapter's subtitle to situate my reading of John within the context and contest of U.S. (multi)cultural dynamics.[8]

Writing Boundary on Papyri

Building community is clearly the purpose of John's Gospel. As Craig Koester points out, the appearance of Jesus' mother at Cana (2:1–12) and at Golgotha (19:16–27) presents an *inclusio* for Jesus' ministry (1995: 214–15). If the prompting of this "woman" leads to Jesus' inaugural "sign" (2:3–4, 11), Jesus' facilitation of a new adoptive relationship between this same "woman" and the beloved disciple fulfills his work on earth, because John immediately comments, "After *this* [what amounts to the formation of a new relational community], . . . Jesus knew that *all* was now finished" (19:28; emphasis mine).[9]

John certainly sees the crucifixion as the "glorification," the goal, and the climax of Jesus' ministry (3:14–15; 12:27–28; 17:1), but John is also adamant that his readers relate Jesus' death to the establishment of "one flock, one shepherd" (10:14–16) and the "gather[ing] into one the dispersed children of God" (11:49–52). Jesus' farewell prayer further confirms that community is the completion of Jesus' ministry and the intention behind his crucifixion. Jesus prays for two things before his arrest and passion: first, he asks God to glorify him (17:1, 5); and second, he asks God to protect the unity or the community of his present and future followers (17:9–11, 20–23).[10]

According to Raymond Williams, the lexical root of the word "community" is "relations or feelings" (1985: 75). Anthony Cohen suggests that community, as a relational idea, is most concerned with boundary; that is, where community begins and ends (1985: 12–13). This is true whether a community comes into being because of external oppression, internal cohesion, or both (Sollors 1986: 175–76).[11] This emphasis on relations and boundary leads Cohen to highlight one common strategy of community construction: that of contrastive definition, which may include naming or even name-calling (1985: 58, 109–110, 115; see also Sollors 1986: 25, 28). As Cohen puts it, "the finer the differences between people, the stronger is the commitment people have to them" (1985: 110).

Contrastive definition is a major strategy in John. One can find it at work within an episode as well as between successive episodes. For example, in another episode that involves a woman (12:1–8), Jesus' friend and foe are clearly defined by Mary's willingness to spend a costly pound of perfume on Jesus' feet, and Judas' accusation of her extravagance.[12] In fact, John "ousts" Judas with two parenthetical statements: one about Judas' habitual greed (12:6) and the other about his eventual decision to betray Jesus (12:4). Similarly, lines are drawn between a Jewish man who comes to Jesus at night in John 3 and a Samaritan woman who is approached by Jesus at noon in John 4. While Nicodemus leaves Jesus in silent ambivalence (Nicodemus gives no response to Jesus' long answer to his question, 3:9–21), the unnamed woman leaves Jesus in spirited communication (4:28–30, 39).

Naming and name-calling are also part of John's repertoire to construct community. In contrast to "disciples" who believe (2:11; 16:27, 29–30), remember or continue in Jesus' word (2:17–22; 8:31; 12:16), and bear fruit (15:8), the "crowd" seeks but misunderstands Jesus' signs (6:2, 22–26; 7:12; 12:17–18, 34–37). In distinction from "disciples" whom Jesus cleanses (13:3–10; 15:3), teaches (13:31–16:33), prays for, and calls his own (17:6–26), the *Ioudaioi* consider Jesus a sinner and demon-possessed (8:48, 52; 9:18–24), and are in turn condemned by Jesus (5:37–47; 8:21–26, 44–47; 10:24–26).[13] Unlike "Galileans" who welcome Jesus (4:45), the *Ioudaioi* complain about Jesus (6:41–42, 52; 7:14–15, 35–36; 8:22, 27), persecute him and his followers (5:16; 9:18–22; 19:38), and seek to kill him (5:18; 7:1; 8:57–59; 10:31–33; 19:7).[14] John basically uses these names to characterize "insiders" and "outsiders" vis-à-vis Jesus' community (C. R. Koester 1995: 263). Later on in the narrative, when Nicodemus speaks up briefly on Jesus' behalf, John indirectly and partially changes his earlier designation of him as "a Pharisee" and "a leader of the *Ioudaioi*" to that of a "Galilean" (3:1; 7:45–52). In contrast, the Roman governor Pilate ironically identifies himself as an *Ioudaios* when he interrogates Jesus for the *Ioudaioi* (18:33–35). After all, Jesus hides and stays away from the "crowd" and from *Ioudaioi* (11:54; 12:34–37), but he stays with "disciples" (1:35–39; 3:22), and addresses them as "friends" (11:11; 15:14–15) and "brothers" (20:17–18).

John uses yet another "name" to perform his contrastive construction of Jesus' community. Despite the distinction that John sometimes draws between the "crowd" and the *Ioudaioi*, both are subsumed under what he calls the "world."[15] This term signifies what is earthly and what is from below, in contrast to Jesus who comes from above. As Jesus is not part of the "world," his community is also not part of the "world" (8:23; 14:18–21; 15:19; 17:6–9, 14). What belongs to the "world," whether it is the provision of food or the power to rule, is also not comparable to what comes from above (6:25–33; 19:8–11).

As the passages referenced here indicate, John does not construct community only through a categorization of (in)difference. He also does it by placing his "community-under-construction" under siege. Jesus' farewell prayer for divine protection of his community is occasioned by a hostile and hateful "world" that rejoices at the community's suffering (16:20). With the tactic of name-calling, John categorizes the "world" as ignorant (1:10; 14:17) and attributes its intolerance to (1) desire for attention (5:44; 12:42–43),[16] and (2) association with the deceitful and murderous devil (3:20; 7:7; 8:44). As a result, the "world" will pursue those who belong to Jesus with the same intensity that it persecutes Jesus (15:20; 16:1–2; 21:18–19). John's naming and name-calling function to highlight the peril that faces Jesus and those who believe in him, and thus belong to Jesus. Recognizing a nemesis, however, can result in a "fortress mentality" that fosters community.[17] It is the same dynamic of singing the song "You and Me against the World"; every time you sing it, the "you-and-me" part becomes closer, stronger, and more real. Without telling us, John actually shows us the desired effect of this emphasis on nemesis in a couple of episodes. The more viciously the *Ioudaioi* attack the congenital blind beggar healed by Jesus, the more tenaciously he commits himself to his healer (9:1–38). Likewise, in response to repeated attempts to stone Jesus on the part of the *Ioudaioi* (8:59; 10:31; 11:7–10), Thomas concludes with the following announcement to his fellow "disciples": "Let us also go [with Jesus to Judea], that we may die with him" (11:16).

Contrastive construction of community also often involves humor or (inside) jokes. Sollors talks about how "communities of laughter arise at the expense of some outsiders," because "a sense of we-ness" develops in laughing with others and/or at others (1986: 132). Irony, of course, is an effective literary strategy for this end (Culpepper 1983:165–80; Tolbert 1989: 98–103; see also Hutcheon 1994). Since there is already a major monograph as well as a major review essay on John's use of irony (Duke 1985; Culpepper 1996b), I will just give some brief examples. A boundary arises between readers and the "world" when the former read and laugh about the latter's inconsistencies: they belong to the devil while they accuse Jesus of demon possession (7:20; 8:48, 52; 10:20); they circumcise on the Sabbath while they criticize Jesus for healing on the same day (7:19–23); they reject Jesus' Galilean origin while they remain ignorant of his origin from above (7:25–29, 52); they murder God's child while they remember the gracious Passover of God with rigid insistence on details to avoid ritual defilement (18:28; 19:31); they charge Jesus with treason against the Roman empire while they ask for the release of a known bandit (18:38–40; 19:12); and they concede loyalty to the Roman emperor while they crucify Jesus for blasphemy (10:33; 19:7, 15). On the other hand, walls of laughter come up *around* readers and Jesus when they read the comment of the unsuspecting steward after Jesus' first "sign," that the "bridegroom" was not like "every man" (2:9–10; see also 3:27–30); when they read about the opening of the "door" to God through Jesus and the closing of the synagogue door by the *Ioudaioi* (9:22; 10:7–10; 12:42; 16:2); or when they read that "the light of the world" exercises authority over those who come with weapons and artificial lights to arrest him in a garden (8:12; 9:5; 18:1–12).

John's use of irony is closely connected with his other strategy of boundary construction. His Gospel is like a shroud of mystery that rises and falls on its characters as well as its readers, thus provoking a potential division between the initiated (those who understand) and the uninitiated (those who do not). Or, to use Norman R. Petersen's words, John uses a "special language" or "anti-language" to create "an anti-society" (1992: 5–6). Anthony Cohen reminds us that "the boundaries of communities perform the same function as do the boundaries of all categories of knowledge" (1985: 14). Alternatively, Benedict Anderson refers to the linguistic diversity that results from the dethroning of Latin and results in the imagination of plural communities (1991: 42–43). What we learn from both Anthony Cohen and Anderson is that knowledge, language, and community are intricately bound. The same point is made not only by the title of Chang-Rae Lee's "spy novel" *(Native Speaker)*, but also by the difficult relationship between its Korean American protagonist and his white, speech therapist wife (1995). What makes people become conscious of their belonging to and participating in a community is the sharing of the same educational and linguistic boundaries. Because of that, the capacity to hold back information or deny linguistic facility is "an essential social and communal weapon" (A. P. Cohen 1985: 87, see also 84, 89).[18] Language, then, has the capacity to create or crush community by conferring or withholding knowledge and information. My use of the word "or" in the previous sentence, however, does not imply two neat and clear separations. In other words, conferring and withholding knowledge and information can both be used to create or crush community. In my opinion, John constructs community precisely by maneuvering his language simultaneously to confer to *and* withhold understanding from his characters and his readers.[19]

Sometimes John does so by manipulating double meanings, like "to be born again and/or to be born from above" (*gennēthēi anōthen*, 3:3), or "spring water and/or living water" (*hydōr zōn*, 4:10). At other times, he does so by mixing metaphorical and literal usages of a word within a single episode, like "temple" in 2:19–21, "food" in 4:31–34, "bread" in 6:32–35, or "sleep" in 11:11–14.[20] Either way, divisions are drawn, as some characters within the Gospel become perplexed or misunderstand while others are able to follow. At the same time, readers are involved in a similar double movement of understanding and misunderstanding as they follow the mixture of comprehension and incomprehension experienced by the characters. Not only will this encounter (much like irony) ally readers with characters who get the picture *over* against characters who do not,[21] its instability will also lure or seduce readers into community with the implied author. The three-step process that Ted Cohen identifies for the functioning of metaphors in a verbal situation is equally applicable to the reading of John's Gospel: "(1) the speaker [John] issues a kind of concealed invitation; (2) the hearer [reader] expends a special effort to accept the invitation; (3) this transaction constitutes the acknowledgment of a community" (1978; cited in C. R. Koester 1995: 231–32). This "transaction" that results in community is premised on the extension and acceptance of an invitation rather than a clear and complete understanding of a metaphor. That is to say, the outcome of a challenge is often secondary to the primary bonding experience of participating in the challenge.

A Community of Confessing Consenters

It should be clear by now that in contrast to those who (1) seek perishable food and drinking water, and (2) thus make up a deceitful and hateful "world," John is constructing a community (or in Petersen's terms, an "anti-society") around Jesus, who is the "bread from heaven," the source of "living water," the witness to truth and the manifestation of love (3:16; 4:13–14; 6:35; 18:37). Jesus' self-identification as "the door" (10:7) certainly indicates an inside and an outside. Moreover, his following elaboration of the metaphor explains not only that Jesus handles all membership exclusively, but also that his community has no previous enrollment (10:8–10). According to John, there is only one way to see, know, believe, and follow God, and that one way is Jesus. All other ways are hazardous and bogus (10:27–30; 12:44–50; 14:6–7). If the "door" metaphor indicates that membership in Jesus' community is exclusive, the "true vine" metaphor illustrates that this membership also requires absolute dependence (15:1, 4–6).[22] These metaphors establish a "centripetal effect, bringing believers into relationship with each other by reinforcing their common relationship to Jesus" (C. R. Koester 1995: 230; see also 5, 84–85). With the cleansing of the temple (2:13–17) and the conversation with the woman at the well (4:1–30, 39–42), Jesus replaces the centers of worship of both the *Ioudaioi* and the Samaritans, and becomes the new center of a new community (Coloe 2001).[23]

What this Christocentric construction of community means is that members must confess Jesus. What confessing Jesus means, in turn, is that membership is based on consent instead of descent. As an alternative community to the "world," Jesus' community is not built upon heredity or ancestry, but on choice and judgment. John makes this point in the first chapter of his Gospel, where he contrasts a nat(ur)al relation to a super-nat(ur)al relation (1:13), and promises community to "all" who believe (1:12). Before John's Jesus performs his first "sign" to begin his ministry, Jesus distances himself from a blood relationship by this statement to his mother, "Woman, what do you have to do with me?" (2:4). As we have already mentioned, the "echo" of this episode in Cana is the scene at the cross, where Jesus addresses his mother again as "woman," and "from that hour," brings her and the beloved disciple together in an adoptive familial relation (19:25–27). This "replacement relation" is particularly unusual because John is clear that Jesus is not the only son of the family, for he concludes the episode at Cana by identifying Jesus' brothers separately from his mother and his "disciples" (2:12). Later on in the Gospel, John will spell out the reason for this separation by having Jesus' brothers make a sarcastic remark about Jesus' need to go public for the sake of the "disciples" (7:1–4). After that remark, we find another parenthetical statement by John: "For not even his brothers believed in him" (7:5). As far as the Gospel is concerned, Jesus and his brothers seem to part ways from that point on (7:6–10), and we find the resurrected Jesus identifying the "disciples" as his new "brothers" near the end of the Gospel (20:17–18). In John, then, community with Jesus is not based on biological descent of the family.

Another illustration of this differentiation between faith and family can be found in the confession on the part of the blind beggar and the aversion on the part of his parents (9:18–23). While the beggar openly confesses Jesus' healing power to the *Ioudaioi*, his parents deny any knowledge of or association with Jesus. Since John gives great emphasis to the congenital nature of the beggar's blindness (9:1, 18–20, 32), one may argue that what this "sign" reveals (9:3) is Jesus' ability to overcome the limits of descent—whether it be biological, familial, or ethnic/national. Jesus, as "the light of the world" (8:12; 9:5), is not limited to Israel. In contrast to the manna of Jewish ancestry, Jesus as "the bread of life" is everlasting, life-giving, and given to "who[m]ever": "anyone," "all," and "everyone" who comes in faith (6:29–51). Jesus, as "the good shepherd" (10:11, 14), is concerned to bring in "other sheep" from "other folds" (10:16). The rest of Jesus' statement to his mother ("My hour has not yet come," 2:4) is repeated several times in John (7:8c, 30; 8:20c). When Jesus finally announces that his hour has come, he is responding to the coming of the Greeks (12:20–23; see also 7:32–36).[24] This "gather[ing] into one the dispersed children of

God" (11:52) is further signified by the multilingual sign above the cross (19:19–20).

This emphasis on consent over descent is evident in the way John attributes the rejection experienced by Jesus to various ancestral concerns of the *Ioudaioi*. They are, for example, baffled by Jesus' untraceable intellectual lineage or his Galilean origin (6:41–42; 7:14–18, 27, 40–52). They are unable to hear Jesus' message because they are adamant about being descendants of Abraham (8:31–59) and "disciples of Moses" (9:28). They are ready to sacrifice Jesus because they grant priority to the preservation of their nation (11:45–50). In many ways, their problem is Nicodemus' problem. Nicodemus, the "Pharisee . . . [and] leader of the *Ioudaioi*" (3:1), is stuck by the "how-can" question, which he asks Jesus twice (3:4, 9). He is stuck because he is not able to shed what is impossible in the old paradigm of biological descent in order to receive what is now possible in the new paradigm of spiritual consent.[25]

Jesus, however, is able to do for the Samaritan woman what he cannot help Nicodemus overcome. For Sollors, marriage is characteristic of consent relations (1986: 6). It is also by now a familiar understanding within Johannine scholarship that the meeting between Jesus and the woman at the well amounts to a betrothal-type scene (see Alter 1981: 51–62; Fehribach 1998: 47–58; J. K. Kim 2004: 98–101).[26] John sets the stage for this betrothal by (1) having Jesus take over the bridegroom's duty to provide wine at the wedding at Cana with his first "sign" (2:1–12); (2) having John the Baptist refer to Jesus as the "bridegroom" (3:25–30); and (3) specifying that the well that forms the backdrop in the meeting between Jesus and the Samaritan woman is none other than the ancestral well of Jacob (4:5–6a). When Jesus approaches the woman for water, she raises several descent-related concerns: (1) the long-standing barrier between *Ioudaioi* and Samaritans because of the latter's mixed lineage (4:9); (2) Jesus' status vis-à-vis "our ancestor Jacob" (4:12); and (3) the different locations of worship according to ancestral traditions (4:19–20). Despite these concerns, her encounter with Jesus ends in her proclamation and the confession by many Samaritans that Jesus is the "savior of the world" (4:28–30, 39–42).[27] In other words, by centering on Jesus, John is constructing a community that goes beyond the limits of descent. Its construction is based on a different paradigm: it is based on faith, confession, or consent.

John's consent, however, should not be understood just as an opposition to descent; it should also be seen as the opposite of dissent. That is to say, John is also constructing a community that emphasizes assent or agreement revolving around the central figure of Jesus.[28] Unlike those who find Jesus' words offensive and leave (6:60–66), the twelve acknowledge his words as "words of eternal life" (6:67–69). Unlike the *Ioudaioi* who refuse to hear what they are told (9:27), the congenital blind beggar follows Jesus' instruction to wash in Siloam and gains sight for the first time in his life (9:6–7, 11). "Disciples" must abide in Jesus' love by obeying his commands (14:15, 21, 23–24; 15:9–10). Or, as Jesus' mother explains to the servants at Cana, "Do whatever he [Jesus] tells you" (2:5; see also 13:12–17). Just like the official who hears Jesus' command to return home and thus witnesses his son's healing (4:46–54), a sheep that belongs to Jesus' flock is identifiable by its hearing of the shepherd's voice (10:3, 16, 27; see also 3:29–30; 5:24–25; 8:43, 47; 18:37).

To construct this community of consent, John proceeds to show and tell the exemplary unity between Jesus and God (17:11). Rather than seeking glory from people like the *Ioudaioi* do (5:44; 12:43), Jesus and God form a "mutual glorification society" (5:41; 8:50, 54). First, Jesus glorifies God by living a life of compliance, which involves being God's "ventriloquized voice."[29] Jesus does not speak for God, but God speaks through him, and Jesus has no voice of his own (7:16–18; 8:28–29; 12:49–50; 14:24). Second, Jesus does nothing on his own. He copies whatever God does, and does whatever God says (5:16–17, 19–21, 30). The clearest proof, and thus the climax of this life of compliance is his crucifixion or his willingness to sacrifice himself in accordance with God's command (10:17–18; 14:30–31; 18:11).[30] As Jesus completes this life in consent to God's decree, God will be glorified and God will glorify Jesus in return (12:27–28; 17:1, 4–5). Thus, Jesus' community is to be a carbon copy of this consenting or assenting relation: to obey Jesus as Jesus obeys God (14:23–24; 15:10; 17:6). What Jesus hears from God and gives to his community is a command to love one another (13:34–35). What Jesus does in obedience and in service to God for his community is also part of that command to love—that is, to be willing to serve and give up life for one another (13:34–35; 15:12–14). In other words, the unity between Jesus and God becomes a model for the community's relation with Jesus, as well as for the internal relations among its members.

Notice that John often represents this emphasis on consent through unity using a language of love. Jesus' obedience to God is a result of God's love for him, causes God to love him, and demonstrates his own love for God (3:35; 10:17; 14:31). Likewise, Jesus loves those who belong to him. Those who belong to him will demonstrate their love for him by obedience, and they will be loved because of their obedience (11:5; 13:1; 14:15, 21, 23–24). What we have then, in John, is a community in the form of an irregular triangle. This is a triangle where God, Jesus, and "disciples" are united by (1) an obedience that goes in one direction and stops at the top (from "disciples" to Jesus, and from Jesus to God);[31] and (2) a love that runs in a circular motion and in both directions (3:16; 15:9; 17:23, 26). In John, obedience, unity, and love are so intertwined that they are essentially inseparable.

What I am suggesting is that John constructs a community that requires confession and demands consent by employing a rhetoric of unity and love. I think this merging or blurring of consent, unity, and love is also at work behind the mystifying role that the beloved disciple plays within the Gospel. As we have already seen, the beloved disciple, being entrusted by Jesus to take care of Jesus' mother (the scene of the cross), is the representative figure John uses to announce the emergence of this new community of consent (19:26–30). John also claims to base his writing on the witness of this beloved disciple (21:24), but he is never named. In fact, he is mentioned late and seldom within the Gospel.[32] While John credits him as the first believer in Jesus' resurrection (20:8), John also states (1) that he, like Peter, "did not understand the Scripture, that he [Jesus] must rise from the dead" (20:9; see also 2:19–22), and (2) that Mary Magdalene was the first one to proclaim Jesus' resurrection. Moreover, John, with one exception (19:26–27), always mentions the beloved disciple along with Peter. In these narratives where they appear together, John always names Peter first and generally devotes more coverage to him.

What can be the benefit to this rhetorical effacement of the beloved disciple in light of John's community construction?[33] First, I think this effacement strengthens John's attempt to construct a community around Jesus. Keeping the spotlight on Jesus, in turn, strengthens John's community building by making it "Jesusian" rather than one that is exclusively tied to the particular lineage of the beloved disciple. Associating Peter with the beloved disciple allows John not only to incorporate Peter's authority when needed, it also bolsters John's emphasis on consent by representing a sort of consensus that Peter and the beloved disciple share as followers of Jesus. It is a move that gives John the flexibility of multiplicity and, at the same time, the authority of unity. It gives credibility as well as content to John's symbolic construction of a consenting community.[34]

An Up-Coming, Never-Ending, and Ever-Growing Community

John's emphasis on consent as both confession and consensus should remind us not to read the preceding section apart from boundary construction. Arguing against descent and dissent does not just construct intra-communal dynamics, it gives "vitality to boundary" (A. P. Cohen 1985: 35–36). Those who do not make a conscious choice to concur with John's Jesus are left out in the dark, deprived of light and direction (12:35–36c). They will remain in the "world" below and die in their sins (8:23–24). In contrast, members of the community are destined to move upward. John stresses that Jesus is from above, and repeatedly refers to his crucifixion as an "up-lifting" experience, or as a prelude to his ascending return to God (3:13–15; 6:62; 8:28; 12:32–34; 13:1, 3; 14:12, 28; 16:4–5, 10, 28; 17:11a–c, 13a; 20:17).[35] Thus, John's Jesus promises that while "outsiders" cannot follow where he goes (7:32–36; 8:21–24), his followers will follow him in this "upward mobility" (12:26; 13:36; 14:1–4; 17:24). As Jesus tells Nathanael in their first encounter, Jesus is both the hub and vehicle of heavenly communication and transportation (1:51).

This "upward mobility" is what John means by "eternal life" (3:16, 36; 5:24; 6:47; 10:28a–b; 12:25, 49–50; 17:3). It includes not just being raised up from physical death (6:39–40, 44, 54; 11:25–26), but also a rise in the quality of life (8:51–53; 10:10; 17:2–3). While Jesus' own resurrection (20:1–20, 24–29) and his raising of Lazarus (11:1–44) show the first nuance of "eternal life,"[36] Jesus' other "signs" portray the second nuance of "eternal life" in John. With Jesus, his followers experience that plainness changes into sumptuousness (2:1–12), sickness into health (4:46–5.9b), paucity into plenty (6:1–14), terror into peace (6:16–21), and darkness into light (9:1–7).

In John's construction, this upward swing will entail a soaring in the community's membership as well. We have already seen that, for John, Jesus' crucifixion, or his being "lifted up," will result in community. John's Jesus is so confident in the "draw" of the cross and the "fruit-bearing potential" of his "disciples" that he ends his farewell prayer interceding for his next generation(s) of followers (12:24, 32; 17:18–23). The success of this growth to come is depicted in the miraculous catch of fish orchestrated by the risen Jesus (21:1–8, 11).[37] Just as Jesus had taught them earlier (15:4–5), the "disciples" come up empty when they go fishing on their own. But when they follow Jesus' direction, they have a large catch. In fact, John makes a point of describing repeatedly the abundance of this catch (21:6, 8, 11).

This up-and-coming community of John's construction is characterized by honor, glory, and expansion. With the freedom and power to conquer (8:31–32; 12:31; 16:33; 17:2), it will march in strides (11:9–10). As John declares, not once, but twice in one verse, "The one who comes from above is above all. . . . The one who comes from heaven is above all" (3:31). In sum, Jesus' community is qualitatively and quantitatively appealing, both in terms of the present and the future.[38] With this construction, John provides an enticing invitation to those outside, but also reinforces the boundary for those inside.

Legitimation, Convolutions, and Contradictions

According to Anthony Cohen, symbolic construction of community often turns to the past for legitimation (1985: 99). This "invention of tradition" (Hobsbawn and Ranger 1983) has been identified by Anderson as fashioning a community "up time" rather than "down time" (1991: 205). In other words, selective memory or creative composition is used to fabricate a history or precedent to make the present construction look valid and natural. Anthony Cohen underscores the emotional investment of this strategy (1985: 102), and thus compares it to Victor W. Turner's "condensation symbols" (1967). It is such a significant part of imagining community that Anderson spends an entire chapter of his book on it (1991: 187–206), and examples of it actually spill over into the other chapters. Whether it is through the "primordialness of language," production of "historical maps," or exhibits in a museum, Anderson shows how looking old can be looking good (1991: 44, 144–45, 174, 181).

Sollors describes one particular maneuver of this "retrospective" and "retroactive" strategy that is, in my opinion, important for John. We may call it the "I-am-third" strategy, although Sollors himself refers to it as the psychoanalytic concept of a "grandfather complex" (1986: 221–23, 230–33). Those who practice this strategy basically claim a third-generation status, thus positioning themselves to "surpass the old ones [second generation or parents] in the name of even older ones [first generation or grandparents]" (Sollors 1986: 230).[39]

We have already talked about the struggle between John's Jesus and the *Ioudaioi* over lineage (6:41–42; 7:14–18, 27, 40–52; 8:31–59). What we must not lose sight of is how consistently John has Jesus invoke an older authority figure to circumvent his opponents. In fact, John has the Baptizer state the operating principle behind the "grandfather complex" early in his Gospel: "After me [the Baptizer] comes a man [Jesus] who ranks ahead of me because he was *before* me" (1:30; emphasis mine [see also 1:15]). It is the priority of precedence. Thus John finds it important, for example, to clarify that circumcision is not from Moses but from the patriarchs (7:22). When the *Ioudaioi* claim the authority of the paramount patriarch—Abraham—John has Jesus either assert his own prior existence (8:48–59) or debate whether they are actually faithful to Abraham (8:39–40). The trump card is, of course, that everything can be overridden in the name of God as "[Grand]Father [*sic*]" (5:15–24; 6:30–33, 43–51, 57–58; 9:28–33). By resorting to the strategic argument of origins, Jesus is able to deflect the criticism about his disregard for the law with the mantra: "I am not swerving, Moses or Abraham. I am serving and fulfilling God. I am I AM" (see Sollors 1986: 230).[40] Jesus is the "good wine" that is delayed (2:9–10). This "grandfather complex"—in terms of Jesus' pre-existence with/as God (1:1–4, 17–18) and/or Jesus' obedience to God—allows John to argue that his community, though late in coming, is "consistent with the law but not derived from the law" (C. R. Koester 1995: 136). The *Ioudaioi* may have been constructing a temple for forty-six years (2:20), but John is going to write the "real" community into existence in twenty-one chapters.

The power of this construction lies in its flexibility to invoke and revoke tradition, because it constructs an "antitype, the redemptive fulfillment of types, of original ancestors" (Sollors 1986: 230). It allows John to do so with Moses (5:45–47; 6:30–33, 49–51, 58; 10:8), or consider Nathanael the "true Israelite" who has no deceit over against the first Israelite (Jacob) who was deceitful (1:47). As the Word that has been there from the beginning and in whom everything has its beginning (1:1–4), Jesus proves himself to be greater than Jacob or any other founding figure. As such, he is able to accuse the *Ioudaioi* of making false claims to paternity (6:25–59; 8:42–44) and incorporate the traditions of Samaria as well as those of the world (4:12, 28–29, 39–42).[41]

This move for legitimation through the "invention of tradition," however, brings to the surface a tension within John's symbolic construction of community. One should remember that Anderson's term for nations, "imagined communities," has a double nuance. In addition to the idea that communities are constructed by the power of imagination, Anderson means for the term to connote also the thought that comradeship and unity are imaginations that cover up actual inequalities and differences (1991: 7; see also Balibar 1991). Or, in the words of Anthony Cohen, "the symbolic repertoire of a community . . . [seeks to construct] the reality of difference into the appearance of similarity," because boundary is the "public mask" that a community puts on to conceal private differences (1985: 21, 108–9). Anderson's emphasis on imagination as a camouflage is also one of the reasons why Bhabha links nation or community to language (1990b: 1–5). Language is inseparable from the construction of nation or community; but nation or community is also like language, because both are full of ambivalence or ambiguities. Bhabha signifies the instability of both nation and language with another playful signifier, "DissemiNation" (1990a). In other words, nation, like language, disseminates and disintegrates in the Derridean sense of *différance* and ambiguity. Why? Because the exterior (boundary) of a nation or community erodes, and its interior interrupts. Bhabha suggests, then, that in one's study of nation or community, one should pay attention not only to the "tension in the creation of community" (2003: 171), but also to the "margins of the nation-space and . . . the boundaries *in-between* nations and peoples" (1990b: 4; emphasis in original).

What would Bhabha's suggestion help uncover in John's community construction? In spite of John's claim that his community is based on consent rather than descent, descent resurfaces throughout his narrative. After all, the entire Gospel, in retelling Jesus' story, is itself a form of "reversed ventriloquism" that creates and claims the authority of lineage or descent by "speak[ing] for the dead" (Anderson 1991: 198). As we have just seen, John is concerned about the future expansion of the community. And this concern, in turn, betrays his concern about the next generation, the passing on of his construction as tradition, and thus his own concern with descent. The same can be said regarding John's selective use of Hebrew Scripture (2:22; 5:39; 6:45; 7:38; 12:13–16, 38–41; 13:18; 15:25; 17:12; 19:23–25, 28; 19:36–37),[42] as well as his pervasive use of kinship and familial language. While hanging on the cross, Jesus brings his mother and the beloved disciple into a fictive familial relation, asking them to address each other as "son" and "mother" (19:26–27). And after the resurrection, he refers to his "disciples" as "brothers" (20:17–18).

John's use of the kinship metaphor goes much deeper. Confessing Jesus is represented as an experience of (re)birth that results in a parent–child relationship with the divine (1:12–13; 3:3). Although John starts his Gospel by (1) contrasting birth by "blood" and by "will" (1:13), and (2) referring to this (re)birth as one of "water and spirit" (3:5), John ends it by showing that this (re)birth through Jesus does involve blood. When the soldier spears Jesus' body after the crucifixion, John tells us that "blood and water came out at once" (19:34). In fact, one should remember that John's Jesus does not just come into the world through a descent from above like the Holy Spirit (1:32–33; 6:38), but as a descendant, a child of God, in order that more divine descendants will be (re)born (1:12, 3:3–7, 13–16).[43] As the Word was a progenitor from the beginning (1:3–4), so Jesus will continue to birth a community.[44]

John's emphasis on consent over against descent is also weakened by traces where will and choice are revealed to be limited in power. All the talk about confessing Jesus notwithstanding, John himself confesses several times that confessing Jesus is impossible without divine initiative. God has to allow it to take place (3:26–27; 6:37, 64b–65), and then also has to make it happen with some kind of a divine magnet-like pull (6:44; 12:32). Quoting the prophet Isaiah, John asserts that without this divine permission and pull, people will not be able to understand and confess Jesus (12:37–41).

This motif of misunderstanding or incomprehension is, of course, all through John's Gospel (see Culpepper 1983: 152–65). And we know that it is not solely due to human refusal, but also results from divine repudiation. From the beginning, John's contrast between birth by blood and birth by will actually contains a specific reference to birth by human will. These traces of emphasis on divine prerogative over human initiative may show that John is not using it as simply another reference to physical birth (a reiteration of birth by blood), but also as a reference to the (futile) human desire and determination to confess Jesus. Given this emphasis on divine descent and a rather deterministic view that is associated with it, I cannot help but wonder if these forms of self-legitimation are not fundamentally in conflict with John's emphasis on consent.

Descent also takes a detour and returns to haunt John's construction of a multi-ethnic community that supposedly finds unity by overcoming descent with consent. We have already seen how John has Samaritans and Greeks coming to confess or admit Jesus (4:28–30, 39–42; 7:32–36; 12:20–23). We have yet to note, however, John's own admission that the *Ioudaioi* do occupy a place of priority in his community of united consensus. For example, John's Jesus admits to the Samaritan woman that he is an *Ioudaios*, and that "salvation is from the *Ioudaioi*" (4:9, 22). Furthermore, this priority of the *Ioudaioi* is evident in the way John puts the term "messiah" in the Samaritan woman's mouth (4:25, 29), although Samaritans of John's time did not use this word to refer to the prophetic figure whom they awaited (C. R. Koester 1995: 43). What looks like a consent of equals may turn out to be a relation of dependence, especially in light of the (patriarchal) marriage metaphor. In John's episode of (communal) erotics, the Samaritans are represented as a woman who must subject herself to the primacy of the male lover. Jesus, as the *Ioudaios* and the "bridegroom," is the one who takes the initiative to approach her and brings her salvation.[45]

These fissures in John's construction of a consenting community are not only applicable to the understanding of consent in contrast to descent, but also applicable to understanding consent in opposition to dissent. In other words, there are cracks in the wall that John constructs to cut off two camps of consensus, and intracommunal conflict is always already taking place alongside intercommunal rivalry. While John generally assumes the "crowd," the *Ioudaioi*, and the "world" to be monolithically anti-Jesus, he occasionally admits that they are "divided" within (7:43; 9:16; 10:19). They debate about Jesus, with opinions ranging from Jesus being the messiah and a prophet to Jesus being demon-possessed (7:31, 40–41; 10:20–21). They take opposing positions about Jesus being a "good man" or a "con man" (7:12). They disagree about whether the messiah's origin is known or unknown (7:27, 42). When a vestige of faith in Jesus is disclosed by the "temple police" (7:45–46), an attempt is made to cover up this fissure in the camp with a reference to the "united" front among the "authorities" and the "Pharisees" against Jesus (7:47–48). Yet John later divulges that there is also no "unity" among those groups (9:16; 12:42). According to him, dissenters within the "crowd" and the "authorities" have to refrain from confessing Jesus because they are afraid of the *Ioudaioi* and the "Pharisees" respectively (7:13; 12:42–43). Nevertheless, we have already seen that consensus among the *Ioudaioi* and the "Pharisees" regarding Jesus is itself a hallucination (8:30–31; 9:16; 11:45; 12:9–11).

In like manner, there is dissension and contradiction within Jesus' camp, despite John's rhetoric of unity and love. Judas Iscariot is, of course, the obvious example. Not only does he steal from the "public purse," he complains about Mary's anointing of Jesus' feet as balmy waste, and finally betrays Jesus to the "other" side (6:70–71; 12:1–6; 13:10–11, 17–18, 21–30). While Judas provides an obvious example, he is not the only example. We find within John other "disciples" who become deserters (6:60, 64, 66), deniers (13:36–38; 18:17, 25–27), or even dissidents who desire Jesus' death (8:31–37).[46]

The relationship between Peter and the beloved disciple affords more ambiguities. It is true that John generally gives Peter first billing as well as more action and conversation. At the same time, John is clear that the beloved disciple precedes Peter in knowing the identity of the betrayer (13:21–26), in reaching and seeing the empty tomb (20:3–5), in believing in Jesus' resurrection (20:8), and in recognizing the risen Jesus beside the sea of Tiberius (21:7). I commented earlier on John's attempt to unite Peter and the beloved disciple in his community construction, but this attempt is seething with underlying tensions and competition. In fact, one may argue that John's attempt to incorporate Peter into his construction of a united community of love blows up at the end, when the risen Jesus tells Peter to care for Jesus' followers *without* concerning himself with the future of the beloved disciple (21:15–17, 20–22).

This discussion surrounding the beloved disciple and Peter leads us to yet another crevice in John's intra-communal and inter-communal construction. If the unnamed disciple who accompanies Peter to the high priest's house after Jesus' arrest is indeed the beloved disciple, then the beloved disciple would have also preceded Peter in entering the courtyard of the high priest (18:15–16).[47] Regardless of the identity of this unnamed disciple, this episode unveils the mingling of Jesus' "friends" and "foes." Peter is able to bypass the guard only because Peter's fellow follower of Jesus is "known to the high priest" (18:15c, 16b–c). In other words, not only are there schisms within each camp, and not only do people change camps, there are ongoing relations between Jesus' "friends" and "foes" even when their attitudes towards Jesus remain unchanged. John's *Ioudaioi*, for example, are there to "console" Mary and Martha because of Lazarus' death (11:19, 31), and they weep together along with Jesus (11:33–37). As Bhabha writes, "The 'other' is never outside or beyond us; it emerges forcefully, within cultural discourse, when we *think* we speak most intimately and indigenously between ourselves" (1990b: 4; emphasis in original). If the "world" below cannot shut out a Jesus who descends from above, then neither can the "disciples" be completely shielded from the *Ioudaioi*.[48]

Contradictions are also present in the center figure around whom John is constructing community. While Jesus announces that "true Israelites" are, unlike their trickster founder Jacob, people without "deceit" (1:47), we find this founding figure of John's community deceiving and double-talking to his brothers about his plan regarding the festival of Booths (7:1–10; see also 7:18). In contrast to his own praise of his pioneer, John the Baptizer, as "a burning and shining lamp" (5:35), Jesus pronounces that "*all* who came before me are thieves and bandits" (10:8, emphasis mine; see also 1:6, 26–27, 29–30). Despite John's attempt to suppress both descent and dissent in his symbolic construction of community, both rise to the surface to contradict his own narrative.[49]

Ambiguous Admittance, Ambiguous Alterity, and Asian Americans

Rey Chow points out that the word "community" is closely related to the word "admittance," and that this latter, ambiguous word has at least three different meanings or connotations (1998: 56–57). Admittance means, first of all, permission to enter a physical space, like going into a country. It means, second, a form of social recognition or acknowledgment that implies a sense of belonging, like being validated as worthy to be part of a school, a discipline, or an association. Finally, the word means confession, like surrendering to face the consequences of a crime, or repenting as a result of a conviction or conversion.

I find Chow's explication of the word extremely helpful in approaching the deep and layered ambiguity in John's symbolic construction of community. For John, admittance into his community (Chow's second definition) hinges on one's admitting faith in Jesus (Chow's third definition). As John requires and demands admittance of Jesus (in the sense of conversion or conviction), will John himself admit the problems that are involved in his construction (in the sense of wrongdoing or crime)? What I find in John is a contradictory impulse to invoke and revoke the power of descent, as well as a contradictory impulse to oust "outsiders" and increase "insiders." As a result, the power of consent that he emphasizes so much actually has hidden limits. Complex relations are reduced to one-dimensional, neatly separable "friends" or "foes." Seepage through and differences within the community of his construction are smoothed over and covered up. Despite his best efforts, what we find in his Gospel is a community that is (1) torn between consent and descent, (2) simultaneously open and closed, and (3) often threatened by potential rupture of difference. Even more disturbing is the fact that his symbolic construction of community implies not just boundary but dehumanizing hierarchy. Those who do not come to Jesus in confessing consent become, in John's construction, part of the "world" below (8:23), "children of the devil" (6:70–71; 8:42–44), and devoid of "life" and "light" (1:5; 3:18–21, 36; 6:53; 8:12, 24; 11:9–10; 12:35–36, 46).

Chow's distinction between the first and second meaning of "admittance" also helps me think about John in terms of U.S. cultural politics. We live in a society where—as we have seen from Nieh's and Chang-Rae Lee's fictions in the beginning of this chapter—an entire apparatus of immigration red tape, structural limits, and glass ceilings functions to "erase," or make invisible different groups of people despite their physical presence within U.S. national borders.[50] In fact, John's construction of community, particularly with its emphasis on consent and "upward" mobility, sounds a lot like the dominant discourse of U.S. society. Although Sollors ends up being more optimistic about the cultural politics of the United States than are many racial/ethnic minority scholars (myself included), he has correctly identified (1) that "the biblical diatribes against Pharisees and hypocrites were mimicked eagerly by the scribes [of the United States]" in the rhetoric of consent over descent (1986: 92) and (2) the tension between consent and descent as "the root of the ambiguity" surrounding U.S. racial/ethnic interaction (1986: 5; see also 4, 6–8).[51] Since the early days of the nation, when consent was used to define itself against its European roots, the dominant culture has been trying to construct and legitimate national unity utilizing John's naturalizing codes, like rebirth and love. It is this rhetoric of consent over descent that makes someone like Milton Gordon suggest the so-called liberal expectancy, when all racial/ethnic affiliation will become insignificant in the United States (1978: 68; cited in Sollors 1986: 20). The emphasis on consent is, of course, intertwined with the accentuation on independence, self-reliance, and thus the myth of upward mobility.

This cultural rhetoric of consent and mobility is, like John, full of contradictions and cover-ups. As Sollors himself admits, U.S. history is besmirched with "descent-based discrimination" like slavery and segregation, and the discourse about "an immigrant nation" ignores the violence done to Native Americans, African Americans, and Chicano Americans (1986: 8, 37). From the perspective of Michael Omi and Howard Winant, the United States has long been a "racial dictatorship" that marginalizes and ostracizes nonwhites (1994: 65–66). What appear as "opportunities" in this land are in fact often constraining circumstances.[52] Likewise, for many in this country, what appear to be issues of "free choice" and "individual consent" are often nothing but "necessary" compromises.

John's ambiguous admittance is especially intriguing to Asian Americans, whom David Kyuman Kim has described as the "ambiguous alterity" within the United States (2003: 328). Kim's term clearly elucidates the "almost-white-but-not-quite" status of Asian Americans in this country. We are part of the "other" of white America, but we are excluded or included by white America depending on the time and occasion. For example, long before the uproar about university admission by affirmative action, Asian Americans were ineligible to receive admission scholarships based on affirmative action in the University of California system. In that sense, we were considered whites. On the other hand, when the Los Angeles Police Department decided to protect the white districts after the verdict involving the police officers who arrested Rodney King, Koreatown was not included in the plan of protection. In that case, we were not considered whites. We are given the title of "model minority" to reinforce the cultural rhetoric of upward mobility, but this image only turns us into "middleman [*sic*] minorities" (Turner and Bonacich 1980) who do the bidding of our oppressors above and deflect the menace of the oppressed below.[53]

We are also an "ambiguous alterity" because many whites cannot (or will not) differentiate between the various ethnic groups within Asian America; we are simply lumped together as an "obscure other." The strategies John uses in his symbolic construction of community are ones that we know well as Asian Americans. For many of us, "naturalization" is not just a strategy of self-legitimation, but a process filled with loops and loopholes. We have been victimized by stereotypical representations and racial jokes.

Our consent to the nation and national competence have been questioned on the basis of descent, despite the cultural discourse on consent. Many of us have also experienced the linguistic barrier to include and exclude that John manipulates (Li 1998: 29, 38). As one critiques how the ambiguous meaning of descent has been used to disqualify Asian Americans in terms of racial lineage, even if they were born in the United States, one must not forget to engage similar contradictions and frictions *within* Asian America communities.

Conclusion

Symbolic construction of community is as important for John as it is for many contemporary Asian Americans. Gish Jen reminds us that "relationships count so heavily that to say something *has no relationship* in Chinese—*mei guanxi*—is to mean, often as not, *it doesn't matter*" (1991: 177–78; emphasis in original). For Nora Okja Keller, sanity itself is dependent on making communication and hence community (1997: 16). Yet, as Maxine Hong Kingston writes, "Community is not built once-and-for-all; people have to imagine, practice, and re-create it" (1989: 306). And it does matter a great deal what kind of community people are imagining, practicing, and re-creating. After reading and thinking about the Gospel of John and U.S. cultural politics in light of each other, I have to admit that I remain ambivalent towards John's ambiguous admittance. On the one hand, I find appealing John's radical vision in which consent or choice frees one from past constraints, and I appreciate the way he gives community a place of prominence, especially in light of the U.S. culture of "possessive individualism" (Li 1998: 103–4). On the other hand, I am apprehensive about John's hierarchical boundary, since within U.S. history "seizure of territory and goods, the introduction of slavery . . . not to mention the practice of outright extermination . . . all presupposed a worldview which distinguished Europeans, as children of God, full-fledged human–beings, etc. from 'others'" (Omi and Winant 1994: 62).

This type of hierarchical boundary, as Tod D. Swanson's reading of the Samaritan episode in John shows (2002), might result in the erasure or extermination of an "other's" ethnic inheritance or cultural traditions—if you like, one's descent—in the name of consent. Consent is, after all, part of Antonio Gramsci's understanding of hegemony (1971).[54] One must not forget that many structural limits that we face as Asian Americans "exist in a definite historical context, having *descended* from previous conflicts" (Omi and Winant 1994: 58; emphasis mine). John himself is eventually unable to sustain his dualistic opposition of consent and descent, because both are power-laden social constructs.[55] In addition, I resist the way John links his articulation of community to consensus, which is akin to what David Spurr has identified as a "colonial rhetoric of affirmation" that (dis)misses difference (1993: 122–24).[56] Although John's appeal to "grandparents" is undoubtedly effective—it is, in fact, employed by many Asian Americans for resistance (Li 1998: 39–41, 77–78, 139–40)—I wonder if this strategy, with its emphasis on "origins," does not lock us into the past and prevent us from looking into the future. Like Buell, I also question how this strategy assumes, and thus reinforces, the patriarchal power differential between (grand)parents and (grand)children (1999: 99).

Finally, I remain ambivalent towards John's Gospel because, as Anthony Cohen reminds us, symbols (including literary texts) that construct community are themselves ambiguous and subject to different interpretations (1985: 14–21). To emphasize this ambiguity of symbols, Cohen suggests that the passing and receiving of symbolic construction of community is more akin to a form of regurgitation than simple digestion (1985: 46). In other words, people have the agency to negotiate and manipulate other people's symbolic constructions and turn them into something else. Sollors has demonstrated that this is indeed the case with the Exodus narrative, which means rather different things in the minds of Puritans and African Americans (1986: 42–48).

Likewise, Craig Koester's study of symbols *within* John has come to a similar conclusion: symbols are ambiguous, and people "may appeal to the same symbol to support conflicting points of view" (1995: 235; see also 14, 17, 24, 221–22). For example, David Rensberger has read John as a helpful voice of protest and emancipation for African American communities, arguing that the contrastive definition used in John's community construction has a liberating political meaning for a community under siege (1988; see also Howard-Brook 1995).[57] Even if Rensberger is correct, however, that John was written out of a context of oppression, one cannot deny the role it has played in inciting and justifying oppression within history. In others words, adapting Ania Loomba's comments about Shakespeare's *Othello*, "even if [John] was originally not [oppressive], its history has made it [so]. . . . Historicizing [John] cannot be a scholarly project that denies us our own histories and politics" (1998: 150; see also Culpepper 1996a: 112–14).

Similarly, Yak-hwee Tan's recent reading of the Johannine community as situated between the "world below" (Roman colonization) and the "world above" (the reign of Jesus and God), and hence a "hybridized" and "advantageous" one with the space for "self-definition" (2006: 178), seems to be just a bit too optimistic or generous. In fact, her generalized reading of hybridity strikes me as falling into what Jonathan Dollimore calls "wishful theory" (1996). Perhaps a helpful balance, if not exactly a corrective, is Jean Kim's more somber and less one-sided reading of John, which suggests that the place between colonialism and nationalism is not exactly hospitable to or helpful for women, whether the women are in John's literary text or in the social texts of modern Korea/America (2004). John's politics of inclusion and exclusion must be scrutinized and remain accountable, even or perhaps especially as his community construction was done in resistance to colonial power. My relations with John can therefore be hardly categorized in terms of a simple consent or dissent. Instead, it is more accurately described by what Emmanuel Levinas says about his Heideggerian lineage: I feel indebted, but this sense of indebtedness is simultaneously filled with regrets (1993: 16; cited in Derrida 1999: 12).

Despite my own ambiguous admittance toward John's ambiguous admittance, there are certain things that I do not want to be ambiguous about. First of all, my ambivalence does not imply a mindless suspension of meaningful judgment or political intervention. While it honestly admits that interpretation of politics and politics of interpretation are messy and complicated businesses, it does not deny the many differences that exist between oppression and liberation. Second, my ambivalence implies an earnest plea that our interpretations of John be carried out in a contextually concrete and specific manner. One must be clear about one's point(s) of departure, goals and interests, as well as the socio-political and ethical implications of one's interpretation (J. K. Kim 2004: 219–24). Last but not least, my ambivalence implies a commitment to "persistent critique" (Spivak 1990: 41, 63). If the Gospel is an ambiguous symbol that is open to a range of interpretation and contains—to use Paul de Man's terms (1984)—both blindness and insight, then our own tasks and texts of interpreting the Gospel are also part of what Spivak calls "a practical politics of the open end" (1990: 105). We must admit that de-colonizing John and our interpretations of John, like de-colonizing the United States, is a continuous process of revision and reevaluation that requires humility, courage, and vigilance.

CHAPTER 4

Overlapping (His)Stories

● ●

Reading Acts in Chinese America

Notwithstanding the contradictions, John's rhetoric regarding a community built upon choice and consent rather than heredity or ancestry (1:13), as well as Jesus' mysterious and mystifying origin (6:41–42; 7:25–29, 40–52; 8:12–19; 9:28–34; 19:7–9), have a special resonance within the history of Chinese America. I am thinking here not of the rhetoric of the dominant culture that presents the United States as a "melting pot," but of the reality of "paper families," which became something like an industry in Chinese America because of (1) the passing of the Chinese Exclusion Act in 1882 that explicitly prohibited Chinese immigrants; (2) the San Francisco earthquake and fires of 1906 that destroyed the town hall and most of its municipal records; and (3) the 1924 National Origins Law or the so-called Second Exclusion Act that established a numerical restriction on immigration to the United States from all non-Western areas, and thus effectually barred Chinese students and Chinese wives of U.S. citizens from entry. "Paper sons" and "paper daughters" were "conceived" to challenge and circumvent these genocidal discriminations that—coupled with both legal and social illegitimacy of miscegenation (see Koshy 2004)—turned Chinese America into primarily a bachelor society.

Set in the context of San Francisco's Chinatown, Fae Myenne Ng's *Bone* (1993) explores how familial relations and responsibilities may still take place in the absence of blood. Ng's story about the family of Leon Leong, himself a paper son as well as the stepfather of Leila, shows that "it's time that makes a family, not just blood" (Ng 1993: 3).[1] Eleven years after the publication of Ng's novel, another Chinese American writer, Gish Jen, ended up exploring a similar subject even when or especially because she was writing in and about a time when trans-Pacific adoption and immigration no longer require deception.[2] In *The Love Wife* (2004), Jen writes about a (Chinese American?) family composed of a mixed couple, two adopted daughters, a biracial son, and an assumed-to-be "second" or "love wife" from China bequeathed by a mother's will. In other words, Jen is also thinking and writing about the possibility of a non-biological family and kinship.

Besides their common interest in constructing a kinship that goes beyond biology, both Ng and Jen seem committed to confounding the question of origin. Unlike what one finds in John and John's portrayal of Jesus, however, Ng never satisfies Leila's—and by extension, Ng's own readers'—desire to know Leon's "real" family or identity. Likewise, the first adopted daughter of Carnegie Wong and Blondie Bailey in Jen's novel is also of questionable origin. Unlike the second daughter, who was adopted from China, Lizzy was an abandoned baby found in front of a church, and Carnegie adopted her as a single man. Not to mention her "original" family, Carnegie and Blondie are not even sure of her ethnic origin: "Was she [Lizzy] part Japanese? Part Korean? Part Vietnamese? Was she any part Chinese at all? Who knew?" (Jen 2004: 106).

The surprise at the end of Jen's novel is that Carnegie himself turns out to be an adopted son, and that the "love wife" is his non-biological sister. Questions of origin and kinship are not only unanswered but also become basically unanswerable within this Chinese/American family. Jen is also careful to hint that these questions surrounding Carnegie's family cannot be limited to his family. Lizzy's feeling of being like "soup du jour" is, for instance, far from benign, because, as she says in response to her white adopted mother's empathetic statement that her own white heritage is also made up of different ethnicities: "Yeah, but it doesn't matter as much because you're white and not adopted. Nobody wonders where you're from, nobody asks you" (Jen 2004: 213). Jen's exploration of origins, family, and kinship must also be read in national and transnational frames.

Marking Contexts, Making Connections

Using her own adoption from Asia into a white family in the United States as a point of departure, Mary F. Foskett has looked at biblical images of adoption in Exodus and Romans (2002). More recently, Foskett has put into dialogue experiences of adoption and the study of or search for Christian origins (2006). In this chapter, I will look at a New Testament book that is most concerned with the origins and the development of the early church community, namely, Acts. Before I do so, however, I would like to go back to the beginning of my last chapter, where I referred to Chang-Rae Lee's *Native Speaker* (1995).

One of the lessons that the protagonist of *Native Speaker*, Henry Park, learns is that even a undercover—and thus undetected—private eye does not and cannot have the "most reasonable eye" (1995: 203). A detached and objective view is impossible, even if he tries to "know nothing of the crafts of argument or narrative or drama," and "stay on the uncomplicated task of rendering a man's life and ambition and leave to the unseen experts the arcane of human interpretation" (1995: 203). Rather than duplicating Park's folly, let me be explicit that my reading of Acts in this chapter is situated in a Chinese American context. Ironically, a recent collection of essays on Acts is titled *Contextualizing Acts* (Penner and Vander Stichele 2003), but its contextualizing acts is almost completely limited to the first-century world from which the book of Acts came. That is to say, the editors and the contributors of that volume seldom if ever contextualize their own location of reading (though they might do so for Luke's writing of Acts or earlier interpreters' reading of Acts). Questioning the knowability and the unity of the ancient world, the volume allows for a "complex readership" or "differing implied reading audiences" (Penner 2003b: 16), but it only does so for the first-century Mediterranean. In contrast, it assumes that the "North American scene" or "context" is unified and knowable; and it is this assumption that causes Penner to "admit" that the volume is "culturally bound," were it not for the contributions to the collection by two Europeans (2003b: 17). Penner does not seem to realize that North America is also consists of a "complex" and "differing readership" of Acts in terms of, among others, race/ethnicity.[3]

Generally speaking, Acts is a narrative with two interconnected foci. First, it sketches the formation, and hence the origin, of the Christ(ian) church community.[4] Second, it depicts the community's missionary expansion into various geographical areas and its conversion of different peoples; such mission and conversion necessarily entail, in turn, further (re)formation of the community.[5] Even a cursory reading of Acts will bring out many intersecting interests with Chinese American communities. Acts has, for example, many episodes that demonstrate an awareness of linguistic and ethnic differences. In addition to the linguistic miracle among ethnic Jews in the Jerusalem Pentecost (2:6–11), one finds the people of Lystra speaking in Lycaonian (14:11), or Paul being fluent in both Greek and Hebrew as an ethnic Jew from Tarsus (21:37, 39–40; 22:2; 26:14). There is also a mixed marriage between Felix and his Jewish wife, Drusilla (24:24). While Lysias' mistake regarding Paul's ethnicity (21:38) may confirm the scholarly argument in our own day that race (being visibly identifiable) and ethnicity are not the same thing, the continuing exchange between Lysias and Paul about their respective Roman citizenship (22:25–29) illustrates the significance of nativity. It is no secret within Chinese America that while native-born Chinese and immigrant Chinese may share a common ethnicity as well as a U.S. passport, barriers and conflicts between the two groups are all too real and prevalent. Given Paul's bilingualism, his Roman citizenship, and his Pharisaic persuasion within Judaism(s), his "multicultural" persona or "multiple identities" (Schwartz 2003: 129) may be comparable to how Chinese Americans have talked about being "multi-hyphenated" (Kuan 2002: 51), or in need of going "beyond the hyphen" (Ty and Goellnicht 2004: subtitle).[6]

The interest of Acts for Chinese Americans can also be seen in the fact that at least three of them have, to my knowledge, chosen to write on the book. First, Khiok-khng Yeo looks at the implications of Paul's preaching in Athens (17:22–31) for inter-religious dialogue (1998: 165–97). Second, David W. Pao scrutinizes the intertextual relations between Acts and the "Isaianic new exodus" (2002). Finally, Timothy Tseng explores the difference between reading a dispute among early Christ-followers (Acts 6:1–7) in terms of an inter-racial/ethnic as opposed to an intergenerational conflict (2002). I would like to follow these three trails to see what Acts and Chinese Americans may have to say about three issues that are of great significance to both parties. Those issues are community integration, religious diversity, and colonialism.

Integration with Qualifications

The historic and continual portrayals of Chinese as "foreign" or "heathen" make it difficult for Chinese to be fully integrated into the mainstream of U.S. society, even if one was born in the United States or has faithfully gone through the process of naturalization. We have already seen from the exchange between Lysias and Paul (22:25–29) Luke's sensibility about the difference that citizenship makes in the larger Roman society (see also 16:35–40). In addition to linguistic and cultural issues (2:5–13; 6:1–7), Luke is also sharp to hint at other problems of integration within the Jewish community. He points to the issue of the Sadducees and the Pharisees (23:6–10), or perhaps even of people belonging to different social status (the "synagogue of the Freedmen" in 6:9). What about the early Christ(ian) community? Is there also a problem of integration in Acts? How about the people who go through the process of conversion in Luke's narrative? This is especially relevant for two reasons: first, Acts seems to link, as sociologists of religion do, conversion with integration into a new community; and second, one of Acts' emphases has to do with the integration of Jews and Gentiles into one people of God through Jesus Christ.

The integration of Jews and Gentiles certainly receives major coverage in Acts, with the length of attention (8:26–15:35) signifying perhaps a long and drawn-out struggle. That is, however, by no means the only source of conflict within the early Christ(ian) community. Timothy Tseng's article (2002) concentrates on the conflict between Hellenistic and Palestinian Jews (6:1–7). In addition, we find Ananias and other Jerusalem disciples being suspicious of a new Christ-follower like Paul (9:10–16, 26). Barnabas is able to help Paul by playing the mediator role (9:27–28), but finds himself falling out with Paul later over John Mark (15:36–41). Does the Christ(ian) community in Acts integrate (new) people into its midst as "peacefully" and seamlessly as 9:31 seems to indicate? Is unity or concord really so characteristic of the Christ(ian) community that, as Pao claims, it stands in vivid contrast in Acts to the "disagreement" or discord of "the Jews" (2003)?

Faith and the Holy Spirit

Paul, in his response to the question of the Philippian jailer, states that faith in Christ is the means to or the requirement for salvation (16:31). However, in the previous chapter we have learned from Peter that, concerning integration into the new community, the giving and the receiving of the Holy Spirit is (at least theoretically speaking) the eraser of (ethnic) difference (15:8–9). The incompleteness or inferiority of faith in Christ without having the Holy Spirit is rather unambiguously implied in the case of the Samaritans (8:14–17) and that of the Ephesians (18:24–19:7). What is tricky in this light is the fact that, in Acts, the Holy Spirit comes and goes as the Holy Spirit pleases (González 2001: 108–109). While the Samaritan followers of Christ experience a time gap or lag between their baptism in Jesus' name and their receiving of the Holy Spirit (8:16), the Ephesian followers seem to receive the Holy Spirit upon (or at least closely following) their baptism in Jesus' name (19:5–6). We must not forget that in the case of Cornelius at Caesarea, the Holy Spirit comes on him and his household before they are even baptized (10:44–48). If faith in Christ is like obtaining a "green card" that grants entry and residency (Rey Chow's first definition of "admission" from my last chapter), the coming of the Holy Spirit is comparable to the naturalization process that (theoretically) turns a "green-card" holder into a citizen eligible for equal rights and benefits (Chow's second definition of "admission"). The difficulty is that, in Acts, it is not up to the newcomer to decide if and when he or she can satisfy the requirement of integration by receiving the Holy Spirit and becoming "naturalized." The matter is simply beyond his or her control.[7]

Money Matters

A closer look at Acts will further reveal that there may well be additional hurdles to being fully integrated into the new people of God beyond the receiving of the Holy Spirit. Shortly after the Pentecost in Jerusalem (2:1–13), we read about the early church as a community with "all things in common" (2:44–45). After a similar description and a positive example of "selling and sharing all" in Barnabas (4:32–37), Acts presents us with a negative example in Ananias and Sapphira (5:1–11). This couple, guilty of withholding for themselves part of the money they receive from selling their property, is struck dead (presumably by the Holy Spirit). Their death, which brings "great fear" upon "the whole church" (5:11), implies that, in addition to receiving the Holy Spirit, members of the Christ(ian) community must further share a specific attitude and action towards material possessions. Otherwise, not only is their integration into the community open to question, but their very presence in the community may also be literally removed.

The importance of money matters in Luke's construction of community is well known. Scattered throughout Acts are Christ believers characterized by works of charity or almsgiving, like Tabitha or Dorcas (9:36), Cornelius (10:2), and the Christians at Antioch (11:25–30). For our investigation of community integration, the most telling story in addition to that of Ananias and Sapphira is arguably that of Simon in Samaria (8:9–24). Luke is clear that Simon has believed and received baptism in the name of Christ (8:13, 16). His desire to purchase the role as an authoritative agent or conduit of the Holy Spirit *after* the Holy Spirit has come upon the Samaritans results, however, in the stern words of Peter that Simon will "have no part or share in this" (8:21). While "this" (literally, "this word or matter") may refer to Simon's specific verbal request (8:19), Peter's specific reference to death or destruction (8:20) implies that what Simon will be deprived of is his very participation in the "word," thus the people/community, of God (8:14). While it is also possible that Peter's threat to remove Simon has to do with Simon's magical worldview, Peter's response in 8:20 locates the problem clearly with a double reference to Simon's (high) view of money.

Suffering Sacrifice

In addition to a proper view of money, Acts has yet another quality or qualification for integration into the Christ(ian) community besides those given by Peter at the Jerusalem Pentecost—namely, professing faith, being baptized, and receiving the Holy Spirit (2:38). Willingness to suffer for one's faith in Christ becomes an issue with the beginning of persecution in Acts 4, when Peter and John receive a verbal warning from the Jewish leaders that they should not "speak or teach at all in the name of Jesus" (4:18). Rather than heeding the warning, Peter and John continue to "evangelize" with the other apostles. As a result, they are jailed, but are miraculously rescued (5:17–23). Then they are re-arrested, helped by Gamaliel's intervention but nevertheless flogged (5:34–40). The apostles finally leave the Jewish council, but they "rejoice" for having been "considered worthy to suffer" in and for Jesus' name (5:41). Other "worthy sufferers" in Acts would include, of course, Stephen (6:8–7:60) and Paul (9:16; 14:19; 16:19–24; 20:23–24, 26–30; 21:13). As Paul and Barnabas return to Lystra, Iconium, and Antioch at the end of their first missionary journey, their encouragement and reinforcement of their converts also include the "must" of sufferings (14:22).[8]

These two additional qualities or qualifications, I would argue, are actually opposite sides of the same coin. Negatively, the quality or qualification of being free from monetary concerns contrasts those who belong to Christ from those who live and act for material gain. In contrast to Christ-followers who sell and share all, we find in Acts some unnamed Philippian slaveholders and one silversmith called Demetrius who, because of falling income, accuse Paul of civic and religious pretenses (16:16–21; 19:23–29). By the time of the Jerusalem council, the experience of suffering persecution has become a distinguishing mark of certain membership in the community (15:26, "certain" in the doubled sense of "some" and "sure"). Unlike the examples of Theudas and Judas the Galilean being given by Gamaliel (5:36–37), the experiences of death and dispersion do not spell an end to the Christ(ian) movement, because certain members of the Christ(ian) community keep evangelizing despite such sufferings (8:1–4; 11:19; 13:44–52; 14:5–6, 19–21; 17:13–17; 20:17–25; 21:10–14; 28:30–31). While one cannot be sure if this positive response to suffering and persecution itself becomes a means of evangelism, one does see that, in the case of Stephen, suffering persecution (in fact, martyrdom) is specifically and directly linked to a welcomed entry into God's community (7:54–60). In other words, the quality or qualification of being worthy of suffering functions positively to legitimate, not just the Christ(ian) community, but also the sufferer's own place in the community. This negative and positive legitimation of one's membership or belonging is clearly seen in Paul's farewell speech to the elders of the Ephesian church at Miletus (20:17–38). In the process of teaching and encouraging the elders, Paul establishes his ethos as a credible leader and teacher in the beginning and at the end of his speech. In the beginning, Paul highlights his endurance of persecution in the past and his present decision to head towards Jerusalem despite certain dangers (20:18–25); in the end, he emphasizes his disinterest in personal material gains (20:32–35).

Acts shows that, despite fulfilling earlier qualifications (faith, baptism, and the ever-elusive coming of the Holy Spirit), one's legitimacy in a community or a larger social body may continue to be questioned on the basis of economics and demonstrated loyalty. Is this why Theophilus, like Apollos in Luke's narrative, needs to be reinstructed even though it is clear that he has already been taught or instructed in the way of Jesus (Luke 1:4; Acts 18:25)? Such a rhetoric of rebirth through a demand of renunciation ("Do you swear to give up . . .") is too painfully familiar to many Chinese Americans who have experienced the process of naturalization. Even a Chinese who was born in the United States may, however, become illegitimate if he or she does not demonstrate loyalty to certain economic or patriotic principles like capitalism, model minority mobility, military "defense," or "homeland security" at the risk of injury or death. As the disputes in Acts over "daily distribution" (6:1–6) and circumcision (10:1–11:30, 13:1–15:35) show, the problem of community integration is entangled with matters of language and ethnic identity.

Ethnic Ceiling

Feminist scholars have already sensitized us to the gender problem in Acts. For instance, only "men" are eligible to be apostles (1:21) or one of the seven "servers" (6:3). Women, in contrast, are generally involved in "the ministry of benefaction and hospitality" rather than that of preaching and teaching (D'Angelo 2002: 68).[9] Referring to the anonymous "slave-girl having a Pythonian spirit" (16:16), Shelly Matthews goes further to state that "[t]he only inspired woman's speech Acts records is . . . said to be mantic rather than prophetic" (2001: 89). What I want to add here is that Acts also has an ethnicity problem. There are many chapters in Acts dealing with the community's mission to Gentiles and the subsequent acceptance of Gentiles, but the work of mission and evangelism is restricted to Jews, whether Palestinian or Hellenistic. This is true not only of the "major" missionaries like Peter, Philip, Barnabas, or Paul, but also of other "minor" ones like Apollos (18:24) or Apollos' "instructors," Priscilla and Acquila (18:1–2,

26).[10] Luke, in other words, does not present the activity of any non-Jewish missionary. This principle of "ethnic monopoly" (which can be translated to the reality of a "glass ceiling" for Gentile Christ-followers) may be why Luke has Paul circumcise Timothy, who has a Greek father and a Jewish mother (16:1–3). Paul's act is especially puzzling because this episode is sandwiched between references to the decision in Jerusalem that Gentile disciples need not be circumcised (15:12–31; 16:4–5). What distinguishes Timothy, of course, is Paul's desire to make him a missionary partner (16:3). Justo L. González may be correct in stating that, as evidenced by the preaching of Stephen, Philip, and Paul in Acts, the Jerusalem apostles' desire to reserve the preaching ministry for themselves (6:2–4) is thwarted by the Holy Spirit (2001: 88–94). There is, however, no thwarting of any kind when it comes to missionary activities on the part of only ethnic or proselyte Jews.[11] If González's argument about Stephen and Philip becoming "preachers" is extendable to the rest of the seven "servers," it may not be insignificant for my own argument here that Luke makes a point to clarify Nicolaus' proselyte status (6:5).

There thus seems to be an unequal inclusion into or integration within the Christ(ian) community on the basis of ethnic identity. Even if the leaders or elders whom Paul appoints "in each church" during his missionary journeys are indeed new Gentile converts (14:23; see also 20:17), there is no reference to their role in preaching or missionary activities. Paul's message to the elders at the Ephesian church refers only to his own preaching (20:25–27), while the elders are specifically charged with the ministry of supervision and care (20:28–30). Note also in this regard Luke's thrice repeated statement that Spirit-filled Gentile disciples are nevertheless required to fulfill certain Mosaic commandments short of circumcision (15:19–21, 28–29; 21:25). The legitimating role that the Jerusalem apostles repeatedly perform upon missions and conversions that they themselves did not begin or mediate (8:14–16; 9:26–29; 11:22–23; 12:24–25; 15:12–35) may further imply other bases of discriminating integration, like language and/or geography.[12]

Obsession with Origin(al)

The legitimating roles of the Jerusalem apostles raise a question regarding how one should interpret the interweaving parallels among the major missionary/preacher figures in Acts as well as between these figures and the Lukan Jesus. Paul's raising of Eutychus (20:7–12), for instance, parallels Peter's raising of Tabitha/Dorcas (9:36–43), and both parallel Jesus' raising of a widow's son in Nain (Luke 7:11–17). Just to give another example,

Jesus' ministry begins in Luke's Gospel with his inaugural sermon, which is followed closely by the act of healing a lame or paralyzed person (4:16–21; 5:17–26). In Acts, this same sequence of and proximity between an inaugural sermon and the healing of a lame person appears in the ministry of Peter (2:14–36; 3:1–10) and Paul (13:13–42; 14:8–11). A key to interpreting these parallels may be the different interactions within these three healing stories (Tannehill 1994: 51–53). In Luke, the scribes and Pharisees accuse Jesus of blasphemies, and Jesus, in challenge to this negative response, affirms his authority to forgive sins as God does by healing the bedridden person (5:21–24). In Acts, people respond so positively to the healing of a lame person that Peter and Paul have to correct, clarify, and confirm their own human status (3:11–12; 14:11–18).

What I am getting at is the concern on Luke's part to emphasize but at the same time discriminate Jesus as the original, and Peter and Paul as the (faithful) copies.[13] Whether it is Peter's explanation of his work among the Gentiles (11:1–18) or Paul's explanation to the Ephesians about the difference between John's baptism and baptism with the Holy Spirit (19:1–7), Luke is consistently directing the reader back not only to the beginning of Acts but also to Luke's Gospel about Jesus (Moessner 1999a: 100–108). Like John's appeal to the "grandfather" that I discussed in the last chapter, this concern of being "faithful to the origin(al)," which is actually already detectable in the preface of Luke's Gospel (1:1–4), is what gives the Jerusalem apostles the privilege of legitimation. Luke has told us early in Acts that having accompanied Jesus from the beginning is a prerequisite for apostleship (1:21–26). In fact, Luke repeatedly legitimates both the ministry of Jesus and the mission to the Gentiles not as "new" developments, but as fulfillments of Hebrew Scripture (3:17–18; 13:22–27, 32–41, 46–48; 15:15–21; 17:2–3; 28:25–28). Likewise, Paul, in his apologetic and/or evangelistic speeches, is always emphasizing his Jewish pedigree, particularly his observance of Torah and other Pharisaic traditions (17:2–3; 21:40–22:21; 23:1–8; 24:10–21; 25:8; 26:1–23, 27). To demonstrate his faithfulness to and observance of such traditions, Paul is willing to follow the advice of James and other elders by joining four other Jews in as well as paying for their Nazarite rite of purification (21:20–26).[14]

As Acts' appeals to *different* "beginnings" (1:22; 10:37; 11:15; 26:4) show, the question of who and what defines the "origin(al)" is important and debatable. For instance, is Luke's Jesus really the "origin(al)," or is he only another copy of Elijah (Brodie 1990), Moses (L. T. Johnson 1992: 12–14), or some other figure(s) or part(s) within Hebrew Scripture (Tiede 1980; Litwak 2005)? This tyranny of the "origin(al)" (however defined) has been a long struggle for many Chinese Americans. Tseng's essay on Acts shows that both mainstream U.S. society and some early members of Chinese American (church) communities have used the "origin(al)" to premise inclusion or integration on acquiescence to tradition, assimilation, and acculturation (2002). It is precisely these opposing but similar tyrannies that Maxine Hong Kingston is struggling against when she writes in succession: "Those of us in the first American generation have had to figure out how the invisible world the emigrants built around our childhoods fits in solid America. . . . Chinese-Americans, when you try to understand what things in you are Chinese, how do you separate what is peculiar to childhood, to poverty, insanities, one family, your mother who marked your growing with stories, from what is Chinese? What is Chinese tradition and what is the movies?" (1976: 5–6). Like Luke's (re)presentation of community and mission, both "solid America" and Chinese "tradition" are claiming the privileged status of original blueprints that others have to "fit in." All these communities are homogenizing presences seeking to authorize who and what is compatible with their respective ideology of the "origin(al)." Such a process of "fitting in" is, as I have shown above, seldom a "finishable" business. Instead, it is a matter of continual—if not eternal—insecurity, whether the rhetoric is the "melting pot" of the United States or the "universalism" of Luke.

Conversion or Conversation?

Yeo argues that Paul's speech in Areopagus (17:16–31) serves as a model for inter-religious dialogue (1998: 165–97). Martin Dibelius, of course, argued for a similar thesis forty years earlier (1956); what Yeo does point to is the significance of religious diversity for Chinese and Chinese Americans. The significance of this issue lies not only in the long history of religious diversity within Chinese America, but also—as I have pointed out in Chapter 2—in the equally long history of marginalization that Chinese Americans face in this society because many of them were not, and are not, Christians.

    In contrast to Yeo, I would suggest, first of all, that Luke, in many places in Acts (including 17:16–31), is not interested in religious diversity or inter-religious dialogue. Acts is, after all, a book of mission and is thus more interested in conversion than conversation (the latter is mostly a means to another end, which is the former). This is particularly visible in Peter's statement that "there is salvation in no one else, for there is no other name under heaven given among mortals by which we must be saved" (4:12).[15] Paul does demonstrate knowledge and even sensitivity to the religious traditions of both Lystra and Athens, and emphasizes to a degree the unity of all human beings (14:16–17; 17:22–28). He nevertheless sees these other religions as "worthless" and "ignorant," and thus argues that their adherents must "turn" and "repent" to faith in the "appointed" and risen Christ (14:15; 17:29–31). Since this need of Jesus Christ seems to be necessary for Jews as well as Gentiles (2:38; 13:36–41; 15:10–11), Luke's goal in Acts seems to be religious monopoly rather than diversity. I therefore do not see Acts' Paul, despite his being persecuted by both Jews and Gentiles in his proclamation of Christ (14:5; 16:19–23; 17:1–7; 18:12–13; 19:23–31; 21:19–22, 27–36), as occupying an interstitial location comparable to Kingston's description above. What Paul promotes in Acts is not an alternative identity for some to stand between Jews and Gentiles, but the elimination of all other ethnic/religious identities for all people. The riot caused by Demetrius' appeal to Artemis (19:23–34), along with the many accounts of persecutions by "Jewish" plots (for example, 20:3, 19; 21:27–31; 23:30), clearly show that Luke is well aware of the conflicts and violence that result from religious and ethnic intolerance. Such awareness does not, however, keep him from pushing for mission and conversion. Instead, as I have proposed previously, Luke presents suffering and martyrdom as legitimation of the Christ(ian) movement as well as verification of one's membership in the community.

One can find within Acts, however, a small but differing thread on this very issue (Tannehill 1994: 330–38).[16] Towards the end of Acts, Paul makes the trip as a prisoner to Rome to appeal his case to Caesar (27:1–28:16). Although there are Roman soldiers, sailors, and other prisoners on board, we do not find any references to Paul preaching or sharing the gospel. In fact, the narrative of this entire treacherous trip contains only two references to religion or divinity. The first is Paul's reference to a divine vision that points, first of all, to his awareness that others on board do not necessarily share his religion; for he specifically refers to God as "the God to whom *I* belong and whom *I* worship" (27:23; emphasis mine). Nevertheless, Paul promises on the basis of this divine vision that everyone on board will be "saved" without (religious) discrimination (27:24–26, 31). The second reference is made by the natives of Malta, when they, upon seeing Paul surviving a viper's bite without any harm, mistake him for "a god" (28:3–6). When comparable mistakes appear previously in Acts, Peter, Barnabas, and Paul have resisted and attempted to correct such mis-identifications (3:11–12; 10:25–26; 14:11–15). In contrast, Herod, who fails to refute a similar misconception others have of him, becomes infested with worms and dies (12:20–23). It is therefore rather surprising that Luke makes no other remarks regarding Paul's response to the islanders' misunderstanding other than his proceeding to perform more miraculous acts of healing on, and for, the island natives (28:7–9).[17] Uncomfortable with Luke's inconsistency on this matter, Charles H. Talbert argues that, when Paul prays (presumably to God) for the healing of the island chief's father (28:8), he is in effect dis-identifying himself from divinity (2003: 184). Even if one accepts Talbert's argument, one will still have to admit that Paul, the great missionary, does not proclaim Christ here the way he and other disciples do in the rest of Acts. That is to say, Paul does not ask the natives of Malta to repent, turn away from other gods, and turn to Jesus alone. Even if one extends Talbert's argument and reads Paul's prayerful healing of the natives as "friendship evangelism," what we have here is at most, in Arthur Darby Nock's categories, an adhesion (adding of new religious traditions *without* leaving or turning away from existing ones) rather than a conversion (see Finn 1997: 32–33).

What seems to be essential to this more tolerant thread in Acts is Paul's alacrity or acknowledgment through the divine vision that—to duplicate Luke's well-known first personal plural in this part of Acts—"we" are literally in the "same boat," and thus "we" will live or die together.[18] This recognition helps Paul to set religious differences and his great missionary zeal aside (if only temporarily, since Paul will quickly resume his missionary acts upon arrival at Rome, 28:23–31), and concentrate on acting for the common good of all. He informs the Roman soldiers of the sailors' plan to "jump ship" (27:27–32) and encourages others on board to eat and keep their strength (and spirits) up (27:33–38). This expression of (unconditional) goodwill causes others to reciprocate, as we see the centurion acting to protect Paul, prevent his soldiers from killing the prisoners, and orchestrate a procedure for all to escape safely to land (27:39–44). This reciprocal goodwill is in operation again on the island of Malta, although Luke is clear that the natives are the initiators and Paul a recipient, this time (28:1–2). When Paul reciprocates by healing many on the island, his reciprocation leads to more reciprocation of goodwill and generous sharing on the part of the natives (28:7–10).

Is this (passing) picture of (religious and ethnic) tolerance and harmony in Acts an affirmative answer to Rodney King's plea after the multi-racial/ethnic uprising in Los Angeles, 1992: "Can we all just get along?" There is no denying that racial/ethnic and religious crises are continuing to mount in the national politics of the United States, as well as in international politics around the globe. What Acts 27:1–28:16 reminds us of is the importance of King's often forgotten, but arguably more insightful, statement that followed his over-quoted question: "We're all stuck here for a while." Diversity and tolerance depend on a deep and durable recognition of everyone's co-existence and interdependence despite, or perhaps even because of racial/ethnic and religious differences. Without that recognition, "all getting along" may be nothing more than a romantic slogan.

From Investigating Intertexts to Challenging Colonialism

According to Pao, Acts is a reproduction of the "Isaianic new exodus" (2002). Like the post-exilic Isaiah (chapters 40–66), Luke struggled to affirm, as he faced the need to redefine and rebuild, the people of God after the trauma of the first Jewish-Roman war. It is, of course, well known that Acts often quotes from the Septuagint, especially Isaiah (Acts 7:49–50; 8:32–33; 13:34, 47; 28:26–27). There are, however, also other more implicit allusions. As Isaiah uses "the way of the Lord" (40:3) to refer to God's "new exodus" for God's people after the Babylonian exile (see also Isaiah 43:16–19), Luke uses "the way" as the self-designation of the early Christ(ian) movement (9:2; 19:9, 23; 22:4; 24:14, 22). In addition, there are many parallel emphases between Isaiah and Acts, like the ingathering of exiles (Isaiah 40:11, 43:5–7; Acts 2:9–11), the universal revelation of God's glory or salvation (Isaiah 40:3–5; Acts 26:23, 28:28), the power of God's word (Isaiah 40:6–8; Acts 6:7, 12:24, 19:20), the centrality of Jerusalem (Isaiah 40:9–11; Acts 1:4–5), the work and power of the Holy Spirit (Isaiah 42:1, 44:1–4, 61:1–2; Acts 2:1–4, 10:38, 13:1–4), the (re)creation of God's people that includes both Jews and Gentiles (Isaiah 43:15–21, 49:6; Acts 10:44–48, 14:1, 15:12–31) as well as other previous outcasts like eunuchs (Isaiah 56:4–5, 8; Acts 8:26–40). The very verse that many have taken as the summary outline of the entire book of Acts, 1:8, captures several main ingredients of Isaiah 40. The geographical sequence of the verse signifies the centrality of Jerusalem ("in Jerusalem [first]"), the reunification of Israel ("in all Judea and Samaria"), and the inclusion of Gentiles ("and to the ends of the earth"). This verse is further bracketed by two references to the focus of the Isaianic new exodus—namely, Israel's restoration or reconstitution. The first is the disciples' question, which prompts the so-called programmatic promise from the resurrected Jesus (1:6). The second, if more indirect, reference is the election of Matthias to replace Judas and thus complete the "twelve," the number of the original apostles as well as the tribes of Israel (1:12–26). Pao, however, ends up using this intertextual connection to argue for a narrower contextual conflict, that is, Luke's concern to establish the church as the true heirs of Israel. What Pao does, then, is in effect (dis)miss the very imperial or colonial dynamics that is present in the exodus from

Egypt, in (deutero-)Isaiah's (post)exilic struggles, as well as in Luke's context of the Jewish-Roman war.

While focusing on another set of intertextual relations, Marianne Palmer Bonz does manage to highlight at the same time inter-contextually (Luke)-Acts' imperial or colonial dynamics (2000). Just as Virgil's *Aeneid* presents the Romans as being ordained by the Gods to take the best out of the ruins of Troy to become the rulers of the world, so Bonz argues that Luke is imitating Virgil but presenting Christ-followers instead as the new ordained conquerors of the universe. Like Virgil, according to Bonz, Luke sees Christ followers emerging as heirs of the very best of the Jewish tradition, despite the destruction suffered by the latter in the first Jewish-Roman war.

My interest here is not to limit or adjudicate Acts' intertextual relations to either Isaiah or Virgil, since I do not think that these are necessarily mutually exclusive.[19] Just as Luke might have employed elements from various literary genres, he could and most likely would have used a number of sources.[20] I will have more to say about the writing and reading of intertexts in Chapter 7; what I want to do here is use both Pao and Bonz together to argue for the anti-colonial implications of Acts (see also Gilbert 2003).[21] Luke is certainly not shy in Acts about Israel's political subjugation. Stephen, for example, does refer back to the slavery in Egypt and the exodus at length and in detail (7:6–38). One also finds in Acts at least a couple of direct references to diasporic existence, Jewish or otherwise (2:5, 9–11; 17:21). As Acts progresses, one finds more and more references to both the presence and the power of Rome (16:12; 18:1–2; 19:35–41). More specifically, both Paul and Paul's opponents have to work through the power of the Romans to achieve their respective ends (16:16–22, 35–40; 17:5–8; 18:12–17; 21:31–32; 23:10; 24:2–3, 10; 25:10–12). At the same time, Acts contains several incisive if indirect jabs at the Romans. Many readers should be familiar with Luke's unflattering representations of the Roman officials surrounding Paul's arrest (Tannehill 1994: 295–313). While Lysias—who did not only mistake Paul's ethnicity and citizenship (21:37–39; 22:22–29) but also seems to be completely ignorant of various Jewish groups within Jerusalem—writes a report to make himself look better than he actually is in order to impress his superior (23:25–30), Felix keeps someone in jail to hope for a bribe from the prisoner (24:26), and Festus (like Felix) is always concerned with accumulating his own political capital (24:27; 25:3, 9, 11). All three of them know Paul to be innocent, but none of them is willing to set Paul free (23:29; 24:22–27; 25:24–27; 26:31–32).

Let me point to one episode that Bonz ignores but will further support her thesis about Acts as a similar yet competing version of Virgil's *Aeneid*. The major character in *Aeneid* who represents the Trojans, migrates to Italy under divine providence, and founds a city that ultimately leads to the triumph of Rome is, of course, Aeneas. Interestingly, there is also a character in Acts with the same name. This Aeneas, however, is a bedridden invalid at Lydda, who is healed by Peter in the name of Jesus Christ (9:32–35). While symbolically Peter's healing of Aeneas may appear to be pro-Roman in one sense, one must remember that this episode involves a clear difference in health and strength. Peter, not Aeneas, is the one who is healthy and strong. Later in Acts, we will find another representative of the new people of God, Paul, making a Roman governor, Sergius Paulus, the first convert of his first missionary journey (13:1–12). Even when Paul comes under Roman custody, he will debate with another Roman governor about "justice, self-control, and the coming judgment," only to have Felix lose in fear and in retreat (24:25). This resistant and subversive move in Acts may also account for Luke's emphasis on how the God of Israel has control over history through Luke's prophecy-fulfillment formula (Tiede 1980). In like manner, one may read Luke's emphasis on God's rejection of (only) unbelieving Jews (13:46–47; 18:6; 28:25–28) as yet another illustration of status reversal (Talbert 2003: 161–73).[22]

As I have intimated from the beginning, this matter of imperialism and colonialism is important to Chinese Americans on two fronts. Externally, China continues to be one of the most desired and feared "partners" of the global world (read: U.S. imperialist) order. Internally, Chinese America, like other racial/ethnic minority Americas, is an internal colony. My reading of Acts becomes uneasily complex, however, when I remember that "manifest destiny" is not only a theme of both Virgil's *Aeneid* and Luke's Acts, but also a claim of both the Romans and the United States in their respective imperialist projects. I also remember that one of the ways in which dominant U.S. society colonizes and racializes its Chinese members is through religion. If Acts was once a tool of resistance against Roman colonialism, its rewriting of Isaiah's rewriting of Exodus has—despite its "intention"—duplicated in effect the lamentable link between (the first) exodus and conquest.[23]

Conclusion

What I hope to have shown here is that Acts is a complex book. Like my yin yang reading of Mark, I find within Acts' pages both liberating and oppressive elements, whether the issue in question is community integration, religious diversity, or colonialism. If Acts is any indication, it indicates that the Bible and the Church are capable at times of inspiring us to be, or to go beyond our very best. At other times, the Bible and the Church can also be sadly like the worst that the world has to offer.

If Acts is a complex book, reading Acts is an even more complex business. Changes in a reader's identification (either of or with different characters in a narrative) will dramatically change the implications of a story, as Tseng's reading of Acts 6:1–7 (2002) shows. My discussion on (anti-)colonial dynamics has shown that the same is true as readers come to Acts with varying and shifting contexts. Readers, however, must deal not only with a context of themselves as readers, but also with that of Luke as author. For example, according to Tannehill, Paul's brief cessation of missionary activities on his trip to Rome (27:1–28:16) may reflect Luke's realization of the minority role that the Christ(ian) movement possessed at the time of a largely non-Christian Roman society (1994: 338–39). Of course, the minority status of the Christ(ian) movement can also account for Luke's overwhelming emphasis on mission and conversion. That is to say, Luke's missionary zeal arises out of his concern over survival; when survival is not in question, then his missionary zeal will also wane. This is not, however, how Tannehill seems to see it. Whether wittingly or unwittingly, Tannehill gives the impression that the picture of religious and ethnic tolerance and cooperation is Luke's compromise with a dominantly non-Christian environment. In other words, for Tannehill, the singularity and brevity of Paul's voyage to Rome in Acts show that mission and conversion are Luke's norm, diversity and tolerance are his exceptions.

Some Chinese American readers, remembering my discussion in Chapter 2 of the frustration that many Chinese American writers have been facing over the politics of the publishing industry, may relate the same episode to a different Lukan context and come up with a rather different interpretation. Instead of the minority status of the Christ(ian) movement, one may relate the differing theology or ideology regarding religious diversity in Acts to Luke's writing under someone's patronage (a likely scenario in Rome's patronage society, despite however fictive the name or figure "Theophilus" [1:1] may be).[24] Again, it is impossible to ascertain which theological or ideological thread is Luke's nod to his patron. Generally speaking, however, the power of the patronage or publishing patrol will steer one to draw exactly the opposite conclusion from Tannehill's. It is precisely the singularity and brevity of Paul's sea voyage to Rome in Acts that evidence diversity and tolerance to be Luke's more treasured, if—or thus—more hidden, perspectives.

Explicitly intercontextual interpretations are therefore admittedly inconclusive interpretations that (ideally) should lead to humble but active engagement with other interpretations. One's comfort or discomfort with such interpretations may also be contextual. My bicultural—or, more accurately, "transcultural"[25]—experience has led me to share Kingston's sentiment: "I learned to make my mind large, as the universe is large, so that there is room for paradoxes" (1976: 29). This contextual sentiment also explains my intention to highlight both the liberating and oppressive elements in Acts. Knowing the importance of religious diversity in general and the role that the Bible has played in the history of racializing Chinese Americans as "foreign heathens" in particular, as well as being sympathetic to the colonial context from which Acts emerged, I have chosen not to be too politically (in)correct about anything, including my act(s) of reading Acts. Reading is intercontextual, and hence too intricately complicated for any simplistic categories, like dominant *or* resistant readings.

CHAPTER 5

Redressing Bodies in Corinth

● ●

Racial/Ethnic Politics and Religious Difference in the Context of Empire

With the growing reliance on science of the early twentieth century came a political ideology representing the nation of the United States as a body threatened by infection. During this time, in the words of David Palumbo-Liu, "[a] particular discursive formation evolved that blended science with politics, economics with sociology, national and international interests, within which the nation was imagined as a body that must, through fastidious hygienic measures, guard against what passes from the exterior, excise the cancerous cells that have already penetrated it, and prevent any reproductive act that would compromise the regeneration of its species in an increasingly massified and mobile world" (1999: 24). Since the "science" that Palumbo-Liu is referring to includes eugenics, this ideology clearly involves not only the national body but also the physical bodies of people who populate the world. As a "medium of culture" (Bordo 1989: 13), a human, physical body is often the site on and through which various cultural and ideological forces compete for inscription and promulgation (see also Smith 1993). By virtue of various factors like race, ethnicity, sexuality, and gender, as well as religion, bodies are also marked, ranked, normalized, and/or pathologized. Deemed to be as undesirable and harmful as viruses or parasites, certain human bodies must be eradicated, or at least removed out of sight and out of mind, if the national body is to remain healthy.

One of the groups that this ideology aims to exclude from the national body—both literally and symbolically—has been Asian-raced bodies. Racialized to be "foreign" (Gotanda 2001), "immigrant" (Lowe 1996), "feminine," and/or "sexually deviant" (Eng 2001), Asian bodies are also often linked with being religiously different or deficient. Two recent books—one on Cambodian Americans (Ong 2003) and the other on Korean Americans (Suh 2004)—have pointed to the challenging dynamics faced by Asian American Buddhists for being a racial/ethnic as well as a religious minority simultaneously.[1]

My point is not to imply that all Asian Americans share the status of being a religious minority. Neither is it my intention to suggest that racial/ethnic differences can be transcended through a shared religion, minority or otherwise. Instead, I have a threefold purpose. First, I want to argue that undesirable bodies often also become disembodied and/or undetectable despite becoming simultaneously marked (I. M. Young 1990: 123; Schlossberg 2001: 4–6). Abject bodies have a way of becoming insignificant and invisible in general and in scholarship in particular, whether American or biblical.[2] Since bodily abjection often involves projections of racial/ethnic "others" in stereotypes, Roland Barthes' description of stereotypes as "emplacement[s] of discourse *where the body is missing,* where one is sure [that] the body is not" (1977: 90; emphasis in original) should give us much food for thought. Second, I want to focus on the importance of interstices, particularly the intersection between body politics and imperial politics, and the connections between race/ethnicity and religion for those living in diaspora. Third, I want to show how experiences of Asian Americans may help to inform a different reading of difference concerning 1 Corinthians.[3]

Embodying Corinthian Rhetoric and Politics

Scholars have long been suggesting that Paul wrote 1 Corinthians to build up the church body in Corinth because its unity or harmony had been torn up by differences that existed within and/or without. These differences were first understood to be mainly doctrinal or theological (Hurd 1983: 97–105; Schrage 1991–2001: 1.38–63). Now scholarly trends have for most shifted to incorporate a material difference, particularly in terms of class or status (Theissen 1982; Marshall 1987; Pogoloff 1992; D. B. Martin 1995: 69–79). I do not need to renew the dated debate about theological ideas or socio-material conditions, as if the two were mutually exclusive. Dale B. Martin's book on Corinthians helpfully points to the "more serviceable concept" of ideology (1995: xiv), since ideology—especially in its Althusserian and Gramscian versions—is an interpretive activity that informs and invents one's existence, inclusive of both thought and practice. I do need to point out, however, that Dale Martin's thesis—namely, that the differences between Paul and (some of) the Corinthians may have boiled down to their different social-status positions, and the corresponding assumptions about the human body—can use greater specificity and further embodiment (see also Glancy 2004).

What Dale Martin seems to have overlooked is the fact or factor that Paul and the Corinthians had different racialized/ethnicized bodies, even though he made a brief mention of racial/ethnic differences to illustrate the Greco-Roman hierarchies of individual and social bodies (1995: 33–34).[4] The same is true of those who attribute the division of the church body at Corinth to class or status difference. If one should prefer the term "status" to "class" because of the latter's modern lineage and its overdetermined association with material wealth (Pogoloff 1992: 208; D. B. Martin 1995: xvi–xvii; Lanci 1997: 34–38), then one should be even more mindful of what race/ethnicity meant to the sociopolitical hierarchization of the Greco-Roman world. Ramsey MacMullen, for example, lists four factors in the Roman status equation: time, money, place, and culture (1974: 122). Although MacMullen does not employ the term "race" or "ethnicity," one can still see their traces in Plutarch's decision to use a foreigner to illustrate someone who does not quite know his place (*Mor.* 615D [*Quaest. Conv.* 1.2]), or in MacMullen's own statement that Roman urban elites "opposed not only *rusticitas* but *peregrinitas* [foreign manners]" (1974: 30–31).[5] In other words, one's distance from Rome may have been more than just a geographical measurement (what MacMullen calls "place"); it may well have involved a racial/ethnic differentiation (my conflation of MacMullen's "place" and "culture").[6] As a colonized people, Jews of the first century were at best clients and at worst abject subjects of their colonial masters, as evidenced by what Peter Schäfer calls "Judeophobia" in the ancient world (1997) or how Benjamin Isaac includes a chapter on attitudes against Jews in his recent work on "racism" in classical antiquity (2004: 440–91; see also Feldman 1993: 123–76).[7] Significantly, the Corinthians were not just any Gentiles or non-Jews. According to most Corinthians scholars, they were mostly made up of Greeks and perhaps even Romans (Hays 1997: 2–4; Lanci 1997: 26–30; Horsley 1998: 22–28). They might not have originated from noble or aristocratic families; but in terms of race/ethnicity, they still belonged to the peoples who succeeded each other in colonizing the Jews of Paul's time.

It is therefore surprising that scholars who talk about the status differences among the Corinthians have failed to mention the status difference— particularly the racial/ethnic difference—between Paul and the Corinthians (for example, Pogoloff 1992; Horsley 1998).[8] It is equally surprising that for all the talk about the prominence of body in 1 Corinthians (even those who dwell on theological difference refer to the letter's theologies of the church body as well as those of the resurrected body), the body of knowledge that has been generated by scholars of 1 Corinthians has paid very little attention to any knowledge of the body, particularly the racial/ethnic difference that is inscribed on the human body. This phenomenon has, of course, much to do with the Europeanization of Paul in particular and the politics of racialization and negation within biblical scholarship in general (Sugirtharajah 2003: 104–109), but the dematerialization of Paul's *Jewish* body is especially ironic given Howard Eilberg-Schwartz's argument of Jews as "people of the body" (1992).[9]

Viewing from the perspectives of contemporary Asian Americans, the power dynamics between Paul and the Corinthians are intriguing enough to warrant investigation and interpretation, since the one who founded, fathered, and now hopes to counsel the mainly Gentile Corinthian church happens to be a Jewish "no-body" (that is, one who is insignificant, invisible, and hence disembodied because his racial/ethnic or bodily inscriptions are often made stereotypical by the dominant culture). This difference becomes even more acute if one pays attention to the status inconsistency facing the Corinthians. While most scholars talk about this in terms of economics, I would like to—again, from the perspectives of contemporary Asian Americans—highlight the importance of religious difference. As Mark D. Nanos insightfully proposes in his work on Galatians, it was not a simple thing for first-century Gentiles to follow the tiny Jewish sect under the name of Jesus Christ (2002).[10] Doing so was to leave the religious majority to become part of a religious minority. Their religious difference, in other words, might bring about a status reduction, if not inversion.[11] Studies of both Korean American Buddhists and Korean American Christians have shown that people experiencing a status inversion in the larger socio-political world—particularly men who find themselves marginalized by their immigrant status and racial/ethnic difference, notwithstanding their difference in being part of a religious majority or minority—become even more anxious about and aggressive in competing for status in a smaller religious setting (Song 1997; Suh 2004). According to Song: "[T]he internal conflicts which lead to schisms [in many Korean American churches] are directly correlated with the heterogeneity of characteristics of the congregation, *status alienation of the immigrants*, and the vested interests of Korean clergymen and lay leaders. . . . Competition for lay leadership positions among Korean men usually evolves into fierce struggle among candidates which frequently accompanies f[r]ictional exaggerated strife within the congregation" (Song 1997: 71; emphasis mine).

What I would like to suggest is that the status inversion suffered by the

Corinthians because of their conversion might help not only explain their well-acknowledged status anxiety, but also give reasons for Paul's problems with them, or their problems with Paul.[12] Their conversion, and hence their status inversion and anxiety, caused them to become even more sensitive and hostile to Paul because of Paul's stigmatized racial/ethnic body as a colonized Jew. This is especially important because, in Paul's time, race/ethnicity and religion were "constitutively interrelated" even if they should not be collapsed into one and the same (Buell 2001: 459–60; see also Beard, North, and Price 1998: 214–15). Going back to MacMullen's Roman status equation, Cicero, for example, singled out religion and cultic/religious practices as *the* "national characteristic" in which Rome was "superior" to "foreign peoples" (*Nat. D.* 2.3.8). If Greco-Roman abjection of Jews had much to do with Jewish religion, hostility against Jews would only intensify in view of what was perceived to be "successful" Jewish proselytism (Schäfer 1997: 9, 32, 77–81, 106–18; Isaac 2004: 453–54, 456–57, 459–62, 466–69, 479–81, 488).[13] After all, Roman writers consistently link the two "expulsions" of Jews from Rome (139 B.C.E. and 19 C.E., respectively) to the threat of proselytism, albeit in differing degrees (Velerius Maximus, 1.3.3; Tacitus, *Ann.* 2.85; and Suetonius, *Tib.* 36). Tacitus, in addition, sees proselytes as "the worst rascals among other [non-Jewish] peoples" (*Hist.* 5.5), and Domitian will lead a "witch-hunt" targeting both Jews and Jewish proselytes to pay the two drachmae of *fiscus Iudaicus* (Suetonius, Dom. 12.1–2).[14] In Greco-Roman eyes, the Corinthians' conversion through Paul was likely to be understood as a case of partial if not (yet) full Jewish proselytism, and thus be a cause of anxiety for the Corinthians. This is evident in Juvenal's narration of the proselytizing progression from Sabbath observance to circumcision, as well as in his conclusion that proselytes "hav[e] been wont to flout the laws of Rome" (14.96–104). In contrast to Nano's reading that the Galatians became anxious to become full proselytes through circumcision, I propose that the Corinthians grew anxious to distance themselves from Paul. In other words, I am suggesting that these Gentile Christ-followers were beginning to try to separate religious affiliation from racial/ethnic filiation. Paul was to make it clear, however, that he would not accept such a separation.[15]

Paul's Rejected Body

Both feminist hermeneutics and ideological criticism have taught us that what is assumed is as important as or perhaps even more important than what is said, since what is said needs to be read in the context of the unsaid.

What Paul does say in the letter has already led many to propose that his status might have been shaky in the eyes of the Corinthians (Wire 1990: 1–11; Horsley 1998: 43, 61, 67–68; Schüssler Fiorenza 1999: 105–28). His decision to preach the Gospel "without charge" (9:18), for example, seems controversial enough to warrant an elaborate exposition or explanation (9:1–18). While many have read this as solely Paul's illustration, or even a self-modeling, of what he is trying to teach the Corinthians (namely, be willing to give up one's own right for the sake of others, 8:1–13; 9:19–23; 10:23–11:1), it is nevertheless important to keep in mind how Paul himself characterizes this drawn-out account. He calls it his "apology" or "defense" (9:3).[16]

Perhaps the icy relationship between Paul and the Corinthians is better seen in an earlier part of the letter. Despite his rhetoric that he considers it "a very small thing" to be judged by the Corinthians or any other human being (4:3), Paul immediately goes on to instruct the Corinthians that they should not judge prematurely, because as God's "attendant" and "steward," Paul will be judged by God when his "master" or "lord" comes sometime in the future (4:4–5). But much more than that, Paul goes on to inform the Corinthians, in a rather sarcastic or even bitter tone, that they are "puffed up" (4:6, 18–19). Rather than judging Paul, they are only qualified to "imitate" him, since Paul is, after all, not just another one of their numerous pedagogues or child-sitters but a spiritual "father" from whom they have received the gospel (4:6–21).

I would suggest that this choice chapter provides not only a lens to (re)view the first three chapters of 1 Corinthians, but also presents a clue to the fundamental problem between the correspondents. After his customary thanksgiving prayer (1:4–9) and an unmistakable statement of his stance against "divisions" (1:10), Paul pits the "foolish" proclamation of the cross against "the wisdom of the world" (1:11–25). Then he reminds the Corinthians of their being called and chosen by God despite their own humble beginnings, and asserts the inappropriateness of self-boasting by any human beings (1:26–31). Next Paul goes back—in both a literary and a historical sense—to acknowledge his own rhetorical deficiencies when he brought the gospel to the Corinthians (1:17a–b, 2:1–2, 4a), though he quickly offers two reasons or remedies for such deficiencies. First, his deficiencies serve to place the attention properly on God's rather than any human power (2:4b–5). Second, Paul's deficiencies must be read with a spiritual rather than physical sense and sensibility (2:6–16). Failing to grasp both of these points (3:1–9, 18–23), these carnal Corinthians, as Paul's spiritual children or posterity, must be careful how they continue to build God's church after

Paul, the "wise builder" (3:10–17). I am suggesting, therefore, not only that the "anyone" in 3:12–15 be taken as referring to the Corinthians, but also that "divisions" (1:10) or "strife(s)" (1:11; 3:3) exist among the Corinthians as well as between Paul and the Corinthians. This is what Paul seems to indicate with that enigmatic statement: "Now these things, brothers, I made into a figure of speech with respect to myself and Apollos for you all, so that through us you may learn" (4:6). In other words, what he has said in the first three chapters about himself and Apollos, as 4:7–21 will help make clear, is actually about the differences between himself and the Corinthians.[17] Of course, while the Corinthians' (mis)handling of the(ir) communion shows that these mainly Gentile converts are anxious and competitive about status among themselves (11:17–34), it is at the same time important to see that at least some if not most of them are also anxious and competitive about status with respect to Paul.[18] From Paul's perspectives, both sets of competition are damaging to the harmony and health of the church body.

Likewise, I will argue that 1 Corinthians 4, particularly when read as a continuation and the culmination of 1 Corinthians 1–3, alerts us to the focus of the Corinthians' anxiety about and hostility against Paul. Coming after Paul's admission of figuration, what follows 4:6 can be read as the main point of Paul's object lesson—namely, the apparent status difference between the Corinthians and the apostles (inclusive of Paul [and Apollos?]). While the Corinthians "became rich," "became kings," are "wise" and "strong" and "honorable," the apostles seem "last," "foolish," "weak," and "dishonorable" (4:8–10). In a way that reflects the Roman stereotypical image of Jews as poor beggars (Martial 12.57.13; Juvenal 3.10–18, 6.542–47), Paul adds other detailed descriptions of the (Jewish) apostles. Besides another reference to their manual labor (4:12a), the apostles are also "condemned to death" (4:9). Furthermore, they "hunger and thirst and are naked, and are beaten and unsettled" (4:11). They are "reviled," "persecuted," and "defamed" (4:12b–13a). As "rubbish of the world," they "became the refuse of all things" (4:13b–c). If Paul is done with using figures of speech in 4:6, he has not exactly given up on using word pictures or emphasizing what is visual in what follows. Paul says the apostles have become "a spectacle to the world" (4:9), and the lesson he wants to teach the Corinthians is partly one of reading and interpreting ("the saying, 'Not beyond what have been written,'" 4:6). The issue, I contend, concerns how the Corinthians would look on the lowly-looking and abject (Jewish) bodies of the apostles, particularly that of Paul.

Remember at this point that Paul's first indication of his "deficiencies" refers to his rhetoric (1:17a–b, 2:1–2, 4a); but then he seems to link his rhetorical inadequacy to his physical weakness (2:3; see also 2 Corinthians 10:10). Ancient Greek rhetoric was, after all, inseparable from the orator's physical or bodily stature, which explains Quintilian's advice that aging and ailing orators should retire to avoid ridicule (*Inst.* 12.11.1–3; see also Pogoloff 1992: 147–49; D. B. Martin 1995: 35, 54–55). Keeping Paul's Jewish body in sight may help explain several things in these first four chapters of 1 Corinthians, such as (1) his emphasis on spiritual (in)sight; (2) his repeated accusation of the Corinthians as "carnal" (3:1, 3); and (3) his references to "flesh" (1:26, 29) and "birth" (high or low, 1:26, 28) in his first specific attempt to cut down the "boasting" Corinthians a size or two (1:26–31). Doing so will also provide greater nuance to later chapters, like Paul's somewhat unexpected comment about his "punished" and "enslaved" body to conclude his "defense" of his manual labor (9:24–27), or his peppered references to racial/ethnic constructions in various parts of the letter (1:22–24; 5:1; 7:18–19; 9:20–21; 10:18, 31–32; 12:2, 13; 14:11, 21). Perhaps most pertinent to my purposes is how Paul clearly described the Corinthians as being "puffed up" (5:2) at the same time making the thirst for "wisdom" a Greek or Gentile characteristic (1:22).

Body Building over Jesus' Dead (Jewish) Body

Let me recapitulate my main arguments before I go any further. I am making a case that, because of Paul's ministry, his Corinthian converts experienced a status inversion in joining a religious minority and thus became even more zealous in their competition for status. As a result, they did not just mishandle the communion of their local church, but they also became more sensitive to and despising of the abject status of Paul's diasporic Jewish body within the imperial ideology of the Roman empire. How, then, does Paul negotiate these difficult dynamics in 1 Corinthians?[19] I would propose that he does so by lifting up Jesus. Or more precisely, Paul lifts himself up through and over Jesus' dead (Jewish) body.

It is by now a common scholarly assumption that the opening thanksgiving prayer, if present, is a good place to locate Paul's major concerns in writing a given letter. In 1 Corinthians, Paul's opening thanksgiving "sets a tone for the whole letter by focusing on Christ" (Horsley 1998: 41). One should not forget, however, that this Christ of Paul will not only return in future, but was also once crucified by the Romans. Jesus on the cross, in the context of the Roman empire, is perhaps the most degraded spectacle of an already degraded Jewish body.[20] For Paul, it is precisely through this other rejected Jewish body that the Corinthians have been enriched in everything and in every way (1:4–5a). After this all-inclusive statement, Paul mentions three specific things that turn out to be main themes of the letter: "words" or "speech," "knowledge," and "gift" (1:5b, 7a). How does Paul relate the crucified and returning Christ to these three elements throughout 1 Corinthians?

Words or Speech

Very quickly after the thanksgiving prayer, Paul goes on to talk about the contrast between wise words and Christ's cross (1:17). One finds in Jesus' dead (Jewish) body God's greater power and wisdom (1:18–25; 4:20). As we have already mentioned, this difference between divine and human power/wisdom changes both the meaning and the merit of Paul's "foolish" and "faulty" speech. If rhetoric is about the body of the orator as much as the body of a speech, the meaning and merit of Paul's Jewish body may also be viewed differently in light of the greater divine power and wisdom being revealed in the crucified Christ. For Paul, the cross reveals God's preferential choice of the less and the least (1:21, 27–28; 3:18–20). Not only does Paul use the Corinthians themselves as an example of this (1:26), he also claims that the same preferential choice should be made for the "weaker," "dishonorable," "shameful," and "lacking" members of the body (12:22–24). Rather than just emphasizing the "diversity and interdependence of the body's members" (Horsley 1998: 171), I think Paul is giving a much more aggressive triple-talk here, since what he says seems applicable to (1) any physical body; (2) the Corinthian church body; as well as (3) his own abject Jewish body. Notice how he has used the same or very similar vocabularies to describe himself (2:3; 4:10–13). The contrast or change between a dead Jewish criminal and God's Christ is the kind of inverted relationship or reversal that enables Paul to transform himself from being a persecutor of the church to being the "last" and "least"—but then finally the hardest-working—apostle (15:9–10).

This divine power or grace changes not only the (spiritual?) status of the Corinthians and Paul, but also alters their relationship with each other within the body of Paul's letter. While the early chapters give the impression that Paul is defending or explaining himself under the judgment of the Corinthians, he performs a great rhetorical reversal in 4:14–21, whereby he transforms himself from the one being judged to a father to be imitated. Paul completes this reversal when he exercises judgment over the Corinthians and instructs them on several issues: (1) fornication and proper judgments within the church body (5:1–6:20); (2) marriage and divorce (7:1–40); (3) the relationship between body (through food and fornication) and idolatry, as well as the relationship between one's own freedom and one's love for others (8:1–14:40); (4) the credibility and consequences of Christ's bodily resurrection (15:1–58); and finally (5) the direction on the offering for the Jerusalem church (16:1–4), which is, for Sze-kar Wan, itself a symbol of Paul's anti-colonial project (2000a). Even Paul's "defense" of his own manual labor is part of this great reversal (9:1–27). Showing himself as one who exemplifies the relinquishment of rights for others' benefit, Paul further establishes himself as a strong person who can discipline his own body. Thus negatively intimating the Corinthians' comparative selfishness and lack of strength, Paul is able to claim for himself a moral high ground that trumps their superior standing in terms of both status and race/ethnicity.

Knowledge

The way in which Paul's words gain both substance and volume over Christ's crucified (Jewish) body is in itself already an illustration of how the same rejected body has enriched "knowledge" (1:5c). Rather than repeating myself about God's greater power/wisdom and newly available spiritual (in)sights (1:17–3:23), let me talk about how Christ's death also brings about knowledge of the other world—or more precisely, knowledge about bodily resurrection. For Paul, it is without question that the dead (Jewish) body of Christ has been raised. This "fact" will, according to Paul, ensure not only the bodily resurrection of all of Christ's followers, but also the continuities and discontinuities between this life and the next life, or the earthly body and the heavenly body (6:13c–14; 15:20–57). If his emphasis on continuities functions to bring about bodily discipline (15:29–37), his talk of discontinuities seem to serve a different purpose. It is important to note here that Paul is well aware and openly acknowledging of the markings and rankings of different bodies. Not only does he talk about the differences among various types of (animal and heavenly) bodies (15:39–41c), he further mentions the differences that exist within each type ("for star from star differs in glory," 15:41d). In other words, Paul is arguing not only for the existence of what he calls "natural/perishable" and "spiritual/imperishable" bodies before and after death (15:42–54a), but he also admits that people do not all have the same "natural/perishable" bodies in this life. His, for example, is racially/ethnically marked "Jewish," and hence ranked as having a lower glory that those marked "Greek" or "Roman."[21]

It is most interesting at this point to see how Paul uses a second strategy to redress his rejected Jewish body. If the cross of Christ implies a reversal that accords greater honor to Paul's "lesser" body, the bodily resurrection of Christ means that Paul's own inscribed body will one day be literally transformed into one with greater glory and power (15:42–44, 51–52). On the one hand, Paul demands that the Corinthians reevaluate his present body; on the other hand, Paul himself seems to have internalized the negative messages about his racialized body to the degree that he does desire a changed body. Frantz Fanon suggested years ago that within the "soul" of the colonized is "an inferiority complex [that] has been created by the death and burial of local cultural originality" (1967: 18). Paul shows us here, however, that this "inferiority complex" goes even deeper. Even when Paul insists on the resurrection of Jesus' and his own (Jewish) body *after* death and burial, he still longs for a different body. Let these "dishonorable," "weak," and "perishable/natural" Jewish bodies die, so they will be raised again alive and anew (15:36, 54–57). Even as Paul writes to resist and reverse Greco-Roman racial/ethnic hierarchies, he is simultaneously subjected to or subjectified by the fantasized and racialized Jewish body as something that is not desirable.[22]

I shall return to Paul's mixture of desire and denigration in 1 Corinthians, but let me proceed now to one final thought about resurrection "knowledge," since it will give us a smooth transition to talk about the relationship between the crucified Christ and "gifts." It is the transformation of Christ's dead body and the appearance of this postmortem body to Paul that turn this other Jewish "no-body" into Paul the ("last," "least" but "hardest-working") apostle (9:1–2; 15:1–11). According to Paul, the office of "apostle" is, of course, the "first" that God has appointed in the church body (12:27–28c). Again, one can see here how Paul's abject body is being lifted or built up over Christ's body, which seems to effect all kinds of changes by occupying what Fanon calls a "zone of occult *instability*" (1963: 227; emphasis mine).

Gifts

Along with various office(r)s (apostles, prophets, and teachers), Paul states that this crucified, risen, and returning Christ has also given to the church body various "gifts" (12:28d–h). Just as different bodies are marked and ranked, so Paul goes on to rank these "gifts," naming "love" and "prophecy" in particular as the "greater gifts" (12:31–14:40). In Paul's eyes, these two "gifts" are clearly "greater" because of what they mean to the harmony of the church body, which is perhaps an even more basic "gift" given by the crucified Christ.[23] Over Christ's dead (Jewish) body comes a new body, namely the church community made up of the individual bodies of those who follow Christ (1:9–13; 5:4; 6:15a; 12:27). This new (or interim?) body of Christ is not only given by Christ, but it also belongs to Christ exclusively (4:1–4; 6:19–20a; 7:23; 10:21–22).[24] Paul's explicit employment of the language of slavery implies the Greco-Roman understanding that slaves are but "surrogate bodies" of their lord or master (Glancy 2002: 15–16; see also Harrill 2006: 19–20, 39). Like any Greco-Roman body, the body of the church is also concerned with issues like internal harmony and external integrity. For Paul, the church body and its many individual bodies must be disciplined—even "enslaved"—to achieve both ends (9:24–27; 15:30–34, 58). Internally, in a passage that sounds like Galen's *On the Usefulness of the Parts of the Body* (1968), Paul plays the role of an ancient physician (if not exactly a dissector) who, with the privilege of (in)sight on the human anatomy, leads the Corinthians in a meditation on the body's divinely designed harmony (12:12–21; see also Kuriyama 1999: 123–28). To preserve this internal harmony, members of the church body, following another aspect of divine design as revealed in Christ, must learn to love and look out for one another's welfare, particularly that of the less and the least (8:1–9:23; 10:23–11:1; 12:22–26; 13:5b). Doing so will bring out unity, since Christ (his body?) is not divided. Doing so is also necessary, as the promise of bodily resurrection implies that even death will not remove one from social relations.

Externally, church members must not associate themselves with idolatry, which may take the form of food and/or fornication, since either will open the body up to undesirable entries or penetrations (5:1–2, 5–13; 6:12–20; 10:1–22). As he has done throughout the letter, Paul supports his arguments with physical allusions to Christ's body. Divisions and strifes because of status difference within the church do not just tear up this body that is given by and belongs to Christ, they are actually murderous acts that crucify Christ's physical body all over again; and these destructive acts perpetrated on Christ's (physical and church) body will result in the bodily destruction of the offenders (8:11–12; 11:17–30; 12:14–30; see also D. B. Martin 1995: 190–95). As I have intimated, Paul's equating of idolatry with food, and particularly fornication, is rather (ideo)logical. In a way that parallels physical combat or competition, opening up one's bodily orifices to another's penetration, in terms of Greco-Roman ideologies, is a submissive act that pronounces one's defeat by a more powerful competitor (D. B. Martin 1995: 178). For Paul, this simply cannot be, because God, upon seeing Christ's crucified body, has already turned Christ into a victor and conqueror (15:24–28).[25]

Paul's Body-Building Projects

One should see that, with his emphases on these church disciplines, Paul is in effect addressing and redressing the Corinthian church body.[26] One should also not lose sight of Paul's own stake in all this: as founder and father of the Corinthian church body, Paul is also one of its members. All the rhetoric about love, being considerate of one another, honoring the weak, unity, and harmony means that the Corinthians must learn to look upon Paul's Jewish body with different eyes. They must learn to see that Jews and Greeks were all baptized in one spirit and into one body (12:13), and that within the body of Christ's church, "circumcision is nothing and uncircumcision is nothing" (7:19).[27]

It is significant that both times Paul makes these statements about racial/ethnic "oneness" within the church, he immediately links them with similar statements about the differences between slaves and free persons (7:20–24; 12:13). Dale Martin has argued that most have under-read or inadequately interpreted Paul's statements about slavery (1990: 63–68). Slaves becoming freed and free persons becoming slaves are, in Greco-Roman household ideologies, not erasures of difference but status reversals, since those who are freed occupy a middle rung between those who are free and those who are enslaved. Given what Greeks and Romans thought of Jewish bodies in the first century, as well as what Paul himself says about God's preferential choice for the less and the least in Christ, I would suggest that Dale Martin's argument about status reversal is also applicable to Paul's view of racial/ethnic differences within the church body. After all, it is an-other rejected Jewish body (Christ) that has been the all-efficient source for the Corinthians when it comes to "speech," "knowledge," and "gift."[28] This reversal of racial/ethnic hierarchy is especially likely if Dale Martin is correct in thinking that when Paul argues that greater honor should be given to the "weaker," "dishonorable," "shameful," "comely," "lacking," but "necessary" body parts (12:22–25), he is in fact employing wordplay and referring to the genitals (D. B. Martin 1995: 94–95). If the "necessary" body part was a euphemism for the penis in Hellenistic writings,[29] the circumcised penis was also the shameful necessity that stigmatized the Jewish (male) body in the Greco-Roman world (1 Maccabees 1:41–49, 60–61; 2:42–48; 2 Maccabees 6:7–11; Tacitus, *Hist.* 5.5; Suetonius, *Dom.* 12.2; Petronius, *Sat.* 102; see also Schäfer 1997: 93, 96–99).[30] As Paul persuades the Corinthians to honor the penis and look out for an-other's interests, Paul the Jew—with his circumcised penis—is actually one of these "others" who stand to benefit. His rhetoric or address to redress the Corinthian church body is also a site through which he might redress his own body and authority as their esteemed founder or respectable father. Ethos and logos feed off of each other.[31] Just as an audience would find the words of a credible orator more convincing, the Corinthians—should they find Paul's rhetoric agreeable— would also find Paul's person more appealing. This is particularly so as his "judgments" on various issues serve to edify and build up the church body. In other words, Paul is clearly presenting himself as occupying all three of the church offices that he mentions (12:27–28c; 14:21–22, 31). He is an apostle, a prophet, and a teacher; he is also not hesitant to tell the Corinthians that he speaks "in tongues more than all of you" (14:18).

In light of the difference in race/ethnicity and thus power dynamics, one may also proceed to read Paul's claim to become a Jew with Jews and a Gentile with Gentiles as having a different nuance (9:19–23).[32] Rather than taking Paul's claim simply as his "assimilation" or, worse, his "transcendence" over race/ethnicity, I contend that it comes across more as a threat. One must keep in mind that within the text of 1 Corinthians, there are all kinds of references to Jewish priority alongside these "all things to all people" statements (9:22; 10:32–33). Not only does Paul use "Gentile" negatively to refer to those who do not follow Christ (5:1; 12:1–2), but he also makes his argument on the basis of Hebrew Scripture (1:19, 31; 2:9, 16; 3:18–23; 9:8–9; 10:7; 14:21; 15:45, 54), and presents Moses and "Israel according to the flesh" as the Corinthians' authority, "ancestors," as well as examples of/for his arguments (10:1–4, 18–22). This simultaneous insistence on Jewish priority and fluidity is comparable to the "chameleonism" that was identified with the Jews of the early twentieth-century United States (Itzkovitz 2001). Not only does this ability and willingness to transform and pass as another race/ethnicity—that is, an "otherness" that can change into another "other" that is the self—*not* dilute Jewish difference, but it may also become the very identification of Jewish difference. Claiming an identity that is "marked at once by indistinguishable sameness and irreducible difference" (Itzkovitz 2001: 43), Paul arouses an anxiety caused by the unclassifiable, or what Zygmunt Bauman calls "proteophobia" (1993: 164–65). Paul becomes in effect a vexing and menacing figure to the Corinthians, especially in light of the socio-cultural mixing, rhetorical self-fashioning, and yet colonial racial/ethnic markings that characterized the Greco-Roman world. Paul claims for himself a reproducible body that is simultaneously a double agent who can disrupt, if not exactly dissolve, the scripted performativity of race/ethnicity by performing its contingency, changeability, and convert-ibility.[33]

In his discussion of the "stereotype," Homi K. Bhabha begins with the emphasis that "[a]n important feature of colonial discourse is its dependence on the concept of 'fixity' in the ideological construction of otherness. Fixity, as the sign of cultural/historical/racial difference in the discourse of colonialism, is a paradoxical mode of representation: it connotes rigidity and an unchanging order as well as disorder, degeneracy and daemonic repetition" (1994: 66). One can understand the importance of "fixity" not only by thinking about what Dale Martin says about the threat of social mobility in terms of status or class in 1 Corinthians (1990: 30–38, 42–44), but also by extending his discussion to consider the fury over fluidity in terms of race/ethnicity. If Paul can turn Gentile and infiltrate the Corinthian world, the Corinthians can also slide down the racial/ethnic scales and become stigmatized Jews. This haunting anxiety is even made explicit by Paul. After repeating a similar emphasis on being "all things to all people" (10:32–33), Paul immediately follows up with a call for the Corinthians to "become imitators of me, as I also am of Christ" (11:1; see also 4:16). The mostly Gentile Corinthians are told, in other words, to become chameleons; that is, they are to become (like) Jews. To the horror of the Corinthians but the advantage of Paul, the differences between Gentiles and Jews are, in the space of one letter, simultaneously solidified and dissolved.[34]

Starting from the cross of Christ, Paul promises a resurrection body, disciplines the church body in Corinth, and in the process also redresses his own rejected body as an-other colonized Jew. Over Christ's dead (Jewish) body, Paul gives not only a glimpse into the future but also a "spiritual" perspective for the present that destabilizes status and identity in order to establish a stable order of a different sort (14:33, 40). Paul does all of this through the textual body of this letter that he wrote to the Corinthians. In different parts of the letter, Paul seems to present himself practically as Christ's spokesperson. While he makes this rather explicit in his statement against divorce (7:10), Paul also makes a more general statement to equate his writing with the Lord's commandment (14:37). Although he seems to draw a distinction between his own words and those of Christ a couple of times (7:12, 25), he nevertheless concludes with the affirmation that he is speaking as one who has "the spirit of God" (7:40b). In contrast to the carnal Corinthians, Paul has "the mind of Christ" (2:16–3:3). As a "spiritual person," Paul "discerns all things," but "he is discerned by no one" (2:15), particularly not the carnal Corinthians. In light of his self-representation as Christ's apostle and spokesperson, when he says that "no one speaking by the spirit of God says, 'Let Jesus be cursed'" (12:3a–b), one wonders if he is not also implying that those who curse or judge him are by definition also not speaking by God's spirit.

(Other) Bodies Feminized and Sexualized

In his various works, Fanon has consistently contended that since colonial power colonizes the geographical space of a people as well as the internal space of a person, one must pay attention to psychic dynamics in thinking about resistance (1965; 1967). Because of this form of internal or psychic colonization, a colonized person is often siding *with* as well as siding *against* his or her colonizer. As Steve Pile points out, Fanon's twin concerns (the ambiguity of resistance and the psychic process of colonization) come together in the work of another diasporic Jew, Sigmund Freud of modern Vienna, since Freud refers to resistance in terms of his patients' *avoidance* of receiving psychoanalytic therapy or his talking cure (Pile 1997: 23–24). Writing about Freud's psychoanalytic ideas as well as his life as a diasporic Jew, Sander L. Gilman argues that psychoanalysis itself was Freud's way of dealing with or "resisting" his own racially/ethnically inscribed body as an European abjection (1993). The problem, according to Gilman, is that Freud's own "resistance" was—in a way that was true to Freud's own theorization—one that also maintained repression or sustained oppression, because Freud ended up deflecting all of his undesirable marginalization as a diasporic Jew onto the female body. Gilman's thesis about race/ethnicity and gender in Freud has been further extended by Daniel Boyarin, who argues that Freud deflected his racial/ethnic abjection as a diasporic Jew not only onto female bodies but also onto homoerotic bodies and relations (1997). In what follows, I will briefly suggest that what Gilman and Boyarin say about Freud's psychoanalytic writings is also applicable to Paul's own body-building project in 1 Corinthians.

Questions of Gender

We have already seen hints of Paul internalizing colonial ideologies in his desire for a new and transformed resurrected body (15:36, 42–44, 51–57). The fact that Paul insists on Christ having a bodily resurrection may be a good indication of what he thinks of masculinity. Christ is, after all is said and done, standing erect as a masculine conqueror and victor over all (15:20–28).[35] As a colonized Jew, however, Jesus' and Paul's masculinity were culturally suspect. Because of its "reputation" for attracting mainly women as proselytes, Judaism was attacked in the Greco-Roman world as a religion of and for women (Matthews 2001). I have already commented

on the connection between Greco-Roman rhetoric and the body of the orator; Maud W. Gleason has further demonstrated a link between rhetorical
and masculine competitions, or more precisely, how rhetoric may signify
legitimate and illegitimate male (1994; see also Gunderson 2000; Richlin
1997).[36] Greco-Roman teachers of rhetoric like Cicero and Quintilian tend
to talk also about the need to gesture and posture in a dignified—meaning masculine—manner. Here a single citation from Quintilian will have
to suffice. He suggests learning from dramatic actors, who perform distinctions among "slaves, pimps, parasites, farmers, soldiers, prostitutes,
maidservants, old men (stern and mild), young men (moral or loose-living),
married ladies, and young girls" (*Inst.* 11.3.74).[37] We can therefore observe
further subtleties in the relations between Paul's rhetorical deficiencies and
his bodily abjection. His bodily abjection as a diasporic and colonized Jew
has to do with Paul's racial/ethnic inscriptions as well as his "feminization"
by the dominant culture of the Roman empire.[38]

Writing about racial relations in the United States, Robyn Wiegman
explains: "In the context of white supremacy, we must understand the threat
of masculine sameness as so terrifying that only the reassertion of a gendered
difference can provide the necessary disavowal. It is this that lynching and
castration offer in their ritualized deployment, functioning as both a refusal
and a negation of the possibility of extending the privileges of patriarchy to
the black man" (1995: 90). Even if the racial/ethnic groups and the exact
practices might differ, the underlying ideology of Wiegman's analysis is still
transferable back to Paul's world. It was a binary imposition so that Greco-
Roman males would have hegemony and monopoly over every masculine
privilege, and the racialized Jew would be pushed into what Wiegman calls
the "corporeal excess of a racial feminization" (1995: 98). Not to be lost or
forgotten here is how Roman ideologies also identified Jewish bodies with
sexual excess or deviance (Martial 7.30, 35, 82; 11.94).[39] In fact, the connection that elite males made between "foreign cults" and women, sexual
immorality, and state subversion is well documented in the Greco-Roman
world (Matthews 2001: 72–82). The intersecting dynamics of race/ethnic-
ity, gender, sexuality, and questions of national loyalty are, of course, also
familiar to many Asian Americans (Eng 2001). It is in resistance or reaction to these dynamics that Frank Chin attempts to (re)masculinize Asian
America not only by attacking Maxine Kong Kingston's "woman warrior"
but also by targeting Fu Manchu as a "homosexual menace" and Charlie
Chan as an "effeminate closet queen" (J. P. Chan et al. 1991: xiii; see also
Chin 1991: 66).[40]

Since many feminist readings of 1 Corinthians have—from various perspectives and with different methodologies—done much to critique the masculinist biases of 1 Corinthians (Wire 1990; Bassler 1998; Schüssler Fiorenza 1999: 105–128; Økland 2004; Penner and Vander Stichele 2005), I have no need to duplicate their helpful and insightful critiques here.[41] I do agree with Kittredge that the gender question should never be subsumed or deflected by any other differential relations of power, be it imperialism and/or race/ethnicity (2000). Let me nevertheless emphasize a need to read Paul's masculinist positions alongside his own "feminization" as a diasporic and colonized Jew. I do so not to excuse or, worse, justify Paul's positions. My hope is to promote a contextual reading that refuses to account for certain gender and/or sexuality problems by simply essentializing a minority person and/or culture (Jewish, Asian American, or whatever) as patriarchal and/or "homophobic," and thus letting the dominant and imperial cultures completely off the hook. The dynamics, deflections, and reduplications of bodily abjection must be teased out and scrutinized.[42] In struggling against this process of racialization *and* feminization, Paul (con)fuses socio-political agency with "manhood" and ends up becoming hysterical about those who are female and what is considered "feminine." In other words, Paul does wrong (about women) even or perhaps especially when he is right (about resisting Roman abjection). As anti-colonial resistance takes place in the form of an antagonistic masculinity between Greco-Roman and Jewish male, competing masculinity also turns into a complementary masculinity in which both groups of men are making and marking their claim through their domination over women (J. K-J. Lee 2004: 134–35). Paul's displacing of his own abjection onto other "others" not only foreshadows Freud and many other colonized and/or racial/ethnic minorities but also echoes those closer to his own time and place. Josephus, for instance, contrasts a high-ranking female convert to Judaism (Fulvia) with an immoral freedwoman who is familiar with the Isis cult (Ida) to refute the charges that Jews attract people from the lower classes onto an-other (*AJ* 18.65–84; see also Matthews 2001: 21–28).

Inseparable from how Paul may have felt "feminized" is perhaps his own ambivalence about masculinity. His "advice" that the Corinthians should put the lesser other first is in a sense an alternative to the agonistic and competitive ethos of the Greco-Roman masculine ideal. One may add to that Paul's whole emphasis on the belonging of a believer's body to the Lord (6:19–20a). This belonging and the subsequent union that exists between Jesus and a follower of Jesus, as Hays points out on the basis of 6:16–17, is for Paul comparable to or even deeper than the sexual union between a man and a *female* prostitute (1997: 104). Since Paul thinks that the bodies of husband and wife belong to each other (7:4), his adamant insistence on the Lord's exclusive rights to his followers (7:23; 10:21–22) may well explain Paul's preference not to take a wife (7:1–9; 9:5). Paul's "heterosexist" assumption regarding sexual union, however, implies that he himself will have to occupy a female or feminine position in his "union" with his Lord. What I am getting at is how Paul's own ambivalence about masculinity (in terms of his non-agonistic advice, his "holy union" with Jesus Christ, and his "feminization" as a colonized Jew) may lead to a haunting anxiety over gender failure that causes him to further solidify gender identity in (re)turn.

Questions of Sexuality

Regardless of whether Paul's list of wrongdoers (5:10–11; 6:9–10) originates from Jewish or Hellenisitic sources and what specific terms may be referring to (Hays 1997: 87–88, 96–97; Horsley 1998: 81–82, 86–87),[43] there is no question that Paul sees—to play on Jonathan Dollimore's book title (1991)—"sexual dissidents" and Christ-following bodies (both collective and individual) as mutually exclusive (6:13c–20). This stigmatization of sexual dissidence as deviance (however defined), when read in light of Greco-Roman degradations of Jews as sexually deviant bodies, becomes triply intriguing. First, Paul seems to suggest that the mostly Gentile Corinthians are actually the ones who are sexually deviant.[44] This is not just true of them before their conversion to follow Christ (6:11), but, to Paul's great amazement and disappointment, their deviant sexuality continues after their participation in the church (5:1–8). Second, Paul's "reversed condemnation" of the Corinthians makes him, though a diasporic and colonized Jew, come across as more Greco-Roman than the Greco-Romans when it comes to matters of sexual "purity." This is especially so since Cicero, for example, has condemned similar incestuous relations (*Clu.* 5.14–6.16).

Writing about the Jews in Algeria in the 1960s, Albert Memmi observes:

> Their constant and very justifiable ambition is to escape from their colonized condition. . . . To that end, they endeavor to resemble the colonizer in the frank hope that he may cease to consider them different from him. Hence their efforts to forget the past, to change collective habits, and their enthusiastic adoption of Western language, culture and customs. But if the colonizer does not always openly discourage these candidates to develop that resem-

blance, he never permits them to attain it either. Thus, they live in constant and painful ambiguity. (1991: 15)

Extending Memmi's obervation in a way, Bhabha suggests that the "almost-white-but-not-quite" dynamics of colonial ideology actually drives both colonizers and colonized to become more and more white (1994: 88). Studies have shown that Asian Americans, finding themselves in the position of being a racial/ethnic *and* religious minority in diaspora, are also driven to employ this strategy. Many Korean American Buddhists, for instance, stress the compatibility between "American values" (particularly being independent, self-reliant, open-minded, and democratic) and Buddhist teachings (especially the need and ability to "find and know one's mind"), and claim as a result that they are indeed "more American" than, say, their Christian counterparts (Suh 2004: 119, 166, 189–90).[45] Todd Penner's reading of Acts, particularly how Luke depicts the Christian community as living up to, modeling, and/or fulfilling various Greco-Roman ideals for its *politeia* (in terms of membership, ethos, constitution, polity, and result), shows that this strategy is not just a modern invention by Asian Americans (Penner 2003a: 84–100). One can easily say the same of Philo, who tries to justify Judaism to Greco-Roman audiences and in Greco-Roman terms. Gregory E. Sterling, for instance, has also shown how diasporic or Hellenistic Jews like Josephus, Demetrius, Artapanus, Pseudo-Eupolemus, and Eupolemus are "national historians—*tout-à-fait*—who claim the superiority of the Jewish nation over both other Oriental people and Greeks" (Sterling 1992: 223) by depicting Moses or Abraham as *Kulturbringer* or benefactor to cultures that had become dominant powers of the historians' own time (see also Holladay 1999: 174–97; and Gruen 1998). In the words of Elizabeth A. Castelli, "one of the important rhetorical strategies of early Christian apologists was to argue for their movement's superior embodiment of the highest virtues from the classical world" (2004: 13).

One will see Paul employing a similar strategy regarding "wisdom." After characterizing wisdom as a Greek thing (1:22), he will proceed to talk about his own (more) "mature" wisdom that is from God (2:6–3:3, 10), as well as needling the Corinthians for resorting to the "wisdom" of "worldly" judges (6:1–6). Likewise, the fact that it is now Paul who reminds the Corinthians to prefer suffering over pursuing prosecution (6:7–8)—a lesson that many Greek and Roman sages (like Plato, Epictetus, and Musonius Rufus) have also spoken and taught (Hays 1997: 95–96)—implies again that Paul is the one who is indeed more "Greco-Roman." Given (1) the Stoic-Cynic emphasis on "freedom," (2) the history of Corinth as "Aphrodite's city" (Lanci 1997: 97–99), and (3) the dominant Roman sensibilities about industry and efficiency, and hence the correlative criticism of the Sabbath as a habit of an idle people worshipping an equally idle God (Schäfer 1997:86–88), one may well say the same thing regarding Paul's teaching of the Corinthians on "freedom" (7:21, 32; 8:9–9:22; 10:23–30), on "love" (8:1–4; 13:1–14:1; 16:14, 24), as well as Paul's own insistence on manual labor (9:1–18) and hard work (4:11–13; 15:9–10, 58). Similarly, given the dominant opinion that Jews are unsocial and peculiar not only because of their dietary rules and circumcision practice but also because of "their belief in a God who does not take human form" (Schäfer 1997: 17; see also Tacitus, *Hist.* 5.5), Paul's insistence on Jesus' bodily resurrection (15:1–58) and the Corinthians as the very (interim?) body of Christ on earth (12:12–30) seems to be just another version of the same strategy.

Third, much like his emphasis on a transformed body in the future, Paul's stigmatization of sexually dissident bodies (whether Jewish or Greco-Roman) in particular, and his claim to be "more Greco-Roman" in general, only end up reduplicating and reinforcing colonial ideologies, whether it is the cult of sexual purity or something else (see also Castelli 2004: 150–51; and Knust 2006). Dionysius of Halicarnassus, the first-century B.C.E. historian, has also used this two-pronged strategy of "appropriation" and transference (Gabba 1991). Writing against anti-Roman sentiments popular among elite Greeks, Dionysius tries to show, on the one hand, in his *Roman Antiquities* that (1) Romans are really Greeks, (2) Roman institutions and morality are similar if not superior to Greek ones, and (3) Rome's power in the world is well deserved (see, for example, 1.4–5, 89; 2.17; 7.66.4–5). On the other hand, Dionysius, in *On the Ancient Orators*, makes a point of pitting Greeks against "Asians" rather than Romans.[46] Cautious about and defensive against what he perceives to be external, foreign, and polluting agents against the personal and/or collective body, Paul's attitude actually resembles the political ideology that represents a nation as a body threatened by infection (for example, Plutarch, *Lyc.* 27.4; see also Isaac 2004: 479).[47] In other words, what Gilman and Boyarin suggest Freud did, Paul also does, as Paul projects his own abjection and stigmatization as being "feminine" and "morally corrupt" onto women and other sexual dissidents. By duplicating and displacing colonial abjection onto people who are also in different ways already subjected, Paul's resistance against colonization and racialization is greatly compromised. He has, in a sense, himself become those who oppress him or what he hates. He is building community on the backs of those whom "everyone" can agree to marginalize and stigmatize. His political view about Jews might well be different, but his political practice ends up duplicating and reinforcing a larger ideological imperative to establish and eschew abject bodies.

Conclusion

Asian Americans are not only familiar with racial/ethnic and religious difference but also well aware of duplication and deflection in our attempts to redress and/or masquerade our own differences. This we do by highlighting, gloating over, and hiding behind other differences. In Hisaye Yamamoto's short story "Wilshire Bus" (2001), a Japanese American woman, Esther Kuroiwa, rides a bus up and down the Wilshire Boulevard of post–World War II Los Angeles twice a week to visit her husband, who is hospitalized because "his back, injured in the war, began troubling him again" (2001: 34). The plot of the story turns on a chance encounter on the bus between Esther and an elderly Chinese American couple, particularly on how Esther changes from acknowledging her similarity with them as "Orientals together on a bus" with a smile (2001: 35) to "detaching" herself from them in silence by "pretending to look out the window" (2001: 36). What causes this change is the verbal assault of a male passenger in the back of the bus made upon the Chinese American woman, because she—though a "nobody" in terms of race, gender, and generation—had dared to turn around and give the man "a quick but thorough examination" upon hearing his loud diatribe against a local sports figure in a public space (2001: 35). As expected, the man's attack consists of his opinion that the Chinese American woman should "get off the bus" and "go back to China" (2001: 35–36).

What is pertinent to our purposes here is Esther's own reflection on the incident. She realizes that her "saving detachment" (2001: 37) has to do with her "gloating over the fact that the drunken man had specified the Chinese [rather than the Japanese] as the unwanted" (2001: 36). The human tendency to duplicate and transfer abjection onto others becomes clear to Esther as she remembers a man she had once seen wearing a placard around his neck in a time of anti-Japanese sentiment during World War II that read "I AM KOREAN" (2001: 36). In other words, Esther realizes that she is deflecting possible denigration or abjection onto others on the bus, just as Chinese and Korean Americans did during the war at the time of the internment of Japanese Americans.

This deflection of one's own abjection onto others is analogous to the projection onto or expulsion of what one feels is unpleasant or undesirable within oneself to the external world. According to Freud, this projection or deflection is known as the psychic process of splitting. For my reading of

1 Corinthians, splitting also signifies what Abdul R. JanMohamed calls a "cleaved subjectivity," in which the subjectivity of a colonized person (like Paul) is bifurcated into two parts—one collaborating with and the other contending against his colonizers (2005: 91). Bhabha has also fittingly compared this splitting process, as a strategy of disavowal, to "a discrimination between the mother culture and its bastards" (1994: 111). What must not be forgotten is that, while a mother may disown her own as bastards, she is nonetheless unable to have bastards on her own: that generally takes the involvement of a third party. In Yamamoto's story, this third and "indispensable" party would be the male passenger in the back of the bus who disrupts a public space with his loud commentary and believes that he (alone) has the right to do and say whatever he pleases without public scrutiny, especially not by an elderly Chinese American woman. One must not focus only on the two Asian American women in reading "Wilshire Bus" and forget that there is another subjection *behind* splitting. As splitting itself is a subjecting act, however, it "disturbs the visibility of the colonial presence and makes the recognition of its authority problematic" (Bhabha 1994: 111). So, one must consider and challenge *both* conditions of subjection, the one behind as well as the one begun in the process of splitting. To return to Paul, one needs to trace, track, or historicize rather than simply essentialize or naturalize his subjection of others. As one rightly and rightfully criticizes Paul's marginalization of women and sexual dissidents in 1 Corinthians, one must also not fail to account for the absent presence of the Roman colonization and racialization of Jews like Paul. Only by doing so will one be able to "show the levels at which opposition can be both contestatory and complicit, and yet still constitute a subversion that matters" (Kondo 1997: 11). If not, one will easily end up—as Spivak has shown with the imperial excuse of "saving brown women from brown men" (1988: 297)—abetting and advancing more imperial violence.

CHAPTER 6

Melancholia in Diaspora

• •

Reading Paul's Psycho-Political Operatives in 1 Corinthians

I suggested in the last chapter that one could and should read 1 Corinthians by paying attention to Paul's Jewish body within the context of other bodies, including (1) the Greco-Roman bodies of the Corinthians, (2) the Corinthian church body, and (3) the political body of the Roman empire. In 1 Corinthians, Paul spins Jesus' crucifixion into a complex cycle of death and rebirth. Not only is Jesus himself risen and assured of a resurrection body, but his death also leads to a new life for Paul. Paul becomes an apostle and, in turn, fathers the rebirth of the Corinthians. I have argued that this complicated cycle of death and rebirth has also allowed Paul to not only (re)claim his Jewish religion and identity but also connect Gentiles with them.

John Ashton, in his comparative or "convergent" study on the "religion of Paul," has proposed that the exchange between Jesus' death and Paul's new life effects an identity for Paul that is structurally comparable to that of a shaman, especially given Paul's own emphasis on the work of (the) spirit in, among other places, his Corinthian correspondences (2000). If Ashton's work focuses more on Paul's own *experience* in becoming a shaman-like figure, T. Lynn Stott's anthropological reading of 1 Corinthians centers on Paul's career as one (1998). In performing a symbolic healing of the Corinthian church body, Stott suggests—albeit only briefly—that Paul is claiming a shaman-like authority and ability to intervene through and intercede with another world for those in need (1998: 11, 14–15, 17).

Reading with Victor Turner's Liminality

To adapt slightly Joseph Roach's work on living effigies as part of what he calls the "circum-Atlantic phenomenon" (1996: 82–83), I would like to suggest that the conditions of doubleness in and through which shamans work are, in Paul's case, related to and overlapped with W. E. B. Du Bois' "double consciousness" in racial/ethnic terms (1990: 8–9). Let me begin with how the suggestion of Paul as a shaman who negotiates between identities, knowledge, as well as body and spirit brings us to the multiple liminalities or in-between-nesses (Turner 1967: 93–111) associated with 1 Corinthians. This is especially important since abjection, which I emphasized in the last chapter regarding Paul's racialized and colonized body, is very much about "frontier" (Kristeva 1982: 9). Thus Shimakawa is correct in stating that "what distinguishes abjection from objectification or fetishization is precisely that indeterminable and dynamic relation between inside and outside" (2002: 82). Liminality, therefore, not only aptly describes Asian Americans who are being racialized as "permanent houseguests in the house of America" (S. C. Wong 1993: 6), but it has also been used by Asian American scholars as a lens to read and/or discuss readings of the Bible (Kuan 2000: 166–67; Kuan 2002: 52–53; A. Y. Lee 2006: 61–62; and Wan 2006).

Many commentators, quoting Strabo (8.6.20), have pointed to Corinth's geographical location as a major thoroughfare or threshold to trading centers in Asia and Italy. We have also seen how both Paul and the Corinthians are liminal as a diasporic Jew and/or a religious minority within the Roman empire. Their liminalities are, however, intensified by their opposite roles in a "both-beyond-and-beneath" site that they share because of their shared faith in a crucified and returning Christ, who is no longer exactly inside but also not quite outside of their communities. While Paul's position as Christ's apostle and founder of the Corinthian church places him beyond the Corinthians, his race/ethnicity as a colonized Jew places him beneath them. As the letter's body emphasizes the new life shared by Paul and the Corinthians—a new life that they all need to live out through their daily and bodily existence, both in terms of the integrity of their individual bodies and of the harmony of the church's collective body—over Christ's dead body, it also enhances the feeling that their present (living out a new life in an old body) is but a transitory stage between their past (living a "pagan" life through their earthly bodies) and their future (living out an eternal life in transformed bodies). This ambiguous position of transition is disturbingly dangerous, because, as Mieke Bal indicates, a premarital bride who exists between fixed positions belongs to no one and is a nobody (1988). If, as I have argued, this is what causes the Corinthians to become hyper-anxious about status as a religious minority and reject Paul's Jewish body, what Paul worries about is the opposite but logical side of that transitional position:

the Corinthians could potentially belong to everybody. This explains why, as we have also seen, Paul emphasizes Christ's exclusive claim on their personal and collective bodies.

Furthermore, the presence/absence dynamics of the letter itself represents the liminality of Paul's authority or his "two contradictory forms of self-articulation" (Bronfen 1992: 12). On the one hand, Paul seems to have established, through this letter and over Christ's (dead) body, his masculinity, his survival, his signature (16:21), and his stature. On the other hand, this letter equally represents and reveals Paul's disempowered or feminized position in his contact with or exposure to the mostly Gentile Corinthian body. For example, although he portrays the Corinthians as immature or underdeveloped believers who are nevertheless standing on the threshold of moral responsibilities, his language of giving birth and providing milk for them (3:1–3) depicts himself as a "feminine" means, vehicle, or channel through whom others may pass, transit, and be nourished into new life. Given also his description that "a necessity is laid on him" by Christ to proclaim the gospel (9:16), one might say—in light of (1) the link between the penis and the word "necessity" that we have discussed, (2) the by now well-known active/passive roles in Greco-Roman sexual understandings, and (3) the corresponding "prophecy as penetration" association (D. B. Martin 1995: 239–42)—that Paul himself has become a hymen, a limen, and a passageway. Having been broken in and broken through by Christ, this penetrated, pregnant, and lactating Paul is—in spite of or in view of his masculine-sounding rhetoric—an indeterminate "he/she" with marginal authority.[1] Unable to resist Christ's call, Paul ends up being able to speak and mediate for others' "healing." In fact, one can say that Paul's shaman-like identity, as far as (he hopes) the Corinthians are concerned, enables and brings Jesus back to voice if not to life, especially since all of the three explicit citations of so-called Jesus' sayings in our extant Pauline corpus are found in 1 Corinthians (7:10–11; 9:14; 11:23–25). Paul is thus helping (the Corinthians) to re-member Christ's body (12:12–31); by doing so, Paul frees Christ's body to speak and do its work in the world again in and through the church. Yet, as John Ashton points out, shamanistic authority is not only premised on experiences of great sufferings and even torments by the power a shaman claims to possess, but it is also contingent on a shaman's ability to persuade others of his or her "authenticity" and sincerity (2000: 33). As a letter of intervention, 1 Corinthians therefore represents both a moment of liminality (because of the uncertainties or indeterminacies regarding its reception) *and* a potential breaking up of that liminal moment (since its arrival might result in a better acceptance or a firmer rejection of Paul).

As an orifice, Paul's bodily existence serves all kinds of thresholds or "passages" in 1 Corinthians. As the link or connection between the Corinthians and Christ, Paul bridges the racial/ethnic divide between Jews and Gentiles; his role as an apostle or a shamanistic messenger also straddles between flesh and spirit, between the earthly and the heavenly, between this and an-other world. He may be despised, but he—along with his circumcised Jewish penis—is a necessary part of the church body. In addition to his pivotal role among the Corinthians, his reference to the collection indicates that he is also a vital conduit of cash flow—a kind of lifeblood?—for the Jerusalem church. His self-articulation about food and sex also gives the impression that while he is no doubt human, he is by no means constrained by the natural urges of his physical body (6:13; 7:1–9, 25–39).[2] His desires for food and sex, for example, seem to be largely mediated through the Corinthians; he is, in other words, more interested in the Corinthians' desires for food and sex than in the food and the sex themselves.

Again, one should remember that this pervasive prominence of liminality or rhetoric of the threshold is implicated in the historical world of racial/ethnic and religious difference within the context of empire. Both Paul and the mostly Gentile Corinthians were in a liminal stage, respectively as a diasporic Jew and as new converts to a minority cult (in both racial/ethnic and religious terms). Both parties found themselves residing on marginal sites or in threshold states, longing to route their hopes for security, safety, and salvation through Christ's dead and resurrected body. It is the dis-eased position of being caught between (unequal) worlds.[3] While—as will become clear in this chapter—even the majority and/or the powerful are haunted in such worlds, most contemporary Asian Americans are familiar with this dis-eased position. Living in diaspora, Asian Americans are liminal figures of abjection on the brink of inclusion/exclusion (Shimakawa 2002: 38).[4] Because of our racially/ethnically marked bodies, and sometimes also because of our religion, Asian Americans are liminal to the boundary of "American-ness." We are neither inside nor outside; or, we are both inside and outside simultaneously. That liminal position makes us threatening and threatened, and that liminality of abjection has led to a couple of psychic processes that are also legible in Paul's "first" letter to the Corinthians: (1) *ressentiment*, and (2) mourning and melancholia.[5]

Reading with Friedrich Nietzsche's *Ressentiment*

The negative implication in Paul's comment on lactation (3:1–3) echoes an even more negative indictment by Frantz Fanon. Calling it "lactification,"

Fanon attacks black women who choose to marry white men to, according to Fanon, achieve upward social mobility for themselves and to "whiten" the entire black race (1967: 47–48). Pointing to Fanon's diatribe, Rey Chow suggests that Fanon's undeniable misogynist view must at the same time be read as a (post)colonial "externalization" of Nietzschean *ressentiment*, and Chow does so by focusing on the timing, targets, and tactics in the acting out of this persistent but generally repressed hostility (2002: 183–91). According to Chow, a colonized person or psyche may, at moments when liberation seems probable, stigmatize, stereotype, scapegoat, and pathologize not only the colonizer, but also those of his/her own racial/ethnic community. In other words, *ressentiment*—a mixture of fear of and desire for the colonizer, and hence a mingling of envy and contempt towards as well as anxiety and defense of one's own—may cause a colonized person to use the very same strategies and tactics of the colonizer on his/her own, especially when another "other" is about to be recognized by the colonizer. And a colonized person/psyche may do this even in the name of anti-colonial resistance. While Chow's interest is clearly the proximity and rivalry within a colonized, racial/ethnic minority community, Paul's letter indicates that *ressentiment* may work against this "other" that is one's own on an even more intimate level. Paul's desire for a transformed resurrection body, even as the founder of the Corinthian community, shows that *ressentiment*, or the internalization and externalization of colonial abjecting dynamics, may also target an "other" that is literally one's own self.[6] This is particularly so if the rhetoric addressing the rivalry against and rejection of Paul in 1 Corinthians is more of Paul's projection on than an actual reflection of the Corinthian situation.[7] If, as I have suggested, abjection is being inside and outside simultaneously, Paul's simultaneous internalization and externalization of abjecting dynamics against himself shows that incorporation of colonial ideology and the racialized gaze is precisely what makes one a colonized and racialized subject. Or, to put this in Foucauldian language, subjection is part of subjectification, even if that subjection is partial and that subjectification divided.[8]

Reading with and against Sigmund Freud's Melancholia

If Paul's *ressentiment* shows that liminality may lead to dissolution *and* reinforcement of binaries and boundaries (as well as their dissolution *through* their reinforcement), Turner himself often links liminality with death (1977). Liminality is, for Turner, the in-between state of life-in-death, death-in-life, or the site of the ghostly double. Paul seems to illustrate this with his concern with not just the death and resurrection of Christ but also the (future) death and resurrection of himself as well as those of the Corinthians. Freud, another diasporic Jew of a later generation, also theorized the psychic processes involved in death and mourning (1953–74: 14.243–58). Mourning, in Freud's exposition, is a process of grieving through which one gradually draws one's libido away from the dead person or lost object to invest instead in a new person or object. Instead of simply emphasizing the termination of liminality and a final regeneration or resurrection like Turner does, Freud also talks about the possibility of a mourning without end. When grief is not resolved and becomes interminable, melancholia—or a state of sustained, hence abnormal and pathological mourning—results.

I must point out, first of all, that melancholia was already recognized and written about in Paul's time (Radden 2002: 55–68). Melancholia is related to the black bile in classical humoral theory, wherein, as in Freud's exposition of melancholia, health or sickness is considered a matter of qualitative and quantitative balance. In other words, both classical and Freudian melancholia have much to do with "the conflictual negotiation *within* the self" (Cheng 2001: 199n18). Reading (1) Aristotle's comments on melancholia in *Problemata* not only as a matter of configuration or materialization in particular bodies but also in relationship to various social domains like education, arts, or politics; and (2) the important role played by classical humoral theory in eighteenth-century discourse about complexion and race (see also Brace 2005: 27), David L. Eng and David Kazanjian point to a need to extend Freud's individualistic frame for melancholia to the socio-material milieu in general and to nationalist/racialized contexts in particular (2003a: 7–12).[9] Separately pursued from but inseparably bound to their suggestion are recent musings that connect postcolonial conditions to both mourning (Durrant 2004) and melancholia (Gilroy 2005).[10] Could a discourse on bodily health, death, and resurrection by a first-century diasporic Jew living under Roman colonization and these modern as well as postmodern theoretical discourses on mourning and melancholia shed light on each other?[11]

According to Freud, the dead or lost object of one's mourning may take various forms, like "a loved person, or . . . some abstraction . . . such as one's country, liberty, an ideal and so on" (1953–74: 14.243).[12] Of course, these various forms of death or loss may occur at one and the same time. This is particularly so for a person like Paul. In addition to or implicated within the death of Jesus, Paul's experience of colonization and diaspora might involve multiple losses, ranging from homeland, family, identity, property, and/or status. Yet another loss from a racial/ethnic minority and (post)colonial perspective is the perpetual inability to be fully integrated because of social dynamics that go beyond the minority person's individual willingness or unwillingness.[13]

Eng and Shinhee Han talk about this in the context of (Asian) America (2003). While the compelling ideal of "whiteness" is foreclosed to Asian-raced bodies, the dominant stereotypical picture of such bodies as "model minority" also dictates a form of mimicry that will lead to what is at best a partial acceptance. They are, in other words, talking about a double loss here. What have been lost are not just the ideal of "whiteness" but also alternative pictures of being "Asian." In contrast to white immigrants who may mourn and eventually become "assimilated" into the mainstream of society, Asian-raced bodies suffer a melancholia of "suspended assimilation" (Eng and Han 2003: 345). As he compares and contrasts anti-Semitism and the ways in which blacks have been racialized and colonized, Fanon also uses the language of mourning to talk about this psychodynamics of being able to neither achieve an idealized "whiteness" nor "recover" from a deformed and deforming racial/ethnic stereotype: "My body was given back to me sprawled out, distorted, recolored, clad in *mourning* in that white winter day" (1967: 113; emphasis mine). Given Fanon's own language of loss, longing, and mourning, what Bhabha calls Fanon's "narcissistic identification" (1994: 88; see also Fanon 1967: 10; and Freud 1953–74: 19.249–50) might be more helpfully understood as Fanon's identifying of, and with, a colonized racial/ethnic minority melancholia.

Fanon's concluding identification of this melancholia as "comparison"—namely, one who suffers from a compulsory comparison to and rejection by a colonial standard of racial/ethnic norms (1967: 211)—sheds yet a different light on Paul's comment on being a Jew to Jews and a Gentile to Gentiles (9:19–21).[14] While these chameleon-sounding verses are, as I suggested in the last chapter, threatening to Corinthian ears, these same verses also betray Paul's melancholic sentiment in facing an impossible Greco-Roman ideal and a denigrated Jewish self. Put differently, a changeable body is menacing because it is generally considered to be abnormal and repugnant. We have already seen, for example, that Paul admits his own failure in achieving the Greco-Roman ideals of rhetorical sophistication and related masculine and bodily ideals (1:17a–b, 2:1–2, 4a). Likewise, as Paul admits the distance between himself and the Gentile desire for wisdom, he also repeatedly admits an unresolved and irresolvable distance between himself and the Jewish demand for signs (1:21–25). Paul's lack of acceptance or his racial/ethnic melancholia becomes even more intense in light of his work with the Corinthians. If one accepts my arguments in the previous chapter

about the conflicts between Paul and the Corinthian church, one is left with
a picture in which Paul feels "unaccepted" by the very people for whom and
with whom he has worked. For Paul, the Corinthian dis-ease is their inability to accept Paul's Jewish body despite "all" the "words," "knowledge,"
and "gifts" that they have received through the dead and resurrected body
of another Jew named Jesus (1:4–7). This diasporic Paul is, in other words,
not just a subject of melancholia who mourns his various losses without
end, he himself is also a lost object of Greco-Roman imperialism. Like a
specter or a ghost, his and other Jewish bodies that have been exploited and
erased continue to haunt the rhetoric of *pax Romana* (Eng and Han 2003:
347–48; see also A. F. Gordon 1997).[15]

Melancholia as Socio-Political Activism

This haunting aspect of the Jewish body provides an opening to follow the suggestion made by Eng and Kazanjian (2003a) to reread, and to
a degree even depathologize, melancholia (see also Cheng 2001: 20–29).
First of all, it should be clear from the above discussion that loss, death,
mourning, and melancholia can all be socio-politically rather than individu-
ally situated.[16] I have already mentioned Turner's linking of liminality and
death, but death for Turner can also be celebrated as a rite of social renewal,
particularly if the dead person is, like a political leader or king, able to capture powerful collective attention (1967; 1977). Second, one's refusal to let
go of a loss—and hence one's "inability" to stop mourning—may actually
be a positive, perhaps even creative, ploy to "resurrect" a "buried" past into
one's present social engagements and political struggles. As Mikhail Bakhtin
suggests, "The most intense and productive life of culture takes place on the
boundaries" (1986: 2), or, in Turner's language, in liminality. Melancholia is not necessarily indecision or inaction, as Freud describes (1953–74:
14.244), but may rather be a form of decision, or even innovation put into
action. In a way akin to Kristeva's reading of Hans Holbein's painting of the
body of the dead Christ (1989: 107–38), I am reading Paul's rhetoric about
the "lost" Jewish body of Jesus as a creative intervention. By refusing to let
it go and get over its loss, Paul insists on both its death and its resurrection
in order to talk about otherness and redress his own body as well as that
of the Corinthian community.[17] Jesus becomes for Paul a lingering though
flickering presence, the unhomely or uncanny that returns, or the ghost that
haunts.[18] Paul as a shaman demonstrates "the cultural politics of memory,
particularly as they are realized through communications between the living
and the dead" (Roach 1996: 34) by speaking the words of the once crucified
Christ. Paul is socio-politically engaged and committed to bring a lost or

dead Jewish body from the past into the present, and he is adamant that this Jew will return or come in a transformed and resurrected body in the future (1 Cor. 15:1–58). In spite of his many losses, this diasporic Paul is no mere victim. He even talks about his own "absent presence" right after a brief call to "grieving" or "mourning" (5:2–5). This melancholic Paul does possess a "keener eye for . . . truth than other people" (Freud 1953–74: 14.246), and this truth is, in contrast to Freud, also much greater than Paul's personal or individual self.

Paul is imaginative and creative because his diasporic and melancholic production is not a return to a simple nationalist and racially/ethnically "pure" politics. What one finds in Paul is not a nostalgia to recover a lost authenticity and/or purity; instead, it is one that incorporates Gentiles through a new racial/ethnic and religious construction. In other words, Paul's diasporic and melancholic production brings about not just a new racial/ethnic or religious being, but also a new communal becoming where the conventional Greco-Roman status system and racial/ethnic rankings are turned upside down. His melancholia does not just turn things inward. He strikes out across racial/ethnic boundaries to build new alternative communities.

With this new racial/ethnic being and new communal becoming, Paul is in fact performing yet another kind of transference. In addition or in contrast to transferring his own abjection to other bodies (female and sexually dissident), his work among the Corinthians is a transferring of his own loss of Jesus (and all that is implicated within) to other racial/ethnic bodies. In calling the Corinthian body (both individual and collective) the body of Christ (6:12–20; 12:12–31), Paul is engineering here nothing less than an inter-racial/ethnic bodily substitution. This is so because Freud suggests that melancholia is not only a presentation but also a precondition of ego formation (1953–74: 14.247; 19.1–59). If one's ego is constituted by the object of one's mourning, Paul's introduction of Jesus to the Corinthians—and hence their regular or repetitive practice of the Eucharist to remember Jesus (11:23–26), or what amounts to performing a rite of passage from life to death that fashions identity and community (Roach 1996: 28)—is making a Jewish (dead but resurrected) body the condition of their (new) being. Put differently, Paul makes the loss of a Jewish Jesus the lost and thus ideal object of the Corinthians' individual and group identification. The Corinthian body or community of love (12:27–13:13) is, in other words, built on and through a racial/ethnic "other" (Jesus and/or Paul). Paul's "love" ethic is therefore thoroughly imbricated with racial/ethnic politics.[19] For Paul, the only way for the Corinthians to preserve this (Jewish) Jesus—their lost, mourned, loved, and longed-for object—is to do so in a sense at the cost of their own (Greco-Roman) selves. If they do not, as Paul clearly states regarding the Corinthians' melancholic meal known as the Lord's Supper, they will be killing (off) their melancholic object (11:27).[20]

Paul's melancholia, in contrast to Freud's, is nothing less than a creative political activism. He is looking for and working toward a body of love that will transform Greco-Roman persons and Greco-Roman values through an insistent preservation of its Jewish part (Jesus and, by extension, Paul). Paul's emphasis on the Lord's Supper in fact might imply that he wants not only the incorporation of the Corinthians, but also that this incorporation comes precisely through a (re)corporealization of the absent (Jewish) Jesus. Through their introjection, ingestion, and digestion of Christ's body and blood, the Corinthians are to be(come), as Paul suggests, the body of Christ (6:19–20; 10:16–17; 12:1–30). In a sense, they are to change places with the crucified (Jewish) Christ and to live his life in and through their individual and collective body. In the language of shamanism, this exchange is nothing less than a possession. For the Greco-Roman Corinthians to be possessed by a Jewish Christ is, of course, the reverse of the colonial possession of Jews by Greeks and Romans.

Melancholia as Inseparable from Mourning

In addition, one must ask what this reading of Paul's melancholia might mean for Freud's theorization of mourning. In "Mourning and Melancholia," Freud differentiates mourning from a pathological melancholia because the former denotes the ability to reinvest one's psychic and emotional energy from a lost to a new object. The tricky part is that Paul's melancholia, in advocating that his own lost love object (Jesus) be a love object of the Corinthians, is simultaneously (re)investing his libido in the Corinthians. Paul's letter(s) to them in general and his familial language in particular (3:1–3; 4:15) show that Paul's (re)cathexis with Christ in fact directs him to other people as his objects of love. Perhaps it is even more accurate to say that Paul's (re)cathexis with Christ takes place only through his reaching out to others. What I am getting at is how Paul's psycho-political investments not only disrupt Freud's reading of melancholia as merely or mostly pathological, but also dispute any neat and ready-made separation between Freud's melancholia and Freud's own mourning.[21] This is especially so given Freud's own uncertainty on the subject, which he expresses at both the beginning and the end of his exploration (1953–74: 14.243, 258).

Melancholia as Subject/Object Reversal

What is disappointing and maddening to Paul is precisely that his love (re)investment in the Corinthians is not coming together as a body of love, either in the Corinthians' relating with each other or with Paul himself. We have seen that in the midst of his arguments, Paul simultaneously defends his manual labor and uses that defense to illustrate how to perform a reversal by giving up self for the benefit of a needy other. Having argued that the following of Jesus by the Corinthians is in fact a tricky reversal of Greco-Roman racial/ethnic ranking, let me also suggest that Paul's reversal involves not only the Corinthians' endless mourning of Jesus but also their endless ritual remembrance of their own state as melancholic objects of an "exclusionary inclusion."[22] In addition to later and more indirect statements of Gentiles as people who do not have the Law (9:21; 14:21), Paul actually begins his letter by reminding the Corinthians of how God "chose" them despite their lack of human qualification (1:26–31). In other words, Paul is asking the Corinthians to face up to the fact that their unexpected entry into the church body is premised on their exclusion. Their loss to God and their exclusion from the church body are not just things of the past, but must be remembered if their being chosen is to be rightly celebrated. To "realize" their chosen-ness (in the doubled sense of comprehending and fulfilling), the Corinthians must keep in mind the haunting conditions of their lack and loss, and witness to their own exclusion. Like colonized Jews within the Roman empire, the Corinthians' identity and membership as Christ-followers are always already mediated through their recovery *of* and *from* their original status as lost, unqualified, or under-qualified "aliens." This constant and continuous recovery process is, like their regularly repeated grieving of Jesus in the form of the Eucharist or thanksgiving celebration, melancholic.[23]

Melancholia as Double Bind

This mixture of grief and celebration points to the postcolonial emphasis on ambiguity, and warns against any premature or overly enthusiastic elation over Paul's psycho-political operations. Let me tie my earlier references to Paul's splitting and (self-)*ressentiment* to the idea of mourning and melancholia through the opening provided by Paul's reference to the Eucharist (10:14–11:34). Paul's emphasis on food in general and on the Lord's Supper in particular "echoes" Freud's reference to melancholia as a nurturing, consuming, or devouring of the lost object. Freud writes, "The ego wants to incorporate this [lost] object into itself, and the method by which it would do so, in this *oral* or *cannibalistic* stage, is by *devouring* it" (1953–74: 14.249–50; emphasis mine).

This literal and intense internalization of or identification with the lost object might, first of all, make one susceptible to *various* forms of—in Althusserian language—interpellation (Cheng 2001: 79). A mouth wide opened to devour all could end up taking in more than what one bargains for. We see this in Freud's guarded statement about how a melancholic subject may turn "manic" when one "plainly demonstrates his [*sic*] liberation from the object which was the cause of his [*sic*] suffering, by seeking like a ravenously hungry man [*sic*] for new object-cathexes" (1953–74: 14.255). We also see this in Paul's reprimand of some Corinthians who end up not only rushing to consume the Lord's Supper but also indulging themselves to the point of getting drunk and clouding their judgment (11:17–34). The same phenomenon is manifest in Paul's own gulping down of and choking on an inferiority complex created by Greco-Roman racialization and abjection of Jewish bodies, and hence his desire for a changed resurrection body (15:35–58).

If Paul in his melancholia incorporates dominant, emergent, and residual cultural ideals (Williams 2001), he will also identify Jesus as both a desirable and a dreaded figure. After all, the Christ with whom he identifies is one who was sacrificed (5:7) and once crucified (1:17–18, 23; 2:2, 8). The "ambivalence" or equivocation (Freud 1953–74: 14.256) that results from this circling or mixing of desire and dread (or death) will now circle back to my earlier discussion about Paul's (self-)*ressentiment* and splitting. On the one hand, Paul's internalization of and identification with the once-crucified Christ makes him resentful, not only over the loss or death of Christ, but also over the very fact that Paul's own cathexis is tied to such a dead and dreadful object or subject.[24] On the other hand, ambivalence leads easily to disavowal or denial, which is in itself a form of exclusion. What I am getting at is how the equivocation, bitterness, and denial that define melancholia ("what-is-gone-cannot-be-gone") might lead to Paul's self-loathing as well as to his displacement of that self-loathing onto other excludable "others" (women and sexual dissidents).[25]

In fact, the same dynamics might bring about another ironic denial and exclusion. As Cheng suggests, "the melancholic would have to make sure that the 'object' never returns, for such a return would surely jeopardize the cannibalistic project that . . . is a form of possession more intimate than any material relationship could produce" (2001: 9). In addition to Christ's bodily resurrection, Paul has certainly included a number of implicit and explicit references to Christ's future return in 1 Corinthians (1:7–8; 4:5; 5:5; 11:26; 15:23), even a prayer in Aramaic that his Lord might hasten his coming (16:22b). There are, however, a couple of points to consider in light of Paul's melancholic identification with Christ.

Paul's claim to have or identify with Christ's mind, first of all, intimates what Bronfen calls a conflation of "the articulating self with its object of articulation" (1992: 72). Paul's representation of himself as Christ's apostle or sent successor turns into an ambiguous condensation of figures. The crucified Christ, the unquestionable object of the Corinthians' desire, will return not only in his resurrected bodily form, but also might—as Paul desires—(re)turn into or be "re-presenced" (Bronfen 1992: 83) through Paul as a temporary and transposed object of desire. One must question if this bodily displacement does not end up being a form of bodily replacement. In other words, Paul himself might be guilty of what he warns the Corinthians of doing; he may have committed what is a second killing of Christ's body by assuming himself to be the bodily double or substitute of his master predecessor. On the one hand, we are thus back to Freud's questionable separation between mourning and melancholia, since Freud's mourning is supposed to be precisely this repeated killing (off) of one's loved but lost object and thus one's affection for it. Instead of being killed by his continual affection for Jesus, we find in Paul such a huge identificatory appetite that it is almost impossible to tell what or whom is being eaten up. On the other hand, one must admit the aptness of Freud's description of melancholic devouring as "cannibalistic." One can readily link Paul's "devouring" of Christ with Freud's exposition of identification in terms of "eating" or as a form of annihilation (1953–74: 18.105). It affirms and lends further nuances to what I said last chapter about Paul building himself up over Jesus' dead body, or how the killing of Jesus brings Paul to life. Yet there is something more, given the conflation or confusion between Paul and his Lord.

If, according to Freud, mourning is the successful killing (off) of the dead and melancholia is endless mourning of the dead, what should one call an incessant attempt to kill and mourn someone who is actually alive? Freud has, of course, made a connection between melancholia and suicide (1953–74: 14.252). What if Paul's incessant mourning or melancholia for Jesus means that Paul so desires to identify with Jesus or let Christ live in him that he wishes to die? Does Paul not say, in arguing for bodily resurrection, that what one sows does not come to life unless it dies (15:36)? Does Paul in that same argument not imply that death is nothing to be afraid of (15:54–57)? What if Paul's melancholia for or identification with Jesus is so deep that it is "killing Paul softly" and Paul is fine with it? What if Paul knows that his melancholia is choking him slowly and, in order to stay alive himself, he feels that he must kill this resurrected Jesus whom he mourns and swallows regularly through the Lord's Supper? Does Paul's description of the Lord's Supper, with its ritualistic remembrance of Christ's dying

(11:23–27), not sound like he is cathected to a resurrected yet perpetually dying Christ? What if the link between melancholia and *ressentiment* I have discussed causes Paul to desire his own death and/or the death of this lost object that he has kept alive?

The presence of the Corinthians shows that mourning/melancholia easily or readily involves a kind of libidinal (re)investment or triangulation. A third party may therefore come into play in this circling of love and hate or mixing of death and life. Take, for example, what Paul says about marriage, a discussion in which the fusion between Paul and his Lord also becomes arguably most confused (7:10, 12, 25, 40). Given (1) his negative view that marriage is a concession and a burden (7:6, 28, 32–35), (2) his negative view against divorce (7:10–14), and (3) his rather triangular or triangulating understanding concerning the relations among a couple and his Lord (7:32–35), would one's melancholia for or identification with the Lord cause one to desire the death of one's spouse, their mutual belonging and concern for each other notwithstanding (7:4, 32–34)? Is Paul not (un)consciously working out this desire when he begins his reflection on the shortness of time with the advice that those who have wives live as if they had none (7:29) and concludes the chapter by imagining a wife who is "happier" with a dead husband (7:39–40)?

Mourning/melancholia is a mixed bag of contradictory emotions, as Paul again shows in his "as-if" statements about mourning and happiness during his discussion about marriage (7:30). More than that, it seems to involve another side, an underside, or an inverted side. What does one call this melancholically linked desire to kill an entwined or even introjected beloved who is still alive and constitutes part of one's self? Perhaps one can call it "suicide" if the living beloved happens to be oneself, "mourning" if it happens to be one's lost object; but what if one desires to kill the closely identified beloved who is a third party, like one's spouse? It is rather surprising to me that the sensitivity to triangulation that Freud demonstrates in his construction of the Oedipus complex is completely absent in his understanding of mourning/melancholia. Melancholia is a triangulating dynamic that is full of self-contradiction: in not being able to kill (off) the dead, life itself becomes a struggle with a desire to kill and/or to die. J. B. Pontalis is most definitely correct in identifying "death-work" of the death drive as a key not only to Freud's dream-work but also to his work on mourning (1978). This is particularly pertinent for Paul in 1 Corinthians since, as I have argued in the last chapter, Paul's whole body-building or life-giving project is founded on Christ's dead body. Perhaps one might even say that Paul's defiant and subversive move to convert Gentiles like the Corinthians is also at least partly fueled by the death drive. That is to say, Paul has to reach out to *other* people because, as a colonized Jew, his life is permeated by death in general and the death of Jesus in particular.

As one thinks about Paul's outreach or body-building project, however, one must also remember that the textual body of 1 Corinthians serves to represent or replace not only Christ's body (dead or resurrected), but also Paul's physical body. While ancient Greek medical practice emphasizes touching the patient's body and thus the very presence of the physician's body (Kuriyama 1999:13, 17–108), Paul writes a letter and plans to send Timothy as his surrogate instead of showing up physically to encounter the diseased church body in Corinth (4:17–21). Perhaps Apollos was Paul's first choice to go to Corinth on his behalf, but Apollos was unwilling to go (16:12). Actually Paul is not finally sure if Timothy will go either (16:10a). In 1 Corinthians, one finds an almost endless deferral of different bodies. In the process of possibly rematerializing Christ's Jewish body, what results is a dematerialization of physically Jewish bodies. What remains seems to be only a textual or textualized body written by a colonized Jew. This, in combination with Paul's expressed desire for a new and renewed resurrection body (15:42–44, 51–52), may betray his ultimate uncertainty of or dis-ease with his own Jewish body.[26] Despite several references to his own return to Corinth (4:18–19; 11:33–34; 16:1–9), Paul becomes only a ghostly presence (5:3–5) who keeps on prolonging his physical absence. If this is true of Paul's "promised coming" as a melancholic object, the same endless deferral might also be true concerning the return of Paul's crucified and resurrected Lord. After all, it is the liminality between absence and presence that defines melancholia.

Is this what Freud meant by melancholia as a process in which a person "knows *whom* he [*sic*] has lost but not *what* he [*sic*] has lost in him [*sic*]" (1953–74: 14.245; emphasis in original)? If nothing else, re-reading Paul through a rethinking of Freud's melancholia immensely complicates any simple and simplistic linear progression from "imitation" to "resistance" through a process of "consciousness-raising" or "self-discovery."

Conclusion

What is clear from 1 Corinthians is that Paul can neither accept nor forget his loss(es) in diaspora, whether the Roman crucifixion of Jesus or his relationship with the Corinthians. If Paul's melancholia embodies these diasporic losses, it is also his way of negotiating with and surviving Roman imperialism and its abjection of Jewish bodies. Melancholia, or the ambivalent self-punishing pleasure of "loss-but-not-loss," is thus also a political double bind with both complicitous and subversive potentials, since memory both prevents and enacts forgetting (Roach 1996: 122). In Paul's remembering as well as our remembering of Paul, it is easy to forget one's own complicit and duplicitous acts.

Because of his racial/ethnic and religious difference, a diasporic subject like Paul finds himself subjected to or living in *ressentiment*, mourning, and melancholia. *Ressentiment*, as a taking in as well as an acting out of colonial abjection, causes Paul not only to disparage women and sexual dissidents, but also to denigrate himself even as he seeks to build himself up over Jesus' Jewish body. Mourning/melancholia, as a simultaneous acknowledgment and disavowal of loss, leads to a duplicitous attitude as well as to a repetitious, doubling, and even splitting desire. Contrary in a sense to the deflection of his own abjection onto other substitutes, Paul's belief in the resurrection and transformation of Christ's dead body also requires the presence of a substitute or double so that Paul can (re)invest his mourning/melancholic desires. This he attempts to do by remaking the Corinthians into his image of or his own modeling of Christ. Doubling as Christ's body, Paul and the Corinthians become living resemblances or copies that enable Paul to deny *and* deal with Christ's death. As such, what Paul seeks in the living (including himself and the Corinthians) are traces of Christ.

Regarding the Corinthians, this desire to mourn or immortalize the dead requires, ironically, the twin process of doubling the dead and congealing the copy. That is to say, while differences between Christ and the Corinthians should be obliterated, there is also a fear that changes in the Corinthians would disclose Paul's "immortalizing" attempt as a failure. Hence one finds in Paul's letter both calls to change and calls to remain unchanged (7:1–40). For Paul, the Corinthians function to give fixture to a dead and lost body of Christ so that, fetishistically, Paul can recognize (in the doubled sense of conceding and refusing) his loss. Regarding himself, mourning/melancholia merges with Paul's self-*ressentiment*, and points to the imbrication of diasporic lives with both hopeful and hopeless politics as well as both defiant and damaging psychic processes. There is no way to dress up or dress down diasporic existence. When one looks at various bodies of evidence—whether it is Paul in the ancient Mediterranean, Freud in modern Europe, or Asian Americans in the postmodern United States—diasporic lives are complicated and often overlaid with racial/ethnic and religious differences. What must be addressed and redressed in the midst of this messy existence is the inseparable link between diaspora and empire. Rather than segregating *ressentiment* and mourning/melancholia as issues, problems, or even pathologies of a certain racial/ethnic and/or religious group, one must scrutinize the colonial and imperial politics and dynamics at work if one is not to redouble the violence already committed.

My reading of 1 Corinthians provides, I hope, something similar to what Fanon had in mind when he called his psychoanalytic project a "sociogeny" (1967: 11). It is a way to think about the complex intersubjective and intrasubjective psyche of a colonized and racialized subject, as well as the convoluted or contradictory agency that such a subject represents. As Judith Butler suggests, political self-empowerment depends, first of all, not on Paul's rhetorical or ideological reversal, but on a "metaleptic reversal" in which one is able to focus on oneself to witness and face (up to) the process of one's formation, including how one comes to (mis)understand one's own agency and power (1997: 15–16).[27] If colonized and racialized subjectivity or agency is—as some minority scholars have chosen to describe it (McBride 2001; Ngai 2004)—"impossible," I will read Butler's suggestion to imply that it is only by honestly facing up to one's "impossibility" that the impossible will have a chance to become possible.

I have argued that the colonized and racialized Paul embodies the ambiguities of empire, but I hope it is by now clear that my goal here is not to pathologize Paul or, worse, to blame the victim. In any case, I do not see Paul as a mere victim but situate him on a liminal fine line between being a fighter and being a victim; accordingly, my reading does not warrant a patronizing attitude toward Paul, either sympathetic or otherwise. Neither is my goal to "solve" or "resolve" Paul's psycho-political struggles. Instead, I want to examine those processes rigorously, even unapologetically and unromantically, by treating 1 Corinthians as a symptomatic text. It shows that racism is more than institutional; it involves both intersubjective *and* intrasubjective processes of racialization (Gilroy 2005: 12). Even as it shows how a racialized and colonized person's subjectivity is by necessity always already compromised, it foregrounds, in my view, one's agency to resist out of circumscribed conditions. In addition to disclosing the possibilities and limits of a racialized and colonized subject, what this symptomatic text finally also points to is not the individual but the imperial ills of empire. Empire must be exposed as the cause of Paul's struggling agency to write himself into the Corinthian picture.

CHAPTER 7

Immigrants and Intertexts

● ●

Biblical In(ter)ventions in Theresa Hak Kyung Cha's *Dictee*

E ver since its "resurrection" from its original publication in 1982, Theresa Hak Kyung Cha's *Dictee* (1995) has attracted considerable critical attention among Asian Americanists.[1] While many have commented on *Dictee*'s language, such as its *heteroglossia* (Spahr 1996: 26, 31), its postmodern tendencies (Kang 1994: 91–92, 95–96), and even its hypertextual sensibilities (Page 1996), no one has given enough critical attention to its use of biblical language or biblical intertexts. For example, Spahr, who skillfully uses Fredric Jameson's characterization of postmodern poetics to argue *against* Jameson's caricature of postmodern politics,[2] lists several intertexts in *Dictee*'s section on "Clio History" that include "F. A. McKenzie's *The Tragedy of Korea,* news releases of the time, and a 1905 letter from the Koreans of Hawaii to President Roosevelt requesting that the United States support Korean autonomy" (1996: 24, 34). Yet she makes no mention of Cha's quotation of Matthew 4:1–11 in the immediately following section on "Calliope Epic Poetry" (Cha 1995: 52–53).[3] Likewise, Walter K. Lew's popular "tracking"—to borrow Rob Wilson's term (1995)—of *Dictee*'s intertexts practically obliterates the Bible without a trace (1982).[4] The same is true of the "intertextual linkages" provided by Kang in MLA's *Resource Guide to Asian American Literature* (2001: 41–42).

I certainly appreciate the warning against any attempt to reduce Cha's multilingual, multigeneric, multimedia (that is, literary and non-literary), and multivalent text into a single channel of focus or argument (S. S. Wong 1994: 135). I would argue, however, that the multi-multiplicities mentioned above are themselves manifestations of a radical intertextuality (Beal 2000: 129), and that the Bible functions precisely, in Cha's reading/writing, as one irreducible and inerasable intertext to accomplish her simultaneous protest against colonial, patriarchal, national, racial, religious, and cultural oppression. One must remember that the Bible is a main part of all these discourses, and particularly so in the United States, where biblical rhetoric has been absorbed into a nationalist rhetoric (Yun 1992: 79–80). In this chapter, I will first argue for a particular relevance that intertexts may carry for immigrants in light of Cha's *Dictee;*[5] then I will turn to the specifics of my reading/writing of Cha's intertextual reading/writing of the Bible.

Textual Intervals and Immigrant Travels

Intertexts, by playing a role in the signification within a new literary context and yet being recognizable as coming from a different literary context, bear the same "insider/outsider," and "present/absent" dynamics or dilemma confronting immigrants (E. K. Min 1998: 319). As Timothy K. Beal correctly points out, intertext or between-text, as "a paradoxical locus of dislocation, without center and without boundaries," is also a theory of intersubjectivity for Julia Kristeva, who first coined the term in 1969 (Beal 2000: 128–29). One should not forget, however, that Kristeva left Bulgaria to settle in France in 1964. In that light, Kristeva's emphasis on intersubjectivity and her use of the psychoanalytic term "transposition" may be closely related to the immigrant experience of transnational transportation and translation. Regardless of Kristeva's interests and intentions, this is precisely how intertexts seem to function in Cha's *Dictee*. One way to get at what I am after is to understand the prefix "inter-" in "intertexts" as one type of intervals—intervals that are spatial as well as temporal. Intertexts provide intervals or openings for the readerly writer or writerly reader to create new meanings, which are desperately needed by immigrants, who often find themselves caught between several national and cultural intervals. Is that not what Cha, who immigrated to the United States from Korea in 1963 when she was twelve years old, seems to imply in the beginning of *Dictee?*[6] Sandwiched between two divisions of language exercise between French and English (1995: 1, 8–9), Cha writes, under the heading "Diseuse":

> She mimics the speaking. . . .
> *She would take on their punctuation. She waits to service this. Theirs. Punctuation. She would become, herself, demarcations. Absorb it. Spill it. Seize upon the punctuation. Last air. Give her. Her. The relay. Voice. Assign. Hand it. Deliver it. Deliver . . .*
>   She takes. She takes the pause. Slowly. From the thick. The thickness. From weighted motion upwards. Slowed. To deliberation even when it

passed upward through her mouth again. The delivery. She takes it. Slow. The invoking. All the time now. All the time there is. Always. And all times. The pause. Uttering. Hers now. Hers bare. The utter. (1995: 3–4; emphasis in original)

"Take on their punctuation." "Seize upon the punctuation." Grab the gap. Capture the opening. Crack open the opening. Remember that a break can serve as a bridge as well as a breach. Remember that "to take on" can mean both adopting and attacking in the English language (Mix 1998: 178; Kang 2002: 224). Remember that "to seize" can mean both capturing, as in taking control of or comprehending, and confiscating, as in taking away from or commandeering. "Take the pause." Take the time. Intervene at the interval. That becomes the key for Cha the immigrant as she finds herself confronted with new languages, new texts, and new cultures that can dis-power as much as empower.

Dictee is about words, language, and power. Perhaps more accurately, dictation is about the power of words and language. We have already seen in discussing John back in Chapter 3 the relationship between language and boundary, as well as an emphasis on consent. It is in this regard worth pointing out the form as well as the content of the preceding dictation/translation exercise that appears on the first numbered page of *Dictee*.[7] While the content of the dictation/translation exercise insinuates an interrogation of a woman who has "come from a far" about her "first-day" experience (Cha 1995: 1), Cha actually chooses to spell and write out some of the punctuation marks as literal words on the page. This practice of "being faithful to a fault" is akin to how the African American writer Richard Wright won his "first triumph" over his "lawgiver" father (1998: 10, 12). When Wright was five years old, a stray cat was keeping his father from sleeping. In frustration, his father barked that Wright should kill the cat. Intentionally literalizing his father's remark, Wright lynched the cat. This is how Wright writes about what he did: "I had had my first triumph over my father. I had made him believe that I had taken his words literally. He could not punish me now without risking his authority. I was happy because I had at last found a way to throw my criticism of him into his face. I had made him feel that, if he whipped me for killing the kitten, I would never give serious weight to his words again" (1998: 13–14).

J. Albert Harrill has also shown, through his work on the Greco-Roman "romance" known as *Life of Aesop,* that people of that time and place were already well aware of the subversive potential of slaves' practicing an extreme literalism (2006: 21–25), and hence Cicero's lament that "the

familiar speech of everyday will not have a consistent meaning if we set verbal traps for one another. Even our authority at home will cease to exist if
we allow our slave-boys to obey our orders to the letter only, without paying
any attention to the meaning implied in our words" (*Caecin.* 18.51–52).

In addition, Cha adopts another tactic to challenge or subvert the
dictate of an authoritative word; she deliberately "mistranslates" various
parts of the French paragraph. Put differently, she engages in what Lowe
calls "unfaithful[ness] to the original" (1994), which is almost diametrically opposed to the "faithfulness to the origin(al)" that we have seen in
both John and Acts in Chapters 3 and 4.[8] Not only does Cha parody and
protest against this "faithfulness" dictate through her literalist transcription and "unfaithful" translation, but she also creates interval or distance
between different languages by literally letting pages pass before translating
(Mix 1998: 175). For example, the English translation of a numbered list
of Chinese characters is only found after almost twenty pages of intervening materials (Cha 1995: 154, 173). Cha seems to suggest that intervening
at intervals and inventing intervals are crucial if translation, transnational,
and transculturational experiences are to become transformative rather
than oppressive for the traveling immigrant. Given (1) the visual affinity
between *diseuse* (French for a female speaker) and dis-use, and (2) the fact
that Chinese, English, and French have all been colonial languages in the
experience of Cha,[9] her investment in intervals as a reservoir for resistance
becomes even starker.

Like punctuations and translations, Cha sees citations of and allusions
to intertexts as other ideal intervals for in(ter)vention. I will further propose
that we are already given a hint of the importance of interval in(ter)ventions
in the title of Cha's book. While many critics have taken the liberty of providing the missing accent mark in Cha's title (for example, E. H. Kim 1994;
Lowe 1994; Kang 1994; and S. S. Wong 1994), I see the elimination of the
accent mark from the French word *dictée* (or dictation), as another example
of "taking on" the "punctuation." It is in the punctuating, in the punctur-
ing, in the "pois[ing] on the in-between" (E. H. Kim 1994: title) that one
can negotiate and appropriate the dictatorial demands of dominant cultures
and dominant cultural texts.[10]

In addition to her experience as an immigrant, Cha's perception and
practice of intertextuality may also be highly informed by her study of film
theory.[11] As another first-generation Asian American, film theorist Trinh
T. Minh-ha points out, by way of Dziga Vertov, who is the focus of three
entries in Cha's edited volume on cinematographic apparatus (Cha 1980: 7–
20), filmmaking is built upon intervals, or the movements between frames;

as such, meanings in films are dependent, not on any single image, but on the "temporal, spatial, rhythmic relations" of multiple images (Trinh 1999: xii). If this emphasis on meaning being relational sounds similar to the theories of both Ferdinand de Saussure and Mikhail M. Bakhtin (itself an intertextual relation upon which Kristeva builds her understanding of intertextuality), Trinh uses Vertov's "theory of intervals" in film to further argue for intervals as ideal for interruptions, irruptions, and impurities (Trinh 1999: xi–xiv).[12] As immigrants seek to establish new relations and create new meanings in their transnational movements, intertexts can become one means by which they can translate—that is, manipulate, negotiate, and thus transform—the dictates of others.

When (Cha's) Word(s) Became Flesh

As I intimated earlier, Cha seems keen to sensitize her readers to oppression besides its transnational and transcultural forms, and to how these various forms of oppression may intersect. As the French term *diseuse* clearly signifies, the subject who travels transnationally, and thus is being confronted with the need to transcribe or translate in different languages, is female. At the same time, Cha hints at the precarious position of a female subject on the first (numbered) page of *Dictee* by translating what is, in French, "someone female" *(quelqu'une)* into simply "someone" in English (1995: 1). In other words, the particularity of gender is often covered over or erased with ease. Immediately following the materials captioned under "DISEUSE," one finds more language exercises involving English and French (Cha 1995: 8–9). The hierarchical relations implied in these exercises are made clear again by both their form and their content. Speaking of form, the statements to be dictated, translated, or conjugated appear as imperative, interrogational, informational, and/or instructional. Speaking of content, while the first two exercises concern language and cultural adjustments of an immigrant experience, statements in the last conjugation exercise read very much like instructions for household chores that are too often identified as "feminine," like wiping the table, grocery shopping, or caring for a child.[13]

If this set of language exercises continues to combine the oppression of immigrants and of women, we find in the next block of materials an attempt to bring together cultural, patriarchal, and religious oppression (Cha 1995: 13–19). After a description of what reads like the ritual of Eucharist, in which the male gender of both Christ and the priest is emphasized, this block of materials contains yet another translation exercise. What is to be translated from English into French this time is a mixture of (1) a religious discourse on sin, penance, and forgiveness; (2) a narrative of a plane trip to Paris, and some scattered sentences about the history of France and the current condition of Paris (probably preparation done by the one flying to Paris); and (3) the lament of a woman who is learning to conjugate, to call, and to believe, but is nevertheless not seen, heard, read, or known by people and/or God. As if she were worried that her readers might not make the connection among colonial, patriarchal, and religious power, Cha concludes with a confession and a "Q-&-A" catechism exercise, in which she emphasizes, *"God who has made me in His own likeness. In His own Image in His Own Resemblance, in His Own Copy, In His Own Counterfeit Presentment, in His Duplicate, in His Own Reproduction, in His Cast, in His Carbon, His Image and Mirror. Pleasure in the image pleasure in the copy pleasure in the projection of likeness pleasure in the repetition"* (1995: 17; emphasis in original). Cha indicates the power dynamics of "Q-&-A" not only by transcribing or translating the French for question mark into "interrogation mark" (1995: 1), but also demonstrates her "ethics of infidelity" in language exercises that, like religion in general and catechism in particular, supposedly require repetition and relish replication. It is therefore no surprise that Cha has this to say about this invisible and inaudible woman who is learning to conjugate a new language to call on people and/or God: "essential words words link subject verb she writes hidden the essential words must be pretended invented she try on different images" (1995: 15).

Make-believe and invention are exactly what one finds in the following confession:

> "Bless me father, for I have sinned. My last confession was . . . I can't remember when . . . These are my sins."
> *I am making up the sins. . . . I am making the confession. To make words. To make a speech in such tongues.* (1995: 16–17, emphasis in original) [14]

Likewise, in the "Q-&-A" catechism, Cha intervenes by inventing and inserting materials into the regular rote responses (Mix 1998: 180–81). To the question, "Who made thee?" Cha answers the expected, "God made me," plus the additional infinitive phrase, "To Conspire in God's Tongue" (1995: 17). To the question, "Where is God?" Cha gives the standard answer, "God is everywhere," along with the extra, "Accomplice in His Texts" (1995: 17). Cha's transcript of this partial "Q-&-A" catechism ends with these words:

> *Acquiesce, to the correspondance [sic]. Acquiesce, to the messenger. Acquiesce, to and for the complot in the Hieratic tongue. Theirs. Into Their tongue,*

the counter-script, my confession in Theirs. Into Theirs. To scribe to make
hear the words, to make sound the words, the words, the words made flesh.
(1995: 17–18, emphasis in original)

We find in this catechism not only references to God's "tongue" and God's "texts," but also an actual insertion of a biblical intertext. There is, of course, a big difference. Cha's insertion of John 1:14 is also an in(ter)vention. The singular and capitalized "Word" in John is now pluralized and de-capitalized. In other words, John 1:14 has been adulterated and resignified. These words, while looking like the so-called Word of God in the Bible, are instead words that Cha makes (up) to "conspire" or "complot." Besides invention or falsification, "making up" also implies atoning for a wrong or supplementing for a deficiency (Kang 2002: 223–24). In Cha's own vocabulary, biblical intertexts become a way for her to write "counter-script" in the form of "counterfeit." Cha is going to cite the Bible, the Word of God, and make it her site of resistance. Reading Cha's in(ter)vention of John 1:14 as a kind of ventriloquist tactic also helps signify the importance of the epigraph at the "beginning" of the book.[15] This epigraph, which is creatively attributed to Sappho, reads: "May I write words more naked than flesh, stronger than bone, more resilient than sinew, sensitive than nerve." While "word(s) becoming flesh" in John refers to incarnation, the phrase in Cha seems to have more to do with resurrection. Cha writes: "Resurrect it all over again . . . resurrect as much as possible. . . . Dead words. Dead tongue. From disuse. Buried in Time's memory. Unemployed. Unspoken. History. Past. Let the one who is diseuse, one who is mother who waits nine days and nine nights be found" (1995: 133). The fact that this book is being rediscovered some thirteen years after Cha was tragically murdered at the age of thirty-one may be evidence that Sappho—in contrast to the irresponsive male God mentioned earlier (Cha 1995: 13–19)—has answered Cha's prayer.[16]

Matthew, Mouth, and Martyrdom

In addition to John 1:14, a much lengthier and more precise biblical intertext is found in the section "Calliope Epic Poetry." As I have already mentioned, Matthew 4:1–11 (the story of Jesus' wilderness temptation by the devil) is cited word-for-word here from the King James or Authorized Version (Cha 1995: 52–53). The insertion of this biblical intertext is, however, itself internally interrupted. In addition to what appears before and after it, Cha has inserted brief interludes after Matthew 4:4 and Matthew 4:7. What may Cha be doing with this intertextual or interval intervention?

I think it is important to point out, first of all, that within Jesus' temptation story in Matthew is an intertextual conflict between various Scripture verses. After Jesus quotes from Deuteronomy 8:3 to shelve the tempter's suggestion that he turn stone into bread (Matthew 4:4), the tempter quotes from Psalm 91:11–12 and suggests that Jesus jump from the temple top (Matthew 4:6). Jesus counteracts, however, by quoting yet another Scripture verse, Deuteronomy 6:16 (Matthew 4:7). What we find in this episode, then, is a clear indication that Scripture is—as we have seen in the multiple or even contradictory strands in Mark, John, and Acts in our previous chapters—not "a monolithic entity in which all of its statements point in one direction" (Snodgrass 1996: 118). It is in this already messy war of (holy) words, or this already cracked-open interval, that Cha intervenes.[17] Second, in the interval between this section and the preceding section, titled "Clio History," are two different types of images. We have a photograph of an execution, with three soon-to-be-executed people standing in line next to each other, all with arms spread out as if already hanging on a cross (Cha 1995: 39). After this non-literary image, we have an image of what looks like a handwritten draft, which contains part of what we have already read in the preceding "Clio History" section, except that the draft here exhibits words or lines deleted, inserted, or replaced in various places (Cha 1995: 40–41). Put differently, Cha's text is shown here, to use the vocabulary of film theory, with its movements between frames—or intervals—swelled up rather than sutured or smoothly covered over. If the photograph of execution reminds one of the focus of "Clio History" (namely, the martyrdom of a young Korean heroine, Yu Guan Soon, during the Japanese colonial rule of the early twentieth century), the handwritten draft seems to suggest that even this feminist version of Korean patriotism (which is often also patriarchal) is itself a sutured variation that is in need of intervention.[18]

Instead of a female martyr, "Calliope Epic Poetry" focuses on a female survivor, Cha's mother. Living in Manchuria during Japan's colonial rule over Korea, Cha's mother is another *diseuse* who becomes "Tri-lingual," speaking mostly Chinese and Japanese, but also her forbidden mother tongue, Korean, in secret (Cha 1995: 45).[19] After several more pages that underscore her fragile body but forbearing spirit (1995: 46–49), Cha describes a dream or a hallucination of heaven that her mother experiences while ill in Manchuria. It is in this dream or hallucination where Cha interweaves and juxtaposes her mother's refusal of three heavenly dishes with Jesus' resistance of three temptations by the devil in Matthew 4 (1995: 50–53).

In contrast to Jesus, who secures angelic service by refusing to eat, to jump from the temple top, or to worship the devil on a mountaintop, Cha's mother, by refusing the angelic service of heavenly food, is pushed from heaven back down to earth by an angel. Many of my readers may well be familiar with an early Christian intertext about a female martyr, Perpetua, who renounces motherhood and tastes heavenly food in a vision (*Passion of Perpetua and Felicitas* [1927]). If this inter(weaving)text signifies Cha's resistance to the Christian heaven, it also signifies her resistance to patriotic martyrdom, since Cha's mother refuses to eat the food of heaven in heaven precisely because she wants to keep eating the food of earth on earth. I want to focus our attention also on how Cha, in her earlier characterization of her mother's patient waiting for a different day and a dissimilar sight despite the long exile in Manchuria, comments: "You cannot ask for more than millet and barley to eat. You take what is given to you. Always do. Always have" (1995: 49). Once in heaven, however, this willingness to eat whatever food is available to stay alive and stay around changes into a refusal to eat, despite the "aroma and the beautiful arrangement" of angel food (Cha 1995: 52). While Matthew's Jesus continues to maintain the priority of heavenly bread (the word of God) over earthly bread after forty days of fasting (Matthew 4:4), Cha has her mother's refusal to consume heavenly dishes sandwiched between two references to eating earthly meals. Before she falls ill, Cha's grandmother "leaves everything to greet you, she comes and takes you indoors and brings you food to eat" (Cha 1995: 49). After she falls from heaven, Cha's mother finds himself back on earth, again in the care of her own parents: "She has eaten nothing your father's voice saying how can she live. Upon hearing this you ask to eat. They say that the dying ask for food as a last wish. They give you to eat" (Cha 1995: 53).

This last quotation demonstrates that this appetite for food is tied to the appetite for life. It also shows the complicated relationship between what David Der-wei Wang calls "two functions of orality": eating food and speaking words (2000: 49).[20] These two oral functions, as we have seen in Paul's concern over "meat" and "tongues" in 1 Corinthians, are by no means neatly separable or even necessarily benign. In the pages of *Dictee*, words turn out to have cannibalistic potential: they can eat or consume the life of a person or a culture. In any case, we find in this episode Cha's mother choosing to favor her father's words about the need for edible food over Jesus's eloquent words about an empty stomach. Eloquent mouths that extol hungry mouths may, in the final analysis, be empty mouths. In other words, Cha is questioning the rhetoric and the logic that tout the capacity to withstand hunger or to suffer martyrdom as a sign of spiritual or patriotic commitment. While Matthew's Jesus ends up dying for God and Yu Guan Soon dying for country, we find Cha's mother trying to stop her own son from buying into this ideology of "dying for a cause" in a later section, "Melpomene Tragedy":

> It is 1962 eighteen years ago same month same day all over again. I am eleven years old. Running to the front door, Mother, you are holding my older brother pleading with him not to go out to the demonstration. You are threatening him, you are begging to him. He has on his school uniform, as all the other students representing their schools in the demonstration. You are pulling at him you stand before the door. He argues with you he pushes you away. You use all your force, all that you have. He is prepared to join the student demonstration outside. You can hear the gun shots. They are directed at anyone. . . . You do not want to lose him, my brother, to be killed as the many others by now already, you say you understand, you plead all the same they are killing any every one. . . . You, my brother, you protest your cause, you say you are willing to die. Dying is part of it. If it must be. (Cha 1995: 83–84)

Rather than understanding one's hunger for food and for life as base appetites that must always be sacrificed to satisfy some higher or heavenly hunger, Cha's biblical in(ter)vention here suggests that such "base" hungers may in fact be basic and crucial to other hungers. For Cha, her mother's hunger for food is linked to a profound hunger for human liberation on earth:

> You know to wait. Wait in the Misere. . . . And you wait. You keep silent. You bide time. Time. Single stone laid indicating the day from sunrise to sundown. Filling up times belly. Stone by stone. Three hundred sixty five days multiplied thirty six years. . . . No more sentence to exile, Mother, no black crows to mourn you. Neither takes you neither will take you Heaven nor Hell they fall too near you let them fall to each other you come back you come back to your one mother to your one father. (Cha 1995: 47, 53)

The way Cha inserts and juxtaposes her mother's refusal of three heavenly dishes into and with the biblical intertext highlights another major difference between Cha's mother and Matthew's Jesus. While Jesus is able to verbally reply and respond to the tempter every time, Cha's mother never speaks her disagreement. Instead, she can only shake her head in refusal. What Cha effectually does, I would argue, is provide the reason behind her mother's refusal to digest rhetoric that dismisses appetites for food and life. Cha's mother is suspicious because she has another oral appetite that has been denied. She is another *diseuse* or female speaker in *Dictee* who gets dictated to but has to struggle to speak.[21] If psychoanalytic theory is right in asserting that eating and speaking are—to use again, that favorite term of Kristeva's theory of intertextuality—"transpositions" of a similar desire to appropriate and incorporate the world (J. W. Brown 1984: 12–13), one of patriarchy's effects is to dictate to women and make them victims of male discourses, and one of such male discourses may well be that of "worthy sacrifice"—whether it be one of food or life, whether it be for God or country. Since the language for desires is dependent on the desire for language, a man like Jesus, with his appetite for speech satisfied, may well be able to afford to forego his appetite for food to pursue other appetites. In contrast, a woman whose appetite for speech remains unsatisfied may well indicate an empty stomach as well as many other unsatisfied appetites. Cha knows that it may be fatal for a woman to have both her oral appetites for speech and food left un(ful)filled. When she writes that "the rain does not erase the [martyr's] blood fallen on the ground" (1995: 85), is she not implying the emptiness of "worthy sacrifice"? Like her practice of interval in(ter)ventions, whether it is in dictation, translation, quotation, or citation, Cha practices an "ethics of infidelity." She is careful not to be too (politically) correct, whatever the cause.[22]

I have been arguing that Cha's gender plays a crucial role in this biblical in(ter)vention. Let me further propose that Cha's "ethics of infidelity" is related to her identity as an immigrant. Many Matthean scholars have pointed out, on the basis of how the tempter begins his first two tests with the same phrase, "if you are the Son of God" (Matthew 4:3, 6), that the entire episode of Jesus' temptation has to do with Jesus' identity, and how it is inseparable from his obedience (Carter 2000: 106; Garland 1993: 39; Pregeant 1996: 206–211; Schweizer 1975: 58).[23] If Jesus' certainty about his identity as God's son helps him not to succumb to the temptations, the opposite is true for Cha and her mother.[24] They do not fall for the potentially victimizing poetics and politics of "higher hunger" or "sacrificial death" precisely because they have an uncertain or unstable identity. Besides the spirit to survive, another consistent theme in Cha's characterization of her mother in this "Calliope Epic Poetry" section is how she and other Koreans have become "Refugees. Immigrants. Exiles" (1995: 45). We have already looked at her stay in Manchuria; immediately after this hallucination of heaven and intertextual in(ter)vention through Matthew, Cha describes how her mother becomes a naturalized U.S. citizen:

One day you raise the right hand and you are American. They give you an
American Pass port. The United States of America. Somewhere someone has
taken my identity and replaced it with their photograph. The other one.
Their signature their seals. Their own image. And you learn the executive
branch the legislative branch and the third. Justice. Judicial branch. It makes
the difference. The rest is past. (1995: 56)

If one is tempted to think that Cha is advocating a return to some kind
of an authentic Korean identity, she immediately removes that temptation
by concluding this section with a description of the impossibility of such a
return:

You return and you are not one of them, they treat you with indifference. All
the time you understand what they are saying. But the papers give you away.
Every ten feet. They ask you identity. They comment upon your inability or
ability to speak. Whether you are telling the truth or not about your nationality. They say you look other than you say. . . . You say who you are but you
begin to doubt. (1995: 56–57; see also 80–81)

Echoing in a way the encounters between Mulberry/Peach and INS
officers in Hualing Nieh's novel that I mentioned in the beginning of Chapter 3 (1988: 3–7, 160–66, 181–82, 204), multiple or impure identity spells
only dishonesty or disloyalty to uniform(ed) police. An immigrant woman
finds herself disqualified because of her inability to speak in her new place
of residence, *and* in spite of her ability to speak in her place of birth. She gets
disqualified every time and everywhere because she does not have the "identity," or the purity, the uniformity that is asked or demanded of her. Her
impure identity, however, also helps her to cross party lines and see through
the victimizing potential of "faultless faithfulness," "higher hunger," and
"meaningful martyrdom."
    Seen in this light, Cha's biblical in(ter)vention as an immigrant woman
may be read as her intertextual reading/writing of Kristeva's theories of
abjection and intertextuality. For Kristeva, as we have seen in the previous
chapters on Paul's 1 Corinthians, abjection is a psychic process that operates on both an individual and a social level. Simultaneously threatened and
attracted by an abject and boundary-crossing impurity (whether in terms of
gender difference like women and/or corporeal associations like food and
waste), one will turn to attack the bodily orifices or social thresholds in an
attempt to bolster the boundary between inside and outside, and between
self and others (Kristera 1982). Cha, an immigrant woman fighting abject to

break out of a dictated space, chooses to chew up intertextual thresholds by churning up, and (ab)using, biblical intertexts that have to do with bodily orifices—that is, eating, speaking, hearing, and reading.

Women Meeting at the Well

In addition to inventing and interrupting biblical intertexts with her own text, Cha also "impurifies" biblical texts with texts of other traditions. The last section of *Dictee*, "Polymnia Sacred Poetry," narrates a story that reminds me of John 4: the story of Jesus meeting the Samaritan woman at the well. In Cha's hands, however, this meeting at the well is no longer between a Jewish man and a Samaritan woman, but between a young girl and a young woman from two neighboring villages. Instead of having the woman at the well go to evangelize her townsfolk upon meeting Jesus at the well as in John, Cha has the women at the well give the young girl some medicine to take home to cure the girl's ailing mother. According to Lew, these differences were not invented by Cha, but incorporated or integrated by her from an ancient Korean shamanistic tradition (1982: 14–21). According to this myth, the young girl is actually a victim of patriarchy. Born after six other sisters to a king who desperately wants a male heir, she is locked in a stone coffin and cast into a pond at birth, but is miraculously saved and taken up to heaven. When she is fourteen, she herself descends from heaven, travels a great distance to secure healing water from a well in the Western sky, and saves her own mother from a deadly illness. It is important to point out, however, that what we find in Cha is actually also an in(ter)vention of this shamanistic tradition, because in Lew's version, the well-keeper is a man, and this man refuses to give the young girl healing water until she marries him and gives birth to seven sons.

As Chew also indicates, "women meeting at a well" is also an allusion to the Greek myth about Demeter and Kore (1995: 221).[25] Kore is Demeter's daughter, but is abducted by Hades into the underworld. To save her daughter, Demeter, as the goddess of agriculture, causes a famine on earth, thus effecting a negotiation that requires Kore to spend half the year in the underworld as Hades' wife, and half on earth with her mother. When Demeter is wandering in search of Kore, she stops to rest at the Kallichoron Well in Eleusis (fourteen miles west of Athens). It is there that she meets the princesses of Eleusis and makes Eleusis her terrestrial home for a while. Later on in *Dictee*, Cha will allude to the myth again. She writes, "Let the one who is mother Restore memory . . . one who is daughter restore spring with her each appearance from beneath the earth" (1995: 133). For my purposes here, let me point out, first, that this negotiation between Demeter and Hades is the result of Kore—unlike Cha's mother, who refuses to partake of any heavenly dish and gets pushed out of heaven for good, *and* unlike Perpetua, who is cut off from her baby but tastes heavenly food— having eaten a few seeds in Hades, which necessitates her return to the earth for six months of the year (Chew 1995: 231). Second, I need to point out that in Nora Okja Keller's novel about a Korean "comfort woman" who actually becomes a shaman to give voice to her past and (re)establish connection with her Korean American daughter, Keller recounts a slightly different version of the Korean shamanistic tale tracked by Lew. According to Keller's protagonist, Akiko, the princess—in a fashion that both mirrors *and* reverses Demeter—goes and distracts the Death Messenger in hell with "handfuls of barley and rice . . . oranges and . . . whiskey" (1997: 49). After successfully identifying her mother through a familiar song, the princess rescues her son-less parents from hell and takes them to the Lotus Paradise.

We find in Cha, therefore, not only in(ter)ventions of both biblical, Korean shamanistic, and Greek mythic intertexts, but also examples of intertextual impurity. Echoing Paul Gilroy's "sound system culture" that features intercultural circulation (1987: 165), the intertexts in Cha are themselves inter-woven, one with another. Archie C. C. Lee has proposed that this kind of textual weaving or cross-textual reading of the Bible is characteristic of Asian biblical hermeneutics (1993; see also A. C. C. Lee 1998; A. C. C. Lee 2004; and Kuan 1999). What are the implications of this practice?

I would argue that this practice, at least as far as the two examples in Cha are concerned, functions to foreground again the gender-specificity of Christian Gospels like Matthew and John.[26] Both times, in contrast to the intimate relationship between the God-Father and Jesus the son, Cha focuses on a mother–daughter relationship.[27] Unlike the male Jesus, whose experience of rebirth and resurrection is full and permanent, the female Kore, the nation Kore-a (Chew 1995: 221–22), as well as Cha's mother, can never have a complete and unproblematic return or recovery after their experiences of violence.[28] In the case of the well-meeting narrative, Cha's interweaving text completely removes John's heterosexually loaded innuendo—whether it is betrothal (the type scene of a man and a woman meeting at a well, John 4:1–7), marriage (the offering of "living water" or sperm by Jesus, John 4:13–16), or family (the birthing of spiritual children by the Samaritan woman for Jesus through her witness to her townsfolk, John 4:28–30, 39–42; see also Fehribach 1998: 45–81). More important, by incorporating and integrating different traditions and intertexts (biblical,

Greek, and Korean) in her *Dictee,* Cha points to competing texts and traditions *alongside* as well as *inside* any dictate.

The Demeter/Kore myth is deeply associated with the ancient mystery religion of Eleusis because of the Eleusinian emphasis on initiating "rebirth," as well as what Luther H. Martin calls "the sovereignty of the feminine" (1987: 58–72). As a result, the myth was certainly in competition with the Christian Gospels in the first four centuries of the Common Era. However, considering their common stress on transworld travels and rebirth, and the fact that the myth and the mysteries both predated the Gospels and continued to be circulated and celebrated in the same geographical and cultural zones of the Gospels,[29] it would be hard to deny the ghostly yet very real presence of this ancient Greek myth within, say, Matthew or John.

It is important to note that Princess Pari Kongju (or Gongju) is generally considered to be the first shamaness of Korea and that her ballad is still being sung in Korean shaman rituals today (Kendall 1985: 153–54). In contrast to the shaman-like and Christ-following Paul discussed in the last chapter, shamans in Korea are predominantly women (Kendall 1988: 6). Furthermore, shamanism is an indigenous Korean religion that has not only survived the importations of Confucianism, Buddhism, and Christianity, but also has become a symbol of anti-colonial resistance and protest in Korea (K.-O. Kim 1994). For example, in Nora Keller's novel *Comfort Woman,* Akiko's shamanism is presented as her choice over and against a Christian missionary religion that parallels Japanese colonization.[30]

One would be wrong, however, to think of resistance solely in terms of rejection, partition, or separation (Cheng 2001: 159). As Laurel Kendall argues, the organizational typology that it is customary in social anthropology to apply to "shaman" or "Buddhist" practices fails to bring out "the complex integration of [religious/cultural] belief and practice" and how people "cross categories" in Korea (1985: 35). If different materials do mingle and mix within a geographical region like Korea (say, between shamanism and Buddhism) or the Mediterranean region (say, between the Gospels and the Demeter/Kore myth), is it not conceivable that Cha's interweaving of John's Gospel with Korean shamanistic traditions might also have already existed?

While it may be easy to see the ancient Korean myth of Princess Pari as a competing but separate tradition of biblical texts, the relationship between the geopolitical East and the biblical texts is actually also more complex. R. S. Sugirtharajah has, for example, pointed to similar thought structure in Buddhism and the Gospel of John. Suggesting that correspondences also exist between Buddhism and Matthew, Sugirtharajah concludes that contributions to the conception of Christianity in general and to the composition of the Gospels in particular must move beyond the Mediterranean milieu or Greco-Judaeo traditions to consider Asian religions and literature (2003: 27–31; see also 107–109).[31] In words that seem to echo Cha's sentiments, Sugirtharajah writes: "Such an acknowledgement and appropriation will enable us to go beyond the traditionally exclusive missionary claims regarding the Christian story. More importantly, it will celebrate the hybridized and eclectic nature of religious stories. It will refuse to be limited by religionist and preservationist imperatives, and ascribe fluidity to the texts" (2003: 31).

Conclusion: Back to the Beginning-*s*

Ironically, Cha's intertextuality seems to ease or erase the anxiety over biblical influence and authority by (1) intimating the influence of other texts on the Bible and (2) disputing the theological or ideological notion about the "oneness" of Scripture and, by extension, the "oneness" of God. I think Cha's practice not only challenges (1) the scholarly differentiation between influence and intertextuality (Clayton and Rothstein 1991) and (2) the scholarly comparison between midrash and intertextuality (Boyarin 1990), but also that her in(ter)ventions of biblical intertexts illustrate—to borrow Bakhtin's vocabulary—a *heteroglossia* that ultimately explodes any dictate, and even the concept of intertextuality. Over twenty years ago, the Canadian literary critic Northrop Frye suggested that one could not understand literature of the Western world without knowledge of the Bible, what he called the "Great Code" (1982). What Cha shows is that this dictate by Frye is nothing less than a suturing act. That is, it presents a pure beginning that conceals or smoothes over other beginnings. Cha shows with the myth of Demeter and Kore that Matthew and John—and by extension the Bible—might themselves hark back to other ancient texts, and such textual trails—as we have seen briefly in Acts in Chapter 4—can become an endless tail or tale. In other words, intertexts can be limitless in width as well as depth, a dictate to repeat is itself infinitely reproducible, and singular lineage or pure genealogy becomes both pluralistic and promiscuous (Cheng 2001: 159). Instead of repeating the dictate that "in the beginning was the Word" and "the Word was made flesh" (John 1:1, 14), Cha inscribes not only that her "words made flesh" (1995: 18) but also insinuates that "in the beginning-*s* were word-*s*." In the early part of *Dictee*, one finds two brief invocations to the Muses. One states:

> O Muse, tell me the story
> Of all these things, O Goddess, daughter of Zeus
> Beginning wherever you wish, tell even us. (1995: 7)

The other is a similar, though by no means a seamless repetition:

> Tell me the story
> Of all these things.
> Beginning wherever you wish, tell even us. (1995: 11)

Cha is asking the Muses, supposedly daughters of Mnemosyne or Memory, to begin "wherever" they wish rather than "from *the* beginning," as in Hesiod's invocation of the Muses in *The Theogony* (1953: 56; emphasis mine). These repeated requests imply that, as I have suggested in the last chapter on Paul, memory and history actually always forget. Cha's invocations are therefore doubling as problematizations. What she problematizes is memory's or history's claim to truth, because both have the "capacity for metamorphosis, an endless recycling of their meaning and an unpredictable proliferation of their ramifications" (Nora 1989: 19).

Kaja Silverman, in a book about "intervals" entitled *The Thresholds of the Visible World,* suggests that one of psychoanalysis's greatest insights is that every memory, every return, every repetition is—to use an immigrant term—a displacement, a different place, a differing beginning (1996: 181). Silverman continues that what this insight encourages is for us to look—and I will add, read—in a way that overlooks and overturns what others want to overdetermine (that is, their dictates of origination, purity, identity, and fidelity).[32] Displacement is what the displaced Cha is doing to her intertexts. Alluding to Hesiod's *Theogony* to talk about her own personal and (inter)national histories, Cha demonstrates that: "[g]enealogists resist histories that attribute purity of origin to any performance. They have to take into account the give and take of joint transmissions, posted in the past, arriving in the present, delivered by living messengers, speaking in tongues not entirely their own. Orature is an art of listening as well as speaking; improvisation is an art of collective memory as well as invention; repetition is an art of re-creation as well as restoration" (Roach 1996: 286).

Michel de Certeau provides perhaps an even better vocabulary to describe Cha's intertextual in(ter)ventions when he suggests that "readers are travellers; they move across lands belonging to someone else, like nomads poaching their way across fields they did not write" (1984: 174). In other words, Cha's intertextual in(ter)vention disregards laws of property and ownership (Spahr 1996: 37) as well as laws of nationality, citizenship, or different "worlds."[33] In that sense, Cha's challenge is not a practice of intertextuality, but *trans*-textuality, with the prefix denoting "both moving through space or across lines, as well as changing the nature of something" (Ong 1999: 4). The point of citing and alluding to biblical intertexts, like her practice of dictation and translation, is not to repeat or transcribe, but to renew, revise, translate, and transform.[34] Ironically, as Rudolf Schnackenburg suggests, this process of transcription and transformation may also be the process of how Scripture like Matthew comes into existence (1996: 252, 264). Paul is, of course, also well known for his free association in his practice of interpreting Hebrew Scripture (Hays 1989: 1–33, 77–83). This process of transmission and transcription does not, however, end with Matthew or Paul. As David C. Parker has demonstrated, the New Testament "is open, and successive generations write on its pages" (1997: 174). Understanding the New Testament as "living texts" (Parker 1997) has enormous implications (see also Alter 2000; Cameron 1991: 5). For example, at least one prominent textual critic has, as a result, proceeded to review what textual criticism means by trying to establish the "earliest" or "original" text of a canonical book (Epp 1999) and to re-vision textual criticism in terms of engaging "multiple variants without resolution about originality" (Epp 2004: 8).

As an in(ter)vention through yet another beginning, let me suggest that de Certeau's understanding of reading as poaching and readers as travelers also sits well with the so-called origin of the word "hermeneutics." The Greek god Hermes, from whom the word "hermeneutics" supposedly derives, has wings on his feet so he can travel back and forth among Gods and between worlds as a *trickster* messenger. In this process of interpretation and in(ter)vention, Cha negotiates and subverts the power of the biblical ca(n)non. In addition, she also revisits and reformulates an ever-changing immigrant identity, because her trafficking and poaching of different texts is "a critique of the desire for documentation" (Cheng 2001: 142), whether that documentation is for or against the traveling subject. The text(s) and trace(s) of (Korea) America, like those about God(s), have multiple beginnings, various versions, as well as intricate inter- and intra-weavings. Rather than assuming a privileged status as the "origin(al)," they are translatable or transportable to copious contexts. As a result, immigrant identity is also *heteroglossic* because of its international or transnational legacy, and inventive in relation to different subject positions. In a way that further facilitates a connection between Cha and the concerns of my previous chapters, Sam Durrant has proposed that the inability to recover the "origin(al)" —and thus to present an integratable narrative—is also the key not only to endless mourning but also to a truly open and inclusive community (2004: 111–17). For both Cha and Durrant, such a community must not only be multi-racial/ethnic in its makeup, but also *inter*national in its scope.

CHAPTER 8

Telling Times in (Asian) America

• •

Extraordinary Poetics, Everyday Politics, and Endless Paradoxes

Almost half a century ago, Ernst Käseman claimed that "apocalyptic is the mother of all Christian theology" (1969: 102).[1] Today, we may wonder not only about his encompassing and totalizing "all," but also about his singular and definitive "mother." Gayatri Chakravorty Spivak, for instance, has declared that Calcutta is her mother, the United States is her stepmother, and that both are nurturing but ugly (1990: 83). To avoid the pitfall of Käseman's generalization, I note at the outset that I am most interested in investigating how the interjections and interruptions from ancient apocalyptic tradition(s) (a pre-post-erity?) inter-act with the present of an "intrusive" and alien-ated (Asian) America, of or from which Spivak is a/part,[2] and that this chapter will focus in many ways only on the apocalyptic tradition(s) that grow(s) out of the book of Revelation in the New Testament. In other words, one will not find here the kind of close reading that is customary for or expected of someone in biblical studies. I take this approach for two main reasons. First, I do not want to reinforce the power of the origin(al), as if the origin(al)—in this case, the book of Revelation—had an essence that, once identified, should and/or could dictate everything that comes afterward. Following Cha's example discussed in the last chapter, I would like to displace so-called origin(al)s, even if my focus is switching to the so-called end of time. Second, as I have done throughout this book, I want to continue to call into question what is considered to be "appropriate" or "inappropriate" subject matter in the field of biblical studies. In addition to arguing that reading theory and read-ing across disciplines may generate new insights into biblical texts, I want to extend the scope of the biblical studies field to include the function of bibli-cal texts in the wider world of literature and culture.[3] In other words, I want to enlarge the "canon" not (only) of the Bible but of biblical studies.

Pervasive yet Particular, Ending but Everlasting

My emphasis on particularity has to do with a paradoxical endlessness that comes with the apocalyptic end. Despite our tendency to associate it solely with right-wing conservatives, there is actually an apocalyptic endemic across the political, ideological, and theological spectrum. As Michel de Certeau observes: "[T]here is vis-à-vis the established order, a relationship between the Churches that defended an *other world* and the parties of the left which, since the nineteenth century, have promoted a *different future*. In both cases, similar functional characteristics can be discerned" (1984: 183; emphasis in original). Since the subtle pervasiveness of apocalyptic has been well argued (Kermode 1966; Dellamora 1995; Robbins and Palmer 1997; C. Keller 1998), I will focus on how this apocalyptic endlessness manifests itself both in scope and in sequence within the culture of the United States today. It is important, however, to underscore first that this apocalyptic endlessness is related to its immense multiplicity and plasticity. Good evidence of that is, of course, the afterlife of apocalyptic even "when prophecy fails" (Festinger, Riecken, and Schachter 1956). This everlasting life expectancy of "expecting Armageddon" (Stone 2000) has to do with more than just sociological and psychological factors. Its endurance also comes partly from apocalyptic's innumerable and infinitely (re)interpretable articulations. Within the Christian Bible, the two most recognized apocalypses, Daniel and Revelation, are, despite many similar characteristics, distinctly different books with different structures to target different enemies.[4] The same is true when it comes to academic studies of ancient Jewish and/or Christian apocalyptic, which have revolved around at least three foci: (1) a genetic concern with sources or origins; (2) a generic emphasis that looks at its literary form, style, and content; and (3) a concentration on generative effects or functions (J. J. Collins 1998: 1–42). Even supposedly rigid premillennialists disagree on the timing of the rapture vis-à-vis the so-called Great Tribulation, and are thus divided into pre-tribulationists, mid-tribulationists, and post-tribulationists (O'Leary 1994: 138–39; S. F. Harding 2000: 238–39). On a broader cultural level, apocalyptic is often used as an effectual but elusive signifier for a positive blooming of utopia and/or a negative catastrophe of gloom and doom.[5]

This is not to say that apocalyptic does not have a stable cast of characters or characteristics (Weber 1999: 32). There is a person or a group receiving a vision or an unveiling of heavenly mysteries (and hence the word "apocalyptic"). This revelation, or at least inspired understanding, is often one of certain coming chaos or calamities that are associated with (the d)evil. This disaster serves, however, as a kind of "ethical" cleansing, out of which a select minority will not only survive but also finally thrive in a new and perfect world. What this somewhat stable if sickening sketch means is, conversely and controversially, dreadfully unstable. While some see apocalyptic as over-turning fatal injustice, others see it as turning over in fatalistic indifference. More important, those who agree on apocalyptic as over-turning may also disagree about what constitutes "justice" and "injustice." On the one hand, Revelation has led to the *Left Behind* series; on the other hand, it has helped to bring about the first mass people's movement in Korea, the 1894 Tonghak Rebellion against foreign occupation (M.-J. Kim 1997). Even if one limits oneself to the *Left Behind* novels, one cannot tell whether readers are responding to the stereotypical domestic woman figure on the basis of her domesticity before her rapture, and/or on her ability to escape domesticity with the rapture (Frykholm 2001: 23–24).[6] Rather than adjudicating whether apocalyptic is in the final analysis a utopian or dystopian vision, or whether its politics is transformative or accommodative, I will make two Derridean moves here. First, apocalyptic can and is likely to be both utopian and dystopian or transformative and accommodative at the same time. Second, the meaning of apocalyptic is relational to or contingent upon its particular use.[7] As Stephen O'Leary notes, "the nature of apocalyptic's appeal should be sought in transactions of texts and audiences" (1994: 11).

In other words, the messy politics of apocalyptic, the politics of time, hinges upon the time of politics. Unlike apocalyptic, however, my appeal to time does not claim to pronounce or produce an end to interpretive conflicts or disagreements. Not only do people read and re-read a text over time and in different spaces, but people who share a context may also read the same text differently. Contextualization therefore cannot and should not end up reifying a certain moment or any singular interpretation.[8] Precisely because apocalyptic time is not monolithic, it is, like time, not static. Despite apocalyptic's linearity, its multiplicity and flexibility make it feasible for social "activists" as diverse as homophobes (see Herman 1997; and Palmer 1997) and environmentalists (M. F. Lee 1997; Lorentzen 1997)—or even as diametrically opposed as Marxists and capitalists—to use basically the same apocalyptic discursive logic.[9] I say this not to undercut but to underscore the significance of interpretive debates. This is particularly so since many people tend to feel helpless when it comes to the book of Revelation, and thus may end up endorsing anyone who is willing and/or able to put forth an interpretation of it.[10]

The multiple, ambivalent, precarious, and volatile tendencies of apocalyptic endlessness can certainly be seen in the context of the United States. Apocalyptic is an undercurrent that informs and implements numerous national(ist) narratives, including the so-called discovery of the "New World," the development of the "frontier," the "Cold War," and its successful accumulation of wealth that leads to the claiming of the twentieth century as an "American" century (Bercovitch 1978; C. Keller 1998: xi, 8–10, 152–69; Stratton 2000). This apocalyptic air is not "out there" as if it were something that is apart, "abnormal," and/or marginal; it is rather "out there" as in "everywhere." It has permeated, even saturated, our literary as well as academic landscapes. We might want to quarantine the *Left Behind* series as a solely fundamentalist or sectarian literary—make it *popular* literary—phenomenon. Douglas Robinson has, however, convincingly argued that mainstream American writers like Emerson, Poe, Hawthorne, Melville, Twain, and Faulkner have all struggled with "the problems raised by the apocalyptic thrust of the American Dream" (1990: 3). Likewise, it is not only academic conservatives like Daniel Bell and Francis Fukuyama who write books with apocalyptic-sounding titles like *The End of Ideology* (Bell 1960) or *The End of History and the Last Man* (Fukuyama 1992). Immanuel Wallerstein, a card-carrying Marxist scholar, also ended up choosing to entitle two of his books, *Utopistics* (1998) and *The End of the World as We Know It* (1999), to signify the shift of paradigms within the social sciences. Contrary to the *Left Behind* series, when it comes to apocalyptic, the Left is actually seldom behind.

In addition to the pervasive scope of apocalyptic, let me use a current event and its lingering effects to illustrate the way in which apocalyptic can become endless by reproducing more apocalyptic sequentially. September 11, 2001, is apocalyptic in several senses; thus it also illustrates apocalyptic's polysemic and multivocal tendencies. In one sense, what happened that day in New York is apocalyptic because it signifies for many the tragic ending of the apocalyptic belief that the United States is the utopia realized or "promised land" achieved.[11] Paradoxically, this apocalyptic ending of an apocalyptic belief only ends up endowing and endorsing more apocalyptic endeavors. As happened before with the involvement of the United States in Vietnam (Stratton 2000: 36–38), failures of apocalyptic proportions paradoxically endear rather than end apocalyptic. At the same time people are mourning the apocalyptic ending of the "American Dream" and/or the "American Century," they are also galvanizing (military) forces to shift the focus from proclaiming the United States the "New World" to committing it to ensure or enforce the "New World Order." The war against Iraq is, for some, a dangerous and an endangering war with (the d)evil, and hence a war of apocalyptic significance. At the same time, apocalyptic also assures these people that they are the (self-s)elect of God, so that God is on the side of the United States and victory is never in doubt.

Apocalyptic has therefore this elasticity—almost a kind of internal, eternal, and endogenous regeneration—that ensures its endlessness. The book of Revelation, for instance, continues to find new life by inspiring modern apocalyptic fiction, like the *Left Behind* series (see also Beal 2002: 82–85). I should be honest here and confess that I have never read any of the best-selling series. I do know of one person who, out of curiosity, picked up a volume to see what all the fuss was about. Later, he told me that he found the book to be so bad that the reading process turned out to be quite an *enduring* experience: he could not wait for this book about the end to end. Ironically, there is literally no end in sight. It has now (re)generated into a serial of seven books, two movies, a radio drama, a children's series, a board game, a Web site, a video game, and who knows what else. This is just like the movie *Terminator,* which is intertextually linked to the Bible, including Revelation 12 (Boer 1995). Rather than terminating, it keeps on showing up from *Term.* I, to *Term.* II, and onto *Term.* III.

The war against Iraq, the *Left Behind* phenomenon, and the *Terminator* movies have another shared commonality in addition to apocalyptic; namely, a focus on science and technology. *Terminator* is, of course, a science fiction. I have just mentioned the *Left Behind* Web site and video game, but I have also learned—if only secondarily through Frykholm's reading of *Left Behind* and *Left Behind* readers (2001: 92–113)—that the series is full of references to computer technology. There were a lot of headlines, especially during the early development of this country's strike against Iraq, concerning our military technology and Iraq's biological weapons. I would suggest that the connection between apocalyptic and science and technology found in these three cases is not coincidental.[12]

Perhaps the statement made by President Clinton during his second inaugural address will provide us with a good entry into this issue. According to Clinton, "scientists now are decoding the blueprint of human life. Cures for our most feared illnesses seem close at hand" (cited in Stratton 2000: 59). He was, of course, referring to the Human Genome Project. Manuel Castells writes, "Prophets of technology preach the *new age*, extrapolating to social trends and organization the barely understood logic of computers and DNA" (1996: 4; emphasis mine). Technoscience is an apocalypse because it allows people to "search" and see all kinds of past record, current account, and future projection on a single computer screen, as well as to unveil or reveal what is literally under the human skin (Gilroy 2000: 37,

43–53; see also A. F. Gordon 1997: 16–17).[13] Technoscience is an apocalypse because the instantaneous and simultaneous capacities of computers and digital communications have supposedly made time end or disappear (Nowotny 1994). Even the punctuation mark that signifies the end of a sentence in writing (a period) is now arguably more widely used as a dot in Web or E-mail addresses like "xxx.edu" (Newman, Clayton, and Hirsch 2002a: 1–2). This apocalypse of technoscience even comes complete with the ambiguity between boom and doom. "[A] specific sense of time," Donna J. Haraway states, is "characteristic of the promises and threats of technoscience" (1997: 9). If the book title *The Eighth Day of Creation* (Judson 1996) promises genome knowledge as the beginning of a new world, others have pointed to the danger of genetic engineering that might lead to selective breeding or genetic essentialism. The idea that one's future is encoded, programmed, readable, and accessible in one's DNA is, of course, in itself apocalyptic. In yet another typical apocalyptic fashion, the (new) age of technoscience may pronounce (new) life for some, but death for others.[14]

Fear of . . . and Desire for Apocalyptic

I have suggested that both the war against Iraq and the technoscientific revolution are apocalyptic; let me now proceed to suggest the connections between these apocalyptic developments and Asian America. The war against Iraq or against terrorism has not only created a climate of xenophobia (there were, for instance, talks of limiting or eliminating visas issued to international students), it has led to hate crimes. One particular problem this has created for Asian Americans is that many in this country are not willing and/or able to differentiate Arabs from South Asians, or Muslims from turban-wearing Sikhs. There have been reports that immediately after September 11 some South Asians and/or Sikhs became victims of hate crimes due to mistaken identity.[15] September 11 has led, of course, to other developments of terror(ism), like the detention of "suspects" without charge.[16] Many Asian Americans are wary of the eerie parallelism between this "patriot act" and the detention of Japanese Americans after Pearl Harbor.[17] Asian Americans, who ironically have long been stereotyped as "naturals" for or genetically inclined towards technoscience, are also well aware that discriminatory practices, whether they are based on genetic or racial/ethnic makeup, happen despite—and sometimes even because of—legal decisions. In Chapter 2, I have written about how the 1982 cult classic *Blade Runner* (starring Harrison Ford) portrays a "Yellow Peril" of the twenty-first century, when wealthy and healthy whites not only live in an "off world" to separate themselves from Asians who are populating the "old world," but they also have to prevent some almost-white-but-not-quite "replicant humans" from passing as lawful (white) residents of the "off world." Fifteen years later, there is another cult classic with reversed roles in a somewhat similar plot. In *Gattaca,* we find a white man (Ethan Hawke) who has not been genetically engineered trying to escape to Titan by adopting another person's genetic identity, as Titan is only for the genetically "perfect." Despite the time difference between these two films, the reversed role of the white male protagonist ironically communicates a uniform and "timeless" message that should be alarming for Asian America: whites (particularly male) are being victimized and are in need of an escape from a world gone wrong because of being populated by beings who are less than one hundred percent human. As Jay Clayton insightfully points out by way of a recent TV commercial for a technoscientific company about the potential of genome research for various persons, the promise of human "improvement" actually targets only those who do not fit into the category of a "healthy, white, adult male," since that category is precisely the one that does not show up in this commercial of genome (re)generation (2002: 31–32, 53–54).[18]

Despite these apocalyptic threats for Asian Americans, one can argue that many Asian Americans and apocalyptic have one important commonality: both involve a moving "beyond" or an "in-between-ness" that implies, among other things, a change in time and space.[19] If people are likely to forget about the spatial dimension of apocalyptic (whether the "New Jerusalem" or "New World" is understood as heaven coming on earth or departing earth for heaven), they also tend to forget that, in dominant ideology, the journey from Asia to the United States often implies an experience of being "fast-forwarded" from some kind of "primitive" or "static" time (McLeod 2000: 44) and/or a linear, chronological progression from being "foreign" to being a "legal alien," and finally to being a "citizen" (Chuh 2001: 286). In addition, there is another sense of "moving beyond" that is important for many Asian Americans—namely, the need and desire to move beyond past and present injustice to a just and radically democratic future. Jacques Lacan (1978: 42–67) and Slavoj Žižek (1989: 44–48) have both suggested that fantasies are instrumental in keeping desires alive and thus in sustaining life. Their suggestion is arguably supported by Nieh's novel, which is full of escape fantasies during her protagonist's fugitive hiding in an attic in Taiwan (1988: 116–54). Recent studies on apocalyptic that focus on function and/or psychology have likewise suggested that apocalyptic might have less to do with time per se than with desire, wish, and need (Yarbro Collins

1984; Strozier 1994; Frykholm 2001). That is to say, it is out of present needs and desires that people seek or hope to see a future (re)vision.

This understanding can be clearly seen in a short story by the Asian American writer Gish Jen, entitled "The Water Faucet Vision" (1999: 37–48). I have already alluded to the root meaning of the word "apocalyptic" as an unveiling or a revelation. Volumes on the topic continue to highlight this aspect of apocalyptic with titles like *Vision of a Just World* (Schüssler Fiorenza 1991: subtitle), *Vision and Violence* (Mendel 1992), *Visions of the End* (McGinn 1998), and *Vision and Persuasion* (Carey and Bloomquist 1999). Paradoxically, Jen's "vision" story is one of lost innocence, or perhaps even lost faith. Adding to the paradox, the narrator of the story does not look ahead, but looks *back* to her grade school days when she used to believe in God, prayer, miracles, and visions. One night, after accidentally dropping her precious prayer beads down a street sewer on her way home from school, Callie had a vision that her lost beads would come back to her. Convinced that the beads would return to her miraculously through the town's water system, Callie got up in the middle of the night and turned on all the faucets in the house. When she woke up the next morning, she did not get her beads back, but she did get into a ton of trouble, not the least of which was the ridicule of her family. What is most telling for our purposes, however, is the closing paragraph of that story:

> Such was the end of my saintly ambitions. It wasn't the end of all holiness. The ideas of purity and goodness still tippled my brain, and over the years I came slowly to grasp of what grit true faith is made. Last night, though, when my father called to say that he couldn't go on living in our old house, that he was going to move to a smaller place, another place, maybe a condo—he didn't know how, or where—I found myself still wistful for the time religion seemed all I wanted it to be. Back then, the world was a place that could be set right. One had only to direct the hand of the Almighty and say, Just here, Lord, we hurt here—and here, and here, and here. (Jen 1999: 48)

Apocalyptic vision then, seems to represent—in both the literary and political sense of the word—human hurts, needs, and desires. Again, let me emphasize here that the specific content of these "hurts," "needs," and "desires" vary with different people, Asian American or otherwise.[20] The title and the theme of Jen's other book, *Mona in the Promised Land* (1996), clearly show that her needs and desires also have something to do with the rude awakening that, for Asian Americans, arriving in the United States is not necessarily the attainment of peace, justice, and security. Or, as another Asian American writer, Lois-Ann Yamanaka, writes in her controversial novel *Blu's Hanging:* "'Mama,' Blu yells into the night, 'Heaven ain't here'" (1997: 260).[21]

As we have seen in the context of September 11, apocalyptic awakening or awakening from apocalyptic does not necessarily lead to the abandonment of apocalyptic. The fact that the so-called New World was not living up to its name in the experiences of many Asian (North) Americans also resulted in Joy Kogawa's novel about the internment experience of many Japanese (North) Americans, *Obasan* (1984).[22] Not only does *Obasan* begin with Revelation 2:17, about hidden manna, white stone, and a new name being promised to the one who overcomes,[23] but this novel also ends by leading to—in typical apocalyptic endlessness—a sequel entitled *Itsuka* (1992). This title, which means "someday," implies the continuation of an apocalyptic vision. Someday in the future, Kogawa seems to be writing to ensure, Japanese (North) Americans will find vindication and compensation through their redress movement.[24] In other words, the novel provides a (moral) vision of a future fulfillment when the injustice suffered by Japanese (North) Americans will finally be rectified. If I may adapt from Walter Benjamin, apocalyptic is "a past[-future] charged by the time of the now . . . blast[ing] out of the continuum of history" (1968: 261) time and again.

Thus I find my writing and reading of apocalyptic comparable to "a persistent critique of what one cannot not want" (Spivak 1996: 28), since apocalyptic may function to identify (meaningful) time, and in the process produce identity (Fradenburg 2002: 215). Apocalyptic, like poetry, can have "power . . . as a vital means of spiritual survival" (cited in Chow 1993: 2). Audre Lorde has, of course, made known the saying "Poetry is not a luxury" (1984). Likewise, Frantz Fanon has suggested that artistic expressions can anticipate and assist other anti-colonial activities by awakening "the native's sensibility of defeat and to make unreal and unacceptable the contemplative attitude or the acceptance of defeat" (1963: 243). Rather than duplicating the binarism of apocalyptic, then, I do not think contemporary Asian America can afford to adopt any clear-cut attitude towards apocalyptic.[25] We have already discussed the problem of essentializing or over-generalizing the politics of apocalyptic, as Fredric Jameson makes the mistake of doing when he homogenizes all so-called third world literature as national allegory (1986). Asian America should be ambivalent about apocalyptic for another reason; namely, its diasporic experiences. If apocalyptic is for many a longing for belonging or "home" (Frykholm 2001: 18, 20), many in diaspora have also learned that this "constant craving" or dreaming for home is simultaneously indispensable and illusory (McLeod 2000: 209–15). The lesson of being in diaspora involves, then, along with the pain of feeling displaced, hopefully an acuity, even a healthy suspicion towards romantic(ized) vision. If I might return to Spivak's comment about having two nurturing but ugly mothers, Spivak concludes her comment by stating that she feels she has "earned the right [and I would add, "found the need"] to critique two places" (1990: 83).

If apocalyptic is at least one of the mothers who nurture our theology and worldview in powerful ways, we must also not hesitate to recognize her imperfections and incompleteness. This is precisely the kind of ambivalence with which Chang-Rae Lee concludes his novel *A Gesture Life:* "Perhaps I'll travel to where Sunny wouldn't go, to the south and west and maybe farther still, across the ocean, to land on former shores. But I think it won't be any kind of pilgrimage, I won't be seeking out my destiny or fate. I won't attempt to find comfort in the visage of a creator or the forgiving dead. . . . I will circle round and arrive again. Come almost home" (1999: 356).

Chang-Rae Lee's narrator, a Korean American who has also been a sub-ject of Japanese colonization, will continue to engage himself in travel and talk of home. At the same time, he will not portend closure. What we find is a circularity that dis-places the certainty of linearity.[26]

Spec(tac)ular Strategy and Ritual Resistance

What Chang-Rae Lee's conclusion also seems to communicate is that completion, certainty, or destiny are not the only alternatives to a dead-end nihilism, nor are they prerequisites for agency (Chuh 2003: 100). The spec(tac)ular aspects of apocalyptic, despite or perhaps even because of its indispensability and its concomitant incompleteness for Asian America, must not distract us from the importance of everyday practice. "I will circle round and arrive again. Come almost home" (Chang-Rae Lee 1999: 356). What is the "everyday"?

> The everyday tells us a story of modernity in which major historical cata-
> clysms are superseded by ordinary chores, the arts of working and making
> things. In a way, the everyday is anticatastrophic, an antidote to the historical
> narrative of death, disaster and apocalypse. The everyday does not seem to
> have a beginning or an end. In everyday life we do not write novels but notes
> or diary entries that are always frustratingly or euphorically anticlimactic.
> In diaries the drama of our lives never ends—as in the innumerable TV soap
> operas in which one denouement only leads to another narrative possibility

and puts off the ending. Our diaries are full of incidents and lack accidents; they have narrative potential and few completed stories. The everyday is a kind of labyrinth of common places without monsters, without a hero, and without an artist-maker trapped in his [*sic*] own creation. (Boym 1994: 20)

This is a fascinating description, except we have already seen that the fantastic category of apocalyptic (Pippin and Aichele 1998) also disseminates and defers endlessly. One must also recognize that the purpose of apocalyptic often involves a prescription for present, everyday living in light of the final outcome.[27] What I am proposing, then, is not the binary viewpoint that sees the everyday as something opposite to or incompatible with apocalyptic. Instead, I would suggest the more paradoxical view that the everyday serves a "supplementary" function, in the Derridean sense that it complements or completes rather than constitutes an appendix to apocalyptic.

According to Rey Chow, de Certeau's distinction between "strategy" and "tactic" is helpful for those writing with a "diasporic consciousness" that critiques apparent opposites, like orientalism and nativism (Chow 1993: 1–26). "Strategy," for de Certeau, represents "the calculation . . . of power relationships that becomes possible as soon as a subject with will and power (a business, an army, a city, a scientific institution) can be isolated" (de Certeau 1984: 36). It involves, in other words, the transformation of historical uncertainties into habitable places (what one may call "home"). In contrast, "tactic," like the "age-old ruses of fishes and insects that disguise and transform themselves," operates for survival and subversion despite "the absence of a proper locus" (de Certeau 1984: xi, 37). It is the difference between securing space of one's own and the need to continue to exercise agency in the space of another. Or, one may translate de Certeau's "strategy" to a coherent agenda, a political program, or even a meta-narrative like apocalyptic, and his "tactic" to a more piecemeal or haphazard maneuver. Chow sees de Certeau's "tactic" as not only more useful for diasporic intervention but also as a "[b]etting on time instead of space" (Chow 1993: 16). It is rather ironic that, even as Chow speaks against apparent binarism, she proceeds to uphold two of her own: strategy versus tactic, and space versus time.

"Tactic" is undoubtedly helpful for diasporic writing and living, given the circularity and uncertainty shown by Chang-Rae Lee above, as well as the ethnographical work on a South Asian American community that I mentioned in Chapter 1 of this book (Ganguly 2001). As R. Radhakrishnan writes about Asian America, "The living and the telling, the experiencing and the meaning-making happen simultaneously much like a radical existential script that begins to exist only when the screen is lifted and the lights turned on" (2001: 259). When Filipino Americans are not sure how things will turn out for them and their future generations in the United States, what sustains them and in fact transforms both them and the larger U.S. culture are mundane everyday routines that "depart from the protocol of the nation by (re)staging alternative and multiple 'origins,'" like family dinners, Friday night karaoke, and weekly mass (Manalansan 2001: 169). As one Filipino American parent puts it, he "can only try to 'inject' a little of the Philippines [for his children] whenever it is possible, and then sit back, maybe bite his lips, and hope for the best" (Manalansan 2001: 163). Yet, despite the absence of an overall plan, such everyday "injections" become the threads and the fabric out of which new cultural traditions are sewn (Lefebvre 1991). Homi K. Bhabha has suggested that "border" or "unhomely lives" require an "art of the present" (1994: 1–18).[28] I would propose that such "art" is often none other than the seemingly "artless" performance of the everyday in the commonplace—like family, work, education, entertainment, or ritual (Iwamura 1996; Bundang 2002). In other words, what Pierre Bourdieu calls "habitus" (1977),[29] or what Patricia Mann calls "micro-politics" (1994).

However, "tactic" (habitus or micro-politics) and "strategy" (habitation or macro-politics) are not necessarily mutually exclusive.[30] Neither are daily ritual or routine and spec(tac)ular apocalyptic.[31] Just as Revelation is not the only book in the New Testament, so apocalyptic is not the only strand in biblical thought.[32] Linear apocalyptic's strategic closure does not negate the importance of everyday tactic. It actually needs the open-endedness of everyday practice to compensate for its blindness and premature certainties.[33] Any coherent political vision or agenda must be subjected to "an indefatigable and illimitable interrogation of myriad relations of power and how they give, shape, and sometimes take life" (Chuh 2003: 150). Between apocalyptic's extravagant promise of utopia on the one hand, and its equally extreme pronouncement of disaster on the other, Asian America needs the calming wisdom to live daily into an open future. We must not allow any particular vision, as important as that vision may be, to blind us to "the diverse, the particular and the unpredictable in everyday life" (Ang 1991: x). Nor can we let any particular vision fool us into thinking that there is an end to everyday politics or political struggle. José Esteban Muñoz, in his attempt to construct for queers of color a practice beyond the binarism of identification/assimilation and counteridentification/utopianism, has similarly and helpfully insisted that one must work "to enact permanent structural change while at the same time valu[e] the importance of local or everyday struggles of resistance" (1999: 11–12).[34]

Conclusion

In sum, there is an endlessness about apocalyptic and an open-endedness in its interpretation. Despite or perhaps even because of its binary tendencies, apocalyptic is something that, I would suggest, (Asian) America cannot fully embrace or fully eliminate. Particular apocalyptic can provide a vision or a strategy for "transformation," but it must inform and be informed by every-day tactic. What I want to emphasize in closing is the importance of human agency. After all, human beings are the ones who (re)write and (re)read apocalyptic. We are actors in this war of wor(l)ds, and we must take on this enduring struggle for progressive ends in (extra)ordinary ways. As we work today under the legacies of the past, we must also realize that the shapes of our future are in no way, as apocalyptic implies, a foregone conclusion. How things will turn out is contingent upon our vision and revision. There is, however, another paradox that we must also keep in mind. Our future is also subject to chance and fortuitous developments that grow out of our everyday practices, despite our plan or intention, or lack thereof. Much as we need apocalyptic (re)visions, we also need a re-visioning that disrupts the teleological theology of the apocalyptic. We cannot be entirely freed from nor entirely framed by apocalyptic. No amount of apocalyptic disclosure can or should foreclose the future. The process of change, including my creation of an Asian American biblical hermeneutics, is always already in process. I must be willing to be attentive to this process of change rather than be too adamant about figuring or fixing its future.[35]

Notes

Chapter 1: What Is Asian American Biblical Hermeneutics?

1. Similarly, in the words of Arjun Appadurai, "diversity is typically the voice of the 'minor' whereas disciplines claim, generally successfully, the voice of the major (in all senses of the senior, the larger, the more important)" (1996: 34). What this "intellectual division of labor and . . . intellectual labor of division" (Debord 1994: 130) bring about is also sanctioned ignorance: whites have no need to learn and know what is happening in racial/ethnic minority scholarship, biblical or otherwise. John Comaroff is right when he states that "the true terror of theory . . . lies in the fact that between sameness and difference lies indifference" (Bhabha and Comaroff 2002: 45).

2. Most point to the post-1965 arrivals of immigrants from South Asia (India and Pakistan) and Southeast Asian (Cambodia, Laos, Malaysia, and Thailand) that make possible the dissolving of the "ethnic monopolizing" (Ono 1995: 71) of East Asians (particularly Chinese and Japanese Americans, but also Korean Americans) within Asian American studies. See, for example, Lowe 1996: 4–7.

3. Filipino Americans have been, for various reasons, an easily forgotten group within Asian American studies, despite their "early" arrival in Louisiana in the mid-sixteenth century. See Chuh 2003: 32–34; Espiritu 1995; and Francia and Gamalinda 1996.

4. The erasure of the hyphen from Asian American is meant to function as a visual protest against the binary separation made between Asian and American. David Palumbo-Liu, on the other hand, uses the slash or the solidus to signify the Asian American experience of being inconclusively shuttled between exclusion and inclusion (1999: 1).

5. This is why I am, in the final analysis, not in agreement with the suggestion that Asian Americans should "bas[e] the identity on politics rather than the politics on identity" (Lowe 1996: 75). I reject this suggestion not because I am not committed to the progressive beginnings of the Asian American movement (although I do, as readers will see in my later chapters, have immense problems with any appeals to

beginnings or origins); nor is it because I am afraid of offending anybody or unwilling to take a stand. I disagree with this suggestion because I think it will inevitably lead to a debate over "authenticity."

6. Readers should not forget that part of Chin's criticism of Kingston centers on Kingston's portrayal or representation of Chinese Americans, particularly Chinese American men as not only patriarchal towards Chinese American women, but also "emasculated" vis-à-vis both white men and white women.

7. In another article, Sau-ling Cynthia Wong talks about "authenticity markers" and "authenticity effects" that an Asian American writer like Amy Tan employs to cater to the desire and demand of a Western readership (1995b). It is worth noting in this regard that Amy Tan's "authenticity markers" and "authenticity effects" turned out to be inadequate to satisfy her readers' desire to "know," since her more recent book, *The Opposite of Fate,* has been advertised as "her first book of nonfiction" (2003: front flap) that supposedly covers her "real" life events and experiences. This burden of representation on the part of the racial/ethnic minority can also be understood in terms of what Albert Memmi calls "the mark of the plural" (1991: 85). For a colonized person, individuality is never allowed; in contrast, he or she is always already assumed to be a component and a copy of his or her collective group.

8. For a recent and far-reaching critique against this postulation of the racial/ethnic minority as a native informant, and thus the practice of reading his/her intellectual work as some kind of "ventriloquism of the speaking subaltern," see Spivak 1999 (255). Related to this is how studying "the native" or "the primitive" often results in a "We think, therefore they are" dictum, or the "occidentalizing-the-world" process (Gewertz and Errington 1993).

Since I have been talking about questions of academic and institutional legitimacy, I should point out Timothy Brennan's observation that this "native informant" assumption also works in the other direction (1997: 114–18). While the claim of being an insider or of uniqueness may be an effective tool or weapon to negotiate "disenfranchisement" (Golden and Toohey 1997: 3), such a claim may limit both the dissemination of knowledge ("whites cannot teach and do not need to know about minority cultures") and the number of racial/ethnic minority professors ("one native informant is sufficient to tell you all you need to know about his/her culture"). In other words, it goes back to the ideology of minoritization, or the tension between what Kwame Anthony Appiah (2005: 101) calls "a politics of recognition" (the need to legitimate a social identity) and "a recognition of politics" (the desire for participation rather than insulation).

9. Rey Chow has recently suggested, mainly through a psychoanalytic lens, that colonized people, upon "decolonization," tend to have an ongoing *ressentiment* towards not whites but members of their own racial/ethnic group (2002: 183–91). I will have more to say about this in Chapter 6, but what is important for our purposes here is how Chow's examples of such *ressentiment* tend to cluster around issues or charges of betrayal and "inauthenticity."

10. Foucault identifies three steps in disciplinary "examination": (1) the economy of visibility, (2) the field of documentation, and (3) the separation into individual(ized) "cases" (1977: 187–92). What these steps clearly show is that power really desires more than visibility; it demands legibility or transparency. Those in power may not find the presence and actions of racial/ethnic minorities agreeable, but they *must* find them knowable and readable. For Meyda Yeğenoğlu, this desire for legibility or transparency also explains the frustration of the Western gaze over the (Islamic) veil (1998: 39–67). This frustration and anxiety increase when it becomes known that veiled women can actually recognize each other with their veils on, because "[t]here are a thousand ways to wear a veil" (cited in Harrison 2003: 122).

11. Putting it in the vocabulary of Stuart Hall (1994: 393–94), identity is a matter of "becoming" as well as (or rather than) "being." In addition, I am arguing that this "becoming" identity is a product of both fortitude and fortune.

12. Related to this is Tina Chen's recent attempt to go beyond the essentialist/constructionist impasse on identity to argue that identity is performed into being through a process of impersonation (2005). Rather than doing an ethnographic study like Ganguly, Chen pursues her argument by looking at the various literary productions within Asian America.

13. Ganguly has also argued that transmission of tradition is a by-product of a community's everyday practice, and is thus a form of dynamic and experiential truth that cannot be distilled and made available in the form of CliffsNotes (2001: 141–70). If one can say the same about racial/ethnic identity, then it is rather ironic that Bible scholars, especially narrative critics who insist on the inseparability of form and content, can become rather desirous or demanding of bare-bone, CliffsNotes script on racial/ethnic identity. Chow's insight on this is also worth quoting at length: "The fact that someone—indeed, one of the same ethnicity—can be attacked for not representing it correctly (for whatever reason) is probably the best evidence for the awareness, however repressed and disavowed, that there is no unanimity, no absolute consensus on this issue; that conflict is actually a locus of reproduction and regeneration; and that even the most long-held and cherished assumptions about the ethnic culture are contestable and potentially dismantleable. Hence the criticism of treachery and betrayal, however justified it may be in some cases, paradoxically always lends credence to the very thing it is trying to condemn—namely, that the representation of the ethnic culture is a historical, discursive event, one, moreover, that is up for grabs and can never be made the exclusive and permanent propriety of any single party, not even a totalitarian regime" (Chow 2002: 189–90).

14. I am aware that several cultural critics of color—most notably, Mudimbe 1988 and Mignolo 2000—have used *gnosis* to argue for the importance of undisciplined or subordinated knowledge. Suffice to say here that I am appreciative of such work, but am referring to a different genealogy here for the purpose of a different argument.

15. In comparison to Hobsbawn, Anderson—with his focus on the mass production and distribution of novels and newspapers—does highlight the importance of literary texts and practices in the invention or construction of national community.

16. I am not suggesting a reference to *only* Asian American scholarship. I am only suggesting that Asian American scholarship be an important part of one's repertoire of reference. There is no fetishizing of my own racial/ethnic group here. In any case, a separatist stance is in the final analysis improper in my view, since (1) my understanding of identity as not inherent but contingent means that Asian American identities are always already shaped—not fully but at least partially—by the larger American society (accordingly, one can say the same about Asian American biblical interpretation), and (2) my earlier reference to the tension between recognition and participation means that both insulation and conversation are part and parcel of Asian American politics, academic and otherwise.

17. To dispel the persistent and perturbing suspicion that this is yet another "bean-counting" case of "politics" over "quality," let me underscore that all of these scholars are holders of earned Ph.D. degrees, full-time professors, and/or published authors. Two anthologies made up of some of their work are now available in Liew and Yee 2002; and Foskett and Kuan 2006.

18. Note that Gates makes a similar argument about the tradition(ing) of African American literary criticism (1988). For him, the tradition is built by African American writers repeatedly referring to and replicating each other's work in a way that is simultaneously a revision and a refiguration (what Gates calls "Signifyin[g]"). Gates also gestures towards a broader implication of his argument when he writes, "Lest this theory of criticism . . . be thought of as only black, let me admit that the implicit premise of this study is that all texts Signify upon other texts. . . . Perhaps critics of other literatures will find this theory useful" (1988: xxiv–xxv). I will argue that this broader implication includes not only its applicability to Asian Americans (see particularly Chapter 7 of this book), but also Eng's connection between canonicity and citational repetitions.

19. A more significant and difficult question is why such cross-referencing has not taken place among Asian American Bible scholars. Is it because "our" number is still too small? Is it because "we" are not writing and publishing enough (if so, one must proceed to investigate its institutional and structural causes)? Is it because "we" have internalized the minoritizing dynamics of both society and academy so much that, when it comes to publication, "we" choose to interact and exchange only with "established" white scholars in the field?

20. I hope my featuring of disagreements here will clarify that my discomfort with who/what arises not out of a fear of conflict or confrontation, but my resistance against making arguments or disagreements in terms of "authenticity." Argue we must, but we should do so on basis other than that of "(in)authenticity."

21. I hope this last point about the "canonical quota of one" shows that my

suggestion to invent and legitimize Asian American biblical hermeneutics through repetition of citation, or re-presenting repeatedly without being referential, has the added advantage of featuring the politics of recognition, both in terms of academic subjects and racial/ethnic subjectivity. I am aware that citing, referencing, and engaging the work of others may potentially turn into a competitive "one-upmanship." There is, however, no foolproof method. All we have are less or more difficult answers.

Since what I said about identity being the product and production of everyday practice and hence becoming recognizable only in hindsight is also applicable to this citational invention of a tradition, one's choice of whom to cite and whom not to refer to becomes a subject or an object of suspicion. Like any "canonical" lists (biblical, racial/ethnic, or otherwise), the list(s) of reference within Asian American biblical hermeneutics must be consistently and insistently problematized, revised, enlarged, and pluralized. Like any other traditions, the tradition being invented for Asian American biblical hermeneutics may also be reformed or revolutionized. Not to be lost in this discussion on the selective nature of reference and citation are the (differing) levels of access that function as both a cause and an effect of such selections.

This discussion on the politics of recognition will not be complete without the reminder that even if the citational invention of tradition makes Asian American biblical hermeneutics legitimate on a discursive level, one must simultaneously work on the institutional level to make sure that Asian American biblical hermeneutics comes into consideration as decisions are made regarding curriculum, research programs, and faculty hiring and tenuring.

22. The importance of repeated performance (which emphasizes agency) and performativity (which emphasizes sociocultural script or dictation) for the constitution of identity is arguably most thoroughly discussed in the work of Judith Butler. See, for example, Butler 1990; and Butler 1993.

23. I say "arguably" because "Signifyin(g)" seems to double for Gates as not only the practice by which an African American literary tradition is made visible and legitimate, but also the content of that very tradition.

24. Bhabha himself does present the "performative" and the "pedagogical" as simultaneous operations, but only to proceed to argue—in his customary way—that this simultaneity presents a splitting because of the contradictory and "contested . . . double-time" (1990a: 297). One biblical scholar who does a bit of such archiving work is R. S. Sugirtharajah. See, for instance, his thoughts on the importance and value of such work in Sugirtharajah 2003: 93–94.

25. The "colonial factor" refers not only to the power move that turns parts into a whole, but also that such turning and definition are often the handiwork of the colonial masters. Nguyen, commenting on Sui Sin Far's "search" for her racial/ ethnic identity in the late nineteenth century ("[w]henever I have the opportunity I steal away to the library and read every book I can find on China and the Chinese";

1995: 222), makes the insightful observation that what she "learns about her 'self' and her history [comes] through books [that are] presumably written by Western orientalists" (2002: 42).

26. Note that, for Bhabha, the splitting or fragmentation of a (national) community is precisely because of the simultaneous but contradictory emphasis of a "pedagogical" representation that implies essentialism and past dictates, and a "performative" repetition that features construction and present agency. One may also compare Bhabha's "performative" and "pedagogical" representation to Paul Gilroy's notions of "routes" and "roots" (1993).

27. According to Radhakrishnan, questions of identity and community are the "cornerstones of diasporic studies" (2001: 259). Kathryn Tanner has also argued for an understanding of Christian culture and community on this alternative basis of engagement rather than agreement; see Tanner 1997.

28. That is to say, legitimacy must not be sought at the cost of uncritically surrendering to dominant or traditional canonicity, whether in terms of referential politics required of racial/ethnic minorities or what is considered to be the acceptable mode of operation in biblical hermeneutics. We Asian Americans need to establish our own claim as Bible scholars and critique the discipline of biblical studies simultaneously.

29. Chuh makes a similar suggestion that one read Asian American literature "as theory"; see Chuh 2003: 16–20. For Chuh, this hermeneutical emphasis also has the advantage of dislodging methodological emphasis from issues of identity and authenticity (2001: 293n7). Another way to approach these questions (not discussed by Chuh) is by way of Pierre Bourdieu's "doxa" (1977; 1990) and John Guillory's "paradoxy" as an extension of Bourdieu (1993: 137–75). Bourdieu's doxa is deep belief that informs one's habitus but is itself beyond declaration, because (unlike orthodoxy or heterodoxy) doxa is beyond controversy and is simply assumed as the way things are. Doxa is thus a construction of truth that is not perceived or received as a construction. For Guillory, paradoxy refers to a (literary) gesture that indirectly points to rather than directly declaring the constructed aspects of doxa. The implications of these concepts for what I am suggesting here should not require any more elaboration, except I do want to point out that while Bourdieu tends to present doxa and habitus as a one-directional influence, I would suggest that habitus (a set of *repetitive* actions governed by doxa for Bourdieu) can also exert a change and an influence on doxa. After all, my argument is that a practice of citational repetition (a habitus), when coupled with a form of paradoxy (reading with and as theory), may both reveal and revise doxa (assumed understandings regarding the goals and practices of biblical hermeneutics). These references to Chuh and Guillory should further indicate that "reading with and as theory" has already made some headway in the broader world of literary/cultural studies even if it has yet to be explicitly articulated within biblical studies. Unlike ideological criticism of the Bible (as it is conventionally practiced), for example, reading the Bible with and as theory (as we will see) does not necessarily imply a negative view of the biblical text.

30. Similar to my earlier emphasis on bypassing authenticity in inventing and legitimating Asian American biblical hermeneutics, reading the Bible with and as theory will also think of interpretation less in terms of accuracy (whether one is reading a text "correctly"), but more in terms of truth production and power deployment (how a text seems to construct certain truth claims and truth effects). If one accepts the contention that to see through power one must learn to view its construction and operation in multiple, overlapping, and contrasting situations, one will further see the significance of the Bible for this purpose. The Bible, as a library of texts rather than a single text, provides divergent wor(l)ds on and for the deployment of power to dominate and/or liberate.

31. This may be a suitable place to explain my use of the word "medi(t)ation" in the subtitle. While "mediation" points to both the mediated dynamics of meaning/reality and the intervening potential of biblical hermeneutics, "medi(t)ation" signifies the importance of theory for in(ter)vention, or reflection as a(n-other) form of action. The word grasps also, of course, the tension I sense in thinking and talking about Asian American biblical hermeneutics, which I addressed in the section, "Before My (Ad)Venture."

32. This doubled view of theory is one important strategy to avoid the doubled trap of exoticism and Eurocentrism that I will identify in Chapter 2. Again, I do not think one can afford to let the—in my view, valid and valuable—concern to challenge Eurocentrism to deteriorate into some kind of a "pure authenticity." If anything, "Asian American" seems to imply a duality or even a multiplicity rather than a kind of separatist singularity. The same is true of, for instance, postcolonial theory, which is often "facilitated by . . . creative dialogues between Western theory and postcolonial contexts" (McLeod 2000: 198). Also relevant and helpful is Chuh's conception of Asian American studies as "collaborative antagonism," where "collaborative [functions] in the doubled sense of working together and working subversively against, and [is] antagonistic in the ways in which diverse approaches to knowledge critique and identify each other's limits (2003: 28).

33. My suggestion of these three sites is indebted to and inspired by Inderpal Grewal, who suggests that South Asian American politics is shaped by three linkages: nationalist politics of contemporary India, colonial discourses, and new affiliations within an immigrant context (1993).

34. Globalization and transnationalism have caused scholars in various fields to question if nation-states are adequate units of analysis, including so-called ethnic studies (like Asian American studies), so-called area studies (like Asian studies), and women's studies. For examples of this trend within Asian and Asian American studies (and the shifting of the latter from "ethnic" to "diasporic" studies), see the many informative essays in Chuh and Shimakawa 2001b; for examples of this in women's studies, see Grewal and Kaplan 1994; Alexander and Mohanty 1997; and Mohanty 2003. As one can see by the authors or editors involved, the line between Asian/American studies and women's studies is itself permeable. For a more suspicious reading of this transnational or cosmopolitan emphasis, see Brennan 1997.

It is worth noting that for some, this transnational linkage has in fact always been there; thus the change from cultural nationalism within Asian American studies to transnationalism is more one of degree than one of kind. One important example is, of course, how the Asian American movement was motivated both by the struggle for national civil rights and by the protest against the imperialist policies of the United States in Vietnam (Mazumdar 1991; see also Nakanishi 1976).

35. An example of an Asian/American biblical scholar who writes and publishes in both Asia and the United States—and in both Chinese and English—is Yeo. For examples of Yeo's work in Chinese, see Yeo 1995; and Yeo 2001.

That is not to say that there are no hesitations being expressed regarding the conflation of Asia and Asian America (both, by the way, are homogenizing terms that cover over a wide range of multiplicity and difference; see Lewis and Wigen 1997), the potential colonization of one field of studies by another, or the possibility that a mutated form of biological or racial/ethnic determinism may (re)emerge (as in "wherever he is, a Chinaman is always a Chinaman, and will forever be a Chinaman"). There is, however, literally a world of difference between making distinctions and insisting on total separation. One should also wonder if the rigid separation of Asian Americans from Asians is not also partly related to "our" own internalization of racist or orientalist views of Asians (Kondo 2001: 32–33, 36; Chuh 2003: 88). Not to be forgotten is also the thought that if Asians have come to America, America has also continued to be present in Asia (Sakai 1989: 113–14; K.-H. Chen 2001: 176–77).

36. Here is an even more daring statement by another Asian American scholar regarding the objective of Asian American (biblical) studies: "to announce and implement dialogism and reciprocity of influence such that the Asianization of America will be perceived as equally valuable as the reterritorialization of Asia in America" (Radhakrishnan 2001: 258).

37. One pragmatic (and ideological) issue that helps block this "traffic" is language. Without denying the fluidity of identity and language, the phenomenon of so-called global English has certainly made non-English scholarship (biblical or otherwise) increasingly less accessible to "English-only" readers. For a more in-depth discussion of this language question, see Spivak 2003: 1–23.

One should keep in mind that the question of language also needs to be raised within Asian American biblical hermeneutics, even if—or perhaps especially—in separation from its exchange with Asian biblical hermeneutics. It should be problematic to think, given the transnational and bilingual scholarship of someone like Yeo, that only publications in English should/could be considered to be Asian American biblical hermeneutics. Doing so will in effect equate Asian American with English-speaking, and English-speaking alone. For a discussion of this language question within (Asian) America, see McKay and S. C. Wong 1988.

38. Or, in the words of Chuh, "By claiming ownership of U.S. national identity, Asian Americanists must also then claim responsibility for the cultural and material imperialism of this nation" (2001: 278).

39. Coalition building is even more significant in light of what Grewal and Kaplan call "scattered hegemonies" (1994). What seems important to add is that such "scattered hegemonies" are actually at work *both* nationally *and* transnationally. It is these "scattered hegemonies" *within* national boundaries that cause different racial/ethnic groups to work at cross-purposes. An example is how African Americans are mobilized to oppose bilingual education and social services for immigrants, while Asian Americans are encouraged to vote against affirmative action (Lipsitz 2001: 298).

40. If the Chin–Kingston controversy is sufficient to illustrate the question of gender, let me point to the possibility that the interethnic conflicts within the racial(ized) group known as Asian American may actually be covering up a class struggle, since "economic inequality within Asian America has often seem to be a function of ethnic difference" (Nguyen 2002: 16).

Chapter 2: Reading with Yin Yang Eyes

1. Throughout this chapter, "Chinese American" refers to any person of Chinese descent who identifies himself or herself as an American. In my opinion, any additional specifications are but attempts to name and to exclude. The work of the self-proclaimed "Chinatown Cowboy," Frank Chin, who presumes Chinese American to be male, U.S.-born, English-speaking, and heterosexual, should be a good warning against any criteria for "authenticity" (see Lowe 1996: 75–76; S. C. Wong 1997: 40).

2. I invoke Lacan here, not because I think that his branch of psychoanalysis is universally valid, but because I want to argue for (and demonstrate) the reality of inter-cultural history on the part of Chinese Americans, as well as our ability to take on the high theory of the geopolitical West. Perhaps more important, as I will argue in greater detail in Chapter 5, psychoanalysis's so-called ahistoricism is itself contextual. What is key for me is not the binarism between "presentism" and "historicism," but how one may learn to use contemporary theory to open one's eyes to different signification at play in a text *without* overlooking the historical contexts from which the text in question and the theory in use emerged respectively.

3. Very interesting and nuanced readings of these two "texts" can be found in R. G. Lee 1999: 91–97, 127–36.

4. As yet another demonstration of inter-cultural mixings, let me point to the Hollywood movie written and directed by M. Light Shyamalan that features Bruce Willis but revolves around a young white boy who has a "sixth sense," or an ability to see dead people. Yin yang is an influential Chinese philosophy or cosmology that emphasizes an organic, fluid, and harmonious relationship between apparent opposites, like female and male, darkness and light, or death and life. A perfect circle that is formed by wavering halves of two opposing extremes conventionally represents this understanding. What is significant about this symbol is that it signifies a continual flow between extremes, as seen by the meandering line in the middle as well as

the presence of one extreme in another. For those who may be interested in reading more about this philosophy or cosmology, see Yeo 1998: 18–21.

5. Note that I am using the word "business" intentionally to denote the economic and materialistic entanglements within the academy.

6. I do want to note, however, that since the dawning of global capitalism, Chinese and other Asian Americans are once again scapegoated for almost everything that seems to go wrong with this country. The most recent and obvious examples are the so-called campaign finance scandal of 1996, the so-called China spy scandal surrounding the nuclear scientist Wen Ho Lee in 1999, and yet another espionage scandal surrounding the Muslim military chaplain James Yee in 2003. If economy, technology, and military are key to globalization, they also become suspect areas through which Chinese—who are by (racialized) definition "foreign" and "alien"—would attempt to infiltrate, pollute, and/or betray the national body of the United States (see also Chuh and Shimakawa 2001a: 1–3). Other examples of alarm include hate crimes against Chinese Americans (like the notorious murders of Vincent Chin in 1982 and Jim Loo in 1989) and a series of Hollywood movies that appear keen to revive the whole idea of a "Yellow Peril" (like *Rising Sun, Falling Down,* and *Menace II Society*). See R. G. Lee 1999: 204–22.

7. Note that my statement here does not dismiss the importance of understanding how specific forms of containment emerge out of specific historical and materialistic occasions. Both Robert G. Lee (1999) and David Palumbo-Liu (1999) have done a splendid job in tracing the emergence of different stereotypical images of Asian Americans in various periods of U.S. history. My concern here is to look for commonalities, which I hope to justify by the fact that these stereotypes and forms of marginalization have, despite their specific beginnings, lingered on rather than disappeared with time.

8. This problem is especially acute in the realm of biblical studies. To my knowledge, there are currently no more than twenty Chinese American Bible scholars who have a full-time, tenure-track, or tenured teaching position in this country. An excellent example of how Chinese Americans have been marginalized within academia can be found in Amy Ling's personal experience as both a student and a researcher (1990: xi–xiii). In that book, Ling also argues that, for Chinese Americans, publication does not depend solely on the "quality" of a work but on many external factors. For example, she suggests that in order for a Chinese American's work to be published, the United States must view China favorably as a potential political ally rather than as an enemy at the time of publication (1990: xiv–xv, 17–20, 85).

9. This is the point that Chin tries to bring out by what he calls "food pornography" or "cultural pornography" (1988: 3); see also Chin et al. 1974: xxii. For those who may be interested in such "exotically different" publications, Ling has provided us with an excellent bibliography under the general heading "alien observer" or "tourist guide" literature (1990: 15–16, 70). What is and is not "exotically different" (in other words, neo-orientalist) is, of course, debatable (see S. C. Wong 1997: 50–52); also debatable is whether such "exotically different" materials are imme-

diately dismissible or potentially disruptive (see T. Chen 2005: 77–78). I have not given a specific example of stripping racial traces, since this maneuver is arguably more easily understood. For those who want to read more about this, however, see David Leiwei Li's discussion of the experiences and work of David Wong Louie in Li 1998: 165–73.

10. The binarism of Asian/American or freezing/melting can mutate into various forms, like culture/geography or ethnic/national (Ono 1995: 69–70). Frantz Fanon, of course, pointed out over forty years ago that "nativism" and "assimilationism" are apparent opposites operating under the same logic of colonialism; he writes: "By its very structure, colonialism is regionalist and separatist. Colonialism does not simply state the existence of tribes; it also reinforces and separates them" (1963: 94). This is also what I see to be the gist of Lowe's celebrated essay on Asian American differences (1996: 60–83). This tricky operation of binarism can also be understood in Lacanian terms, in which the central concern of the self/other binarism is not difference, but the sameness of the self (Lacan 1977: 1–7). Or, as Robert Lee demonstrates, people who argue for and those who argue against imperialistic expansions may actually share the same basic racist orientation (1999: 137–40).

11. For the term *huaqiao*, see S. C. Wong 1997: 39–40. The term *zhuoxing* refers to the long pole that many Chinese workers and farmers used to carry things in the past. The pole, hollow on the ends but solid in the center, gives the illusion that an object may be passed through the pole from end to end. However, because of the solid center, this is not possible. The parallel drawn by this "nickname" is that one will have a tough time communicating with, or getting through to a second- or third-generation Chinese American, who appears to know both Chinese and English (the hollow ends), but in actuality knows them only half-well. The term "bananas" should be self-explanatory; it refers to someone who is "yellow on the outside, but white on the inside." See also L. L. Wang 1995 for what he calls the "dual domination" of assimilation and loyalty demanded of Chinese Americans from both sides of the Pacific.

12. According to Chow, Chinese from mainland China are generally viewed by the geopolitical West as the most "authentic," those from Hong Kong as the least "pure," and those from Taiwan somewhere in between (1991: 94).

13. I am borrowing here the vocabulary of Caren Kaplan, who warns against separatism as a formation of "theoretical tourism" (1990: 361). An example of one literary theorist who seems to be advocating separatism at times is Henry Louis Gates, Jr., who goes so far as to advocate an exclusion of any methodology or theory of study that originates outside one's racial/ethnic traditions (1990). For a good rebuttal of such a position, see Ling 1987: 154.

14. The problem of a rigid identity politics, even in the name of race/ethnicity, has also been scrutinized lately by Paul Gilroy. Gilroy's last two books (2000; 2005) have both been critiques of what he calls "purity seekers" (2005: 151), or how identity politics may and have become hindrances to a humanism that cuts across national and/or racial/ethnic lines. See also Kwame Anthony Appiah's argument

against the "Medusa Syndrome" (a gaze that turns to stone or, in my language, freezes and fossilizes) and for a "rooted cosmopolitanism," in Appiah 2005.

15. I am using the pronoun "me" rather than "us" here to indicate that I do not presume to speak for all Chinese Americans, since we are diverse in terms of class, gender, sexuality, nativity, language, citizenship, age, religion, occupation, geographical location, and political affiliation. This acknowledgment, however, should not be taken as an espousal of a rugged individualism, because the main reason for this chapter is precisely my desire to submit my ideas for a communal discussion.

16. Since my focus here is more on Chinese American biblical hermeneutics and less on Mark, I will devote only limited space to this Gospel text. For my fuller treatment of this Gospel, see Liew 1999. In fact, this chapter is partly my "second-step" effort to think through in a systematic and sustained manner, within the context of Chinese America, what I have done with Mark in that earlier monograph.

17. In contrast to Bhabha, who presents "mimicry" as mainly a "menace" (1994: 88) to the colonizer, I am using "mimicry" to refer to a reinscription or a duplication of colonial ideology by the colonized. This actually brings up a need that has been suggested by many within postcolonial and ethnic studies; namely, the need to give greater specificity to the term "hybridity" (which, along with "ambivalence," is central to Bhabha's positive use of "mimicry") rather than assuming that all hybrids are necessarily and equally liberating. See, for example, Burton 1998; Loomba 1998: 143–51; and Palumbo-Liu 1995b: 59.

18. For example, see Phillips 1990. I say that the emphasis on aesthetic experimentation and indeterminate free play is obsolete because a second generation of deconstructionists has politicized deconstruction by applying it to specific struggles for liberation; see Clayton 1993: 50–59. A similar shift is detectable in biblical scholarship that is associated with poststructuralism in general or Jacques Derrida in particular. This is arguably best illustrated in the changing or evolving scholarship of Stephen D. Moore (1992; 1996; 2001; 2004).

19. An almost immediate response to the denial or problematization of biblical authority is that one is then no longer working within the so-called Christian tradition (in the singular). However, as I have argued in the last chapter, tradition is an invention (Hobsbawm and Ranger 1983). Also important in this regard is Paul Ricoeur's distinctions between traditionality, tradition, and tradition-s (1984–88: 3.219–29). For me, Christian culture, like any other culture, is an ongoing process of invention and modification. Mary Ann Tolbert has helpfully suggested that biblical authority itself is a rather recent "invention," and that a difference be made between discarding the Bible and disputing biblical authority (1998). I should also mention in passing the Lacanian emphasis that "*[s]ome* resistance is a sign of taking an idea or proposition seriously" (Grosz 1990: 11; emphasis in original). For Lacan, the purpose of reading Sigmund Freud "is not to be able to imitate him but rather to discover the principles that govern his discourse" (Payne 1993: 57; see also Lacan 1977: 8, 31–34). In fact, as Jonathan Dollimore suggests, the vigor of contempo-

rary psychoanalysis is built upon people's honest struggles with and *against* Freud (1998: 272). In my opinion, if we have the courage to give up fetishizing (to use another psychoanalytic concept) the Bible and using it to ventriloquize our views, we may actually invigorate Christianity by being able to discuss openly with each other the "whats," "hows," and "whys" we desire in our Christian lives (see also Weeks 1995). Although Mark Poster is talking about computers, what he says about becoming subjected to one's subject of study is also relevant to our discussion here (1990: 146–49).

20. See also Sollors 1986: 81–86 for the relationship between the New Testament and the "melting-pot" language of both J. Hector St. John de Crevecoeur and Israel Zangwill.

21. As Loomba and Orkin remind us, "the concept of 'race' not only shifts in meaning . . . but its connotations also vary *within* each historical context. . . . Both *religion* and colour can be understood as central but fluctuating markers of racial, national and cultural difference" (1998a: 13; emphasis mine). For the process of racialization in the United States, see Omi and Winant 1994.

22. A dramatic example of this Chinese/Christendom binarism can be found in the August 16, 1999, newsletter from the conservative but "popular" Christian clergyman John MacArthur (available in excerpts at http://www.aamdomain.com/cac). Claiming that his information was based on the *New York Times,* MacArthur suggested that divine providence "preserved the New World for the spread of Christianity" when an internal power struggle broke out in China in 1424 and kept the Chinese admiral Zheng He and his navy from reaching the Americas. According to MacArthur, God did this because China "has always been—and continues to be—a bastion of spiritual darkness."

23. Again, Robert Lee (dis)misses this important reference to the Bible, as he reads the story as one of "racial transgression . . . framed as a *moral* transgression" (1999: 95; emphasis mine). For a nuanced reading of this story in terms of race, gender, *and* sexuality (since Ah Wee, the female murder victim, had dressed and lived publicly as a man), see Okihiro 2001: 81–83.

24. As Walter Benjamin teaches us, there is a politics (as well as a hermeneutics) that can only be "nourished by the image of enslaved ancestors rather than that of liberated grandchildren" (1968: 260). See also Taylor 1998: 130–32.

25. Allow me to illustrate this dynamics from a personal experience. In the PBS program "Chinese Americans" (August 1999), religious diversity and religious tolerance are featured as characteristics of Chinese America. Immediately after the broadcast, I received an E-mail through my subscription of a Chinese American Christians discussion list (http://www.aamdomain.com/cac). The sender of this message suggests that one should read Romans to correct the "misguided" emphasis on religious diversity and toleration among Chinese Americans. Considering the "Christian nation" rhetoric and how the Bible has been used to racialize and colonize people within the United States, I have serious doubts if an endorsement of

biblical authority will help bring about much liberating change. Once again, location matters immensely. Even assuming the same commitment to progressive social change, one may still view and use biblical authority very differently if one is a Chinese American Christian in the United States or a Dalit Christian in India.

26. The word "often" is crucial, and thus should not be overlooked. Chinese Americans do not all occupy the same class position; among us are factory and restaurant workers as well as business executives and professionals.

27. Mark's treatment of these two particular issues ("scapegoating" and violence) has become the topic of two monographs that view Mark much more positively than I do here. While Robert G. Hamerton-Kelly (1994) uses René Girard's theory of the "scapegoat" and Robert R. Beck (1996) depends on Gene Sharp's "nonviolent action," both argue that Mark stops rather than stays on the course of violence. Both readings are, from my perspective, undercut by the way they (dis)miss the apocalyptic violence promised against Jesus' opponents in, say, the parable of the wicked tenants (12:9). I must further point out that Hamerton-Kelly, by seeing Jesus as the only scapegoat within Mark's narrative, does not only write off the way Mark may be scapegoating the Jewish authorities for the evil of Roman imperialists; he may also be guilty of anti-Jewish implications by emphasizing that Mark provides a necessary corrective to the scapegoating violence of Hebrew Scripture.

28. Examples of Jesus' constrained movements include his being "sent out" to the desert by the Holy Spirit (1:12), his undesired retreat into the outskirts of towns because of some unsolicited free publicity (1:40–45), his being asked to leave Gerasene almost immediately upon arrival (5:1–20), his double change of plans after the disciples return from a mission (6:30–44), his frustrated attempt to hide out in Tyre (7:24–27), and his divinely ordained trip to Jerusalem (8:31). For examples regarding Jesus' problems with his disciples and opponents, see Kingsbury 1989: 63–117.

29. This politics of alliance is, in my view, one good way to theorize and problematize the often complex relations between the freeing and confining aspects within any single progressive endeavor. As I tried to indicate in reference to the concept of biblical authority, a great deal hinges on whether one is willing to critique one's own authority and refuse the temptation to idealize (Kondo 1995: 96–97).

30. One should also remember in this regard that as objects of white gaze, Chinese Americans are generally feminized and categorized as a deviant "third sex" (see R. G. Lee 1999: 83–105). I am not encouraging here a "benevolent" attempt to include women, but arguing that women define my understanding of Chinese American resistance and my use of yin yang eyes. Lowe has further argued that women of color have done the best job in theorizing how social subjects are "sites of a variety of differences . . . constructed across a multiplicity of social relations" (1996: 74).

31. Although, linguistically speaking, there is no way to identify if the second-person plural pronoun "you" (16:7) is masculine or feminine (or both), the fact that the alluded promise of a future reunion in Galilee is given by Jesus to his male disciples right after their private, "for-male-only" Passover together (14:26–28) should

be enough evidence to argue that the women are not included in the second-person plural pronoun of 16:7.

32. This endorsement of interdisciplinary studies should not be taken as an uncritical embrace of everything that other disciplines have to offer. After all, Palumbo-Liu is also very critical of Asian Americanists who adopt postcolonial and postmodern theories in a predominantly aesthetic way that denies historical and materialistic specificities (1995a).

33. I am aware that some Markan scholars (Myers 1992: 190–94; Waetjen 1989: 115–17) understand the demon's name "Legion" as a Latin term that refers to the Roman armies, and thus the entire pericope to be a coded anti-Roman or anti-colonial protest (see also Moore 2004: 134–38). For them, then, the demoniac's condition is comparable to the "mental disorder" that Fanon links to colonialism (1963: 249–310). Without disputing the evil of colonialism or necessarily Fanon's own reading, I would like to question if we should keep pathologizing a non-unified self or keep condemning "children of colonialism" to some form of schizophrenia as individual or personal sickness. I shall return to this question in Chapter 6.

In addition to calling for greater specificity, both Dollimore (1996) and Palumbo-Liu (1995b: 59–60) have questioned the effectiveness of assuming a hybrid or multiple identity as a strategy of resistance. Actually, both wonder if the talk of hybridity or multiplicity is but a form of "wishful thinking." As a response, I will admit, first of all, that one's use of hybridity or multiplicity should indeed be thought through in context-specific and task-specific ways. Second, I would suggest that hybridity or multiplicity does not *guarantee* results; but then no strategy does. Third, I would say that if wishful thinking is in any way linked to the power of human imagination, I will pronounce myself an unashamed advocate of it (see Lorde 1984). Note also that in her attempt to argue for the continuing importance of "claiming America" within Asian American studies (an attempt that I agree with and support), Sau-ling Wong has also questioned if this emphasis on hybridity or multiplicity is an upper-class privilege (1995a: 14–15).

34. I am somewhat surprised that in his struggle with a similar problem, DuttaAhmed ends up suggesting a tactic of "absence" or "invisibility" (1996: 345–48) when he himself argues in the beginning of his article that "negation of authorship is a luxury we cannot afford just yet" (1996: 338). I would argue that negation of presence is also a luxury that we cannot afford, thus a ghostly or phantom-like presence is a more effective strategy to counteract the problem of representational fixity that DuttaAhmed correctly identifies.

35. A fine reading of this film is again provided by Robert Lee (1999: 196–203). Although he does not comment on this film's similar emphasis on Chinese American eyes, he does provide a context to help account for the emergence of both *Blade Runner* and *Year of the Dragon* in the 1980s; see R. G. Lee 1999: 180–91.

36. My contention here is, of course, indebted to feminist standpoint theory; see, for example, S. Harding 2004.

Chapter 3: Ambiguous Admittance

1. To continue my questioning, in a note to chapter 2, of the conventional practice of pathologizing schizophrenia, Tina Chen has recently suggested a fascinating reading of Nieh's schizophrenic protagonist, Mulberry/Peach, as a performance against national and cultural insistence on fixity and singularity (2005: 89–112). In addition, one may look at the more abstract and ambitious reading of schizophrenia in Deleuze and Guattari 1983.

2. Sau-ling Wong (2001) has helpfully pointed out that even the novel itself is not a single entity, given its publication history of having appeared in various forms (serialization, translations, and editions with multiple excisions and additions).

3. Calling the figure of an Asian spy (for instance, Earl Derr Biggers' Charlie Chan) a "cultural convention," Tina Chen repeatedly argues that the construction of this convention is connected to the way Asians are racialized in this country, not only as "foreign," but also as "sneaky," "secretive," and "inscrutable" (2005: xviii, 18, 178–79).

4. For arguably the most influential attempt to reconstruct the community behind John's Gospel, see R. E. Brown 1979. Despite recent emphasis that language *constitutes* reality, the deep-rooted understanding that language reflects reality dies hard. For example, Sharon H. Ringe, in her study of John, proceeds to spend an entire chapter describing (or more accurately, inscribing) the "language," "location," and "social composition" of the Johannine community (1999: 10–28) almost immediately after a brief comment that "performative language . . . builds . . . community" (1999: 2). Likewise, Adeline Fehribach ends her fine analysis by briefly questioning whether reconstructions of an egalitarian Johannine community honestly take into consideration John's androcentric and patriarchal characterization of women (1998: 178–79). What is at issue for her then is the result, not the nature, of such reconstructionist projects. Lest I be misunderstood, I will clarify that my resistance to historical reconstructions does not mean that I advocate an ahistorical understanding or practice an acontextual interpretation of John. In fact, I think that every interpretation is contextual; the difference is whether an interpreter is self-reflexive about the contextual nature of his or her interpretation.

5. It is important to point out that, for Anthony Cohen, this shift of emphasis (from our reconstruction of John's community to John's construction of community) should not be understood simplistically as a shift from an etic view of the outsider to an emic view of an insider, because any singular emic view may itself be an etic view of an interpreter (1985: 72).

6. Admittedly, Anderson's work has a narrower focus than Anthony Cohen's. Anderson is interested in the emergence of nation-states since the end of the eighteenth century, but I believe his thesis that imagination brings about a sense of (be)longing is still applicable to other forms of communities from an earlier time. This is particularly so given (1) Anderson's own account of the many parallels between the imaginings of earlier religious and later nationalist communities (1991: 10–19), and (2) the

parallel between Anderson's emphasis on nation as a "non-face-to-face" community (1991: 6) and John's concern to construct a community that transcends geographical and temporal distances (11:52; 17:20–26). Anderson's "imagined communities" thesis is, of course, not without problems. In fact, the thesis seems to have a colonizing (under)current that attributes the "models" of imagining nations solely to Europe and the Americas (1991: 67–82). For an attempt to decolonize Anderson, see Chatterjee 1996.

7. In his last chapter, Craig R. Koester does address the relationship between John's symbolic construction and community construction (1995: 220–56). His insights into this topic, however, are muddled by his attempt to reconstruct the Johannine community behind the Gospel (thus the chapter ends up demonstrating a "mix-and-match" attitude toward the historical-critical, the literary-rhetorical, and the social-scientific approach to John). This illustrates, yet once more, the hegemonic power of the "text-as-window" mentality, because Koester actually prefaces his reconstruction with warnings against such endeavors (1995: 221–23). Since most studies on community within New Testament scholarship continue to focus on definition, structure, and social fact (see, for example, Richard S. Ascough's survey on such studies of Pauline churches [1998]), it is worth pointing out that, for Anthony Cohen, moving to focus on the symbolic construction of community is a helpful shift to bring to the foreground the long-neglected questions of culture and meaning.

8. The Bible has, of course, been a galvanizing force within U.S. national and nationalist politics for a long time; see Sollors 1986: 40–65. For an insightful account that has relevance for the dynamics of "internal colonization" within the United States in both the past and the present, see Priscilla Wald 1993. "Internal" and "external" colonizations are, of course, related and provide fuel for each other; see, for example, Anderson 1991: 83–111; and Rowe 1994.

9. Reading John as a nationalist narrative in the context of Roman colonization, Jean K. Kim has not only suggested that the community John attempts to construct is a national one, but also critiqued how John exploits and, in turn, enforces the "mother-nation" ideology by featuring Jesus' mother precisely, and only, at moments of crisis in the national community to help bring about national solidarity (2004: 61–89, 169–94).

10. Community is also what Jan A. Du Rand seems to mean when he concludes that John's entire plot has to do with "God's commitment through *relationships* for salvation renewal" (1998: 17; emphasis mine). John's connection between crucifixion, glorification, and community is also rather intricate. Crucifixion is glorification for both God and Jesus in John, because it manifests Jesus' unity with God, and this manifestation of unity will result in a community that also manifests the unity between God and Jesus. This double manifestation will, in turn, be a witness that leads to belief, and thus even a larger community and a greater glorification (13:31–35; 17:11, 20–23).

11. Two projects that deal with similar issues (racial or ethnic communities in the United States) end up taking these opposing emphases regarding the reason

behind the formation of such communities. For Michael Omi and Howard Winant, racial formation is a result of domination (1994). For Paul Spickard and W. Jeffrey Burroughs, ethnic community is the result of internal group processes (1999). The difference between race and ethnicity is, of course, itself significant in accounting for this difference. As we shall see in John's mixing of consent and descent, religion and race/ethnicity have a rather curious relationship. While Anderson talks about the practice of "ethnicizing" religion with the example that Malays were equated as Islamic during the days of colonial Malaya (1991: 170), Wayne A. Meeks has also suggested that early Christians were often ridiculed as "the third race" (1993: 9). I will have more to say about this complicated relationship in Chapters 5 and 6, but for those who want to explore further, Sollors 1986: 21, 54–56 and Buell 2005 are two good places to start.

12. Many have pointed out the relationship between this episode and John 13, where we find Jesus washing the disciples' feet as well as Judas departing to betray Jesus. For a more affirmative reading of this connection or parallel, see Ford 1997: 136, 140; for a more suspicious reading, see J. K. Kim 2004: 162–67.

13. I have chosen to use the Greek transliteration not only because of the anti-Jewish implications of the conventional translation of *Ioudaioi* as "Jews" (see, for instance, Reinhartz 2001:15), but also because of the recent work by Obery M. Hendricks, Jr. (1995) and Daniel Boyarin (2002). According to both, *Ioudaioi* refers to an elitist group within but not representative of Israel; as a result, John's named attack on the *Ioudaioi* does not imply a disidentification with all Jews or all of Israel on his part. See also Reinhartz 1998: 254–55.

14. Although John also names "the chief priests" and "Pharisees," and sometimes distinguishes them as the leaders of the *Ioudaioi* (3:1; 11:45–47), he basically groups them together by giving them common perceptions and actions against Jesus. For example, both groups call Jesus a "sinner" (9:13–16, 18–24), try to arrest/kill him (10:31–39; 11:45–50, 53, 57), harass his followers (9:22; 12:10, 42), and finally demand that Pilate crucify him (19:6, 14–16). The most telling sign of their interchangeability may be the way in which John identifies those who send people to interrogate John the Baptizer first as the *Ioudaioi* (1:19), and later as "the Pharisees" (1:24).

15. John says that the "crowd" is, for example, afraid of the *Ioudaioi* (7:12–13), but uses the same verb, "astonished" *(thamazō)*, in the same episode to describe the response to Jesus on the part of both groups (7:15, 20–21). Correspondingly, while the "chief priests and Pharisees" accuse the "crowd" of being ignorant of the law (7:49), their own knowledge of the law is immediately shown to be inadequate (7:50–51; C. R. Koester 1995: 60–61). Depending on how one interprets the genitive, one may well argue that John is identifying the "crowd" with the *Ioudaioi* with his curious turn of phrase, "the great crowd of the *Ioudaioi*" (12:9). As I mentioned earlier, John makes it clear that Jesus distances himself from both groups (11:54; 12:34–37).

16. Craig Koester suggests that some of John the Baptizer's disciples also demonstrate their membership in this "worldly" group by virtue of their jealous resentment of Jesus' popularity (3:25–26, 31; 4.1); see C. R. Koester 1995: 165.

17. "Fortress mentality" is the term that Philip E. Hammond and James D. Hunter use to describe the outlook of evangelical college students in the United States (1984; cited in Busto 1999: 180). Craig Koester (1995: 224) also has a brief but good discussion of this mentality in John through the work of John Elliott (1994).

18. Anderson argues for the political implications of linguistic boundary by pointing to the "massacre" or "retreat" of native language and the invention of "venomous argots" (like "gooks") in colonial situations (1991: 148, esp. n. 2). For Anderson, gaining access to a foreign language is a form of social penetration. Colonizers often produce and employ pejoratives like "gooks" to vent their frustration over their inability to penetrate the language world of the natives, as opposed to the ability and need of the colonized to penetrate the language world of the colonizers.

19. For me, the impasse within current discussions about John's language (including his use of irony) has much to do with a rigid assumption that John uses *either* "stable irony" (resulting in a scenario where readers of the Gospel understand clearly what characters within the Gospel do not) *or* "unstable irony" (resulting in a scenario where readers of the Gospel, along with characters within the Gospel, fail to understand and thus feel victimized; see, for example, Culpepper 1996b; and C. R. Koester 1995: xi, 232). Instead, John can be using *both,* and misunderstanding, understanding, and lack of understanding in reading John can be an open, continual, and shifting process. Using Herbert A. Simon's notion of "satisficing" (1957), Eric Rothstein points out that intriguing texts always involve their readers in a dance between understanding *and* not understanding (1991: 124–27). In Johannine terms, it is this mixture that keeps "drawing" its readers back to the "well." If John uses only "stable irony," and readers always understand, as R. Alan Culpepper claims, then Culpepper would have relatively little motivation to read John over and over again in the "last fifteen years" (1996b: 205). To prepare for the development of this chapter, let me also point out that there is a difference between the claim that John uses "unstable irony" to victimize readers (Culpepper 1996b: 193–94) and my view that John himself is betrayed by the contradictions or ambiguities of his own construction.

20. For Petersen, John's creation of a "special language" depends on a heavy dose of "contrast, negation, and inversion" regarding "everyday experience" in general and the Mosaic traditions in particular (1992: 5–6).

21. I emphasize the word "over" because, as John's Jesus makes "blindness" an occasion for revelation (9:3), the inability to understand on the part of some characters reveals that (in accordance with Johannine understanding) they are from below and of the "world," unlike those who understand and will join Jesus in the realm above (8:21–27; 14:1–3).

22. The "fruitlessness" of discipleship independent of Jesus is later exemplified

by Peter's fishing expedition (21:1–6). The "disciples" are not able to catch anything by themselves; with Jesus' company and command, they have a full catch.

23. Anderson suggests that imaginings of (national) communities often involve a center, whether it is realized vertically (as in belief in God or loyalty to a king), or experienced geographically (through religious, administrative, or educational pilgrimages); see Anderson 1991: 15–16, 19–20, 53–58, 121–32.

24. Note also that the coming of the Greeks is, in turn, preceded by the ironic remark of the "Pharisees" that "the world has gone after him" (12:19). This "world" thus carries the implication of tribes and traditions that go beyond those of Israel, not to mention the *Ioudaioi*.

25. I am indebted to Ingrid Rosa Kitzberger for using paradigmatic vacillation as a lens to view the interaction between Jesus and Nicodemus (1998). Yet, Kitzberger never identifies the paradigms at play *within* this Gospel narrative; instead, she is using it as a launching pad to put into dialogue two methodological paradigms in Johannine studies (feminist and theological interpretations).

26. Sollors' idea of marriage is, of course, based on the romantic notion of courtly love. As courtly love was a European development in the medieval period, it should not be confused with ancient practices of betrothal and marriage. Without equating these different understandings of love and marriage, one could or should still realize that ancient marriage was often also an arrangement by consent, although this consent was generally not made between the bride and the groom but their respective fathers/guardians (see Bremen 1996: 265n100).

27. Exactly how Jesus brings about this change in the Samaritan woman is, of course, a matter of interpretation. He seems to have done so by (1) clarifying the superior nature of the "living water" that he has to offer (4:10, 13–14), (2) detailing her personal marital history (4:16–18), and (3) "spiritualizing" true worship that transcends traditional prescription and geographical location (4:21–24). Although the woman's personal marital history is placed in the middle of the progression, according to her own confession (4:29), that is the most effective of Jesus' strategies. If one is willing to take this piece of marital history as a reference to Samaria's national history (2 Kings 17:24), one may understand 4:16–18 as an important exchange over matters of lineage; see, for example, Fehribach 1998: 63–69. While Jean Kim does not agree with this "allegorical" reading of the woman's marital history, she nevertheless brings questions of lineage into the discussion by way of Ezra and Nehemiah (2004: 101–10).

28. In that sense, John is constructing what Anderson calls "a community of verticality" (1991: 20, 24). According to Anderson, this principle of community construction (linking members vertically to a central figure, be it king, God, or Jesus) overcomes temporal separation and lies behind the sexual politics of dynastic marriages that bring diverse populations together. We can see both of these factors at work in John: Jesus' farewell prayer includes a petition for unity between his present and future followers (17:20–21), and we have already mentioned the meeting between Jesus and the Samaritan woman as a "betrothal" (4:1–30, 39–42).

29. I borrow this term from the title of Elizabeth D. Harvey's study on gender politics and gendered poetics during the Renaissance (1991).

30. As Craig Koester suggests, John's passion account is full of correlations between Jesus' "experiences" and Hebrew Scripture, thus showing that Jesus' suffering and death are indeed in fulfillment of God's will (1995: 194–96). In a typical move of Johannine irony, this unique unity that Jesus claims to have with God is what the *Ioudaioi* consider profane and what they kill him for (5:18; 10:33; 19:7). While they think they are putting an end to Jesus' blasphemy by depriving him of life, by that act they facilitate Jesus' fulfilling this life of compliance and self-sacrifice that he claims is demanded by God.

31. I readily admit that there are some passages in John that imply Jesus and the "disciples" have an influence on God, such as 9:30–31; 11:22, 41–42; 14:12–14, 16; 15:7, 16; and 16:23–24. While these verses promise that God will hear or listen to either Jesus or the "disciples," the verb that describes what Jesus and the "disciples" do is not "command" *(entellō)* but "ask" *(aiteō or erōtaō).* Needless to say, these two verbs imply very different power relations.

32. He is specifically mentioned only in 13:23–26; 19:26–27; 20:1–10; and 21:7, 20–24. His presence at the scene of the cross (and his habitual association with Peter) may suggest that he is also the unnamed disciple who accompanies Peter in Peter's attempt to follow Jesus after Jesus' arrest (18:15–18). I will return to this episode a little later.

33. I owe much of the following development to Denise Kimber Buell, whose work on Clement of Alexandria's writings provoked many of my thoughts regarding John's strategic employment of the beloved disciple as a representative figure in his Gospel (see particularly 1999: 7, 84–86).

34. The potential problem John faces in pushing the figure of the beloved disciple more to the foreground may be illustrated in Anderson's discussion about the "backfire" that dynasts after the mid-nineteenth century risked in identifying themselves with the "particular-national" tendencies within their empires (1991: 84–85). John's double reference to his having left out from his Gospel "other" materials about Jesus (20:30; 21:25) may be another power move on his part: as we discussed earlier, there is power in withholding knowledge and information. Doing so (or at least claiming to have extra materials not accessible in writing) may not only reinforce John's own place in the community he is seeking to construct, but it can also further enhance its uniformity by keeping its members "deprived" and dependent.

35. Despite their shared anxiety over influence (whether John was influenced by Jewish, Hellenistic, or Gnostic texts), both Wayne A. Meeks (1972) and Charles H. Talbert (1976) have done much to alert Johannine scholars to this downward and upward emphasis in the Fourth Gospel.

36. Craig Koester argues that Lazarus' resurrection functions to foreshadow Jesus' own resurrection rather than the resurrection to be experienced by believers, because Lazarus obviously will die again (1995: 110). But if Lazarus' second death disqualifies it from being a model of the promised resurrection of believers, why is

it acceptable as a symbol for Jesus' resurrection? In other words, why is the implication of a second death not agreeable for believers, but agreeable for Jesus?

37. John's idea(l) of an expanding community can be seen in his emphasis on the need for the "disciples" to testify or "bear fruit" (1:19–51; 4:28–30, 39–42; 9:13–34; 15:1–8, 16, 27; 17:18, 20). Of course, the aforementioned emphasis on a "world" that "hates" and "persecutes" will lead to trials, and trials are but another forum for testimonies. Put differently, I do not think that one can rigidly make a division between an emphasis on communal survival and an emphasis on communal expansion, since the two are intricately related in John.

38. John therefore gives priority to what is on top, on high, and in bulk. Admittedly, he does connect glorification with death (12:23–26) and emphasizes God rather than humans as the true giver of honor (5:41, 44; 8:50, 54; 12:42–43). The promise of an escalating membership shows most clearly, in my opinion, that these moves on John's part provide nothing more than different routes of travel to the same destination. That is to say, John confirms rather than contests the existing "cultural capital" of honor, power, and number in constructing Jesus' community.

39. Boyrain has also recently pointed to this strategy within the discourse of both Jewish and Christian "orthodoxy" (2004: 59).

40. The double "I am" here is meant to duplicate John's manipulation of language. It can function as an emphatic affirmation of what precedes (the fulfillment of divine purposes) and it can mean something more—namely, the claim to be divine (Jesus is not only fulfilling God, but is God).

41. John shows that Anthony Cohen's differentiation between "creation of community" (signified by a rejection of existing norms) and "continuity of community" (signified by a reassertion of existing norms) is not sustainable in practice (1985: 63). While the distinction may be helpful conceptually, these two emphases are more often than not combined in the actual practice of community construction.

42. Since implicit allusions to Hebrew Scripture can be matters of intense debate, I am limiting my examples here to John's explicit allusions. I do not deny, however, that John may contain many other allusions to Hebrew Scripture that are not explicitly stated.

43. Anderson also relates this invention of fictive kinship to the patriotic demand for self-sacrifice, since such a demand becomes more cogent when connected with "purity and fatality" (1991: 143). Anderson's suggestion itself becomes more pertinent in light of John's emphasis on sacrifice. John's Jesus defines a "good shepherd" by his or her willingness to sacrifice life (10:11–18), and John later links Jesus' thrice-repeated command to Peter to care for the flock with Peter's upcoming martyrdom (21:15–19). All this becomes even more alarming when one remembers John's affirmative response to Caiaphas' statement that sacrificing one to save a nation is an expedient arrangement (11:50–52).

44. Buell helpfully reminds us that procreation language and kinship language are both symbols that function to "naturalize" one's proposition. As such, both are deeply imbricated with power, particularly the power to claim legitimacy and

demand conformity. In that sense, John's descent language is in line with his construction of a compliant community, if not in line with his contrast between consent and descent. Buell is careful to point out at the same time that argumentation using these symbols has "vastly different consequences according to the relative cultural, social, or political power of its proponents" (1999: 9; see also 3–4, 12–13).

45. The qualifying statement of the Samaritans also establishes the primacy of what is male and *Ioudaioi* when they say that their belief is predicated on Jesus' own words rather than the woman's testimony (4:39–42); see Fehribach 1998: 75–79; and J. K. Kim 2004: 106–115. This confession of the Samaritans may have yet another implication. Given the classical Athenian equation of marriage with procreation (see Buell 1999: 36n14), their confession may signify a birthing on the part of the Samaritan woman, and thus the consummation of the betrothal between Jesus and the woman. For an insightful critique of the marginalization of women within so-called progressive communities, see Chow 1998: 55–73.

46. It is telling that within the short span of one chapter, John uses the same verb, "complain" (*gongyzō*, 6:41, 61) to describe the response that the *Ioudaioi* and the "disciples" make to Jesus (C. R. Koester 1995: 59).

47. In addition to the unknown identity of the unnamed disciple, this episode also contains the confounding identity of the high priest (Annas or Caiaphas). For a fascinating reading of this bewildering question, see Staley 1995: 85–109.

48. The ambiguity, contradiction, and confusion around John's construction of the *Ioudaioi* is already recognized by Culpepper, who also proceeds to question the practice of translation (1996a: 115).

49. At times, both Anderson and Anthony Cohen give the impression that a nation or community inevitably sows its own seed of further break-up as it constructs its boundary. Anderson does this more through examples, showing how the teaching of European "national history" and administrative pilgrimages in colonies end up contributing to anti-colonial nationalism (1991: 110–11, 118, 113–40, 163–85). Anthony Cohen, on the other hand, states that community construction contains "the domino theory of politics: once one group marks out its distinctiveness, others feel compelled to follow suit" (1985: 110). If one is willing to follow Raymond Brown's traditional stance that 1 John reflects a later development in which intercommunal conflicts of the Johannine community turn intracommunal, then one may also claim to have a biblical example of this "domino theory."

50. David Leiwei Li concurs that a nation is made up of both "the institutional and the imaginary, the political that regulates the juridical and territorial boundaries, and the cultural that defines origins and continuities, affiliations and belongings" (1998: 7). This differentiation (and contradiction) notwithstanding, Li further points out that the "cultural wars" over nation and community are tied to the understanding of the institutional and the political. For Li, the U.S. rhetoric of "volitional allegiance" is consistently opposed by an insistence on the nation's power to refuse consent to membership, thus giving the established community undue favors over the rights of the prospective citizen (1998: 3). According to Li, this opposition itself

results from the simultaneous embrace of Lockean "individualistic liberalism" and the Machiavellian spirit of imperial governance within the understanding of "Atlantic Republicanism."

51. For specific references to John in the construction of consent in the United States, see Sollors 1986: 85–86, 94. Part of Sollors' (over)optimism is due to his (over)readiness to make race an aspect of ethnicity. For a good critique of this elision of race and ethnicity, see Omi and Winant 1994: 14–23, 53–91.

52. For an excellent discussion of the "politics of mobility" from one Asian American perspective, see S. C. Wong 1993: 118–65.

53. According to Busto, this "model minority" image also functions to pressure young Asian Americans into subscribing to the cultural emphasis on material success and conformative citizenship (1999: 178). For an interesting illustration and insightful critique of this kind of cultural consent to upward mobility, see Jen 1991.

54. For Gramsci, the difference between hegemony and ideology lies precisely in the difference between consent and contest, or between calm practices and clamorous protests. That is to say, when articulation is needed to defend or argue for a position, that position is already exposed as contestable ideology. Hegemony (or the highest form of ideology), on the other hand, is what we do in silence and live out as "it-goes-without-saying." It is taken for granted, it is understood as a given, it is simply assumed; there is no question raised or any inquisition made. In sum, it is given in "consent."

55. For an explication of ethnicity as a social construction, see Anthony Cohen 1985: 104–105.

56. Much of what Drucilla Cornell calls "the postmodern challenge to the ideal of community" concerns issues of consensus, difference, and "otherness" (1992). In recent years, some reflections on and suggestions have been made about how communities may exist and persist *with* conflict and disagreement; see, for example, Tanner 1997 (who focuses on the community of Christendom) and Warnke 1992 (who focuses on the community of U.S. society).

57. If interested, one can find two more examples of liberational reading of John in Culpepper 1996a: 119–21. See also Rensberger 2002, where he reads John, or the incarnation of the Logos, as a radical "downward mobility." What Rensberger ignores, in my view, is that this "downward mobility" ends with an "upward mobility" in the Fourth Gospel. For a helpful critique of how "downward mobility" or "voluntary weakness" might actually reinforce one's power (even if the critique is done more through Paul than John), see Caputo 2006.

Chapter 4: Overlapping (His)Stories

1. I should add that Ng's story does not romanticize families, biological or otherwise. After all, the story begins with the alarming news that Leon and Leila's mother are no longer living together. This "separation" is at least partly because their daughter, Ona, has committed suicide by jumping off a building in a local

housing project. "Paper families," as Tina Chen correctly reminds us, "reveal a very situated sense of obligation as well as exploitation" (2005: 26).

2. This change has to do with (1) the repeal in 1943 of both the Exclusion Act and the National Origins Law; and (2) the Immigration Act of 1965, which removed "national origins" as the basis of U.S. immigration legislation, and thus also its previous bias for European immigrants.

3. As I hope will become clear in my next chapter, Penner's attempt to defer and deflect a consideration of why the collection focuses on referencing Greek and Roman rather than Jewish writers (2003b: 19) is itself both a sign and a cause of the volume's inattention to racial/ethnic issues. I would also suggest that this ignorance of or inattention to racial/ethnic difference within both the first-century Mediterranean world and contemporary North America is not unrelated to another acknowledged lack within the collection; namely, the lack of attention given to the religious context of the Greco-Roman world (Penner 2003b: 18). As will become more apparent in my next two chapters, religion and race/ethnicity were very much intertwined concepts for people of the first-century Mediterranean world, inclusive of Greeks, Romans, and Jews.

An inattention to gender may well be another possible reason for—and result of—this lack in contextualizing their own readings of Acts even as the volume's editors and contributors work to contextualize Acts' writing. Out of its twelve entries, only the last one has much to comment on gender (Vander Stichele 2003). I am afraid Elisabeth Schüssler Fiorenza is correct in her observation that feminist biblical scholarship is still seldom read by male scholars (1999: 3). She has, for example, already argued for the need for rhetorical criticism to examine the context, location, and interests not only of the biblical writers but also of the contemporary biblical scholars (1999; see also Schüssler Fiorenza 2005). This critical turn to self, along with her call to examine the constructive power of language, are both fundamental to Schüssler Fiorenza's ethical project, which she advocates in the name of the polis (understood in the sense of the public). Despite the pervasive references in *Contextualizing Acts* to sociorhetorical criticism, and a lengthy discussion surrounding precisely the same term, polis, by one of the volume's co-editors (Penner 2003a: 66–78), the reference to gender and reading location in general, as well as the citation of Schüssler Fiorenza in particular by the volume's other co-editor (Vander Stichele 2003: 321–29), are unable to move this volume to contextualize beyond the past.

What this collection of essays seems to demonstrate is that the study of Acts has, in a time lag, duplicated the development that has taken place in the study of Revelation. In other words, its emphasis has shifted from genetic (the study of sources) to generic (the study of genres) and now to generative (the study of functions, including sociopolitical ones) concerns. I will refer to this development within the study of Revelation again in Chapter 8, but let me simply point out that *male* interpreters of Revelation have by now also begun to contextualize their own interpretive work (for example, Ruiz 2003: 135; Rhoads 2005; and Blount 2005). This is a next step that I think interpreters of Acts must also begin to take. It is in fact ironic that while most interpreters who contextualize Acts would argue or agree that Luke's writing of Acts has theological or socio-political reasons that go beyond mere antiquarian interest, these same interpreters would continue to understand their own reading of and writing on Acts as arising out of antiquarian interests, and thus beyond the need of contextualization.

Finally, lest I be misunderstood, let me clarify that my comments above have to do with the volume rather than the editors. To be fair, Penner and Vander Stichele have since collaborated on a couple of articles—on Acts (Penner and Vander Stichele 2004) and on 1 Corinthians (Penner and Stichele 2005) respectively—with a more pointed focus on gender and their own reading location.

4. Although the word "Christian" is used in Acts 11:26 and 26:28, Daniel Boyarin has helpfully argued that the separation between Judaism and Christianity as two different religions might not have occurred until the fourth century C.E. (2004). I am therefore intentionally using the term "Christ(ian)" throughout this chapter as a visible reminder of Boyarin's argument.

5. Most New Testament scholars agree that Acts is related to the Gospel of Luke, because the same person authored both books. Beyond that, scholars disagree on the specific nature of that relationship—for instance, if Luke-Acts is a two-volume work, if Acts is a later sequel to Luke's Gospel, or if the books share a coherent outlook. For arguably the best, or at least the most convenient, reference to this issue, see Parsons and Pervo 1993.

6. Acts is also intriguing to me because its history of interpretation has been infused with orientalizing strategies (see Wordelman 2003: 205–17) as well as justifications for missionary activities and colonial expansion (see Staley 2004: 177–79).

7. Eckhard Plümacher has argued, on the basis of Acts 10 and 13, that the descending of the Holy Spirit on Cornelius and his household is connected with preaching or the proclamation of the Word (1999: 253–55). Plümacher's main argument is, of course, the importance of speeches in Acts, and hence Acts' association with historiography, given the latter's emphasis on speeches as "causes" of historical events. One runs into two difficulties, however, should one try to extend Plümacher's argument to other comings of the Holy Spirit in Acts. In the case of the Ephesians (18:24–19:7), one will have to differentiate among different proclamations or proclaimers of the Word, since Apollos' proclamation is clearly inadequate. I will have more to say about the differentiation of preaching or preachers, but now let me get to the second and greater difficulty. In the case of the Samaritans (8:14–17), their receiving of the Holy Spirit is not based on preaching or speech. Even if one attributes the delay of the Holy Spirit's coming to Philip's "inadequate" preaching, one cannot attribute the Spirit's final descent to preaching, since Peter and John did not preach at all; instead, they prayed for and laid hands on the Samaritans (8:14–17). In fact, Luke seems to confirm through Simon the magician that, at least in this case, the Spirit's descent is connected with the laying on of hands (8:18). Again, my point is that Acts refuses to be consistently specific about the cause or the timing of the Spirit's descent on people.

8. For R. S. Sugirtharajah, the emergence of many missionary societies in the eighteenth and nineteenth centuries coincided with the scholarly observation of this missionary-journey structure in Acts (2003: 21–24, 103–105).

9. Although Amy-Jill Levine chooses to emphasize the debates between "feminist advocates" and "feminist detractors" of Acts (2004b:1), her first footnote nevertheless refers to the work of Turid Karlsen Seim, who suggests that one can find a "double message" regarding women in both Luke's Gospel and Acts (1994). Two of the contributors to Levine's edited volume *A Feminist Companion to the Acts of the Apostles* (2004a) do choose to make Seim's thesis more of a "consensus" among feminist readings of Acts (Burrus and Torjesen 2004: 171n1). Most of the contributors to the same volume seem to share this "consensus" understanding, although comparatively some do seem to be more hopeful or less hopeful about Acts' overall treatment of gender.

10. Levine has questioned if Priscilla is a Gentile, since only Aquila is called a "Jew" in Acts 18:2 (2004b: 16). Even if Levine is correct, the close working relations between Priscilla and Aquila would imply that she is more likely than not a proselyte to Judaism.

11. González has also failed to deal with the gender question in his more affirmative reading of Acts 6. Barbara E. Reid, for example, has wondered if the complaint of the Hellenistic widows has less to do with their being recipients than with their being practitioners of ministry, whether that is understood in terms of distributing elements of the Eucharist or distributing financial resources (2004). If so, Reid would be correct to point out that the so-called resolution of the apostles bars the widows from receiving any ministerial assignments.

12. Note also that the Jerusalem apostles also legitimize the ministry of the seven "servers" by praying and the laying on of hands (6:6).

13. Other parallels among Jesus in Luke's Gospel and Peter as well as Paul in Acts might include their experiencing of heavenly vision, their facing of trial, their imprisonment, and their miraculous "deliverance" (see, for example, Luke 3:21–22, 9:28–36, 22:47–24:53; Acts 9:1–9, 10:1–12:17, 16:16–40). If these pertain to their experiences, there are also parallels between their speeches; examples would include an emphasis on acceptance or inclusion of Gentiles (Luke 4:16–27; Acts 3:25–26, 10:34–35, 15:6–12, 17:22–31) or an emphasis on a close connection between God's promise to David and Jesus as the Messiah (Luke 20:41–44; Acts 2:22–36, 13:13–41). Others have interpreted such parallelization by Luke as his desire to present a "consensus document" of and for the early church (H. Koester 1982: 2.318–23; Tyson 2003: 27). One can also add Stephen to this mix. For example, while Stephen's martyrdom parallels that of Jesus (Luke 23:32–47; Acts 7:51–60), Stephen's suffering as a witness for Jesus also parallels the suffering of Paul; like Stephen, Paul has the experience of being stoned (7:58; 14:5, 19). See also Moessner 1999b.

14. For more on Luke-Acts as a continuation of Israel's story, see Loveday Alexander 1999, where she argues that the theme of Israel actually frames Luke-Acts (since Israel is featured in the beginning of Luke's Gospel [1–4], the beginning

of Acts [1:6], and the end of Acts [27–28]). Many, because of Acts' emphasis on incorporating Gentiles and its appeal to Jewish traditions, have read Acts as mainly an attempt to legitimate its mission or community; for example, see Esler 1987; and Sterling 1992. This legitimation thesis implies, of course, a major concern that is shared by most if not all Chinese Americans—namely, a crisis of identity.

15. This issue of religious diversity or inter-religious dialogue touches on the question of Judaism(s) in Acts. Since I will not be addressing this question directly or explicitly, interested readers may want to consult, for instance, Tyson 1992; and Tyson 1999.

16. This is far from the being the only issue in Acts in which a contradiction can be found. For example, in the midst of Paul's many vigorous defenses of his beliefs in and faithfulness to the Torah, he also surprisingly declares once that the Torah is, unlike faith in Jesus Christ, unable to free one from sins (13:39). There is, in addition to the "double message" regarding women, also a mixed message about possessions. I have already talked about an emphasis on "selling and sharing all" in the early chapters of Acts. As one reads on, however, one will find that some Christ(ians) are in fact able to retain their own personal wealth, as long as they use what they have to help spread the message and expand the community. Examples of this later and latter strand include the house-owning and slave-keeping Mary (12:12–13), some Greek "leading" women in Thessalonica as well as the "prominent" women and men in Berea (Acts 17:4, 12), and perhaps also the purple-cloth-dealing merchant Lydia (16:13–15) or the charity-giving Tabitha/Dorcas (9:36–39). Even Paul is suspect on this front, since Acts ends by stressing that he is able to rent his own place in Rome for two years (28:30). One question that is well worth asking is if and how economic difference might circle back to impact our earlier question about community integration, particularly if (as the episode involving Mary and Rhoda seems to imply) a Christ(ian) household is made up of slaves and those who own them. Other scholars have also pointed to the multiplicity, even contradictory elements, within Acts in different ways. For example, Vernon K. Robbins, focusing on form rather than content, has suggested that Acts contains "multiple generic features" (1999: 65) or "different modes of discourse" (1999: 68).

17. On the basis of Luke's identification of the islanders as "foreigners" or "barbarians" (28:2), Amy L. Wordelman tries to make sense of this contradiction or "abnormalcy" in Acts by suggesting that Paul's sermon-less service or performance might have to do with the presence of an unbridgeable language barrier, since "barbarian" basically means in this context "non-Greek-speaking" (2003: 217). Note, however, not only Wordelman's admission that "it is dangerous to attribute too much to absence in a text" (2003: 217) but also how Wordelman's "language gap" fails to account for Paul's "tolerance" in the first half of his trip, or throughout the entire chapter that immediately precedes his arrival at Malta.

18. Besides 27:1–28:16, the narrator of Acts also uses first-person-plural pronouns in 16:10–17; 20:5–15; and 21:1–18.

19. For example, David L. Balch has read Luke-Acts alongside Greco-Roman historical and biographical foundation narratives like those by Dionysius of Halicarnassus and Plutarch (2003); Dennis R. MacDonald has read Homer and Euripides as Acts' intertexts (2003; 2004); and F. Scott Spencer has found one helpful echo of Ovid in Acts (2004: 139–40).

20. Not everyone is ready to grant Luke this liberty on both fronts. For example, Daryl D. Schmidt is willing to admit Luke's Jewish and Greco-Roman influences only after he has limited Acts' genre to historiography (1999: 60). Even if one wants to identify Acts as a type of historical writing, I think Dennis C. Duling and Norman Perrin are correct in stating that Luke has at least four webs of "influence": (1) Greco-Roman historical writing, (2) Greco-Roman popular romance, (3) the Hebrew Bible, and (4) the Gospel of Mark (1994: 379).

21. Although both are more concerned with identifying the genre or at least the generic association of Acts, J. C. O'Neill (1961) and Gregory E. Sterling (1992) have managed to place Acts within a broader cultural—perhaps even a socio-political if not yet exactly an anti-colonial—frame when they suggest that Acts is an apologetic work that takes its cue from diasporic or Hellenistic Jews who needed to defend or justify their faith and way of faith. Earlier scholarship, particularly those done out of Europe, tended to understand Luke's apologetic in Acts as an attempt to appease rather than to compete with Rome; see, for example, Haenchen 1971: 105–107.

22. Walter T. Wilson has recently compared the founding of Gentile churches in Acts to the ancient foundation narratives of Greco-Roman colonies (2001). Given Luke's emphasis on tying the early church movement to its Jewish roots, as well as what I have mentioned regarding the work of Bonz and Pao, Wilson's analysis might lead to a rather radical reversal; namely, the founding of colonies by a colonized people.

23. Penner and Vander Stichele come to a similarly mixed conclusion on Luke's gendering of violence in Acts; see Penner and Vander Stichele 2004: 203.

24. For a helpful and convenient summary of various options on understanding Theophilus, see Loveday Alexander 1993: 187–200.

25. The term "transcultural" here does not refer to a transcendence of or over culture, but only that the mixing and mingling, or the challenging and exchanging, dynamics I have in mind involve actually more than just two cultures.

Chapter 5: Redressing Bodies in Corinth

1. In addition to featuring two different ethnic groups within Asian America, there is yet another important difference between the work of Ong and Suh. While Suh, comparatively speaking, concentrates on the dynamics between Korean American Buddhists and Korean American Christians, Ong pays greater attention to the dynamics between Cambodian Americans and European Americans. Both, however, use the language of "hiding" to communicate the marginal position occupied and

felt by a religious minority group, whether in relationship to a co-ethnic group or an entirely different racial/ethnic group altogether (Ong 2003: title; Suh 2004: 4, 165, 187, 195).

2. Here is an intriguing irony that can use more exploration. Racial difference is visible, but that visibility has only made racial minorities undetectable and unseen in this country. Tina Chen has chosen to signify this irony with her strategic use of the term "in/visibilities" (2005: 6, 160). In those same pages, she has also suggested, to counter Peggy Phelan's thesis about the power of being unmarked or unseen (1993), that a distinction needs to be made between being invisible and being unmarked.

3. I trust that my reasons for choosing 1 Corinthians will become clear as I develop my arguments in this chapter. Suffice it to state now that one prominent commentator, after describing Corinth as "a city only a few generations removed from its founding by colonists seeking upward social mobility," compares the Corinthians of Paul's days to the commentator's own "American readers" (Hays 1997: 3). As we shall see, what this commentator fails to recognize—like Penner's introduction to *Contextualizing Acts* (2003b)—is the racial/ethnic differences that exist between the Corinthians and Paul as well as among his "American readers."

4. Dale Martin does mention that Paul's body was an issue for his critics at Corinth. However, he sees this—as he does with the matter of Paul's manual labor—as becoming a "real" issue only in 2 Corinthians, and he also limits Paul's bodily problem to "illness, disfigurement, or simply constitutional infirmity" (1995: 53–55, 83–86). Martin never explains or elaborates on what he means by "constitutional infirmity," but the thought that Paul's body is racially/ethnically marked as Jewish does not seem to cross his mind. Perhaps Martin, in correctly refuting the assumption that so-called Judaism and Hellenism must be mutually exclusive when it comes to Paul's cultural heritage, influence, and repertoire (2001), has gone too far and ends up (dis)missing Paul's racially/ethnically marked body as a Jew altogether. Again, a helpful corrective might be found in contemporary Asian American experiences: their bodies are still raced and stigmatized as "Asian" even when they are fluent and knowledgeable in things both "Asian" and "American." In other words, Dale Martin's call to rethink "culture" within Pauline studies (2001: 59–61) must be supplemented with a thinking of race/ethnicity. As we shall see later in this chapter, influence and resistance are also not necessarily mutually exclusive. Instead of giving an example from Asian America, let me, for now, point to the wisdom tradition of Ben Sira, a Jewish teacher from the Hellenistic period; one will find in that tradition both uses and critiques of Greek thought and rhetoric (see Pogoloff 1992: 163–67).

Pauline scholars of earlier generations did talk about Jewish-Gentile difference in 1 Corinthians. However, they did so by completely separating racial/ethnic and religious issues from the context of imperial politics, and by completely subsuming racial/ethnic issues as questions of religious practices in one direction (that is, whether Jewish Christ-followers would or should accept Gentiles who followed Christ without taking on certain Jewish practices like circumcision); see, for instance,

Baur 1831. It is important to note that this trail of scholarship has continued within Pauline studies in general, even if not in the study of 1 Corinthians in particular. More recently, studies of Paul from the "new perspective" would emphasize Paul's Jewishness to interrogate the continuity and permeability between Jews (who are not followers of Christ) and Christ-followers more than the dynamics between Christ-followers who were Jewish and Christ-followers who were Gentile. These studies have also concentrated less on 1 Corinthians than on Romans and Galatians. Two representative scholars to look at in this regard could be E. P. Sanders (1977; 1983) and Daniel Boyarin (1994; 2004).

Despite the view that "race" is a modern invention and the many attempts to distinguish "race" from "ethnicity," I will couple the terms together as "race/ethnic-ity" in this chapter for the same reasons that Denise Kimber Buell has given (2001: 450n3): (1) to acknowledge the two terms' intricate relationship and implications for each another in ancient and modern times, and (2) to acknowledge that understand-ings and knowledge of the past and the present are informative of and influential upon each other in all intellectual endeavor (regarding anti-Semitism in particular, see also Schäfer 1997: 2–3). On top of that, I also want to honor the work of Afri-can American scholars who argue, not only for the presence of blacks in the Bible, but also against the assumption that biblical Jews were necessarily "whites" (see, for example, Copher 1991; Felder 1993). Michael Joseph Brown has recently ques-tioned this practice of identifying black presence by fellow African American Bible scholars because the concept of "race," as I mentioned, is a modern construction (2004: 52). Note, however, that a couple of recent works have helpfully indicated that color-coded prejudice was very much alive in antiquity regardless of whether the term "race" was employed (Isaac 2004) or not employed (Byron 2002; see also Harrill 2006: 42–43, 46).

For my immediate purposes, let me point out that, if one is willing to grant (1) the association of blackness with Egyptians and (2) the relevance of Acts for Pauline studies, then Lysias' mistaken identification of Paul as an Egyptian in Acts 21:38 might be taken as an indication of Paul's blackness. In the final analysis, however, my emphasis on racial/ethnic difference in this chapter is not dependent on the actual color of Paul's skin. One must remember, first, taking the example of the Irish—they were first deemed to be (like) "black" but later deemed to be "white" (Ignatiev 1995)—that skin color is not necessarily "color" (Drake and Cayton 1945: 503n), but that phenotypical differences are "something that we learn to see" (Nguyen 2002: 169). That is to say, color, race, or ethnicity (including "Jewishness" in Paul's time) is like the emperor's "new clothes"; it is a display of power—a fantasy of power and a powerful fantasy—in which physical evidence is secondary to observer compliance. In addition to the extant educational and ideological work on how to view Jews from the Greco-Roman world, it is important to recognize that, aside from the general question on the visibility or readability of Jewish difference, Paul himself is not shy in owning up to his race/ethnicity as a Jewish person (1 Corinthi-ans 10:1–6; 2 Corinthians 11:22). For my own understanding of race and ethnicity, see Liew 2005: 114–21. I would also like to thank here both Randall C. Bailey and Gay L. Bryon for pushing me to think through the idea of black presence in the Bible by providing both conversations and bibliographical recommendations.

5. I will not confine my Greco-Roman references to those that are known to have existed before the time of Paul, since my use of them is not motivated by a search for source or influence, but by a desire to understand the cultural sensibilities of the general time period.

6. For example, Romans saw the Greeks as "the world's greatest chatterboxes. Not only did they talk too much, but at the wrong time. The learned Greek . . . was often gauche, *ineptus*, a bore. . . . They talked shop, their own shop, in a manner offensive to polite conversation" (cited in Pogoloff 1992: 266). See also Juvenal, where he satirizes the Greeks with the prefatory remark that they are "the race which is most dear to our rich men" (3.58–125). What is clear is the existence of a social and racial/ethnic scale within the Roman empire (see also Goldhill 2001). For example, *barbarus* gradually became a negative term for all those who were not Greek or Roman in the Greco-Roman world (Byron 2002: 2).

7. I am therefore suggesting that the picture of diasporic Jewish communities as one of "people secure in their self-understanding, loyal to their traditions but open to their neighbors and (with the exception of the aristocracy) respected by their Gentile and later Gentile Christian neighbours" (Gaston 2005: 253) is skewed and overly optimistic. It (dis)misses underlying and at times explosive racial/ethnic tensions. One should also keep in mind that such underlying racial/ethnic tensions are arguably more often and more keenly felt by marginalized racial/ethnic groups, and that in Paul's portrayal, the Corinthians are longing for status—and thus aristocratic identifications, including a lack of respect for Jews?—even if they were not originally of high birth (1:26–31; 4:6–19; 11:17–34).

Gaston's essay is part of a larger and recent collection of essays on and responses to the "new perspective" on Paul as a Christ-follower who remains Jewish. While this collection as a whole seems to acknowledge the importance of race/ethnicity for Greco-Roman religion in general and hence to Pauline studies in particular, it very quickly seems to reduce everything back down to religion and religion alone. Despite the fact that four out of seven contributors footnoted Shawn Kelley's book *Racializing Jesus* (2002; see, for instance, N. Elliott 2005: 248n26; Nanos 2005: 263n32 and 266n38; Johnson Hodge 2005: 271n2; Campbell 2005: 306n25), only one is substantial in her investigation of Paul's ethnicity or racialization (Johnson Hodge 2005). What one finds in this collection is a paradox of referring to race/ethnicity and then just as quickly allowing it to evaporate into (almost) non-existence.

Of immense significance is the fact that neither Schäfer nor Isaac limits prejudice against Jews to a merely "Christian" hostility but both see it as a much wider phenomenon of the Greco-Roman world. In fact, Isaac intimates more than once that Greco-Roman hostilities towards Jews tended to be more intense outside than inside Judea (2004: 442, 456, 467, 478). If that was true, a diasporic Jew like Paul would have been more vulnerable to racial/ethnic discrimination. Perhaps the best-known attacks on Jews in the Greco-Roman world are those by Tacitus (*Hist.* 5.4–5) and Juvenal (14.96–106); for an example of a Greek author, see Cassius Dio, 37.16.5–17.4. Of no less importance is also Schäfer's thesis that Egypt (both before and during its hellenization) rather than Syria-Palestine in the second century B.C.E. was the "'mother' of anti-Semitism" (1997: 11). Given Schäfer's German heritage and his own admission of the long and problematic relations between Germans and Jews (1997: 1–2), his thesis reads like an attempt to shift the blame. This is particularly troubling given the link that some African American Bible scholars make among Egypt, Africa, and black persons and presence. Does Schäfer's thesis, whatever his intentions, have the effect of shifting at least part of the responsibility for "anti-Semitism" from (mainly white?) Europeans to (mainly black?) Africans? I will have more to say about this "shifting" or transferring dynamics to another vulnerable minority population in a latter part of this chapter.

8. Horsley's disregard of racial/ethnic differences in 1 Corinthians is especially problematic, as it leads him to the (con)fusion of Hellenistic Jews and Gentiles, as seen by his rather pervasive use of Philo to illustrate or argue for what he sees to be representative of the Corinthians; see, for example, Horsley 1998:117–21, 181–82, 211–12. As I have tried to point out in reference to Dale Martin, there is an immense spread of social space between complete isolation and total assimilation in which racial/ethnic minority groups might operate in any given society. It is equally important to remember that both the area and the approach of that operation are often contested and limited by various dominant cultural forces.

Commenting on the controversial casting of Jonathan Pryce as an Asian or Eurasian in the first performances of *Miss Saigon* in New York, Karen Shimakawa indicates that such "cross-castings" (of whites playing Asian/American-s)—by making Asian/American-s disembodied and invisible—on stage might be a "more comprehensible" and "more pleasurable" experience for dominant audiences, and hence also a "more profitable" setup for producers (2002: 46, 48). Given the long-standing and perhaps willful anti-Jewish and anti-Semitic practice in biblical studies in general (Tyson 1999; Kelley 2002) and in Pauline studies in particular (D. B. Martin 2001), I wonder if the same comment cannot be made of "our" academic research and publishing. Mindful of modern racism and anti-Judaism, Buell is correct in calling scholars of early Christianity to pay greater and better attention to questions of race/ethnicity (2005). Although her earlier article tends to focus on how early Christians adapted Jewish rhetorical uses of ethnoracial concepts to construct a new race/ethnicity rather than transcended the racial/ethnic particularity or exclusivity of Judaism (2001), her more recent collaboration with Caroline Johnson Hodge (2004) does focus more on Paul's identity as a diasporic Jew or Judean.

9. Part of the problem has to do, I think, with the conventional understanding that Paul is about "transcending" or "overcoming" racial/ethnic divides. Thus, what Theodor W. Adorno says about interpreting in general is applicable to interpreting race in Paul in particular: "The person who interprets instead of accepting what is given and classifying it is marked with the yellow star of one who squanders

his intelligence in impotent speculation, reading things in where there is nothing to interpret" (1991–92: 1.4). Perhaps a bigger part of the problem is the fact that many people are simply not comfortable talking about race. Gilroy makes the insightful observation that many in the twenty-first century have tried to avoid the question of race by making it a distinctively mid-twentieth-century problem (2005: 13–14). That is to say, they say race and racism are really problems of the past, and that present generations should be given the freedom to move on rather than being dragged down or, worse, made responsible for them. This avoidance of race is, however, not just done by burying race as a concern of the past; it is also done through the charge of anachronism or, ironically enough given Gilroy's observation, "presentism." According to this view, race is a modern fifteenth- or sixteenth-century construct, so any talk about race before that time frame—for example, during the Greco-Roman world of the first century—is illegitimate. In other words, race is bracketed and safely quarantined within several hundred years of human history. It is a fantasy or a fabrication to talk about race in antiquity, and it is mere or unhealthy nostalgia to talk about race in the present.

Related to this is also Butler's reflection on how masculine disembodiment is achieved through the reduction of women to corporeality or bodily forms (1987: 133). Of course, I need to point out here that what Butler identifies (the rendering of an "other" as "essentially body") happens not only to women but also to people of color. Since the guild of biblical studies is still predominately white and male, these white male scholars' tendency to identify with Paul often ends up—following Butler's rationale—turning Paul into yet another noncorporeal soul or spirit.

10. One must not fail to forget, as Pamela Eisenbaum reminds us, that Paul was writing before the twin births of rabbinic Judaism and Christianity as separate "religions" (2005: 237). While these twin births have traditionally been understood as having taken place at the end of the first century C.E., some are suggesting now that the so-called parting of the way did not happen until as late as the fourth century C.E.; see, for example, Boyarin 2004.

11. For a brief but helpful survey of the Corinthian "context," including the major Gentile or Greco-Roman religious streams, see Horsley 1998: 22–28. While this kind of "background" or "contextual" information is routinely given in commentaries on the Corinthian letters, not enough nuanced attention has been given to how religious difference (particularly in majority/minority terms) is played out in the letters themselves. Neither has adequate attention been paid to the intersection between race/ethnicity and religion. Again, as I have mentioned in an earlier footnote, questions have pretty much been limited to those about Gentile Christ-followers and Jewish circumcision, though without the kind of socio-political framing that Nanos proposes. One scholar who does talk about both ethnic and religious difference in 1 Corinthians is Brad Ronnell Braxton (2003), but he limits his inquiry to the issue of circumcision in 1 Corinthians 7:17–24. Moreover, Braxton seems to be reading 1 Corinthians through Nanos' reading of Galatians in the way he attributes to the Corinthians a desire to be circumcised and accounts for that desire. Finally,

Braxton reads (and critiques) Paul as (naively) advocating a transcendence over ethnic differences in 1 Corinthians. I do not think that ethnic issues can be limited to a single chapter or a single issue in 1 Corinthians, nor do I agree with Braxton's reading that Paul is elevating one's allegiance to Christ to the overwhelming or exclusion of all other ethnic identities or allegiances (since in my view, Paul continues to see race/ethnicity and religion as closely connected). I would furthermore like to insist that one should read 1 Corinthians in terms of 1 Corinthians rather than through another Pauline letter.

12. As we only have the letter(s) of Paul, and thus only one side of the conversation, it is practically impossible to know to what extent his rhetoric is a reflection or Paul's own projection of the Corinthian situation. Either way, I am suggesting that paying attention to both racial/ethnic and religious differences will add much to one's reading of 1 Corinthians. For the sake of readability, my language in the rest of the chapter will not make that differentiation between reflection and projection, but readers should nevertheless keep in mind that delicate but decisive distinction.

13. I am emphasizing Greco-Roman perceptions here because I do not want to imply that Greco-Roman Judaisms were necessarily all zealous in missionary activities and at all times. For a helpful discussion of that topic, see Goodman 1994. My interest here has less to do with how conversions by non-Jews to Judaisms took place but more with how Greco-Romans tended to see and respond to the presence of Jews and such conversions by non-Jews. That is to say, I am also paying attention to what might in fact be anticipation of or anxiety over *potential* proselytism as well as actual proselytism. While Schäfer is (like me) not concerned with whether Jews of the ancient world were active in mission, he is (unlike me) still concerned with whether proselytism had factually taken place or not.

14. While Schäfer helpfully suggests how proselytes are part of the "hunted," he is in my view mistaken to conclude that "we have to regard Domitian's vigorous enforcement of the *ficus Iudaicus* not as a measure against proselytes (he only wanted them to pay the tax)" (1997: 115, 113–16). Who needs to pay tax and who does not need to pay tax is, however, always already a matter of politics and power relations. Again, a look at Asian American history will be of help here. For example, money was clearly not the only issue when a "Foreign Miners' Tax" was passed in 1850 and then reenacted in 1852 primarily against Chinese, or, in 1870—at a time when Chinese laundrymen in San Francisco were known for delivering laundry without using horses—that a city-wide stipulation was made to charge laundry shops a higher quarterly fee for laundry deliveries made without horses (see S. Chan 1991: 46).

15. This reading is actually consistent with Boyarin's recent (re)constructionist history of Judaeo-Christian relations (2004). For Boyarin, the births and more or less simultaneous separation between rabbinic Judaism and Christianity were a long process of negotiation that extended from the end of the first century C.E. to the fourth century C.E. What is significant is that on the "Christian" side, Boyarin sees *Gentile* followers of Christ (in other words, not Paul himself) to be the main play-

ers in the construction of heresiology, and hence the construction of Christianity as a "religion" that is no longer understandable in terms of a race or a *genos* (2004: 4, 16–17, 29, 59, 62, 65–67, 72–73). While Boyarin begins his investigation of the process with Justin Martyr, my reading of 1 Corinthians might be read as an earlier or even pioneering engagement of that long negotiation between race/ethnicity and religion.

16. I am therefore suggesting that there is no need to read this account single-dimensionally. As I will proceed to show in the latter parts of this chapter, Paul may well be working on several fronts with this single account.

17. Many before me have questioned the factuality of the four Corinthian factions that Paul describes in 1:12, since he seems to focus on the conflict between the "weak" and the "strong" as he progresses in the letter. See, for example, Mitchell 1991: 83–86; D. B. Martin 1995: 58; Horsley 1998: 34–35, 44–45.

18. I am thus arguing that conflicts and divisions in 1 Corinthians not be limited to those at Corinth, but on the basis of race/ethnicity, be extended to problems between the Corinthians and Paul, a colonized Jew. Notice in this regard that the four teachers Paul names (himself, Apollos, Cephas, and Christ) in 1:12 are, if we can trust Acts' account of Apollos, all Jews. The same is also true of the apostles, whom Paul, as we will see, contrasts with the Corinthians in 4:8–13. Nils Dahl (1977) has suggested that 1 Corinthians 1:10–4:21 should not be read as (Paul's) "apologetic," because Paul seems to be critical also of those who claim allegiance to himself (1:13; 3:4–9; 4:6). In the next section, I will talk about how Paul argues for his authority, not by directly affirming or asking for personal allegiance, but by appealing indirectly to an-other Jewish body (that of Christ's). In other words, since the conflict involves racial/ethnic difference, Paul is building up for his own apology not only a united Jewish front but also one that is fronted by Christ. One should remember also that Dahl does admit after all that the first four chapters of 1 Corinthians contain "apologetic elements" (1977: 61n50).

Note also that Cynthia Briggs Kittredge has made a similar (but more one-sided) revisionary reading of Paul's letter to the Philippians on the basis of gender. Instead of seeing—as scholars used to do—the two women mentioned in 4:2 (Euodia and Syntyche) as opposing each other, Kittredge suggests that they might in fact be presenting a united front against Paul (1998: 53–110).

19. Scholars who are adamant that 1 Corinthians is a piece of deliberative rhetoric (Mitchell 1991; D. B. Martin 1995: 38–39) might see my reading here as a plug for taking the letter as a piece of forensic rhetoric, but I am personally less concerned with such deliberations and delineations. These definitions of rhetorical genres are in my view often too neat, too rigid, and thus too limiting. In practice, types of rhetoric are usually mixed and messy, just as logos, ethos, and pathos are interconnected and inseparable elements of any speech making. I would further contend that my reading provides greater continuity between 1 and 2 Corinthians than readings that (dis)miss Paul's "apology" or "defense" in 1 Corinthians as "merely" rhetorical (for example, D. B. Martin 1995: 52–53).

20. Forms of Roman punishment were contingent on not only the nature of the crime but also the status of the offender. Punishment and status were hence mutually constitutive, and "disciplinary" in a most profound manner. See Castelli 2004: 39–41.

21. Buell, commenting on the existence of racial/ethnic hierarchies in the Greco-Roman world, quotes Philo's wish that with the beginning of the Roman imperial period would come "a fresh start" for the Jews (*VM* 2.44; 2001: 469). The articulation of this wish betrayed not only the low ranking hitherto suffered by Jews, but also turned out sadly to be a wish unfulfilled. For more on such racial/ethnic hierarchies in antiquity, see Byron 2002; and Isaac 2004.

22. Similar dynamics were at work in the attempt to reverse the Jewish practice of circumcision by and among some Jews within the Greco-Roman world. Paul himself mentions circumcision and uncircumcision in 1 Corinthians (7:18–19), I will also have more to say about the Jewish circumcised penis a little later on in this chapter.

23. According to Dale Martin (1995: 96–103), Paul's evaluation of these gifts also has to do with his desire to reverse status, since prophecy was generally associated with the lower *nous* (mind) while tongues or esoteric speech was generally associated with the higher *pneuma* (spirit).

24. Ernst Kantorowicz has suggested that it is from medieval Christology (Christ as having the corporeal duality of human and God) that the English and the French developed the doctrine of the "king's two bodies"—namely, the king's body natural and body politic (1957). I am not sure if one cannot actually attribute this doctrine more directly to Paul's explication in 1 Corinthians on Christ's physical body and church body. The irony in all this is that I read Paul's argument about Christ's dual corporeality as at least partly a challenge to the colonialism of the Roman Caesar, while Kantorowicz proposes that the corporeal duality of the English and French monarchs functioned to ensure the indestructibility of the king's sovereignty, and hence the dual idea of sovereign succession and the indestructibility of English and French body politics. Both ideas being suggested by Kantorowicz have, of course, a role to play in the subsequent development of English and French colonial projects.

25. Since Paul uses the same "master-and-slave" or "ownership" vocabularies not only to describe the relations between Christ and his followers but also to underscore the (bodily) obligation that Christ-followers have to each other (9:19–27) as well as the (bodily) obligation that married couples have to each other (7:4), a potential dilemma arises for followers who are married to an "unbeliever." Paul awkwardly dances around this problem by asserting that within marriage and family the cleansing power of the follower is greater than the contaminating influence of the unbeliever (7:12–16). Nevertheless, Paul is clear that the best thing for a Christ-follower to do is to remain celibate and abstain from sex altogether (7:5–7, 15). See also D. B. Martin 1995: 209–219.

26. Hays refers to this as a process of "resocialization" on the part of the Corinthians (1997: 4, 11–12, 63, 98, 111).

27. One must not collapse Paul's various letters together as if what he says in one is unproblematically transferable to another. Therefore, one must not (*pace* Braxton 2003) assume because of Galatians that Paul's statement about circumcision and uncircumcision being "nothing" is a reaction to the Corinthians' also wanting to be circumcised. Note that Paul's statement in 7:19 is preceded by 7:18, where he discourages the "correction" or removal of circumcision as much as he does the seeking of it. I am therefore suggesting that Paul's statement here functions to remedy or correct a negative view that the Corinthians had about Jewish men and their circumcised penises.

28. As Buell and Johnson Hodge have argued on the basis of Romans and Galatians, Paul's incorporation of Gentiles "in Christ" is not racially/ethnically neutral, since he is using a Jewish or Judean rhetorical strategy (regarding racial/ethnic inheritance through generations) to "graft" Gentiles onto a Jewish or Judean ancestry under Abraham, and thus the God of Israel, even if these Gentiles do not necessarily have to become Jewish or Judean in all of their practices (2004: 247–50; see also Gaston 2005: 267–68; Johnson Hodge 2005: 276).

Notice also that, throughout the letter, Paul uses Jewish Scripture as yet another weapon to correct or counteract the Corinthians' obsession with "wisdom," which Paul also stereotypes as a Greek or Gentile characteristic. Stephen M. Pogoloff, for example, has suggested, after typifying rhetoric as a(nother) form of (Greco-Roman?) cultural wisdom and thus an index of social status, that Paul cited Jewish or Hebrew Scripture in 1:19 (Isaiah 29:14), 1:26–31 (Jeremiah 9:22–23), and 3:19 (Job 5:12–13 and Psalm 93:11) to recommend a different but good kind of wisdom. This (Jewish) wisdom teaches not exaltation of one's own status but humility before God, which is also commended by Paul through his citing of Isaiah 64:4 in 2:9 and Isaiah 40:13 in 2:16 (Pogoloff 1992: 54, 140, 156–58). Much work has been done on the importance of Hebrew Scripture for Paul's 1 Corinthians; see, for example, Stanley 2004: 75–96; and Heil 2005.

29. One may extend Dale Martin's point and further tie the "necessary" to Paul's other adjectives in 12:22–25 as all being references to the circumcised penis, because Greeks were against the Jewish practice of circumcision, seeing it as a mutilation of an otherwise perfect body and hence as a crude and ugly violation of beauty (Dover 1989: 124–35).

30. As Johnson Hodge correctly points out (2005: 270), Paul himself sees circumcision as the Jewish or Judean identity marker in Galatians 2:7–8.

31. For my purposes, let me reiterate what one's body (including one's race/ethnicity) might have meant to one's ethos in the Greco-Roman world. Theon, for example, discusses ethos in three main categories: (1) external qualities like education, friendship, reputation, and wealth; (2) bodily qualities like health and beauty; and (3) virtues and deeds (*Prog.* 9.15–24, 10.13–18). Not only does the body of the orator occupy a separate category, markings of the body can also be found beyond the category of "bodily qualities." For example, included under "external qualities" is one's breeding or birth, which might well involve one's race/ethnicity.

32. Johnson Hodge argues that the "lawlessness" in 1 Corinthians 9:21–22 refers to a moral deficiency (as in "evil") rather than a racial/ethnic designation (as in "Gentile"). In the literary context of 1 Corinthians, I do not see the two as necessarily mutually exclusive. For Paul, as we shall see, Gentiles are also morally suspect.

33. African American critics have suggested that the practice of "passing" does not only "turn what [is] conceived of as a natural opposition into a societal one" (Fabi 2001: 5) but also indicates a desire "to control the terms of . . . racial definition, rather than be subject to the definitions of white supremacy" (G. Wald 2000: 6). At the same time, I do not deny that "passing" or "chameleonism" may be—for some—a matter of survival, and that it may have both accommodative and subversive effects.

34. Johnson Hodge, arguing for a more fluid understanding of ethnic identity in Paul, also discusses 1 Corinthians 9:19–22, although she does so through Clarence Glad's "psychagogy" (Johnson Hodge 2005: 282–85). The "individual dispositions" and "communal context" of Glad's "psychagogy" (Glad 1995) are in my view inadequate for the Corinthian passage in question because psychagogy does not take into consideration the racial/ethnic rankings at work within the larger imperial dynamics of the Roman empire. As a result, Johnson Hodge, despite her own reference to how colonization created multiple identities in ancient Sicily (2005: 274), presents Paul's desire to live "gentilelishly" to fulfill his hope for Israel's restoration, as if the (imperial) power relations within Paul's context were either inconsequential or at most one-dimensional. That is to say, in Glad's formulation, and hence Johnson Hodge's application of "psychagogic" and pedagogical dynamics, the teacher (Paul) is always already the one who has the power over the students, and hence the emphasis or the burden is consistently on the teacher's willingness and ability to be flexible to adapt and meet the changing "dispositions" of those students (2005: 283–85). Power dynamics within a teaching and learning community are, however, often much more complicated and even confrontational. What is not emphasized enough is precisely the power differentials between a teacher who is a colonized Jew (Paul) and a student audience made up of mainly Greco-Roman colonizers (the Corinthians). Put differently, Paul's "adaptability" is not necessarily accepted or appreciated by the Corinthians, just as a predominantly white institution is not necessarily ready to adopt a racial/ethnic minority faculty member, even if—or perhaps especially—because he or she is willing to talk and act white. I also think Johnson Hodge's concluding remarks about Paul's prioritizing of "in-Christness" over other available identities a little confusing, because it once again sounds like being in Christ is subsuming if not transcending other ethnic identities and identifications. It would be helpful to clarify here again that being in Christ is, as Johnson Hodge has argued alone and along with Buell, being incorporated into Israel's larger story or into a Jewish/Judean ancestry (Johnson Hodge 2005: 276; Buell and Johnson Hodge 2004: 247–50). In other words, the effect of prioritizing "in-Christness" is not the suppression of racial/ethnic difference; instead, since Christ is Jewish, its

effect has more to do with—negatively speaking—not discriminating against Jews or—positively speaking—even the endorsing or endearing of Jewish identities. If racial/ethnic identities are multiple and malleable, as Johnson Hodge is arguing, I would suggest that, in the context of the Roman empire, the malleability of racial/ethnic identities in a Jew and in a Corinthian carries vastly different significations and implications.

35. Elisabeth Bronfen, writing about the pervasive portrayals of women dying in modern narratives and paintings, refers also to Freudian psychoanalysis to suggest that this representation, repetition, or continuation is a simultaneous acknowledgment and denial of the threats of death in life (1992: 30, 65, 102, 120). By portraying and mourning the death of an-other, Bronfen contends, the speaker or spectator is at the same time able to enjoy a moment of self-congratulatory satisfaction for having survived. This portrait, literary or otherwise, functions therefore, in a sense, as the survivor's immortalizing self-portrait. For Bronfen, this sense of satisfaction or superiority, as well as being the transposing or ciphering act of the surviving speaker or spectator, makes and marks the survivor as culturally, even if not biologically, masculine.

36. Richard B. Hays gets very close to this idea when he compares Greco-Roman orators to "movie stars and sports heroes" (1997: 30), though he never articulates "masculinity" as an issue in rhetorical competitions; see also Hays 1997: 27, 35. For more on masculinity and Paul's Corinthian correspondence in particular, see Larson 2004; for masculinity and Pauline studies in general, see Clines 2003.

37. Quintilian's suggestion also shows, in my view, the complex relations between rhetoric and masculinity. Actors were generally considered to be part of the undesirable *infames* in Roman society (Edwards 1997). What it points to, then, is what Schüssler Fiorenza calls "the feminine typecasting of rhetoric" (1999: 63) vis-à-vis the pursuit of a masculine philosophy (and one can readily include performance in that "feminine typecasting"). If rhetoric and performance were both always already suspect in terms of Greco-Roman masculinity, the insistence that rhetoric become a performance of masculinity might be an attempt to defend or shore up an acknowledged lack or conscious threat. As we shall see, I think this dynamics has implications for Paul's own gender understanding within 1 Corinthians.

38. Despite Isaac's statement that Jews "are not usually accused of softness or effeminacy," he does refer to Rutilius Namatianus' comment in the fifth century C.E. that the Jewish God, by reason of the Sabbath rest, must be soft or effeminate (2004: 464, 471–72). Harrill also reads the Corinthians' attack on Paul's body and rhetoric (2 Cor. 10:10) as their view of Paul as slavish and lacking in manhood (2006: 35–57). What Harrill seems to have forgotten in that reading is a point that he himself emphasizes repeatedly throughout his larger project on New Testament slavery; namely, that Greco-Roman slavery does not connect only with issues of masculinity, since slaves, women (hence the issue of masculinity), barbarians or foreigners (hence the issue of race/ethnicity), and beasts (hence the issue of humanity or human-ness) slide into and intersect with each other (2006: 37, 41–42, 47, 69, 124, 130, 136–37).

In other words, Harrill has overlooked Paul's body as also "Jewish" even though he cites Cicero's statement that "Jews and Syrians" are "born to be slaves" (*De provinciis consularibus* 5.10; cited in Harrill 2006: 44).

39. Schäfer, in his reading of Martial, argues for a particular connection that the Roman writer makes between a circumcised penis and a fantasized sexual potency as well as lustfulness on the part of the Jews; see Schäfer 1997: 99–102.

40. Of course, my point here is not to argue for the portrayals of Fu Manchu and Charlie Chan as positive, but to demonstrate how Chin ends up buying into and collaborating in the abjection of effeminacy and homosexuality in the name of a progressive racial politics.

41. Not only does Paul seem to have intentionally left out the "no longer male and female" part of the baptismal formula in 12:13, but he also explicitly argues for a "natural" or "divinely ordained" ordering of men over women in 11:3–10, as well as commands women to silence in 14:33b–36. Others have pointed out how Paul, in contrast to what one finds in Acts, places Aquila before Prisca in 16:19, or how he interrupts his practice of addressing both men and women when he comes to the question of "virgins" in 7:25–38. For a helpful discussion of this interruption in particular and Paul's treatment of women in 1 Corinthians in general, see also D. B. Martin 1995: 227–49.

42. This is why I am not satisfied with the otherwise very fine article by Buell and Johnson Hodge, because they simply conclude that Paul's vision of race/ethnicity is not ideal, because it "structurally subordinates one ethnoracial group [Gentiles] to another [Jews/Judeans]," as some German Christians did during the Third Reich (2004: 250). Read in the imperial context of the first century C.E., Paul's reversal of dominant Greco-Roman racial/ethnic hierarchies does have an element of (anti-colonial) protest and resistance; it might even be his strategy for survival. One must not forget the reality of *different* power differentials when one evaluates this admittedly imperfect and inadequate move by Paul (say, between Paul and Greeks/Romans and between Hitler's German Christians and Jews). Differences in social location and in race/ethnicity do bear weight even if the rhetoric and the concepts seem to be similar. Again, my goal here is not to defend Paul, but to insist on a more nuanced reading that teases out the complexities even as one brings out the complicities in Paul's efforts to resist.

43. The most controversial terms here are undoubtedly *malakoi* and *arsenokoitai* (6:9), which the New Revised Standard Version translates as "male prostitutes" and "sodomites" respectively. For a detailed discussion of both terms, see D. B. Martin 1996; and Nissinen 1998: 113–18.

44. This is, of course, part of the stereotypical portrayal of Gentiles by Jews; see Buell and Johnson Hodge 2004: 244. In other words, both Jews and Romans used the strategy of "oppositional ethnic self-definition" (J. M. Hall 1997: 47), albeit from very different positions of power. Just as Tacitus attacks the Jews for their dietary and sexual practices (*Hist.* 5.5), so Paul is accusing the Corinthians of idolatry in the form of food and/or fornication (5:1–2, 5–13; 6:12–20; 10:1–22).

45. Other early Christ-followers after Paul (including Clement, Athenagoras, and Justin) would continue to use this strategy to justify their following of Christ as they simultaneously worked to negotiate what "being Roman" might mean; see Buell 2001: 460–66.

46. Here I am, of course, only comparing Paul and Dionysius in terms of their strategies, not the purpose or direction of those strategies. That is to say, I am not suggesting with this comparison that Paul is pro-Roman or engaging in an apologetic on behalf of Rome.

47. Paul would, however, speak of the influence of a Christ-follower in cleansing rather than contaminating terms (7:12–16). Using a similar language of pollution against the body to explain 1 Corinthians, Dale Martin nevertheless argues that Paul is worrying about a fundamental and internal polluting agent that is more threatening than women who do not follow Christ (since he does allow marriages between followers and non-followers to continue in 7:12–16) and other sexual dissidents (1995:198–228). Paul is most afraid of desire, which is also assumed to be particularly dangerous and tempting for women.

Chapter 6: Melancholia in Diaspora

1. As Christ's open vessel, Paul is free to acknowledge his rhetorical inadequacies (1:17; 2:1–4). By doing so, he seems to place himself among the "weak" and "foolish" ones who are nonetheless chosen by God. At the same time, Paul's apparent placing of himself among the "weak" (e.g., 2:3; 4:10) is countered by his self-articulation as one of the "strong" (e.g., 9:22). Dale Martin is correct that this ambiguity has much to do with Paul's rhetorical goal in 1 Corinthians; namely, to promote unity by persuading people of high status (the "strong") to also accept willingly positions and people of low status (the "weak"; 1995: 61–68). I would add, however, that this ambiguity also fits well with his self-portrait and self-understanding as a "he/she" in 1 Corinthians. This ambiguity is, moreover, consistent not only with what I said earlier about status being a complicated composite of various factors like birth, wealth, education, race/ethnicity, and religion (thus varietal status occurs precisely when a person scores high in some of these areas but low in others), but also with the fact that people can have multiple identities (see Buell and Johnson Hodge 2004: 248). If we can trust Acts, Paul is, for instance, both a Jew and a Roman citizen. Since the meaning of status is relational, it may change and fluctuate depending on the specific terms and relations under consideration. In addition to all these factors, my argument that Paul is working on at least two fronts here (status conflicts among the Corinthians and status conflict between the Corinthians and himself) makes it futile and less than helpful to try to identify and stabilize "the weak" as only one (racial/ethnic) group of people.

2. Paul's liminal or threshold state between the mystical and the material will become even more pronounced in 2 Corinthians, where he couples his other-worldly travels with a thorn in his flesh (12:7).

3. Although I place a major emphasis on racial/ethnic difference throughout this chapter, I must point out that race/ethnicity, religion, and politics are often linked and overlap each other. Such mixing and mingling were particularly true of the Greco-Roman world. Dale Martin, for example, suggests that Paul in 1 Corinthians is pitting the "somewhat hidden world of [Jewish?] apocalyptic reality" against "the Greco-Roman world of rhetoric and status"; perhaps more important, Dale Martin is also quick to point out that Paul "in some sense 'mirrors' the values of 'this world' but in another sense counters and overturns those values" (1995: 57). In other words, Paul is not ideologically "pure"; instead, he does straddle between both worlds.

4. The same can be said not only of Paul but also of the women and sexual dissidents onto whom Paul transfers his own abjection. In addition to that of Julia Kristeva, various theories on sacrifice and surrogation have emphasized this link between abjection and liminality; see, for example, Roach 1996 (esp. 40–41, 148).

5. I put "first" in quotes to signify the ongoing debate among scholars about the integrity of Paul's Corinthian correspondence. See, for example, Snyder 1992: 8–14; and Wan 2000c: 1–10.

6. In a way comparable to the choice of some Asian Americans to surgically change the frequency of epicanthic fold above their eyes (Palumbo–Liu 1999: 92–104; Gilman 1999: 98–111), some Jews of the Greco-Roman world also chose to reverse the marks of their circumcision (1 Maccabees 1:15; Josephus, *AJ* 12.241; see also S. J. D. Cohen 1999: 39–40; Gilman 1999: 137–44). These procedures are at least partly connected to the psychic process of *ressentiment*. *Ressentiment,* or the internalization and externalization of colonial abjecting dynamics, may also provide one possible "answer" to Claudia Setzer's question about why Paul is opposed to Gentiles being circumcised if Paul "remains a robust Jew and maintains the election of Israel" (2005: 293), especially since the Jewish practice was tied to the promise of Abraham becoming the "father" of many nations in Genesis 17. Gilman, although he does not use the term or idea of *ressentiment,* has suggested how Freud (that diasporic Jew of another era) also so internalized the cultural stigmatization of Jews that he decided not to circumcise even his own sons (1993: 86).

7. I am indebted to Theodore W. Jennings, Jr., for pointing out to me Martin Heidegger's comment that linking Paul to *ressentiment*, as Nietzsche does, shows "only that one has understood nothing" (Heidegger 2004: 86). To be very brief here, let me suggest a succession of thoughts without much elaboration. First, the projects of Nietzsche and Heidegger share two concerns: (1) both place a high premium on individuals making self-conscious choices independently of traditional views or conventional values, and (2) both make a close connection between being and time. Second, Nietzsche's project depends on a nostalgic return to a form of aristocratic elitism that values a particular type of being. Third, this type of particular being (the "overman" or "superman"), for Nietzsche, is able to accept and will an eternal recurrence as an existential challenge to create a new vision of life. Fourth, Nietzsche despises Paul for representing a slave mentality and a slavish or colonized

Jewish people that seek revenge on their masters by way of a transcendent God and a set of "universal" moral values (like pity) that end up devaluing this life in favor of the next. Fifth, Nietzsche seems to understand *ressentiment* in general and Paul's *ressentiment* in particular as a reactive or reactionary response to a fateful and transitory passing of time (this is especially so when Nietzsche reads Paul under Martin Luther's influence [1997: 39–55]). Sixth, Heidegger's negative assessment of Nietzsche at this point has to do with at least their different opinions on time, on Paul, and on the place of theology within German philosophy. For Heidegger, Paul's apocalyptic thought seems to (courtesy of Rudolf Bultmann?) represent an understanding of time that is no longer fated, and thus provides an opening for an "authentic" existence.

It is important to point out that, despite its more recent publication in English, Heidegger's *The Phenomenology of Religious Life* (2004) is actually a collection of his lectures given back in the late 1910s and early 1920s, and Heidegger's thought certainly also evolved with the passing of time. By the time of his *What Is Called Thinking?* (1968), Heidegger makes not only a distinction between "going to the encounter" of previous thinkers and "going counter to" previous thinkers but also a more sustained effort to (re)read Nietzsche that is more characteristic of an "encounter."

Thus I am also reading Nietzsche's reading of Paul here in the later Heideggerian sense of a "transformative" (re)reading (see Wood 2002), particularly given the aphoristic nature of Nietzsche's writing. Despite Nietzsche's tendency to enamor elitism and thus his reading of Paul as a "priestly" Jew in contrast to "other" Jews, his contextualizing of Paul and other Jews as being colonized and resistant to the Romans is a helpful resource to re-read Paul in a way with which Nietzsche himself might not agree or anticipate. For example, Nietzsche's comment that "[o]ne would no more choose to associate with 'first Christians' than one would with Polish Jews" (1990: 171) points to Paul's abjection as a Christ-following Jew, particularly if one remembers that Paul's resurrection rhetoric is always already premised on Christ's crucifixion by the Romans. As I hope to show in the next section, if one reads Paul's emphasis on Christ's crucifixion and resurrection as melancholic resistance against the Romans, then Paul's *ressentiment* is not necessarily other-worldly or doomed to drown in an individualistic psychology. At the same time, my reading will not, as both Nietzsche and Heidegger did, (over)emphasize individual agency so much that it becomes a desire and advocate for mastery.

8. I should also point out in light of Krister Stendahl's often-cited essay on "The Apostle Paul and the Introspective Conscience of the West" (1976: 78–96) that while Stendahl is critiquing the practice of reading Paul in terms of guilt and individualism, my reading focuses on the psychic processes of subjection that are not individualistic. Not only must one realize the differences between the first-century Greco-Roman world and the twenty-first-century United States, one must also recognize differences among various psychological readings of Paul. One should also recall that Greco-Romans did talk about *psychē* and divided selves *(akrasia)*; the

Stoics even had a theory regarding transference of subjectivity *(oikeiōsis)* that will be relevant to a later part of this chapter (see Harrill 2006: 19, 27–28, 30, 91).

9. This "socializing" or "culturalizing" of psychoanalysis is, of course, in keeping with Pauline studies in many ways. Not only was Stendahl's "classic" essay on "The Apostle Paul and the Introspective Conscience of the West" (1976: 78–96)— which is often seen as one of the early stimuli to a rethinking and thus the "new perspective" on Paul—first delivered to the 1961 Annual Meeting of the American Psychological Association, but there is also now a steady insistence that Paul should be read as relating to "peoples" rather than "individuals" (Setzer 2005: 293).

10. While Durrant reads the novels of J. M. Coetzee, Wilson Harris, and Toni Morrison as continual (and thus endless?) mourning over the traumatic histories of racial oppression, Gilroy's "postcolonial melancholia" refers to the imperial pathology of refusing to recognize the loss of (the British) empire. In comparison to Gilroy, I will focus more on the melancholia of the colonized and less on melancholia as a pathology.

11. In a sense, the bridging between colonialism and psychoanalysis has been well paved and prepared by the work of Bhabha, who has consistently and insistently turned to psychoanalysis and turned it into a tool to interrogate and indicate what colonialism has repressed.

12. My move from Nietzschean *ressentiment* to Freudian mourning and melancholia is actually not as "baseless" as it might look. Not only has Freud credited Nietzsche with having "a more penetrating knowledge of himself than any other man who ever lived or was likely to live" (Jones 1953–57: 2.344), but he has also admired the psychoanalytic work of and exchanged letters for over two decades with the woman who rejected Nietzsche's marriage proposal, Lou Salomé (Jones 1953–57: 2.176–77, 421; 3.208, 213, 453).

13. This statement does not imply a return to the "older" understanding of Jews as a separate group of people who had no interaction with non-Jewish social sectors (Eisenbaum 2005: 235). As current Asian Americans know, there is a vast space between being fully isolated in a racial/ethnic ghetto and being fully integrated into the mainstreams of a society.

14. Bhabha's "mimicry," or the colonial injunction to be white but not quite, seems to point to similar psycho-political dynamics (1994: 85–92). At least Cheng does see Bhabha's "mimicry" and Fanon's "comparison" as two fundamentally related activities (2001: 79). My reading of Paul's melancholia as a double loss or a double bind is also comparable to the way in which Kaja Silverman reads the melancholic female subject (1988: 148–59). According to her, female melancholia is a result of being simultaneously pushed by the Oedipus complex to dis-identify and pulled by cultural pressures to identify with one's mother. If Paul and the women he marginalizes and excludes actually share similar psycho-political traumata, then the idea that Paul's "splitting" is a rejection of an "other" that is part of oneself also takes on an added level of meaning.

15. As Cheng suggests, melancholia could and should be read as a psycho-

political dynamics impacting a colonized racial/ethnic minority as well as the entire "nation," particularly if the latter is built upon the consumption and denial as well as the exclusion and retention—thus, in a word, abjection—of racialized/ethnicized others (2001: x, 10–13). Although Cheng has in mind the nation of the United States or the American empire during the so-called American century, what she says is, I think, also applicable to the Roman empire of the first century. See also Gilroy 2005: 98–106.

16. This is especially so given Gilman's thesis that psychoanalysis is Freud's displaced or disguised study of anti-Semitism (1993).

17. Kristeva has, of course, linked her exploration of abjection, the Freudian understanding of melancholia, and her critique of (hetero)sexism through what she calls the "black sun" (1989). As will become apparent, Kristeva's emphasis on a melancholic double bind will be very important for my reading of Paul in 1 Corinthians. Since I am relating Paul's melancholia to Jesus, I was tempted to play on Kristeva's notion and call it Paul's "black son" (given Paul's representation of Jesus as "God's son," 1:9; 15:28) to point to the absence of racial/ethnic considerations in Kristeva's reflection (as well as my desire to at least keep the possibility of an Afro-Asiatic Jesus open). I decided not to do so, however, because Paul's gender problem in 1 Corinthians (not only his abjection of women but also his emphasis on God as Father and Jesus as son) is precisely what Kristeva is targeting in presenting melancholia as the incomplete or unsuccessful detachment from the mother.

18. Interestingly enough, not only has the "messiah" of the Ghost Dance religion been called "Christ," but the Ghost Dance is also meant to dance dead Native Americans back to life and thus functions to reclaim a Native American identity as well as to restore a Native American world (Porcupine 1973; see also Smoak 2006). Here one witnesses the amazing twists and turns of intercultural contacts and contexts. The Ghost Dance is able to "incorporate" Christian elements to resist the colonialism being carried out partly through Christianity. At the same time, if one follows my argument about Paul in this chapter, one can also say that the Native Americans also have an insight about Paul that has been overlooked (intentionally or unintentionally) by white Christians.

One might wonder if, in accordance with Christian traditions that maintain Paul never met the fleshly Jesus, why Paul would mourn and become melancholic over the loss of someone whom he has never met. In some ways I find this fascinating question almost impossible to answer, since one of psychoanalysis's deepest insights is the displacement and hence the almost irrecoverable loss of "origin." In other words, an identifiable melancholic object might itself be just a link within an ever differing and deferring chain of significant significations. Jesus, for example, might be representative of Paul's own dissatisfaction with the colonizing Romans and/or Paul's ideal of a peaceful multi-racial/ethnic community, so his continuous mourning for Jesus might actually be his yet-to-be-articulated melancholia for his lost ideals.

19. I am, in effect, reversing Cheng's analogical reading of melancholia and assimilation as internalization of an "other" (2001). While Cheng scrutinizes the

effects of this racial melancholia in terms of a minority's assimilation of an idealized "whiteness," I am arguing that Paul is asking his Gentile Corinthians to internalize Jesus and hence assimilate under the God of Israel, if not into the people of Israel.

20. This "second killing," or forgetting, of the lost object is, ironically enough, what defines "proper mourning" for Freud (1953–74: 14.244–45). It is precisely Paul's refusal to "disparage," "denigrate," or "kill" (Freud 1953–74: 14.257) Jesus (again) that constitutes what I call his "melancholia."

21. Perhaps this helps to explain why and how Freud, in a subsequent exploration, presents melancholia as the precondition for both ego formation and mourning (1953–74: 19.1–59). Freud does mention three features that exist in melancholia to distinguish it from mourning: (1) a low self-regard (1953–74: 14.244), (2) an unconscious dimension (1953–74: 14.245), and (3) a sense of ambivalence (1953–74: 14.256). In any case, the two concepts turn out to be so intertwined that it seems highly questionable to me that one can really differentiate or detach them, in pathological terms or otherwise. See also Cheng 2001: 95–99, 104–105.

22. Despite Paul's reversal project and my own understanding of power relations as something other than one-directional or one-dimensional, I nevertheless would not want to run the risk of collapsing the power differential between the colonizer and the colonized. To signify that differential, I am using "exclusionary inclusion" to refer to the state of the Corinthians, but—following Abdul JanMohamed's reading of black exclusion in Jim Crow society (2005: 233)—"included exclusion" to refer to the state of Paul and other colonized and racialized Jews within the Roman empire.

23. In 1 Corinthians, Paul refers to the common meal more literally as "the Lord's Supper" (11:20) rather than the more ritualistic Eucharist or "thanksgiving meal." In what follows, I shall proceed to argue that there are in fact good reasons for this more literal naming of the meal.

24. Freud at times also explains the self-denigration of the melancholic as a transference between the lost object and the melancholic. For Freud, the experience of loss may lead the melancholic to shift from missing to blaming and then to hating the lost object. When this hatred of the lost object is transferred to the melancholic self, self-denigration results. See Freud 1953–74: 14.244, 248.

25. As I indicated earlier, low self-regard or self-loathing is a key defining characteristic of melancholia for Freud (1953–74: 14.244, 246–48, 251–52). In addition to his desire for a changed body in 15:35–58, another passage that may indicate Paul's self-loathing is 4:9–13. Perhaps the proximity or the "transference" between melancholia and self-*ressentiment* is why Freud reads melancholia as a potentially dangerous psychic process that might lead to the extreme act of suicide (1953–74: 14.252). Of course, in Paul's case, this transference of melancholia into self-*ressentiment* is even easier. As a diasporic Jew living within the Roman empire, Paul has more than an indirect memory of Jewish abjection through Jesus; it is his "lived" reality. Abjection is, after all, what he believes he is partly facing with the Corinthians. Paul's melancholia as a colonized Jew with an abject body also presents a chal-

lenge to Freud's understanding that melancholia has to do with "dissatisfaction with the ego on moral grounds . . . [but] concerns itself much less frequently with bodily infirmity, ugliness or weakness, or with social inferiority" (1953–74: 14.248).

26. Daniel Punday, in his book on "narrative bodies," has raised a similar point about the power differential between "the embodiment of the masses" and the disembodiment of, or at least a disembodied space before, the elite analyst (2003: 174). While one should not lose sight of the status reversal Paul performs here as a colonized Jew, the fact that he does so through a "disembodying" move is also worth pondering. For more on the operation of power between medicine and human/social bodies within a specific Asian or Cambodian American context, see Ong 2003: 91–95, 103, 109.

27. I believe Bhabha is thinking in similar terms when he suggests that, rather than merely judging or condemning a stereotype (which would certainly include a racialized and colonized subject), one must "change the object of analysis itself" to construct a stereotype's "regime of truth," or to understand "the *processes of subjectification* made possible (and plausible) through stereotypical discourse" (1994: 67, 70; emphasis in original).

Chapter 7: Immigrants and Intertexts

1. Cha's *Dictee* was first published by Tanam Press in 1982, and was republished by Third Woman Press in 1995. Its new acclaim can be most readily seen in the publication of a collection of essays on *Dictee* (E. H. Kim and Alarcón 1994) as well as a more recent volume on Cha (Lewallen 2001). For many critics, *Dictee*'s "resurrection" has to do with the changing emphasis within Asian American studies since the 1990s, when diversity began to problematize the previous concern to cultivate "common ground" to "reclaim America," and thus a more rigid understanding of identity politics. See, for example, Choy 1999: 95–98; and S. S. Wong 1994: 103–104.

2. For Jameson, the way postmodern texts employ quotations and insert foreign languages results in a bricolage that is but another "specialized global space" that distances, alienates, and colonizes readers into political depression and inaction (1991: 49, 140–43).

3. Kristina Julie Chew, on the other hand, does acknowledge this biblical intertext, but she mistakes the passage as a quotation from Luke 4, which, unlike Matthew, places the temptation of worldly kingdoms before the "capering challenge" (Chew 1995: 231). Neither does Chew follow up on that acknowledgment of allusion with any kind of analysis.

4. The only possibility of such a trace in Lew is through his "tracking" of *Dictee*'s intertextual relations with Marguerite Yourcenar's *Fires*, since both are structured into nine sections named after figures in classical Greek stories. In Lew's blurry reproduction of Yourcenar's text, one can see a reference to "Mary Magdalene" and "St. John" (Lew 1982: 2–3). Yourcenar's intertextual relations to the Bible are more

explicitly acknowledged by Shu-mei Shih in a footnote (1997: 162n24), but that acknowledgment does not lead Shih (like Chew) to pay any particular attention to the Bible in Shih's reading of Cha's *Dictee*.

5. Note that I am using the word "may" to connote possibility in two senses. First, it connotes a potentiality rather than a certainty; that is to say, the actual effect of intertextuality on different readers is never guaranteed. Second, it connotes a multiplicity rather than a singularity; that is to say, there is no one definitive understanding of intertextuality. Interpretations of this very concept vary in accordance with "specific social and ideological agendas and perspectives" (Allen 2000: 4). Lisa Lowe is, of course, correct that Asian Americans have been racialized as "immigrant" and hence "perpetual foreigners" in the United States (1996). One must not, however, let this process of racialization lead to a kind of knee-jerk reaction that ends up—like Frank Chin does—creating a false binarism between immigrants and Asian Americans as if the two are by definition mutually exclusive.

6. It is important to point out that Cha proceeds to problematize the conventional assumption of immigrants as people who resettle transnationally out of "free choice." This is arguably best seen in the way she describes Koreans living in Manchuria during Japanese colonial rule over Korea as "Refugees. Immigrants. Exiles" (Cha 1995: 45), thus signifying the blurred lines among these categories and the impurity of so-called free choice.

7. Immediately before this first numbered page, *Dictee* contains a page that looks like a table of contents. However, the heading of the first section, "Clio History," does not appear until twenty-three pages later. I will return to this issue of "beginning" in *Dictee* toward the end of this chapter. I should also take this opportunity to thank Professor Andre LaCocque of Chicago Theological Seminary for helping me with the French in *Dictee*.

8. For examples of such inaccurate and/or inappropriate translations here and elsewhere in Cha's *Dictee*, see Mix 1998: 177–78. In this regard, one can also question if the distinction that Foucault draws between the episteme of correspondence in the pre-Classical eras and the episteme of causality in the Cartesian world is not a bit overdrawn (1970: 17–77). If not an epistemology, there is at least a long-lingering ethics of correspondence, conformity, or uniformity.

9. The role that Chinese and English play in Korean and Korean American lives should be well known. What may be less known is the strong missionary presence that French Catholics had in nineteenth-century Korea (Mix 1998: 180). Cha herself started studying French at a Catholic school in San Francisco and spent a year attending the Centre d'Études Américains du Cinéma in Paris. For a helpful narrative chronology of Cha's short life, see Susette Min 2001. Cha's emphasis on French may also have to do with the thought that, as Immanuel Wallerstein argues, the French Revolution of 1789 led to the concept of "citizens" (1999: 106–107). As we shall see, Cha does mention the French Revolution in *Dictee* (1995: 14), and citizenship and inclusion are ideas that she struggles with throughout her book.

Many critics have also pointed out how an assumption of cultural hierarchy operates within the practice of translation, and thus how the untranslated Korean writing in Cha's *Dictee* (1995: frontispiece) denotes Korea's "inferior" position within the dominant cultural hierarchy. See, for instance, Lowe 1994: 41–42; Mix 1998: 175; E. K. Min 1998: 314; and E. H. Kim 1994: 4, 8–10. I think Cha has also subtly pointed to the cultural hierarchy—or, in fact, cultural violence—that is involved in language dictation or translation with the very first French phrase on the very first (numbered) page of *Dictee*. What is translated or written out in English as "open paragraph" can also be translated as "go to the line." This reveals not only an enforcement of certain standards but also reminds me of a photograph of an execution line in *Dictee* (1995: 39).

10. There may be several reasons for Cha's choice of title. First, dictation is often used to teach foreign languages. Second, dictation, like other dictates, demands faithful reproduction and repetition. Third, dictation involves an inherent contradiction: though it demands faithful reproduction, it also demands a *change* from what is verbal into what is written, not to mention the likelihood that the "dictator" may himself or herself be reading from a written text. For a good and thorough essay on the figure of dictation in Cha, see E. K. Min 1998.

11. As note 9 indicates, film theory was the subject of Cha's focus during her year of study in Paris. Cha has produced not only two films but also an edited volume on film theory, entitled *Apparatus* (1980). For a catalog of various forms of Cha's artistic productions, see Lewallen 2001: 155–67. One can also find within the pages of *Dictee* descriptions of the cinema experience; see, for example, Cha 1995: 94, 149.

12. Laura E. Donaldson has also advocated using the filmic act of suturing to understand intertextuality as a "transnational critical practice" (1995). Donaldson focuses, however, only on the imperial violence that suturing, intertextuality, and transnationalism entail. Her own emphasis on (re)introducing agents who operate out of different power positions (1995: 283), as well as her appeal to Homi K. Bhabha (1995: 290), should have alerted her to the possibilities that these same acts and theories may become avenues of subversion and resistance in the hands of the colonized. Within the theory of intertextuality, especially in the case of Kristeva, this emphasis on specificity can also be understood in terms of the contrasting focus between Bakhtin *(parole)* and Saussure *(langue)*.

13. In contrast to dictation and translation and their demand for faithful repetition, Shelley Wong suggests that conjugation indicates the relationship between language and subject position, as well as the dictate against multiple subject positions (1994: 120).

14. Yi-chun Tricia Lin understands this paragraph as Cha "undoing the religiosity of the entire passage" (1997: 138). In other words, Cha's "making up" or "making" of confession is a replacement of religious speech by human speech, and *Dictee* her confession of human deeds or sins. This becomes Lin's way to link various parts of *Dictee* together, highlighting particularly the imperial injustice in Korea's history, whether in the hands of Japan or those of the United States.

15. What really counts as the "beginning" of Cha's *Dictee* is, as is true in the case of Luke's Acts, both confusing and debatable. Let me repeat my promise that I will have more to say about this in the final part of this chapter.

16. Note that Lin also understands Cha to be referring to the centrality of language in human experience with the phrase "words made flesh" (1997: 174–75).

17. In addition to being known for quoting from Hebrew Scripture, Matthew is also known for containing many inter-scriptural or verbal conflicts. One can think of, for example, the controversy of the disciples plucking grain on the Sabbath (12:1–8) or the disagreement between the Pharisees and Jesus on the matter of divorce (19:1–9; see Carter 2000: 265–66, 378–82). One can also think of the six antithetical statements Jesus makes in the Sermon on the Mount, each beginning with "you have heard that it was said . . . but I say to you" (5:21–48; see also 15:1–20). It is also interesting to point out in this regard that many of Matthew's so-called quotations are not exact copies of either the Hebrew Masoretic text or the Greek Septuagint, such as 1:22–23; 2:15; 4:15–16 (see Carter 2000: 114; Schweizer 1975: 27–28, 42). For more on Matthew's use of the Hebrew Scripture, see Garland 1993: 29.

18. While Elaine Kim agrees that Cha has a tenuous relationship with Korean nationalism or patriotism, she nevertheless argues for a more positive reading of Yu and martyrdom in *Dictee* (1994: 16–17).

19. Note that I am using the present tense throughout because this is the tense that Cha herself uses. Yi-chun Lin suggests that Cha is doing so to protest against what official history leaves out (especially the experiences of women) and to reveal the inseparability between historiography and present concerns (1997: 139–40).

20. What I am developing here is greatly indebted to Wang's fascinating and thought-provoking essay about "hungry women," despite the fact that his essay is about modern Chinese fiction rather than Cha or the Bible.

21. Not only do the parallel stories in the "Erato Love Poetry" section (Cha 1995: 91–119) tie together the oppression of women and that of religion, they also highlight the gender difference vis-à-vis speech. For Cha, coming to speech or language is an extremely physical experience, which she expresses by linking, for example, ink with blood, and by providing numerous drawings of the human body to accompany her description of one struggling with speech, in the "Urania Astronomy" section (1995: 61–75).

22. One should remember that the term "political correctness" was first coined by the Left to promote vigilance within its own critical efforts, but was then "translated" by the Right to dismiss *all* critical efforts of the Left (Scott 1995: 4). In addition to the mistranslations between French and English and the additions in the "Q-&-A" catechism that we have looked at, Cha's "ethics of infidelity" also extends to the speaking of the marriage vow and the naturalization oaths of U.S. citizenship (Lowe 1994: 37).

23. For Pregeant's overall argument regarding the importance of Jesus' identity throughout the Gospel of Matthew, see 1996: 213, 216–17, 220, 223.

24. It is virtually impossible to draw a clean distinction between Cha and her mother. As Cha writes, "Mother inseparable from which is her identity, her presence. . . . Mother, I dream you just to be able to see you. . . . I write. I write you. Daily. From here. If I am not writing, I am thinking about writing. I am composing" (1995: 49, 56).

25. As Chew correctly points out, Kore is also better known as Persephone, or Proserpina in Latin (1995: 273n28). Kore, the "girl" or "maiden," is often used for the sake of simplicity, but such a practice also renders Persephone nameless.

26. One can further point out an intertextual relation between Matthew 4 and John 4 that may be of significance to (my reading of) Cha. Both chapters have Jesus emphasizing a "higher hunger." We have already talked about the Scripture that Jesus quotes in response in Matthew 4:3–4. In John, sandwiched between the witness of the Samaritan woman and the response of her townsfolk is Jesus refusing an offer of food from his disciples, saying, "My food is to do the will of him who sent me and to complete his work" (John 4:34). I also wonder if Cha focuses on these two Gospels because they are best known for containing several long discourses or dictates by Jesus.

27. Note, in this regard, how in the "Calliope Epic Poetry" section, the difference between the silence of Cha's mother and the speech of Matthew's Jesus in their respective "temptations" is presented in the context of the relationship between Cha and her mother.

28. *Dictee*'s frontispiece is supposedly a picture of a mine in Japan. Since it was mined by Korean slaves, what was scratched on the wall is in Korean. While Cha does not provide a translation for the writing to indicate Korea's subaltern cultural position, the writing reads: "Mother, I want to see you / I am hungry / I want to go home." As Cha's *Dictee* clearly indicates in the "Melpomene Tragedy" section (1995: 77–89), the end of Japan's occupation does not mean the end of Korea's troubles; it has been divided into two. In a paragraph that particularly evokes the myth of Demeter and Kore, Cha writes: "The population standing before North standing before South for every bird that migrates North for Spring and South for Winter becomes a metaphor for the longing of return. Destination. Homeland" (1995: 80). In the case of Cha or Cha's mother, her "return" is also partial, because (as I have already pointed out) what immediately follows is her naturalization as a U.S. citizen, and then her unsatisfactory "return" trip to (South) Korea.

29. The Demeter/Kore myth originated from the *Homeric Hymn to Demeter* of the seventh century B.C.E.; the Eleusinian mysteries were also well established by that time. Based at Eleusis but embraced popularly by people all over the Mediterranean, the mysteries were finally eclipsed by Christianity in the fifth century C.E. See L. H. Martin 1987: 62–63, 69, 71–72.

30. Arguably, one of the best ways to get at this is through Akiko's relationship with her husband, who is a Euro-American Christian minister. Particularly helpful, perhaps, are Akiko's narratives on her baptism, her first sexual experience with her minister husband, and their travel around the United States (N. O. Keller 1997:

99–113). For a discussion of the role or function the Princess Pari tale plays in Nora Keller's *Comfort Woman,* see K. J. Lee 2004.

31. I am indebted to Fernando F. Segovia for pointing my thought in this direction, and to Gay L. Byron for providing me with the specific bibliographical reference.

32. I have long been puzzled by the way Cha's *Dictee* is set up. Before the first numbered page, we have the frontispiece of untranslated Korean inscriptions, a dedication to her parents, the epigraph attributed to Sappho, and what looks like a table of contents, where the names of the nine Muses are listed along with their respective areas of supervision. Between this table of contents and the first "chapter" ("Clio History") are, however, over twenty pages of intervening materials. I would like to suggest that these twenty-some pages (the sandwich of language exercise–"DISEUSE"–language exercises; the block of materials on language, discourse, and religion; and the two pleadings to the Muses inserted before and after the second set of language exercises) function like Jacques Derrida's "exergue" in *Of Grammatology* (1976: 3–5). Literally translatable as "outside-the-work" (from the Greek, *ex-ergon*) but nevertheless part of the text, the exergue is also the small space on the reverse side of a coin, usually below the main inscription and often giving the date and place of engraving. Whatever "exergue" may mean for Derrida, it seems to point to a marginal space, an "other" text, or a hidden beginning that threatens to return or invade. There are always already "other" beginnings, "other" words. As Shelley Wong suggests, this disruption of one single beginning can be seen in the way Cha places Sappho, the traditional tenth and mortal Muse who presides over lyric, in front of the other Muses and the epic tradition of singular beginning (1994: 115–16). Wherever one begins and whatever one says (or as Cha puts it, "beginning wherever you wish, tell"), one is involved in a suturing act. Such suturing points not only to the violence of reading/writing but also provides, at least for Cha, the potential for in(ter)ventions. I should also point out that Cha's invocation of the Muses, in a way akin to her intertextual in(ter)ventions, seems to correspond to and compete with the Catholic practice of novena or nine prayers (1995: 19), as well as the list of ten elements in Taoist cosmology at the end (1995: 173–74; see also Lin 1997: 162–63). Again, Cha's in(ter)vention means that neither the list of the Muses nor the list of Taoist cosmological elements is "accurate." Regarding the Muses, she has the traditional "Euterpe" as "Elitere," and "Polyhymnia" becomes "Polymnia" (E. K. Min 1998: 319). Regarding the Taoist element, the last item on the list seems to be using the wrong Chinese character, which, in turn, leads to a bad transliteration, *Chung Wai* (Cha 1995: 154, 173). While Shih sees this as a "misrecognition" (1997: 162n26), I am more inclined to see it as just another one of Cha's in(ter)ventions.

33. Cha does that not only in her own reading/writing of her intertexts, but she also encourages her readers to do so in reading her text. Critics are correct to point out how reading *Dictee* has to be an active, creative, even a displaced and displacing experience. This is particularly true when readers encounter languages that they cannot read; to avoid feeling displaced or disoriented, one has simply to displace or

disregard those parts of the book. Another good example of this is the "Erato Love Poetry" section, where the odd-numbered pages and the even-numbered pages tell a different story (Cha 1995: 94–118). Readers experience a narrative discontinuity despite the spatial continuity, and they have to make a choice as to which story to follow and which story to forsake. The same is true of the way Cha writes many sentences without punctuation, thus giving readers the responsibility, and the freedom, to make things up as they go along. As Eun Kyung Min suggests, naming her book *Dictee* (or dictation) may also have been Cha's way of releasing ownership of this text to others, namely her readers (1998: 309–10).

34. Sugirtharajah is referring to something very similar by way of Paul de Man and postcolonial palimpsest (2003: 48). In fact, he also refers to de Certeau in his discussion of how popular press and newspapers cite and allude to biblical texts (2003: 80–85).

Chapter 8: Telling Times in (Asian) America

1. Following Käseman, I will also use the adjective "apocalyptic" as a substantive throughout the chapter to emphasize how, in my view, apocalyptic outlooks cannot and should not be limited to any particular genre or to the realm of the literary.

2. While the United States is seen as "intrusive" and imperialistic by many nations around the world, some in the United States see themselves as isolated for the "just" cause that the Bush administration has taken towards Iraq. Regarding Asian America, many Asian Americans feel alienated because some fellow Americans look upon them as "intruders" who do not really belong to this national body. Indebted to the provocative title of a recent anthology on South Asian Americans, *A Part yet Apart* (Shankar and Srikanth 1998), I am using "a/part" to signify the tangential position many South Asian Americans find themselves in both the United States and Asian America.

3. Note that a new journal, *Postscripts* (edited by Elizabeth Castelli and Yvonne Sherwood), has been created to push biblical studies precisely in this direction.

4. Timothy K. Beal has recently argued, for instance, that the book of Revelation is different from previous apocalyptic of the Jewish traditions in two ways: first, Revelation involves a clear binarism between Satan and God; and second, it involves extreme violence (2002: 82).

5. Some social scientists have chosen to differentiate between these two outlooks, using the word "millennial" to signify a utopian beginning of a new world and reserving the word "apocalyptic" to signify catastrophic, world-ending events or sentiments. See, for example, Nichols 2002: 185.

6. Frykholm's dissertation (2001) has now been revised and published; see Frykholm 2004.

7. The ambiguous politics of apocalyptic is demonstrated time and again in readings of Revelation. For almost every book that argues for the "liberating" message of Revelation (Boesak 1987; Schüssler Fiorenza 1991; Richard 1995), there

is another one that points to the book's oppressive potential, particularly in terms of gender and violence that "liberating" readings tend to overlook (Pippin 1992; Moore 2001: 173–99). Yet even such matters as gender and violence in Revelation are subject to diverse interpretations. To give just one example, is voyeurism of violence committed against women through Revelation (like Revelation 17–18) turning women readers into "powerless voyeurs of their own abjection" rather than (or as well as) turning the gaze of (male) readers to the atrocities of (their own) criminality (Ashcroft 2001: 121)? One can find a similar debate within the broader world of cultural studies. For instance, Matthew Wray (1997) views apocalyptic affirmatively as a discourse of resistance, while Lee Quinby sees it negatively as a dangerous worldview (1994). I agree with Frykholm that the problem of them both—and I would add, the problem of the entire debate—is that people are operating out of a premise that is "too narrow, too fixed and too simple" (2001: 44). The politics of apocalyptic is not, and should not be, an "either-or" issue. This is helpfully and powerfully illustrated in Toni Morrison's *Paradise* (1998), where a small group of blacks is driven out of their home in Haven, travels across the United States, and eventually settles in a new town called Ruby. Paradoxically, this group ends up turning Ruby into just another Haven, because the nine "original" families that comprise it proceed to exclude anyone who is not an "original," and its patriarchal culture is threatened by a community of women in a nearby convent. The genius of Morrison's *Paradise* lies partly in how she has this black group reenacting (and reacting to) not only the experiences of the early pilgrims who came to the "New World" to escape persecution, but also their acts of reinscribing the very intolerance that had victimized them in the first place (hence their displacing and destruction of Native Americans).

8. To say the least, I find extremely problematic the presupposition that every phenomenon has only one context, only one cause, and only one effect. Bill Ashcroft has recently argued for a "constitutive" theory of textual meaning, which involves a dynamic but unstable convergence of text, writer, and reader, as well as a blurring between a writer who reads and a reader who writes (2001: 56–81). While I find myself agreeing with Ashcroft's theory in many ways, I also find myself resisting his optimism. Ashcroft, in his attempt to celebrate postcolonial agency, seems to (dis)miss the thought that the same "interpolative" (2001: 45–55) or transformative agency belongs to the colonial masters as well as to the once colonized. Thus Ashcroft ends up seeming to say that postcolonial writers, through the art of appropriation and interpolation, can manage to bring about transformation of textual meaning in a definitive (as in "over and done with") way. There seems to be no knowledge, at least no acknowledgment, that this postcolonial transformation may itself be appropriated, interpolated, and transformed again by the colonizers. What is missing from Ashcroft's "constitutive" theory of textual meaning is that constitution of meaning is a never-ending struggle and process.

9. The apocalyptic dimension in Karl Marx's history of class conflict should be well known. More striking is how apocalyptic has also been functioning for

capital(ism) in recent history. The apocalyptic scare involving Y2K has, according to one report, generated and supported a four-hundred-billion-dollar "remedial" industry (Quayson and Goldberg 2002: xv). The Y2K scare is, of course, coterminous with the *Left Behind* phenomenon, which has also generated an incredible amount of dollars. Frykholm has further argued that the *Left Behind* novels themselves reveal a "deep investment" in the technological and consumerist culture of the contemporary United States (2001: 93); see also S. F. Harding 2000 for a similar argument regarding the ironic relations between fundamentalism and modernity.

10. For me, these interpretive debates should not necessarily be conducted on the premise of different applicable interpretations, but should also involve debates on whether various aspects of a text (biblical or otherwise) should be applied or be found applicable in the first place. Otherwise, what we end up with could turn into a kind of fundamentalism of the Right and of the Left, with both sides insisting that the point of reading the Bible is to "apply" the word directly to one's own world. I do not mean here that the debates have to be done in terms of a rigid binary between "applicable" and "inapplicable," nor that "applicability" should be the sole concern of interpretive debates. I believe Jacques Derrida was referring also to this double heterogeneity (of text and of reading practice) when he stated in an interview, "when I try to decipher a text I do not constantly ask myself if I will finish by answering *yes* or *no*" (1981: 52; emphasis in original).

11. As Jon Stratton points out (2000: 27), it is "a likely touch of Baudrillardian irony" that Jean Baudrillard uses "Utopia Achieved" as a heading for a section of his book, *America* (1988: 75–105). What is even more ironic in the aftermath of September 11 is Baudrillard's choice to entitle the immediately following section "The End of US [*sic*] Power?" (1988: 107–18).

12. The connection between technology and apocalyptic has also been argued by Lieb (1998). While Lieb makes this connection through the book of Ezekiel, a link between Lieb and Revelation is nevertheless available via Jean-Pierre Ruiz's work on the intertextual relations between Ezekiel and Revelation (1989).

13. Some have argued further that information or computer technology and the genome project are related, if not one and the same. See, for example, Richard Dawkins, who makes the memorable pronouncement that "DNA is ROM" (1996: 117).

14. In addition to matters of the human genome, one can point to the development of global capitalism, in which the technoscientific capacity to bring about speed and simultaneity has become the key to separate the rich from the poor. With what he calls a "nanocracy," Richard H. Roberts has suggested that with global capitalism, God and capital—both being given the characteristics of omnipresence and simultaneity, and hence also omniscience and omnipotence—have basically mixed and merged into one for many, if not most, people (2002: 277–78, 280–81).

15. I am indebted to Jaideep Singh for relating these reports to me.

16. Here is a timely, and choice, quote from Ngugi wa Thiongo, although it was

written over two decades ago: detention without charge is "a terrorist programme for the psychological siege of a whole people" (1981: 14).

17. Of particular horror regarding the World War II internment of Japanese Americans is the way in which racism was used to justify adopting more racist measures. The argument was that, since many Japanese Americans had not found welcome in the United States, it was even more likely and understandable that they would collaborate with the Japanese government rather than the U.S. government (Chuh 2003: 67).

18. Clayton also provides a nuanced reading of *Gattaca* (2002: 48–53). Although Clayton does not mention apocalyptic, his reading of the movie as simultaneously criticizing and romanticizing the determinism or triumphalism signified by the genome project has important implications for apocalyptic. The same is true of Clayton's comments on the movie's heterosexist cleansing, since the homophobic movement has at times portrayed the so-called gay agenda as the very coming of the apocalypse (see, for example, Herman 1997). To push Clayton's reading a step further, what *Gattaca* implies is that, should the so-called gay gene ever be "found," gay persons would likely be the very first to be put through the process of genetic "modification."

19. This connection between the apocalyptic and the diasporic is actually already found in the New Testament; see especially the letter known as 1 Peter.

20. The same applies to the issue of power or powerlessness. I do not want to deny here the need to differentiate between personal malice and systemic oppression. Neither do I want to downplay the helpful distinction between perceived or "real" powerlessness. I do want to emphasize Michel Foucault's relational understanding of power. For Foucault, power is not a zero-sum game. That is to say, power relations are complex and multidirectional. One feels power and/or powerlessness in relation to different groups and different settings. As a result, claiming the need to read apocalyptic from the standpoint of the "powerless" does not necessarily resolve the complexity of the situation.

21. My focus here on the injustice facing Asian Americans is not meant to dismiss problems within Asian America or other brutal human realities that are national and/or global. The scope and scale of these problems only serve to support my contention that apocalyptic desires belong not only to the conservatives.

22. I am using the term "Asian (North) American" here to acknowledge that Kogawa is Canadian, and that her books are about (Japanese) Canadians rather than people of the United States.

23. For a helpful reading of how this verse might function in the novel, see Iwamura 2002.

24. I should add here that if one looks at Kogawa's *Obasan* and *Itsuka* together, what one sees is a convoluted chrono-logic somewhat comparable to Michael J. Fox's "back to the future." If it is not exactly the "undoing plot" (Gallagher 2002) of "back to the future," it nevertheless involves a trip back to re-do or re-write his-

tory (the accounting or recounting of the internment experience in *Obasan*) for the purpose of bringing about a different future (the "someday" of *Itsuka*). The same can be said of much revisionary work on Asian American history; see, for example, Takaki 1989; and S. Chan 1991. Edouard Glissant, speaking of the *present* need for the colonized to have a *history* that is often denied them as they seek to envision a different *future*, suggests a similar conflation of time with what he calls "a prophetic vision of the past" (1989: 64). While Glissant chooses to use the adjective "prophetic," I would like to point to a similar conflation of time in the fantastic and apocalyptic book of Daniel. Daniel wrote in the second century B.C.E. a narrative situated *back* in the sixth century B.C.E. to "foretell" the *future* in order to forestall or protest the attempts or atrocities of Antiochus IV Epiphanes to "hellenize" the Jewish people who were Daniel's own *contemporaries* (Lacocque 1988). I have already suggested that this collapse of past, present, and future made possible by the instantaneity and simultaneity of computer and digital communications is one of the characteristics of the apocalypses of "our times." Note also that in the last few years Asian Americanists have become more self-critical and self-reflexive about the presuppositions, purposes, and practices of revisionary historiography; see, for instance, Kang 2002: 114–63.

25. What Michel Foucault writes about Georg Wilhelm Friedrich Hegel is particularly applicable to what I want to say about apocalyptic:

> [O]ur age, whether through logic or epistemology, whether through Marx or through Nietzsche, is attempting to flee Hegel. . . . But to truly escape Hegel involves an exact appreciation of the price we have to pay to detach ourselves from him. It assumes that we are aware of the extent to which Hegel, insidiously perhaps, is close to us; it implies a knowledge, in that which permits us to think against Hegel, of that which remains Hegelian. We have to determine the extent to which our anti-Hegelianism is possibly one of his tricks directed against us, at the end of which he stands, motionless, waiting for us. (1972: 235)

For our purposes, the significance of this long quote lies not only in how Foucault ends with an apocalyptic image (Hegel waiting for us at the end), but also in Hegel's apocalyptic understanding of history as the process of Reason's own self-revelation (not to mention Hegel's view on Christianity as the highest form of consciousness or the most absolute form of religion). In that light, what Paul de Man writes about Hegelians is also applicable to what I want to say about apocalyptic: "Whether we know it, or like it, or not, most of us are Hegelians and quite orthodox ones at that" (1982: 763). Another paradox I insist on is that no Hegelian synthesis can resolve our paradoxical relationship with apocalyptic.

Not to be (dis)missed in this relationship between Hegel and apocalyptic is the relationship between Hegel and racism, and thus the potential link also between apocalyptic and racism. I have already referred to this potential link in my discussion of the apocalyptic aftermath of September 11 as well as of the apocalyptic implications of technoscience. I will simply point here to a recent book by Shawn Kelley (2002), where Kelley investigates the racializing effects of Hegel and Martin Heidegger on the biblical scholarship that is dependent on their philosophy, like the Tübingen school, Rudolf Bultmann, and the parable scholarship of Robert Funk and Dominic Crossan. Kelley is certainly right that both Hegel's and Heidegger's philosophies are deeply imbricated with and implicated by the racializing discourse of their times. What Kelley does not pay enough attention to in that book is how those philosophies are also deeply imbricated with and implicated by apocalyptic. I have already mentioned the apocalyptic dimension in Hegel's philosophy; let me simply point to Heidegger's apocalyptic by way of his being influenced by Søren Kierkegaard, his dissatisfaction with the "everyday," as well as the telling title of his article "Only a God Can Save Us" (1993). Not to be forgotten also is Bultmann's own emphasis on "eschatology" in his appropriation of Heidegger's existentialism (Kelley 2002: 139) or the fact that Käseman (whose statement on apocalyptic is used by me to begin this chapter) was a student of Bultmann's. My point is that the "ethical" cleansing within the apocalyptic trope is easily translatable to racial/ethnic cleansing. The paradox that Revelation was most likely targeting the Romans whereas Hegel and Heidegger were targeting other racial/ethnic groups (not the least of which were the Jews) only serves to illustrate apocalyptic's ambiguity and agility.

26. I am indebted to a provocative reading of Chang-Rae Lee's novel by Chuh (2003: 100–109). However, I disagree with Chuh's more binary reading of its conclusion. Rather than reading Chang-Rae Lee's circular language as a displacement of linear progression, Chuh takes it (mistakenly in my view) as a "replacement" (2003: 106).

27. De Certeau would suggest that the same is true for the writing of history (1988). That is to say, the concern with the past is always already a concern with the present.

28. In using the term "unhomely" to describe the "border," Bhabha is referring to the Freudian idea that something that has previously been concealed or forgotten may return to haunt us (1994: 10). In addition to Bhabha's use of the "unhomely" for the diasporic, this Freudian idea can also speak to the apocalyptic, since many people would like to deny the pervasiveness of apocalyptic, only to find it returning in surprising and haunting ways and places (see Beal 2002: 4–5, 71–85).

29. A helpful but highly paradoxical definition of habitus is "the durably installed generative principle of regulated improvisations" (Bourdieu 1977: 78).

30. For a critique of de Certeau's binary understanding of strategy/space and tactic/time through the work of Fanon, see Pile 1997: 14–23.

31. I do not agree, therefore, with Toni Morrison's rhetoric of moving "away from pathetic yearning and futile desire; away from an impossible future or an irretrievable and probably nonexistent Eden to a manageable, doable, modern human activity" (1997: 3–4). I have already mentioned how much recent theory on the diaspora presents home precisely as this kind of an "irretrievable and probably nonexistent" imaginary that *may* end up enabling "manageable, doable . . . human activity."

Admittedly, there is yet another paradox here: one desires apocalyptic because of the "hurts" and "needs" of everyday existence, but then everyday practice is also a (re)source for "transformation" (however defined).

32. Let me clarify here that one should not read this sentence as implying that apocalyptic is contained neatly and entirely within the book of Revelation.

33. For Spivak, "persistent critique" makes intellectual work comparable to the domestic work of (mostly) women (1989: 89). Both involve an endless and regular processing of doing, undoing, and redoing.

34. Muñoz calls this non-binary mode or practice of resistance "disidentification" (1999).

35. This is another reason why I am not keen to suggest a hermeneutics in terms of rules and regulations. Doing so would, I am afraid, turn biblical studies in general and Asian American biblical interpretation in particular into a technique or another school of trade rather than a cultivation of sensibilities and exploration of perspectives. For similar concerns and sentiments within biblical studies, see Schüssler Fiorenza 1999: 42, 59, 68; within the larger world of literary/cultural studies, see Spivak 2003.

Works Cited

Adorno, Theodor W.
  1978   *Minima Moralia: Reflections from Damaged Life.* Trans. E. F. N. Jephcott. New York: Verso.
  1991–92   "The Essay as Form." Pp. 1.1–23 in *Notes to Literature,* ed. Rolf Tiedemann, trans. Sherry Weber Nicholsen. 2 vols. New York: Columbia University Press.
Alexander, Loveday C. A.
  1993   *The Preface to Luke's Gospel: Literary Convention and Social Context in Luke 1.1–4 and Acts 1.1.* New York: Cambridge University Press.
  1999   "Reading Luke-Acts from Back to Front." Pp. 419–46 in *The Unity of Luke-Acts,* ed. Jozef Verheyden. Louvain: Peeters.
Alexander, M. Jacqui, and Chandra Talpade Mohanty, eds.
  1997   *Feminist Genealogies, Colonial Legacies, Democratic Futures.* New York: Routledge.
Allen, Graham
  2000   *Intertextuality.* New York: Routledge.
Alter, Robert
  1981   *The Art of Biblical Narrative.* New York: Basic Books.
  2000   *Canon and Creativity: Modern Writing and the Authority of Scripture.* New Haven, CT: Yale University Press.
Anderson, Benedict
  1991   *Imagined Communities: Reflections on the Origins and Spread of Nationalism.* Revised ed. New York: Verso.
Ang, Ien
  1991   *Desperately Seeking the Audience.* New York: Routledge.
Appadurai, Arjun
  1996   "Diversity and Disciplinarity as Cultural Artifacts." Pp. 23–36 in *Disciplinarity and Dissent in Cultural Studies,* ed. Cary Nelson and Dilip Gaonkar. New York: Routledge.

Appiah, Kwame Anthony
  2005 *The Ethics of Identity.* Princeton, NJ: Princeton University Press.
Ascough, Richard S.
  1998 *What Are They Saying about the Formation of Pauline Churches?* New York: Paulist Press.
Ashcroft, Bill
  2001 *Post-Colonial Transformation.* New York: Routledge.
Ashton, John
  2000 *The Religion of Paul the Apostle.* New Haven, CT: Yale University Press.
Bailey, Randall C.
  1995 "'Is That Any Name for a Nice Hebrew Boy?'—Exodus 2:1–10: The De-Africanization of an Israelite Hero." Pp. 25–36 in *The Recovery of Black Presence: An Interdisciplinary Exploration,* ed. Randall C. Bailey and Jacquelyn Grant. Nashville: Abingdon.
Bakhtin, Mikhail
  1986 *Speech Genres.* Ed. Carol Emerson and Michael Holquist. Austin: University of Texas Press.
Bal, Mieke
  1988 *Death and Dissymmetry: The Politics of Coherence in the Book of Judges.* Chicago: University of Chicago Press.
Balch, David L.
  2003 "ΜΕΤΑΒΟΛΗ ΠΟΛΙΤΕΙΩΝ: Jesus as Founder of the Church in Luke-Acts." Pp. 139–88 in Penner and Stichele, eds. 2003.
Balibar, Etienne
  1991 "Racism and Nationalism." Pp. 37–67 in Etienne Balibar and Immanuel Wallerstein, *Race, Nation, Class: Ambiguous Identities.* Trans. Chris Turner. New York: Verso.
Barthes, Roland
  1977 *Roland Barthes.* Trans. Richard Howard. New York: Hill and Wang.
Bassler, Jouette M.
  1998 "1 Corinthians." Pp. 411–19 in *Women's Bible Commentary,* ed. Carol A. Newsom and Sharon H. Ringe. Expanded ed. with Apocrypha. Louisville, KY: Westminster John Knox.
Baudrillard, Jean
  1988 *America.* Trans. Chris Turner. New York: Verso.
Bauer, David R., and Mark Allan Powell, eds.
  1996 *Treasures New and Old: Contributions to Matthean Studies.* Atlanta: Scholars.
Bauman, Zygmunt
  1993 *Postmodern Ethics.* Cambridge: Blackwell.
Baur, F. C.
  1831 "Die Christus Partei in der korinthischen Gemeinde." *Tübinger Zeitschrift für Theologie* 5: 61–206.

Beal, Timothy K.
  2000   "Intertextuality." Pp. 128–30 in *Handbook of Postmodern Biblical Inter-pretation,* ed. A. K. A. Adam. St. Louis, MO: Chalice.
  2002   *Religion and Its Monsters.* New York: Routledge.
Beard, Mary, John North, and Simon Price
  1998   *Religions of Rome. Volume I: A History.* New York: Cambridge University Press.
Beck, Robert R.
  1996   *Nonviolent Story: Narrative Conflict Resolution in the Gospel of Mark.* Maryknoll, NY: Orbis.
Bell, Daniel
  1960   *The End of Ideology: On the Exhaustion of Political Ideas in the Fifties.* Glencoe, IL: Free Press.
Benjamin, Walter
  1968   *Illuminations.* Ed. Hannah Arendt, trans. Harry Zohn. New York: Schocken.
Bercovitch, Sacvan
  1978   *The American Jeremiad.* Madison: University of Wisconsin Press.
Bhabha, Homi K.
  1990a "DissemiNation: Time, Narrative and the Margins of the Modern Nation." Pp. 291–322 in Bhabha, ed. 1990c.
  1990b "Introduction: Narrating the Nation." Pp. 1–7 in Bhabha, ed. 1990c.
  1994   *The Location of Culture.* New York: Routledge.
  2003   "On Writing Rights." Pp. 162–89 in *Globalizing Rights: The Oxford Amnesty Lectures 1999,* ed. Matthew J. Gibney. Oxford: Oxford University Press.
  2005   "Adagio." *Critical Inquiry* 31: 371–80.
Bhabha, Homi K., ed.
  1990c *Nation and Narration.* New York: Routledge.
Bhabha, Homi K., and John Comaroff
  2002   "Speaking of Postcoloniality, in the Continuous Present: A Conversation." Pp. 15–46 in Goldberg and Quayson, eds. 2002.
Bhabha, Homi K., Paul Gilroy, and Stuart Hall
  1991   "Threatening Pleasures." *Sight and Sound* 1: 17–19.
Bhalla, Alok
  1993   "A Plea against Revenge Histories: Some Reflections on Orientalism and the Age of Empire." Pp. 1–13 in *Indian Responses to Colonialism in the Nineteenth Century,* ed. Alok Bhalla and Sudhir Chandra. New Delhi: Sterling.
Bierce, Ambrose
  1946   "The Haunted Valley." Pp. 451–60 in Ambrose Bierce, *The Collected Writings of Ambrose Bierce.* New York: Citadel.

Blount, Brian K.

1998   *Go Preach! Mark's Kingdom Message and the Black Church Today.* Maryk-
        noll, NY: Orbis.

2005   *Can I Get a Witness? Reading Revelation through African American Cul-
        ture.* Louisville, KY: Westminster John Knox.

Boer, Roland

1995   "Christological Slippage and Ideological Structures in Schwarzenegger's
        Terminator." *Semeia* 69/70: 165–93.

Boesak, Allan A.

1987   *Comfort and Protest: Reflections on the Apocalypse of John of Patmos.*
        Philadelphia: Westminster.

Bonacich, Edna

1988   "Teaching Race and Class." Pp. 85–93 in *Reflections on Shattered Win-
        dows: Promises and Prospects for Asian American Studies,* ed. Gary Y.
        Okihiro, Shirley Hune, Arthur A. Hansen, and John M. Liu. Pullman:
        Washington State University Press.

Bonz, Marianne Palmer

2000   *The Past as Legacy: Luke-Acts and Ancient Epic.* Minneapolis: Fortress.

Bordo, Susan

1989   "The Body and the Reproduction of Femininity: A Feminist Appropriation
        of Foucault." Pp. 13–33 in *Gender/Body/Knowledge: Feminist Recon-
        structions of Being and Knowing,* ed. Alison M. Jaggar and Susan R.
        Bordo. New Brunswick, NJ: Rutgers University Press.

Bourdieu, Pierre

1977   *Outline of a Theory of Practice.* Trans. Richard Nice. New York: Cam-
        bridge University Press.

1990   *The Logic of Practice.* Trans. Richard Nice. Stanford, CA: Stanford Univer-
        sity Press.

Boyarin, Daniel

1990   *Intertextuality and the Reading of Midrash.* Bloomington: Indiana Univer-
        sity Press.

1994   *A Radical Jew: Paul and the Politics of Identity.* Berkeley: University of
        California Press.

1997   *Unheroic Conduct: The Rise of Heterosexuality and the Invention of the
        Jewish Man.* Berkeley: University of California Press.

2002   "The *Ioudaioi* in John and the Prehistory of 'Judaism.'" Pp. 216–39 in
        Pauline Conversations in Context: Essays in Honor of Calvin J. Roetzel, ed.
        Janice Capel Anderson, Philip Sellew, and Claudia Setzer. Sheffield (UK):
        Sheffield Academic.

2004   *Border Lines: The Partition of Judaeo-Christianity.* Philadelphia: University
        of Pennsylvania Press.

Boym, Svetlana
1994   *Common Places: Mythologies of Everyday Life in Russia.* Cambridge, MA: Harvard University Press.
Brace, C. Loring
2005   *"Race" is a Four-Letter Word: The Genesis of the Concept.* New York: Oxford University Press.
Braxton, Brad Ronnell
2003   "The Role of Ethnicity in the Social Location of 1 Corinthians 7:17–24." Pp. 19–32 in *Yet with a Steady Beat: Contemporary U.S. Afrocentric Biblical Interpretation,* ed. Randall C. Bailey. Atlanta: Society of Biblical Literature.
Bremen, Riet van
1996   *Limits of Participation: Women and Civic Life in the Greek East in the Hellenistic and Roman Periods.* Amsterdam: Gieben.
Brennan, Timothy
1990   "The National Longing for Form." Pp. 44–70 in Bhabha, ed. 1990c.
1997   *At Home in the World: Cosmopolitanism Now.* Cambridge, MA: Harvard University Press.
Brodie, Thomas L.
1990   "Luke-Acts as an Imitation and Emulation of the Elijah-Elisha Narrative." Pp. 78–85 in *New Views of Luke and Acts,* ed. Earl Richard. Collegeville, MN: Liturgical Press.
Bronfen, Elisabeth
1992   *Over Her Dead Body: Death, Femininity and the Aesthetic.* New York: Routledge.
Brown, James W.
1984   *Fictional Meals and Their Function in the French Novel, 1789–1848.* Toronto: University of Toronto Press.
Brown, Michael Joseph
2004   *Blackening of the Bible: The Aims of African American Biblical Scholarship.* Harrisburg: Trinity International.
Brown, Raymond E.
1979   *The Community of the Beloved Disciple: The Life, Loves and Hates of an Individual Church in New Testament Times.* New York: Paulist Press.
Bruns, Gerald L.
1992   *Hermeneutics Ancient and Modern.* New Haven, CT: Yale University Press.
Buell, Denise Kimber
1999   *Making Christians: Clement of Alexandria and the Rhetoric of Legitimacy.* Princeton, NJ: Princeton University Press.
2001   "Rethinking the Relevance of Race for Early Christian Self-Definition." *Harvard Theological Review* 94: 449–76.

2005   *Why This New Race: Ethnic Reasoning in Early Christianity.* New York: Columbia University Press.

Buell, Denise Kimber, and Caroline Johnson Hodge
  2004   "The Politics of Interpretation: The Rhetoric of Race and Ethnicity in Paul." *Journal of Biblical Literature* 123: 235–51.

Bundang, Rachel A. R.
  2002   "Home as Memory, Metaphor, and Promise in Asian/Pacific American Religious Experience." *Semeia* 90/91: 87–104.

Burrus, Virginia, and Karen Torjesen
  2004   "Afterword to 'Household Management and Women's Authority.'" Pp. 171–76 in Levine, ed. 2004a.

Burton, Jonathan
  1998   "'A Most Wily Bird': Leo Africanus, *Othello* and the Trafficking in Difference." Pp. 43–63 in Loomba and Orkin, eds. 1998b.

Busto, Rudy V.
  1999   "The Gospel according to the Model Minority? Hazarding an Interpretation of Asian American Evangelical College Students." Pp. 169–87 in *New Spiritual Homes: Religion and Asian Americans,* ed. David K. Yoo. Honolulu: University of Hawai'i Press.

Butler, Judith
  1987   "Variations on Sex and Gender: Beauvoir, Wittig and Foucault." Pp. 128–43 in *Feminism as Critique: On the Politics of Gender,* ed. Seyla Benhabib and Drucilla Cornell. Minneapolis: University of Minnesota Press.
  1990   *Gender Trouble.* New York: Routledge.
  1993   *Bodies That Matter: On the Discursive Limits of "Sex."* New York: Routledge.
  1997   *The Psychic Life of Power: Theories in Subjection.* Stanford, CA: Stanford University Press.

Byron, Gay L.
  2002   *Symbolic Blackness and Ethnic Difference in Early Christian Literature.* New York: Routledge.

Cain, Maureen, and Christine B. Harrington
  1994   "Introduction." Pp. 1–11 in *Lawyers in a Postmodern World: Translation and Transgression,* ed. Maureen Cain and Christine B. Harrington. New York: New York University Press.

Cameron, Averil
  1991   *Christianity and the Rhetoric of Empire.* Berkeley: University of California Press.

Campbell, William S.
  2005   "Perceptions of Compatibility between Christianity and Judaism in Pauline Interpretation." *Biblical Interpretation* 13: 298–316.

Caputo, John
  2006   *The Weakness of God: A Theology of the Event.* Bloomington: Indiana
          University Press.
Carey, Greg, and L. Gregory Bloomquist, eds.
  1999   *Vision and Persuasion: Rhetorical Dimensions of Apocalyptic Discourse.*
          St. Louis, MO: Chalice.
Carter, Warren
  2000   *Matthew and the Margins: A Sociopolitical and Religious Reading.* Mary-
          knoll, NY: Orbis.
Cassel, Susie Lan, ed.
  2002   *The Chinese in America: A History from Gold Mountain to the New Mil-
          lennium.* Walnut Creek, CA: AltaMira.
Castelli, Elizabeth A.
  2004   *Martyrdom and Memory: Early Christian Culture Making.* New York:
          Columbia University Press.
Castells, Manuel
  1996   *The Rise of the Network Society.* Malden, MA: Blackwell.
Cha, Theresa Hak Kyung
  1995   *Dictee.* Berkeley, CA: Third Woman.
Cha, Theresa Hak Kyung, ed.
  1980   *Apparatus—Cinematographic Apparatus: Selected Writings.* New York:
          Tanam.
Chakrabarty, Dipesh
  1992   "Postcoloniality and the Artifice of History: Who Speaks for 'Indian'
          Pasts?" *Representations* 37: 1–26.
  2001   "Notes toward a Conversation between Area Studies and Diasporic Stud-
          ies." Pp. 107–29 in Chuh and Shimakawa, eds. 2001b.
Chakravarti, Uma
  1990   "What Happened to the Vedic Dasi? Orientalism, Nationalism, and a
          Script for the Past." Pp. 27–87 in *Recasting Women: Essays in Colonial
          History,* ed. Kumkum Sangari and Sudesh Vaid. New Brunswick, NJ: Rut-
          gers University Press.
Chan, Jeffery Paul, Frank Chin, Lawson Fusao Inada, and Shawn Wong
  1991   "Introduction." Pp. xi–xvi in *The Big Aiiieeeee!: An Anthology of Chinese
          American and Japanese American Literature,* ed. Jeffery Paul Chan, Frank
          Chin, Lawson Fusao Inada, and Shawn Wong. New York: Penguin.
Chan, Sucheng
  1991   *Asian Americans: An Interpretive History.* Boston: Twayne.
Chatterjee, Partha
  1996   "Whose Imagined Community?" Pp. 214–25 in *Mapping the Nation,* ed.
          Gopal Balakrishnan. New York: Verso.

Chen, Kuan-Hsing
  2001 "Missile Internationalism." Pp. 172–86 in Chuh and Shimakawa, eds.
        2001b.
Chen, Tina
  2005 *Double Agency: Acts of Impersonation in Asian American Literature and
        Culture.* Stanford, CA: Stanford University Press.
Cheng, Anne Anlin
  2001 *The Melancholy of Race: Psycholanalysis, Assimilation, and Hidden Grief.*
        New York: Oxford University Press.
Cheung, King-Kok
  1990 "The Woman Warrior versus the Chinaman Pacific: Must a Chinese Ameri-
        can Critic Choose between Feminism and Heroism?" Pp. 234–51 in *Con-
        flicts in Feminism,* ed. Marianne Hirsch and Evelyn Fox Keller. New York:
        Routledge.
  1997a "Re-Viewing Asian American Literary Studies." Pp. 1–36 in Cheung, ed.
        1997b.
Cheung, King-Kok, ed.
  1997b *An Interethnic Companion to Asian American Literature.* New York: Cam-
        bridge University Press.
Chew, Kristina Julie
  1995 "Pears Bearing Apples: Virgil's 'Georgics'—Plato's 'Phaedrus'—Theresa
        Hak Kyung Cha's 'Dictee.'" Ph.D. diss., Yale University.
Chin, Frank
  1981 *The Chickencoop Chinaman and The Year of the Dragon: Two Plays.*
        Seattle: University of Washington Press.
  1988 *The Chinaman Pacific and Frisco R. R. Co.: Short Stories.* Minneapolis:
        Coffee House.
  1991 "Come All Ye Asian American Writers of the Real and the Fake." Pp. 1–92
        in *The Big Aiiieeeee!: An Anthology of Chinese American and Japanese
        American Literature,* ed. Jeffery Paul Chan, Frank Chin, Lawson Fusao
        Inada, and Shawn Wong. New York: Penguin.
Chin, Frank, Jeffery Paul Chan, Lawson Fusao Inada, and Shawn Hsu Wong, eds.
  1974 *Aiieeeee! An Anthology of Asian-American Writers.* Washington, DC:
        Howard University Press.
Chow, Rey
  1991 "Violence in the Other Country: China as Crisis, Spectacle, and Woman."
        Pp. 81–100 in *Third World Women and the Politics of Feminism,* ed. Chan-
        dra Talpade Mohanty, Ann Russo, and Lourdes Torres. Bloomington: Indi-
        ana University Press.
  1993 *Writing Diaspora: Tactics of Intervention in Contemporary Cultural Stud-
        ies.* Bloomington: Indiana University Press.
  1998 *Ethics after Idealism: Theory-Culture-Ethnicity-Reading.* Bloomington:
        Indiana University Press.

2002   *The Protestant Ethnic and the Spirit of Capitalism.* New York: Columbia University Press.

Choy, Gregory
   1999   "Sites of Function in Asian American Literature: Tropics of Place, Agents of Space." Ph.D. diss., University of Washington.

Chuh, Kandice
   2001   "Imaginary Borders." Pp. 277–95 in Chuh and Shimakawa, eds. 2001b.
   2003   *Imagine Otherwise: On Asian Americanist Critique.* Durham, NC: Duke University Press.

Chuh, Kandice, and Karen Shimakawa
   2001a "Introduction: Mapping Studies in the Asian Diaspora." Pp. 1–21 in Chuh and Shimakawa, eds. 2001b.

Chuh, Kandice, and Karen Shimakawa, eds.
   2001b *Orientations: Mapping Studies in the Asian Diaspora.* Durham, NC: Duke University Press.

Clayton, Jay
   1993   *The Pleasures of Babel: Contemporary American Literature and Theory.* New York: Oxford University Press.
   2002   "Genome Time." Pp. 31–60 in Newman, Clayton, and Hirsch, eds. 2002b.

Clayton, Jay, and Eric Rothstein, eds.
   1991   *Influence and Intertextuality in Literary History.* Madison: University of Wisconsin Press.

Clifford, James
   1988   *The Predicament of Culture: Twentieth-Century Ethnography, Literature, and Art.* Cambridge, MA: Harvard University Press.

Clines, David J. A.
   2003   "Paul, the Invisible Man." Pp. 181–92 in *New Testament Masculinities,* ed. Stephen D. Moore and Janice Capel Anderson. Atlanta: Society of Biblical Literature.

Cohen, Anthony P.
   1985   *Symbolic Construction of Community.* New York: Tavistock Publications and Ellis Horwood.

Cohen, Shaye J. D.
   1999   *The Beginnings of Jewishness: Boundaries, Varieties, Uncertainties.* Berkeley: University of California Press.

Cohen, Ted
   1978   "Metaphor and the Cultivation of Intimacy." *Critical Inquiry* 5: 3–12.

Cohn, Norman
   1993   *Cosmos, Chaos, and the World to Come: The Ancient Roots of Apocalyptic Faith.* New Haven, CT: Yale University Press.

Collins, John J.
  1998   *The Apocalyptic Imagination: An Introduction to Jewish Apocalyptic Lit-
          erature.* 2nd ed. Grand Rapids, MI: Eerdmans.
Collins, Patricia Hill
  2000   *Black Feminist Thought: Knowledge, Consciousness, and the Politics of
          Empowerment.* 2nd ed. New York: Routledge.
Coloe, Mary L.
  2001   *God Dwells with Us: Temple Symbolism in the Fourth Gospel.* Colleg-
          eville, MN: Liturgical Press.
Copher, Charles B.
  1991   "The Dark Presence in the Old Testament." Pp. 146–64 in *Stony the Road
          We Trod: African American Biblical Interpretation*, ed. Cain Hope Felder.
          Minneapolis: Fortress.
Cornell, Drucilla
  1992   "The 'Postmodern' Challenge to the Ideal of Community." Pp. 39–61 in
          Drucilla Cornell, *The Philosophy of the Limit*. New York: Routledge.
Culler, Jonathan
  2000   "The Literary in Theory." Pp. 273–92 in *What's Left of Theory? New
          Work on the Politics of Literary Theory,* ed. Judith Butler, John Guillory,
          and Kendall Thomas. New York: Routledge.
Culpepper, R. Alan
  1983   *Anatomy of the Fourth Gospel: A Study in Literary Design.* Philadelphia:
          Fortress.
  1996a "The Gospel of John as a Document of Faith in a Pluralistic Culture." Pp.
          107–127 in *"What Is John?" Readers and Readings of the Fourth Gospel,*
          ed. Fernando F. Segovia. Atlanta: Scholars.
  1996b "Reading Johannine Irony." Pp. 193–207 in *Exploring the Gospel of John:
          In Honor of D. Moody Smith,* ed. R. Alan Culpepper and C. Clifton Black.
          Louisville, KY: Westminster John Knox.
Dahl, Nils
  1977   "Paul and the Church at Corinth according to 1 Cor. 1:10–4:21." Pp. 40–
          61 in Nils Dahl, *Studies in Paul: Theology for the Early Christian Mission.*
          Minneapolis: Augsburg.
D'Angelo, Mary Rose
  2002   "The *ANHP* Question in Luke-Acts: Imperial Masculinity and the Deploy-
          ment of Women in the Early Second Century." Pp. 44–69 in *A Feminist
          Companion to Luke,* ed. Amy-Jill Levine (with Marianne Bickenstaff).
          New York: Sheffield Academic.
Dawkins, Richard
  1996   *The Blind Watchmaker: Why the Evidence of Evolution Reveals a Universe
          without Design* With a New Introduction. New York: Norton.
Debord, Guy
  1994   *The Society of the Spectacle.* Trans. Donald Nicholson-Smith. New York:
          Zone.

de Certeau, Michel
  1984 *The Practice of Everyday Life.* Trans. Steven Rendall. Berkeley: University of California Press.
  1988 *The Writing of History.* Trans. Tom Conley. New York: Columbia University Press.
Deleuze, Gilles, and Félix Guattari
  1983 *Anti-Oedipus: Capitalism and Schizophrenia.* Trans. Robert Hurley, Mark Seem, and Helen R. Lane. Minneapolis: University of Minnesota Press.
  1990 "What Is a Minor Literature?" Pp. 59–69 in *Out There: Marginalization and Contemporary Culture,* ed. Russell Ferguson, Martha Gever, Trinh T. Minh-ha, and Cornel West. Cambridge, MA: MIT Press.
Dellamora, Richard, ed.
  1995 *Postmodern Apocalypse: Theory and Cultural Practice at the End.* Philadelphia: University of Pennsylvania Press.
de Man, Paul
  1982 "Sign and Symbol in Hegel's *Aesthetics.*" *Critical Inquiry* 8: 761–75.
  1984 *Blindness and Insight: Essays in the Rhetoric of Contemporary Criticism.* Rev. ed. Minneapolis: University of Minnesota Press.
Derrida, Jacques
  1976 *Of Grammatology.* Trans. Gayatri Chakravorty Spivak. Baltimore: Johns Hopkins University Press.
  1981 *Positions.* Trans. Alan Bass. Chicago: University of Chicago Press.
  1998 *Monolingualism of the Other, or the Prosthesis of Origin.* Trans. Patrick Mensah. Stanford, CA: Stanford University Press.
  1999 *Adieu to Emmanuel Levinas.* Trans. Pascale-Anne Brault and Michael Naas. Stanford, CA: Stanford University Press.
Desmond, Jane, and Virginia Dominguez
  1996 "Resituating American Studies in a Critical Internationalism." *American Quarterly* 48: 475–90.
Dibelius, Martin
  1956 "Paul on the Areopagus." Pp. 26–83 in *Studies in Acts of the Apostles,* ed. Heinrich Greeven, trans. Mary Ling and Paul Schubert. London: SMC.
Dollimore, Jonathan
  1991 *Sexual Dissidence: Augustine to Wilde, Freud to Foucault.* New York: Oxford University Press.
  1996 "Bisexuality and Wishful Theory." *Textual Practice* 10: 523–39.
  1998 "Shakespeare and Theory." Pp. 259–76 in Loomba and Orkin, eds. 1998b.
Donaldson, Laura E.
  1995 "A Response—When Jesus Rewrote the Corn Mothers: Intertextuality as Transnational Critical Practice." *Semeia* 69/70: 281–92.
Dover, Kenneth James
  1989 *Greek Homosexuality.* Cambridge, MA: Harvard University Press.

Drake, St. Clair, and Horace R. Cayton
  1945 *Black Metropolis: A Study of Negro Life in a Northern City.* New York: Harcourt, Brace and Company.
Du Bois, W. E. B.
  1990 *The Souls of Black Folk.* New York: Vintage.
Duke, Paul D.
  1985 *Irony in the Fourth Gospel.* Atlanta: John Knox.
Duling, Dennis C., and Norman Perrin
  1994 *The New Testament: Proclamation and Parenesis, Myth and History.* 3rd ed. Fort Worth, TX: Harcourt Brace.
Du Rand, Jan A.
  1998 "Reading the Fourth Gospel like a Literary Symphony." Pp. 5–18 in Segovia, ed. 1998.
Durrant, Sam
  2004 *Postcolonial Narrative and the Work of Mourning: J. M. Coetzee, Wilson Harris, and Toni Morrison.* Albany: State University of New York Press.
DuttaAhmed, Shantanu
  1996 "Border Crossings: Retrieval and Erasure of the Self as Other." Pp. 337–50 in *Between the Lines: South Asians and Postcoloniality,* ed. Deepika Bahri and Mary Vasudeva. Philadelphia: Temple University Press.
Edwards, Catherine
  1997 "Unspeakable Professions: Public Performance and Prostitution in Ancient Rome." Pp. 66–95 in *Roman Sexualities,* ed. Judith P. Hallett and Marilyn B. Skinner. Princeton, NJ: Princeton University Press.
Eilberg-Schwartz, Howard, ed.
  1992 *People of the Body: Jews and Judaism from an Embodied Perspective.* Albany: State University of New York Press.
Eisenbaum, Pamela
  2005 "Paul, Polemics, and the Problem of Essentialism." *Biblical Interpretation* 13: 224–38.
Elliott, John
  1994 *A Home for the Homeless: A Social-Scientific Criticism of 1 Peter, Its Situation and Strategy.* Minneapolis: Fortress.
Elliott, Neil
  2005 "An American 'Myth of Innocence' and Contemporary Pauline Studies." *Biblical Interpretation* 13: 239–49.
Eng, David L.
  1998 "Queer/Asian American/Canons." Pp. 13–23 in *Teaching Asian America: Diversity and the Problem of Community,* ed. Lane Ryo Hirabayashi. Lanham, MD: Rowman and Littlefield.
  2001 *Racial Castration: Managing Masculinity in Asian America.* Durham, NC: Duke University Press.

Eng, David L., and Shinhee Han
  2003 "A Dialogue on Racial Melancholia." Pp. 343–71 in Eng and Kazanjian,
        eds. 2003b.
Eng, David L., and David Kazanjian
  2003a "Introduction: Mourning Remains." Pp. 1–25 in Eng and Kazanjian, eds.
        2003b.
Eng, David L., and David Kazanjian, eds.
  2003b *Loss*. Berkeley: University of California Press.
Epp, Eldon Jay
  1999 "The Multivalence of the Term 'Original Text' in New Testament Textual
        Criticism." *Harvard Theological Review* 92: 245–81.
  2004 "The Oxyrhynchus New Testament Papyri: 'Not without Honor Except in
        Their Hometown'?" *Journal of Biblical Literature* 123: 5–55.
Esler, Philip Francis
  1987 *Community and Gospel in Luke-Acts: The Social and Political Motivations
        of Lucan Theology*. New York: Cambridge University Press.
Espiritu, Yen Le
  1992 *Asian American Panethnicity: Bridging Institutions and Identities*. Philadel-
        phia: Temple University Press.
  1995 *Filipino American Lives*. Philadelphia: Temple University Press.
Fabi, M. Giulia
  2001 *Passing and the Rise of the African American Novel*. Urbana: University of
        Illinois Press.
Fanon, Frantz
  1963 *The Wretched of the Earth*. Trans. Constance Farrington. New York:
        Grove.
  1965 *A Dying Colonialism*. Trans. Haakon Chevalier. New York: Grove.
  1967 *Black Skin, White Masks*. Trans. Charles Lam Markmann. New York:
        Grove.
Fehribach, Adeline
  1998 *The Women in the Life of the Bridegroom: A Feminist Historical Literary
        Analysis of the Female Characters in the Fourth Gospel*. Collegeville, MN:
        Liturgical Press.
Felder, Cain Hope
  1993 "Cultural Ideology, Afrocentrism and Biblical Interpretation." Pp. 184–
        95 in *Black Theology: A Documentary History*, ed. James H. Cone and
        Gayraud S. Wilmore. 2 vols. Maryknoll, NY: Orbis.
Feldman, Louis H.
  1993 *Jew and Gentile in the Ancient World*. Princeton, NJ: Princeton University
        Press.
Festinger, Leon, Henry W. Riecken, and Stanley Schachter
  1956 *When Prophecy Fails*. Minneapolis: University of Minnesota Press.

Finn, Thomas M.
 1997 *From Death to Rebirth: Ritual and Conversion in Antiquity.* New York: Paulist Press.

Ford, J. Massyngbaerde
 1997 *Redeemer, Friend and Mother: Salvation in Antiquity and in the Gospel of John.* Minneapolis: Fortress.

Foskett, Mary F.
 2002 "The Accidents of Being and the Politics of Identity: Biblical Images of Adoption and Asian Adoptees in America." *Semeia* 90/91: 135–44.
 2006 "Obscured Beginnings: Lessons from the Study of Christian Origins." Pp. 178–91 in Foskett and Kuan, eds. 2006.

Foskett, Mary F., and Jeffrey Kuan, eds.
 2006 *Ways of Being, Ways of Reading: Asian American Ways of Reading the Bible.* St. Louis, MO: Chalice.

Foucault, Michel
 1970 *The Order of Things: An Archaeology of the Human Sciences.* New York: Pantheon.
 1972 *The Archaeology of Knowledge and the Discourse of Language.* Trans. A. M. Sheridan Smith. New York: Pantheon.
 1977 *Discipline and Punish: The Birth of the Prison.* Trans. Alan Sheridan. New York: Pantheon.
 1980 *Power/Knowledge: Selected Interviews and Other Writings, 1972–1977.* Ed. Colin Gordon, trans. Colin Gordon, Leo Marshall, John Mepham, and Kate Soper. New York: Pantheon.
 1988 *Politics, Philosophy, Culture: Interviews and Other Writings, 1977–1984.* Ed. Lawrence D. Kritzman, trans. Alan Sheridan and others. New York: Routledge.

Fradenburg, L. O. Aranye
 2002 "Group Time: Catastrophe, Survival, Periodicity." Pp. 211–37 in Newman, Clayton, and Hirsch, eds. 2002b.

Francia, Luis H., and Eric Gamalinda, eds.
 1996 *Flippin': Filipinos on America.* New York: Asian American Writers' Workshop.

Freud, Sigmund
 1953–74 *Standard Edition of the Complete Psychological Works of Sigmund Freud.* Ed. and trans. James Strachey. 24 vols. London: Hogarth.

Frye, Northrop
 1982 *The Great Code: The Bible and Literature.* Toronto: Academic.

Frykholm, Amy Johnson
 2001 "Reading the Rapture: Christian Fiction and the Social Structures of Belief." Ph.D. diss., Duke University.
 2004 *Rapture Culture: Left Behind in Evangelical America.* New York: Oxford University Press.

Fukuyama, Francis
1992 *The End of History and the Last Man.* New York: Free Press.
Gabba, Emilio
1991 *Dionysius and the History of Archaic Rome.* Berkeley: University of California Press.
Galen, Claudius
1968 *On the Usefulness of the Parts of the Body.* Trans. Margaret Tallmadge May. 2 vols. Ithaca, NY: Cornell University Press.
Gallagher, Catherine
2002 "Undoing." Pp. 11–29 in Newman, Clayton, and Hirsch, eds 2002b.
Ganguly, Keya
2001 *States of Exception: Everyday Life and Postcolonial Identity.* Minneapolis: University of Minnesota Press.
Garland, David E.
1993 *Reading Matthew: A Literary and Theological Commentary on the First Gospel.* New York: Crossroad.
Gaston, Lloyd
2005 "The Impact of New Perspectives on Judaism and Improved Jewish-Christian Relations on the Study of Paul." *Biblical Interpretation* 13: 250–54.
Gates, Henry Louis, Jr.
1988 *The Signifying Monkey: A Theory of African-American Literary Criticism.* New York: Oxford University Press.
1990 "Authority, (White) Power, and the (Black) Critic; It's All Greek to Me." Pp. 72–101 in JanMohamed and Lloyd, eds. 1990.
1992 *Loose Canons: Notes on the Culture Wars.* New York: Oxford University Press.
Gewertz, Deborah, and Frederick Errington
1993 "We Think, Therefore They Are? On Occidentalizing the World." Pp. 635–55 in Kaplan and Pease, eds. 1993.
Gilbert, Gary
2003 "Roman Propaganda and Christian Identity in the Worldview of Luke-Acts." Pp. 233–56 in Penner and Stichele, eds. 2003.
Gilman, Sander L.
1993 *Freud, Race, and Gender.* Princeton, NJ: Princeton University Press.
1999 *Making the Body Beautiful: A Cultural History of Aesthetic Surgery.* Princeton, NJ: Princeton University Press.
Gilroy, Paul
1987 *"There Ain't No Black in the Union Jack": The Cultural Politics of Race and Nation.* Chicago: University of Chicago Press.
1993 *The Black Atlantic: Modernity and Double Consciousness.* Cambridge, MA: Harvard University Press.
2000 *Against Race: Imagining Political Culture beyond the Color Line.* Cambridge, MA: Belknap/Harvard University Press.

2005   *Postcolonial Melancholia.* New York: Columbia University Press.
Glad, Clarence
  1995   *Paul and Philodemus: Adaptability in Epicurean and Early Christian Peda-gogy.* New York: Brill.
Glancy, Jennifer A.
  2002   *Slavery in Early Christianity.* New York: Oxford University Press.
  2004   "Boasting of Beatings (2 Corinthians 11:23–25)." *Journal of Biblical Lit-erature* 123: 99–135.
Gleason, Maud W.
  1994   *Making Men: Sophists and Self-Representation in Ancient Rome.* Prince-ton, NJ: Princeton University Press.
Glissant, Edouard
  1989   *Caribbean Discourse: Selected Essays.* Trans. J. Michael Dash. Charlottes-ville: University Press of Virginia.
Goldberg, David Theo
  1993   *Racist Culture: Philosophy and the Politics of Meaning.* Cambridge, MA: Blackwell.
Goldberg, David Theo, and Ato Quayson, eds.
  2002   *Relocating Postcolonialism.* Malden, MA: Blackwell.
Golden, Mark, and Peter Toohey
  1997   "General Introduction." Pp. 1–9 in *Inventing Ancient Culture: Historicism, Periodization, and the Ancient World,* ed. Mark Golden and Peter Toohey. New York: Routledge.
Goldhill, Simon, ed.
  2001   *Being Greek under Rome: Cultural Identity, the Second Sophistic, and the Development of Empire.* Cambridge: Cambridge University Press.
González, Justo L.
  2001   *Acts: The Gospel of the Spirit.* Maryknoll, NY: Orbis.
Goodman, Martin
  1994   *Mission and Conversion: Proselytizing in the Religious History of the Roman Empire.* Oxford: Clarendon.
Gordon, Avery F.
  1997   *Ghostly Matters: Haunting and the Sociological Imagination.* Minneapo-lis: University of Minnesota Press.
Gordon, Milton
  1978   *Human Nature, Class, and Ethnicity.* New York: Oxford University Press.
Gotanda, Neil T.
  2001   "Citizenship Nullification: The Impossibility of Asian American Politics." Pp. 79–101 in *Asian Americans and Politics: Perspectives, Experiences, Prospects,* ed. Gordon H. Chang. Stanford, CA: Stanford University Press.
Gramsci, Antonio
  1971   *Selections from the Prison Notebooks.* Ed. and trans. Quinton Hoare and Geoffrey Nowell Smith. New York: International.

Grewal, Inderpal

1993 "Reading and Writing the South Asian Diaspora: Feminism and Nationalism in North America." Pp. 226–36 in *Our Feet Walk the Sky: Women of the South Asian Diaspora*, ed. Women of South Asian Descent Collective. San Francisco: Aunt Lute.

Grewal, Inderpal, and Caren Kaplan, eds.

1994 *Scattered Hegemonies: Postmodernity and Transnational Feminist Practices.* Minneapolis: University of Minnesota Press.

Grosz, Elizabeth

1990 *Jacques Lacan: A Feminist Introduction.* New York: Routledge.

Gruen, Erich S.

1998 *Heritage and Hellenism: The Reinvention of Jewish Tradition.* Berkeley: University of California Press.

Guillory, John

1993 *Cultural Capital: The Problem of Literary Canon Formation.* Chicago: Chicago University Press.

Gunderson, Erik

2000 *Staging Masculinity: The Rhetoric of Performance in the Roman World.* Ann Arbor: University of Michigan Press.

Haenchen, Ernst

1971 *The Acts of the Apostles: A Commentary.* Trans. Bernard Noble and Gerald Shinn. Philadelphia: Westminster.

Hall, Jonathan M.

1997 *Ethnic Identity in Greek Antiquity.* Cambridge: Cambridge University Press.

Hall, Stuart

1994 "Cultural Identity and Diaspora." Pp. 392–403 in *Colonial Discourse and Post-Colonial Theory: A Reader,* ed. Patrick Williams and Laura Chrisman. New York: Columbia University Press.

1996 "The After-Life of Frantz Fanon: Why Fanon? Why Now? Why *Black Skin, White Masks?*" Pp. 12–37 in *The Fact of Blackness: Frantz Fanon and Visual Representation*, ed. Alan Read. Seattle, WA: Bay Press.

Hamerton-Kelly, Robert G.

1994 *The Gospel and the Sacred: Poetics of Violence in Mark.* Minneapolis: Fortress.

Hammond, Philip E., and James D. Hunter

1984 "On Maintaining Plausibility: The Worldview of Evangelical College Students." *Scientific Study of Religion* 22: 221–38.

Haraway, Donna J.

1997 *Modest_Witness@Second_Millennium. FemaleMan©_Meets_OncoMouse™: Feminism and Technoscience.* New York: Routledge.

Harding, Sandra, ed.
  2004   *The Feminist Standpoint Theory Reader: Intellectual and Political Controversies.* New York: Routledge.
Harding, Susan Friend
  2000   *The Book of Jerry Falwell: Fundamentalist Language and Politics.* Princeton, NJ: Princeton University Press.
Hardt, Michael, and Antonio Negri
  2000   *Empire.* Cambridge, MA: Harvard University Press.
Harrill, J. Albert
  2006   *Slaves in the New Testament: Literary, Social, and Moral Dimensions.* Minneapolis: Fortress.
Harrison, Nicholas
  2003   *Postcolonial Criticism: History, Theory and the Work of Fiction.* Malden, MA: Polity.
Harvey, Elizabeth D.
  1991   *Ventriloquized Voices: Feminist Theory and English Renaissance Texts.* New York: Routledge.
Hays, Richard B.
  1989   *Echoes of Scripture in the Letters of Paul.* New Haven, CT: Yale University Press.
  1997   *First Corinthians.* Louisville, KY: John Knox.
Heidegger, Martin
  1968   *What Is Called Thinking?* Trans. Fred Wieck and J. Glenn Gray. New York: Harper and Row.
  1993   "Only a God Can Save Us." Pp. 91–116 in *The Heidegger Controversy: A Critical Reader,* ed. Richard Wolin. Cambridge, MA: MIT Press.
  2004   *The Phenomenology of Religious Life.* Trans. Matthias Fritsch and Jennifer Anna Gosetti-Ferencei. Bloomington: Indiana University Press.
Heil, John Paul
  2005   *The Rhetorical Role of Scripture in 1 Corinthians.* Atlanta: Society of Biblical Literature.
Hendricks, Obery M., Jr.
  1995   "A Discourse of Domination: A Socio-Rhetorical Study of the Use of *Ioudaios* in the Fourth Gospel." Ph.D. diss., Princeton University.
Herman, Didi
  1997   *The Antigay Agenda: Orthodox Vision and the Christian Right.* Chicago: University of Chicago Press.
Hesiod
  1953   *The Theogony.* Trans. Norman O. Brown. Indianapolis: Bobbs-Merrill.
Hobsbawm, Eric
  1983   "Introduction: Inventing Traditions." Pp. 1–14 in Hobsbawm and Ranger, eds. 1983.

Hobsbawm, Eric, and Terence Ranger, eds.

1983   *The Invention of Tradition.* New York: Cambridge University Press.

Holladay, Carl R.

1999   "Acts and the Fragments of Hellenistic Jewish Historians." Pp. 171–98 in Moessner, ed. 1999c.

Hom, Sharon K.

2001   "Cross-Discipline Trafficking: What's Justice Got to Do with It?" Pp. 76–103 in Chuh and Shimakawa, eds. 2001b.

Horsley, Richard A.

1998   *1 Corinthians.* Nashville: Abingdon.

2001   *Hearing the Whole Story: The Politics of Plot in Mark's Gospel.* Louisville, KY: Westminster John Knox.

Horsley, Richard A., ed.

2000   *Paul and Politics: Ekklesia, Israel, Imperium, Interpretation.* Essays in Honor of Krister Stendahl. Harrisburg: Trinity International.

Howard-Brook, Wes

1995   *Becoming Children of God: John's Gospel and Radical Discipleship.* Maryknoll, NY: Orbis.

Hurd, John Coolidge

1983   *The Origin of 1 Corinthians.* 2nd ed. Macon, GA: Mercer University Press.

Hutcheon, Linda

1994   *Irony's Edge: The Theory and Politics of Irony.* New York: Routledge.

Ignatiev, Noel

1995   *How the Irish Became White.* New York: Routledge.

Inden, Ronald B.

2000   *Imagining India.* Bloomington: Indiana University Press.

Irwin, Wallace

1906   "Young Mr. Yan." Pp. 13–18 in Wallace Irwin, *Chinatown Ballads.* New York: Duffield.

Isaac, Benjamin

2004   *The Invention of Racism in Classical Antiquity.* Princeton, NJ: Princeton University Press.

Itzkovitz, Daniel

2001   "Passing like Me: Jewish Chameleonism and the Politics of Race." Pp. 38–63 in Sánchez and Schlossberg, eds. 2001.

Iwamura, Jane Naomi

1996   "Homage to Ancestors: Exploring the Horizons of Asian American Religious Identity." *Amerasia Journal* 22: 162–67.

2002   "The 'Hidden Manna' That Sustains: Reading Revelation 2:17 in Joy Kogawa's *Obasan.*" *Semeia* 90/91: 161–79.

Jameson, Fredric

    1986   "Third-World Literature in the Era of Multinational Capitalism." *Social Text* 15: 65–88.

    1991   *Postmodernism: Or the Cultural Logic of Late Capitalism.* Durham, NC: Duke University Press.

JanMohamed, Abdul R.

    2005   *The Death-Bound-Subject: Richard Wright's Archaeology of Death.* Durham, NC: Duke University Press.

JanMohamed, Abdul R., and David Lloyd, eds.

    1990   *The Nature and Context of Minority Discourse.* New York: Oxford University Press.

Jasper, David

    2004   *A Short Introduction to Hermeneutics.* Louisville, KY: Westminster John Knox.

Jen, Gish

    1991   *Typical American.* Boston: Houghton Mifflin.

    1996   *Mona in the Promised Land.* New York: Alfred A. Knopf.

    1999   *Who's Irish?* New York: Vintage.

    2004   *The Love Wife.* New York: Alfred A. Knopf.

Jeung, Russell

    2005   *Faithful Gernerations: Race and New Asian American Churches.* New Brunswick, NJ: Rutgers University Press.

Johnson, Luke Timothy

    1992   *The Acts of the Apostles.* Collegeville, MN: Liturgical Press.

Johnson Hodge, Caroline

    2005   "Apostle to the Gentiles: Constructions of Paul's Identity." *Biblical Interpretation* 13: 270–88.

Jones, Ernest

    1953–57   *The Life and Work of Sigmund Freud.* 3 vols. New York: Basic Books.

Judson, Horace Freeland

    1996   *The Eighth Day of Recreation: The Makers of the Revolution in Biology.* Expanded ed. New York: Cold Spring Harbor Laboratory.

Kang, Laura Hyun Yi

    1994   "The 'Liberatory Voice' of Theresa Hak Kyung Cha's *Dictée.*" Pp. 73–99 in Elaine Kim and Alarcón, eds. 1994.

    2001   "*Dictee* by Theresa Hak Kyung Cha." Pp. 32–44 in *A Resource Guide to Asian American Literature,* ed. Sau-ling Cynthia Wong and Stephen H. Sumida. New York: The Modern Language Association of America.

    2002   *Compositional Subjects: Enfiguring Asian/American Women.* Durham, NC: Duke University Press.

Kantorowicz, Ernst

    1957   *The King's Two Bodies: A Study in Mediaeval Political Theory.* Princeton, NJ: Princeton University Press.

Kaplan, Amy, and Donald E. Pease, eds.
  1993 *Cultures of United States Imperialism*. Durham, NC: Duke University
        Press.
Kaplan, Caren
  1990 "Deterritorializations: The Rewriting of Home and Exile in Western Femi-
        nist Discourse." Pp. 357–68 in JanMohamed and Lloyd, eds. 1990.
Käseman, Ernst
  1969 *New Testament Questions of Today*. Trans. W. J. Montague. Philadelphia:
        Fortress.
Keenan, Thomas
  1997 *Fables of Responsibility: Aberrations and Predicaments in Ethics and Poli-
        tics*. Stanford, CA: Stanford University Press.
Keller, Catherine
  1998 *Apocalypse Now and Then: A Feminist Guide to the End of the World*.
        Boston: Beacon.
Keller, Nora Okja
  1997 *Comfort Woman*. New York: Penguin.
Kelley, Shawn
  2002 *Racializing Jesus: Race, Ideology and the Formation of Modern Biblical
        Scholarship*. New York: Routledge.
Kendall, Laurel
  1985 *Shamans, Housewives, and Other Restless Spirits: Women in Korean Ritual
        Life*. Honolulu: University of Hawai'i Press.
  1988 *The Life and Hard Times of a Korean Shaman: Of Tales and the Telling of
        Tales*. Honolulu: University of Hawai'i Press.
Kermode, Frank
  1966 *The Sense of an Ending: Studies in the Theory of Fiction*. New York:
        Oxford University Press.
Kim, David Kyuman
  2003 "Enchanting Diasporas: Asian Americans, and the Passionate Attachment
        of Race." Pp. 327–40 in *Revealing the Sacred in Asian and Pacific America*,
        ed. Jane Naomi Iwamura and Paul Spickard. New York: Routledge.
Kim, Elaine H.
  1982 *Asian American Literature: An Introduction to the Writings and Their
        Social Context*. Philadelphia: Temple University Press.
  1994 "Poised on the In-between: A Korean American's Reflections on Theresa
        Hak Kyung Cha's *Dictée*." Pp. 3–30 in Elaine Kim and Alarcón, eds. 1994.
Kim, Elaine H., and Norma Alarcón, eds.
  1994 *Writing Self, Writing Nation*. Berkeley, CA: Third Woman.
Kim, Elaine H., and Lisa Lowe
  1997 "Guest Editors' Introduction." *positions: east asia cultures critique* 5: v–
        xiv.

Kim, Jean K.
  2004 *Woman and Nation: An Intercontextual Reading of the Gospel of John from a Postcolonial Feminist Perspective.* Leiden: Brill.
Kim, Kwang-Ok
  1994 "Rituals of Resistance: The Manipulation of Shamanism in Contemporary Korea." Pp. 195–220 in *Asian Visions of Authority: Religion and the Modern States of East and Southeast Asia,* ed. Charles F. Keyes, Laurel Kendall, and Helen Hardacre. Honolulu: University of Hawai'i Press.
Kim, Min-Jung
  1997 "Moments of Danger in the (Dis)continuous Relation of Korean Nationalism and Korean American Nationalism." *positions: east asia cultures critique* 5: 357–89.
Kim, Uriah Y.
  2005 *Decolonizing Josiah: Toward a Postcolonial Reading of the Deuteronomistic History.* Sheffield (UK): Sheffield Phoenix.
Kingsbury, Jack Dean
  1989 *Conflict in Mark: Jesus, Authorities, Disciples.* Minneapolis: Fortress.
Kingston, Maxine Hong
  1976 *The Woman Warrior: Memoirs of a Girlhood among Ghosts.* New York: Putnam.
  1989 *Tripmaster Monkey: His Fake Book.* New York: Alfred A. Knopf.
Kittredge, Cynthia Briggs
  1998 *Community and Authority: The Rhetoric of Obedience in the Pauline Tradition.* Harrisburg: Trinity International.
  2000 "Corinthian Women Prophets and Paul's Argumentation in 1 Corinthians." Pp. 103–109 in Horsley, ed. 2000.
Kitzberger, Ingrid Rosa
  1998 "How Can This Be?' (John 3.9): A Feminist-Theological Re-reading of the Gospel of John." Pp. 19–41 in Segovia, ed. 1998.
Klein, Julie Thompson
  1996 *Crossing Boundaries: Knowledge, Disciplinarities, and Interdisciplinarities.* Charlottesville: University Press of Virginia.
Knust, Jennifer Wright
  2006 *Abandoned to Lust: Sexual Slander and Ancient Christianity.* New York: Columbia University Press.
Koester, Craig R.
  1995 *Symbolism in the Fourth Gospel: Meaning, Mystery, Community.* Minneapolis: Fortress.
Koester, Helmut
  1982 *Introduction to the New Testament.* 2 vols. New York: de Gruyter.
Kogawa, Joy
  1984 *Obasan.* Boston: Godine.
  1992 *Itsuka.* New York: Viking.

Kondo, Dorinne

1995   "Poststructuralist Theory as Political Necessity." *Amerasia Journal* 21: 95–100.

1997   *About Face: Performing Race in Fashion and Theater.* New York: Rout-ledge.

2001   "(Un)Disciplined Subjects: (De)colonizing the Academy? Pp. 25–40 in Chuh and Shimakawa, eds. 2001b.

Koshy, Susan

2000   "The Fiction of Asian American Literature." Pp. 467–96 in *Asian Amer-ican Studies: A Reader,* ed. Jean Yu-wen Shen Wu and Min Song. New Brunswick, NJ: Rutgers University Press.

2004   *Sexual Naturalization: Asian Americans and Miscegenation.* Stanford, CA: Stanford University Press.

Kristeva, Julia

1982   *The Power of Horror: An Essay on Abjection.* Trans. Leon S. Roudiez. New York: Columbia University Press.

1989   *Black Sun: Depression and Melancholia.* Trans. Leon S. Roudiez. New York: Columbia University Press.

Kuan, Kah-Jin Jeffry

1999   "Asian Biblical Interpretation." Pp. 1.71–77 in *Dictionary of Biblical Interpretation,* ed. John H. Hayes. 2 vols. Nashville: Abingdon.

2000   "Diasporic Reading of a Diasporic Text: Identity Politics and Race Rela-tions and the Book of Esther." Pp. 161–73 in Segovia, ed. 2000.

2002   "My Journey into Diasporic Hermeneutics." *Union Seminary Quarterly Review* 56: 50–54.

Kuriyama, Shigehisa

1999   *The Expressiveness of the Body and the Divergence of Greek and Chinese Medicine.* New York: Zone.

Kwok, Pui-lan

1998   "Jesus/the Native: Biblical Studies from a Postcolonial Perspective." Pp. 69–85 in Segovia and Tolbert, eds. 1998.

Lacan, Jacques

1977   *Écrits: A Selection.* Trans. Alan Sheridan. New York: Norton.

1978   *The Four Fundamental Concepts of Psychoanalysis: The Seminar of Jacques Lacan Book XI.* Ed. Jacques-Alain Miller, trans. Alan Sheridan. New York: Norton.

Lacocque, André

1988   *Daniel in His Time.* Columbia: University of South Carolina Press.

Lai, Him Mark

2004   *Becoming Chinese American: A History of Communities and Institutions.* Walnut Creek, CA: AltaMira.

Lanci, John R.
  1997   *A New Temple for Corinth: Rhetorical and Archaeological Approaches to Pauline Imagery.* New York: Peter Lang.
Larson, Jennifer
  2004   "Paul's Masculinity." *Journal of Biblical Literature* 123: 85–97.
Lee, Andrew Yueking
  2006   "Reading the Bible as an Asian American: Issues in Asian American Biblical Interpretation." Pp. 60–69 in Foskett and Kuan, eds. 2006.
Lee, Archie C. C.
  1993   "Biblical Interpretation in Asian Perspective." *Asia Journal of Theology* 7: 35–39.
  1998   "Cross-Textual Interpretation and Its Implications for Biblical Studies." Pp. 247–54 in Segovia and Tolbert, eds. 1998.
  2004   "Cross-Textual Reading Strategy: A Study of Late Ming and Early Qing Chinese Christian Writings." *Ching Feng: A Journal on Christianity and Chinese Religion and Culture* 4:1–27.
Lee, Chang-Rae
  1995   *Native Speaker.* New York: Riverhead.
  1999   *A Gesture Life.* New York: Riverhead.
Lee, James Kyung-Jin
  2004   *Urban Triage: Race and the Fictions of Multiculturalism.* Minneapolis: University of Minnesota Press.
Lee, Kun Jong
  2004   "Princess Pari in Nora Okja Keller's *Comfort Woman.*" *positions: east asia cultures critique* 12: 431–56.
Lee, Martha F.
  1997   "Environmental Apocalypse: The Millennial Ideology of 'Earth First!'" Pp. 119–37 in *Millennium, Messiahs, and Mayhem: Contemporary Apocalyptic Movements,* ed. Thomas Robbins and Susan J. Palmer. New York: Routledge.
Lee, Robert G.
  1991   "*The Woman Warrior* as an Intervention in Asian American Historiography." Pp. 52–63 in *Approaches to Teaching Kingston's* The Woman Warrior, ed. Shirley Geok-Lin Lim. New York: Modern Language Association of America.
  1999   *Orientals: Asian Americans in Popular Culture.* Philadelphia: Temple University Press.
Lefebvre, Henri
  1991   *Critique of Everyday Life.* Trans. John Moore. New York: Verso.
Levinas, Emmanuel
  1993   *Dieu, la mort et le temps.* Paris: Grasset.
Levine, Amy-Jill, ed. (with Marianne Blickenstaff)
  2004a   *Feminist Companion to the Acts of the Apostles.* Cleveland, OH: Pilgrim.

Levine, Amy-Jill
  2004b "Introduction." Pp. 1–21 in Levine, ed. 2004a.
Lew, Walter K.
  1982 *Excerpts from: Dikte for Dictee*. Chongno Gu: Yeul Eum Publishing.
Lewallen, Constance M.
  2001 *The Dream of the Audience: Theresa Hak Kyung Cha (1951–1982)*. Berkeley: University of California Press.
Lewis, Martin W., and Kären E. Wigen
  1997 *The Myth of Continents: A Critique of Metageography*. Berkeley: University of California Press.
Li, David Leiwei
  1998 *Imagining the Nation: Asian American Literature and Cultural Consent*. Stanford, CA: Stanford University Press.
Lieb, Michael
  1998 *Children of Ezekiel: Aliens, UFOs, the Crisis of Race, and the Advent of End Time*. Durham, NC: Duke University Press.
Liew, Tat-siong Benny
  1999 *Politics of Parousia: Reading Mark Inter(con)textually*. Leiden: Brill.
  2001 "(Cor)Responding: A Letter to the Editor." Pp. 182–92 in *Queer Commentary and the Hebrew Bible*, ed. Ken Stone. Cleveland, OH: Pilgrim.
  2002a "Introduction: Whose Bible? Which (Asian) America?" *Semeia* 90/91: 1–26.
  2002b "More Than Personal Encounters: Identity, Community, and Interpretation." *Union Seminary Quarterly Review* 56: 41–44.
  2005 "Margins and (Cutting-)Edges: On the (Il)Legitimacy and Intersections of Race, Ethnicity, and (Post)Colonialism." Pp. 114–65 in *Postcolonial Biblical Criticism: Interdisciplinary Intersections*, ed. Stephen D. Moore and Fernando F. Segovia. New York: Continuum.
Liew, Tat-siong Benny, and Vincent L. Wimbush
  2002 "Contact Zones and Zoning Contexts: From the Los Angeles 'Riot' to a New York Symposium." *Union Seminary Quarterly Review* 56: 21–40.
Liew, Tat-siong Benny, and Gale A. Yee, eds.
  2002 *The Bible in Asian America*. *Semeia* 90/91. Atlanta: Society of Biblical Literature.
Lin, Adet [pseudonym: Tan Yun]
  1943 *Flame from the Rock*. New York: John Day.
Lin, Yi-chun Tricia
  1997 "Translating Cultures and Re-writing Boundaries: Maxine Hong Kingston, Joy Kogawa, and Theresa Hak Kyung Cha." Ph.D. diss., State University of New York at Stony Brook.
Ling, Amy
  1987 "I'm Here: An Asian American Woman's Response." *New Literary History* 19: 151–60.

1990   *Between Worlds: Women Writers of Chinese Ancestry.* New York: Pergamon.

Lipschits, Oded, Yaacov Shavit, and Omer Sergey
2006   "Review of Uriah Y. Kim, *Decolonizing Josiah: Toward a Postcolonial Reading of the Deuteronomistic History.*" *Review of Biblical Literature.* Accessible at www.bookreviews.org/pdf/4975_5222.pdf.

Lipsitz, George
2001   "'To Tell the Truth and Not Get Trapped': Why Interethnic Antiracism Matters Now." Pp. 296–309 in Chuh and Shimakawa, eds. 2001b.

Litwak, Kenneth Duncan
2005   *Echoes of Scripture in Luke-Acts: Telling the History of God's People Intertextually.* New York: T and T Clark International.

Loomba, Ania
1998   "'Local-Manufacture Made-in-India Othello Fellows': Issues of Race, Hybridity and Location in Post-colonial Shakespeares." Pp. 143–63 in Loomba and Orkin, eds. 1998b.

Loomba, Ania, and Martin Orkin
1998a   "Introduction: Shakespeare and the Post-colonial Question." Pp. 1–19 in Loomba and Orkin, eds. 1998b.

Loomba, Ania, and Martin Orkin, eds.
1998b   *Post-Colonial Shakespeares.* New York: Routledge.

Lorde, Andre
1984   "Poetry Is Not a Luxury." Pp. 36–39 in Andre Lorde, *Sister Outsider: Essays and Speeches.* Trumansburg, NY: Crossing Press.

Lorentzen, Lois Ann
1997   "Phallic Millennialism and Radical Environmentalism: The Apocalyptic Vision of Earth First!" Pp. 144–53 in *The Year 2000: Essays on the End,* ed. Charles B. Strozier and Michael Flynn. New York: New York University Press.

Lowe, Lisa
1994   "Unfaithful to the Original: The Subject of *Dictée.*" Pp. 35–69 in Elaine Kim and Alarcón, eds. 1994.
1995   "On Contemporary Asian American Projects." *Amerasia Journal* 21: 41–52.
1996   *Immigrant Acts: On Asian American Cultural Politics.* Durham, NC: Duke University Press.

McBride, Dwight A.
2001   *Impossible Witnesses: Truth, Abolitionism, and Slave Testimony.* New York: New York University Press.

MacDonald, Dennis R.
2003   *Does the New Testament Imitate Homer? Four Cases from the Acts of the Apostles.* New Haven, CT: Yale University Press.

2004   "Lydia and Her Sisters as Lukan Fictions." Pp. 105–10 in Levine, ed. 2004a.

McGinn, Bernard
1998   *Visions of the End: Apocalyptic Traditions in the Middle Ages.* With a new preface and expanded bibliography. New York: Columbia University Press.

McKay, Sandra Lee, and Sau-ling Cynthia Wong, eds.
1988   *Language Diversity, Problem or Resource? A Social and Educational Perspective on Language Minorities in the United States.* New York: Newbury House.

McLeod, John
2000   *Beginning Postcolonialism.* New York and Manchester (UK): Manchester University Press.

MacMullen, Ramsey
1974   *Roman Social Relations: 50 B.C. to A.D. 284.* New Haven, CT: Yale University Press.

Manalansan, Martin F., IV
2001   "*Biyuti* in Everyday Life: Performance, Citizenship, and Survival among Filipinos in the United States." Pp. 153–71 in Chuh and Shimakawa, eds. 2001b.

Mann, Patricia
1994   *Micro-Politics: Agency in a Postfeminist Era.* Minneapolis: University of Minnesota Press.

Marshall, Peter
1987   *Enmity in Corinth: Social Conventions in Paul's Relations with the Corinthians.* Tübingen: J. C. B. Mohr.

Martin, Dale B.
1990   *Slavery as Salvation: The Metaphor of Slavery in Pauline Christianity.* New Haven, CT: Yale University Press.
1995   *The Corinthian Body.* New Haven, CT: Yale University Press.
1996   "*Arsenoloitēs and Malakos:* Meanings and Consequences." Pp. 117–36 in *Biblical Ethics and Homosexuality: Listening to Scripture,* ed. Robert L. Brawley. Louisville, KY: Westminster John Knox.
2001   "Paul and the Judaism/Hellenism Dichotomy: Toward a Social History of the Question." Pp. 29–61 in *Paul Beyond the Judaism/Hellenism Divide,* ed. Troels Engberg-Pedersen. Louisville, KY: Westminster John Knox.

Martin, Luther H.
1987   *Hellenistic Religions: An Introduction.* New York: Oxford University Press.

Marx, Karl
1977   *Karl Marx: Selected Writings.* Ed. David McLellan. Oxford: Oxford University Press.

Matsuoka, Fumitaka, and Eleazar S. Fernandez, eds.
  2003 *Realizing the America of Our Hearts: Theological Voices of Asian Americans.* St. Louis, MO: Chalice.
Matthews, Shelly
  2001 *First Converts: Rich Pagan Women and the Rhetoric of Mission in Early Judaism and Christianity.* Stanford, CA: Stanford University Press.
Mazumdar, Sucheta
  1991 "Asian American Studies and Asian Studies: Rethinking Roots." Pp. 29–44 in *Asian Americans: Comparative and Global Perspectives,* ed. Shirley Hune, Hyung-chan Kim, Stephen S. Fugita, and Amy Ling. Pullman: Washington State University Press.
Meeks, Wayne A.
  1972 "The Man from Heaven in Johannine Sectarianism." *Journal of Biblical Literature* 91: 44–72.
  1993 *The Origins of Christian Morality: The First Two Centuries.* New Haven, CT: Yale University Press.
Memmi, Albert
  1991 *The Colonizer and the Colonized.* Expanded ed. Trans. Howard Greenfeld. Boston: Beacon.
Mendel, Arthur P.
  1992 *Vision and Violence.* Ann Arbor: University of Michigan Press.
Mignolo, Walter D.
  2000 *Local Histories/Global Designs: Coloniality, Subaltern Knowledges, and Border Thinking.* Princeton, NJ: Princeton University Press.
Min, Eun Kyung
  1998 "Reading the Figure of Dictation in Theresa Hak Kyung Cha's *Dictée.*" Pp. 309–324 in *Other Sisterhoods: Literary Theory and US Women of Color,* ed. Sandra Kumamoto Stanley. Urbana: University of Illinois Press.
Min, Susette
  2001 "Narrative Chronology." Pp. 151–54 in Lewallen 2001.
Mitchell, Margaret Mary
  1991 *Paul and the Rhetoric of Reconciliation: An Exegetical Investigation of the Language and Composition of 1 Corinthians.* Louisville, KY: Westminster John Knox.
Mix, Deborah Marie
  1998 "Re-Writing the Wor(l)d: Experimental Writing by Contemporary American Women." Ph.D. diss., Purdue University.
Moessner, David P.
  1999a "The Appeal and Power of Poetics (Luke 1:1–4): Luke's Superior Credentials (παρηκολουθηκότι), Narrative Sequence (καθεξῆς), and Firmness of Understanding (ἡ ἀσφάλεια) for the Reader." Pp. 84–123 in Moessner, ed. 1999c.
  1999b "'The Christ Must Suffer': New Light on the Jesus-Peter, Stephen, Paul

Parallels in Luke-Acts." Pp. 117–53 in *The Composition of Luke's Gospel: Selected Studies from Novum Testamentum*, ed. David E. Orton. Leiden: Brill.

Moessner, David P., ed.

1999c *Jesus and the Heritage of Israel: Luke's Narrative Claim upon Israel's Legacy*. Harrisburg: Trinity International.

Mohanty, Chandra Talpade

2003 *Feminism without Borders: Decolonizing Theory, Practicing Solidarity*. Durham, NC: Duke University Press.

Moore, Stephen D.

1992 *Mark and Luke in Poststructuralist Perspectives: Jesus Begins to Write*. New Haven, CT: Yale University Press.

1996 *God's Gym: Divine Male Bodies of the Bible*. New York: Routledge.

2001 *God's Beauty Parlor: And Other Queer Spaces in and around the Bible*. Stanford, CA: Stanford University Press.

2004 "Mark and Empire: 'Zealot' and 'Postcolonial' Readings." Pp. 134–48 in *Postcolonial Theologies: Divinity and Empire*, ed. Catherine Keller, Michael Nausner, and Mayra Rivera. St. Louis, MO: Chalice.

Morrison, Toni

1997 "Home." Pp. 3–12 in *The House That Race Built*, ed. Wahneema Lubiano. New York: Vintage.

1998 *Paradise*. New York: Alfred A. Knopf.

Moy, James S.

1993 *Marginal Sight: Staging the Chinese in America*. Iowa City: University of Iowa Press.

Mudimbe, V. Y.

1988 *The Invention of Africa: Gnosis, Philosophy and the Order of Knowledge*. Bloomington: Indiana University Press.

Muñoz, José Esteban

1999 *Disidentifications: Queers of Color and the Performance of Politics*. Minneapolis: University of Minnesota Press.

Myers, Ched

1992 *Binding the Strong Man: A Political Reading of Mark's Story of Jesus*. Maryknoll, NY: Orbis.

Nakanishi, Don T.

1976 "Minorities and International Politics." Pp. 81–85 in *Counterpoint: Perspectives on Asian America*, ed. Emma Gee. Los Angeles: UCLA Asian American Studies Center.

Nanos, Mark D.

2002 *The Irony of Galatians: Paul's Letter in First-Century Context*. Minneapolis: Fortress.

2005 "How Inter-Christian Approaches to Paul's Rhetoric Can Perpetuate Negative Valuations of Jewishness—Although Proposing to Avoid That Outcome." *Biblical Interpretation* 13: 255–69.

Newman, Karen, Jay Clayton, and Marianne Hirsch
2002a "Re-Reading the Present." Pp. 1–7 in Newman, Clayton, and Hirsch, eds. 2002b.

Newman, Karen, Jay Clayton, and Marianne Hirsch, eds.
2002b *Time and the Literary.* New York: Routledge

Ng, Fae Myenne
1993 *Bone.* New York: Hyperion.

Ngai, Mae M.
2004 *Impossible Subjects: Illegal Aliens and the Making of Modern America.* Princeton, NJ: Princeton University Press.

Ngugi wa Thiongo
1981 *Detained: A Writer's Prison Diary.* London: Heinemann.

Nguyen, Viet Thanh
2002 *Race and Resistance: Literature and Politics in Asian America.* New York: Oxford University Press.

Nichols, Stephen G.
2002 "Re-Reading the Apocalypse: Millennial Politics in 19th- and 11th-Century France." Pp. 183–209 in Newman, Clayton, and Hirsch, eds. 2002b.

Nieh, Hualing
1988 *Mulberry and Peach: Two Women of China.* Trans. Jane Parish Yang and Linda Lappin. Boston: Beacon.

Nietzsche, Friedrich Wilhelm
1967 *On the Genealogy of Morals.* Trans. Walter Kaufmann and R. J. Hollingdale. New York: Vintage.
1990 *Twilight of the Idols and the Anti-Christ.* Trans. R. J. Hollingdale with an introduction by Michael Tanner. New York: Penguin.
1997 *Daybreak: Thoughts on the Prejudices of Morality.* Trans. R. J. Hollingdale. Cambridge: Cambridge University Press.

Nissinen, Martti
1998 *Homoeroticism in the Biblical World: A Historical Perspective.* Trans. Kirsi Stjerna. Minneapolis: Fortress.

Nora, Pierre
1989 "Between Memory and History: *Les Lieux de Mémoire.*" *Representations* 26: 7–25.

Nowotny, Helga
1994 *Time: The Modern and Postmodern Experience.* Cambridge: Polity.

Okihiro, Gary Y.
1994 *Margins and Mainstreams: Asians in American History and Culture.* Seattle: University of Washington Press.
2001 *Common Ground: Reimagining American History.* Princeton, NJ: Princeton University Press.

Økland, Jorunn
  2004   *Women in Their Place: Paul and the Corinthian Discourse of Gender and Sanctuary Space.* London: T and T Clark.
Olbricht, Thomas, and Anders Eriksson, eds.
  2005   *Rhetoric, Ethic, and Moral Persuasion in Biblical Discourse: Essays from the 2002 Heidelberg Conference.* New York: T and T Clark International.
O'Leary, Stephen
  1994   *Arguing the Apocalypse: A Theory of Millennial Rhetoric.* New York: Oxford University Press.
Omi, Michael, and Howard Winant
  1994   *Racial Formation in the United States: From the 1960s to the 1990s.* 2nd ed. New York: Routledge.
O'Neill, J. C.
  1961   *The Theology of Acts in Its Historical Setting.* London: SPCK.
Ong, Aihwa
  1999   *Flexible Citizenship: The Cultural Logics of Transnationality.* Durham, NC: Duke University Press.
  2003   *Buddha Is Hiding: Refugees, Citizenship, the New America.* Berkeley: University of California Press.
Ono, Kent A.
  1995   "Re/signing 'Asian America': Rhetorical Problematics of Nation." *Amerasia Journal* 21: 67–78.
Page, Barbara
  1996   "Women Writers and the Restive Text: Feminism, Experimental Writing and Hypertext." *Postmodern Culture* 6: 196. Accessible at http://muse.jhu.edu/journal/postmodern_culture/v006/6.2page.html.
Palmer, Susan
  1997   *AIDS as an Apocalyptic Metaphor in North America.* Toronto: University of Toronto Press.
Palumbo-Liu, David
  1995a "The Ethnic as 'Post-': Reading Reading the Literatures of Asian America." *American Literary History* 7: 161–68.
  1995b "Theory and the Subject of Asian America Studies." *Amerasia Journal* 21: 55–65.
  1999   *Asian/American: Historical Crossings of a Racial Frontier.* Stanford, CA: Stanford University Press.
Pao, David W.
  2002   *Acts and the Isaianic New Exodus.* Grand Rapids, MI: Baker.
  2003   "Disagreement among the Jews in Acts 28." Pp. 109–18 in *Early Christian Voices: In Texts, Traditions, and Symbols. Essays in Honor of François Bovon,* ed. David H. Warren, Ann Graham Brock, and David W. Pao. Leiden: Brill.

Park, Eung Chun
  2003   *Either Jew or Gentile: Paul's Unfolding Theology of Inclusivity.* Louisville,
         KY: Westminster John Knox.
Parker, David C.
  1997   *The Living Texts of the Gospels.* New York: Cambridge University Press.
Parsons, Mikeal C., and Richard I. Pervo
  1993   *Rethinking the Unity of Luke and Acts.* Minneapolis: Fortress.
Payne, Michael
  1993   *Reading Theory: An Introduction to Lacan, Derrida, and Kristeva.* Cam-
         bridge: Blackwell.
Penner, Todd
  2003a "Civilizing Discourse: Acts, Declamation, and the Rhetoric of the *Polis*."
         Pp. 65–104 in Penner and Vander Stichele, eds. 2003.
  2003b "Contextualizing Acts." Pp. 1–21 in Penner and Vander Stichele, eds.
         2003.
Penner, Todd, and Caroline Vander Stichele
  2004   "Gendering Violence: Patterns of Power and Constructs of Masculinity in
         the Acts of the Apostles." Pp. 193–209 in Levine, ed. 2004a.
  2005   "Unveiling Paul: Gendering Ethos in 1 Corinthians 11.2–16." Pp. 214–37
         in Olbricht and Eriksson, eds. 2005.
Penner, Todd, and Caroline Vander Stichele, eds.
  2003   *Contextualizing Acts: Lukan Narrative and Greco-Roman Discourse.*
         Atlanta: Society of Biblical Literature.
[Perpetua]
  1927   *The Passion of S. Perpetua.* Trans. R. Waterville Muncey. London: J. M.
         Dent.
Petersen, Norman R.
  1992   *The Gospel of John and the Sociology of Light: Language and Character-
         ization in the Fourth Gospel.* Valley Forge, PA: Trinity.
Phelan, Peggy
  1993   *Unmarked: The Politics of Performance.* New York: Routledge.
Phillips, Gary A., ed.
  1990   *Poststructural Criticism and the Bible: Text/History/Discourse. Semeia*
         51. Atlanta: Scholars.
Pile, Steve
  1997   "Introduction: Opposition, Political Identities and Spaces of Resistance."
         Pp. 1–32 in *Geographies of Resistance*, ed. Steve Pile and Michael Keith.
         New York: Routledge.
Pippin, Tina
  1992   *Death and Desire: The Rhetoric of Gender in the Apocalypse of John.* Lou-
         isville, KY: Westminster John Knox.
Pippin, Tina, and George Aichele
  1998   "Introduction: Fantasy and the Bible." Pp. 1–7 in *Violence, Utopia and the*

Kingdom of God: Fantasy and Ideology in the Bible, ed. George Aichele and Tina Pippin. New York: Routledge.

Plümacher, Eckhard

1999   "The Mission Speeches in Acts and Dionysius of Halicarnassus." Pp. 251–66 in Moessner, ed. 1999c.

Pogoloff, Stephen M.

1992   *Logos and Sophia: The Rhetorical Situation of 1 Corinthians.* Atlanta: Scholars.

Pollock, Sheldon, Homi K. Bhabha, Carol A. Breckenridge, and Dipesh Chakrabarty

2000   "Cosmopolitanisms." *Public Culture* 12: 577–89.

Pontalis, J. B.

1978   "On the Death-Work in Freud, in the Self, in Culture." Pp. 85–95 in *Psychoanalysis, Creativity, and Literature: A French-American Inquiry,* ed. Alan Roland. New York: Columbia University Press.

Porcupine

1973   "Account of the Messiah." Pp. 793–96 in *The Ghost-Dance Religion and Wounded Knee,* ed. James Mooney. New York: Dover.

Poster, Mark

1990   *The Mode of Information: Poststructuralism and Social Context.* Chicago: University of Chicago Press.

Pregeant, Russell

1996   "The Wisdom Passages in Matthew's Story." Pp. 197–232 in Bauer and Powell 1996.

Pulido, Laura

2006   *Black, Brown, Yellow, and Left: Radical Activism in Los Angeles.* Berkeley: University of California Press.

Punday, Daniel

2003   *Narrative Bodies: Toward a Corporeal Narratology.* New York: Palgrave.

Quayson, Ato, and David Theo Goldberg

2002   "Introduction: Scale and Sensibility." Pp. xi–xxii in Goldberg and Quayson, eds. 2002.

Quinby, Lee

1994   *Anti-Apocalypse: Exercises in Genealogical Criticism.* Minneapolis: University of Minnesota Press.

Radden, Jennifer

2002   *The Nature of Melancholy: From Aristotle to Kristeva.* New York: Oxford University Press.

Radhakrishnan, R.

1990   "Ethnic Identity and Post-structuralist Difference." Pp. 50–71 in JanMohamed and Lloyd, eds. 1990.

2001   "Conjunctural Identities, Academic Adjacencies." Pp. 249–63 in Chuh and Shimakawa, eds. 2001b.

Razack, Sherene H.

  1998 *Looking White People in the Eye: Gender, Race, and Culture in Court-rooms and Classrooms*. Toronto: University of Toronto Press.

Reid, Barbara E.

  2004 "The Power of the Widows and How to Suppress It (Acts 6:1–7)." Pp. 71–88 in Levine, ed. 2004a.

Reinhartz, Adele

  1998 "On Travel, Translation, and Ethnography: Johannine Scholarship at the Turn of the Century." Pp. 249–56 in Segovia, ed. 1998.

  2001 *Befriending the Beloved Disciple: A Jewish Reading of the Gospel of John*. New York: Continuum.

Rensberger, David

  1988 *Johannine Faith and Liberating Community*. Philadelphia: Westminster.

  2002 "Spirituality and Christology in Johannine Sectarianism." Pp. 173–88 in *Word, Theology, and Community in John*, ed. John Painter, R. Alan Culpepper, and Fernando F. Segovia. St. Louis, MO: Chalice.

Rhoads, David, ed.

  2005 *From Every People and Nation: The Book of Revelation in Intercultural Perspective*. Minneapolis: Fortress.

Rich, Adrienne

  1979 "Disloyal to Civilization: Feminism, Racism, Gynephobia." Pp. 275–310 in Adrienne Rich, *On Lies, Secrets, and Silence: Selected Prose, 1966–1978*. New York: Norton.

Richard, Pablo

  1995 *Apocalypse: A People's Commentary on the Book of Revelation*. Maryknoll, NY: Orbis.

Richlin, Amy

  1997 "Gender and Rhetoric: Producing Manhood in the Schools." Pp. 90–110 in *Roman Eloquence: Rhetoric in Society and Literature*, ed. William J. Dominik. New York: Routledge.

Ricoeur, Paul

  1984–88 *Time and Narrative*. Trans. Kathleen McLaughlin and David Pellauer. 3 vols. Chicago: University of Chicago Press.

Ringe, Sharon H.

  1999 *Wisdom's Friends: Community and Christology in the Fourth Gospel*. Louisville, KY: Westminster John Knox.

Roach, Joseph

  1996 *Cities of the Dead: Circum-Atlantic Performance*. New York: Columbia University Press.

Robbins, Thomas, and Susan J. Palmer, eds.

  1997 *Millennium, Messiahs, and Mayhem: Contemporary Apocalyptic Movements*. New York: Routledge.

Robbins, Vernon K.
  1999   "The Claims of the Prologues and Greco-Roman Rhetoric: The Prefaces to Luke and Acts in Light of Greco-Roman Rhetorical Strategies." Pp. 63–83 in Moessner, ed. 1999c.
Roberts, Richard H.
  2002   *Religion, Theology and the Human Sciences.* New York: Cambridge University Press.
Robinson, Douglas
  1990   *American Apocalypses: The Image of the End of the World in American Literature.* Baltimore: Johns Hopkins University Press.
Rohmer, Sax
  1939   *The Drums of Fu Manchu.* Garden City, NY: Crime Club-Doubleday, Doran and Company.
Rosaldo, Renato
  1989   *Culture and Truth: The Remaking of Social Analysis.* Boston: Beacon.
Rothstein, Eric
  1991   "Diversity and Change in Literary History." Pp. 114–45 in Clayton and Rothstein, eds. 1991.
Rowe, John Carlos
  1994   "Melville's *Typee:* U.S. Imperialism at Home and Abroad." Pp. 255–78 in *National Identities and Post-Americanist Narratives,* ed. Donald E. Pease. Durham, NC: Duke University Press.
Rubin, Gayle
  1975   "The Traffic in Women: Notes on the Political Economy of Sex." Pp. 157–210 in *Toward an Anthropology of Women,* ed. Rayna Reiter. New York: Monthly Review.
Ruiz, Jean-Pierre
  1989   *Ezekiel in the Apocalypse: The Transformation of Prophetic Language in Revelation 16:17–19:10.* New York: Peter Lang.
  2003   "Taking a Stand on the Sand of the Seashore: A Postcolonial Exploration of Revelation 13." Pp. 119–35 in *Reading the Book of Revelation: A Resource for Students,* ed. David L. Barr. Atlanta: Society of Biblical Literature.
Said, Edward W.
  2003   *Freud and the Non-European.* New York: Verso.
Sakai, Naoki
  1989   "Modernity and Its Critique: The Problem of Universalism and Particularism." Pp. 93–122 in *Postmodernism and Japan,* ed. Masao Miyoshi and H. D. Harootunian. Durham, NC: Duke University Press.
Sánchez, María Carla, and Linda Schlossberg, eds.
  2001   *Passing: Identity and Interpretation in Sexuality, Race and Religion.* New York: New York University Press.

Sanders, E. P.

 1977   *Paul and Palestinian Judaism: A Comparison of Patterns of Religion*. Phila-
        delphia: Fortress.

 1983   *Paul, the Law, and the Jewish People*. Philadelphia: Fortress.

Schäfer, Peter

 1997   *Judeophobia: Attitudes toward the Jews in the Ancient World*. Cambridge,
        MA: Harvard University Press.

Schlossberg, Linda

 2001   "Introduction: Rites of Passing." Pp. 1–12 in Sánchez and Schlossberg, eds.
        2001.

Schmidt, Daryl D.

 1999   "Rhetorical Influences and Genre: Luke's Preface and the Rhetoric of Hel-
        lenistic Historiography." Pp. 27–60 in Moessner, ed. 1999c.

Schnackenburg, Rudolf

 1996   "Matthew's Gospel as a Test Case for Hermeneutical Reflection." Trans.
        Ronald D. Witherup, S.S. Pp. 251–69 in Bauer and Powell, eds. 1996.

Schrage, Wolfgang

 1991–2001   *Der erste Brief an die Korinther*. 4 vols. Zurich and Braunschweig:
             Benziger Verlag and Neukirchener Verlag.

Schueller, Malini Johar

 1992   *The Politics of Voice: Liberalism and Social Criticism from Franklin to
        Kingston*. Albany: State University of New York Press.

Schüssler Fiorenza, Elisabeth

 1991   *Revelation: Vision of a Just World*. Minneapolis: Fortress.

 1999   *Rhetoric and Ethic: The Politics of Biblical Studies*. Minneapolis: Fortress.

 2005   "Disciplinary Matters: A Critical Rhetoric and Ethic of Inquiry." Pp. 9–32
        in Olbricht and Eriksson, eds. 2005.

Schwartz, Saundra

 2003   "The Trial Scene in the Greek Novels and in Acts." Pp. 105–137 in Penner
        and Stichele, eds. 2003.

Schweizer, Eduard

 1975   *The Good News according to Matthew*. Trans. David E. Green. Atlanta:
        John Knox.

Scott, Joan W.

 1995   "Multiculturalism and the Politics of Identity." Pp. 3–12 in *The Identity in
        Question*, ed. John Rajchman. New York: Routledge.

Segovia, Fernando F., ed.

 1998   *"What Is John?" Volume 2: Literary and Social Readings of the Fourth
        Gospel*. Atlanta: Scholars.

 2000   *Interpreting beyond Borders*. Sheffield (UK): Sheffield Academic.

Segovia, Fernando F., and Mary Ann Tolbert, eds.

 1998   *Teaching the Bible: The Discourses and Politics of Biblical Pedagogy*. Mary-
        knoll, NY: Orbis.

Seim, Turid Karlsen

1994 *The Double Message: Patterns of Gender in Luke and Acts.* Nashville: Abingdon.

Setzer, Claudia

2005 "Does Paul Need to Be Saved?" *Biblical Interpretation* 13: 289–97.

Shankar, Lavina Dhingra, and Rajini Srikanth, eds.

1998 *A Part Yet Apart: South Asians in Asian America.* Philadelphia: Temple University Press.

Shih, Shu-mei

1997 "Nationalism and Korean American Women's Writing: Theresa Hak Kyung Cha's *Dictee.*" Pp. 144–62 in *Speaking the Other Self: American Women Writers,* ed. Jeanne Campbell Reesman. Athens: University of Georgia Press.

Shimakawa, Karen

2002 *National Abjection: The Asian American Body Onstage.* Durham, NC: Duke University Press.

Shukla, Sandhya

1997 "Building Diaspora and Nation: The 1991 'Cultural Festival of India.'" *Cultural Studies* 11: 296–315.

Silverman, Kaja

1988 *The Acoustic Mirror: The Female Voice in Psycholanalysis and Cinema.* Bloomington: Indiana University Press.

1996 *The Thresholds of the Visible World.* New York: Routledge.

Simon, Herbert A.

1957 *Models of Man, Social and Relational.* New York: John Wiley and Sons.

Slemon, Stephen

1991 "Modernism's Last Post." Pp. 1–11 in *Past the Last Post: Theorizing Post-Colonialism and Post-Modernism,* ed. Ian Adam and Helen Tiffin. Calgary: University of Calgary Press.

Smith, Sidonie

1993 *Subjectivity, Identity, and the Body: Women's Autobiographical Practices in the Twentieth Century.* Bloomington: Indiana University Press.

Smoak, Gregory E.

2006 *Ghost Dances and Identity: Prophetic Religion and American Indian Ethnogenesis in the Nineteenth Century.* Berkeley: University of California Press.

Snodgrass, Klyne

1996 "Matthew and the Law." Pp. 99–127 in Bauer and Powell, eds. 1996.

Snyder, Graydon F.

1992 *First Corinthians: A Faith Community Commentary.* Macon, GA: Mercer University Press.

Sollors, Werner

    1986   *Beyond Ethnicity: Consent and Descent in American Culture.* New York: Oxford University Press.

Song, Young In

    1997   "Critical Feminist View of Patriarchal Structure of the Korean American Christian Church." Pp. 67–93 in *Korean American Women Living in Two Cultures,* ed. Young In Song and Aileen Moon. Los Angeles: Keimyung-Baylo University Press.

Spahr, Juliana M.

    1996   "Postmodernism, Readers, and Theresa Hak Kyung Cha's *Dictee.*" *College Literature* 23: 25–43.

Spencer, F. Scott

    2004   "Women of the 'Cloth' in Acts: Sewing the Word." Pp. 134–54 in Levine, ed. 2004a.

Spickard, Paul, and W. Jeffrey Burroughs

    1999   "We Are a People." Pp. 1–19 in *We Are a People: Narrative and Multiplicity in Constructing Ethnic Identity,* ed. Paul Spickard and W. Jeffrey Burroughs. Philadelphia: Temple University Press.

Spivak, Gayatri Chakravorty

    1988   "Can the Subaltern Speak?" Pp. 271–313 in *Marxism and the Interpretation of Culture,* ed. Cary Nelson and Lawrence Grossberg. Urbana: University of Illinois Press.

    1989   "Naming Gayatri Spivak: Interview by Maria Koundoura." *Stanford Humanities Review* 1: 84–97.

    1990   *The Post-Colonial Critic: Interviews, Strategies, Dialogues.* Ed. Sarah Harasym. New York: Routledge.

    1996   "Bonding in Difference: Interview with Alfred Arteaga." Pp. 15–28 in *The Spivak Reader: Selected Works of Gayatri Chakravorty Spivak,* ed. Donna Landry and Gerald MacLean. New York: Routledge.

    1997   "Teaching for the Times." Pp. 468–90 in *Dangerous Liaisons: Gender, Nation, and Postcolonial Perspectives,* ed. Anne McClintock, Aamir Mufti, and Ella Shohat. Minneapolis: University of Minnesota Press.

    1999   *A Critique of Postcolonial Reason: Toward a History of the Vanishing Present.* Cambridge, MA: Harvard University Press.

    2003   *Death of a Discipline.* New York: Columbia University Press.

    2005   "Touched by Deconstruction." *Grey Room* 20: 95–104.

Spurr, David

    1993   *The Rhetoric of Empire: Colonial Discourse in Journalism, Travel Writing, and Imperial Administration.* Durham, NC: Duke University Press.

Staley, Jeffrey L.

    1995   *Reading with a Passion: Rhetoric, Autobiography, and the American West in the Gospel of John.* New York: Continuum.

2004   "Changing Woman: Toward a Postcolonial Postfeminist Interpretation of Acts 16.6–40." Pp. 177–92 in Levine, ed. 2004a.

Stanley, Christopher D.
2004   *Arguing with Scripture: The Rhetoric of Quotations in the Letters of Paul.* New York: T and T Clark International.

Stendahl, Krister
1976   *Paul among Jews and Gentiles.* Philadelphia: Fortress.

Sterling, Gregory E.
1992   *Historiography and Self-Definition: Josephus, Luke-Acts and Apologetic Historiography.* Leiden: Brill.

Stone, Jon R., ed.
2000   *Expecting Armageddon: Essential Readings in Failed Prophecy.* New York: Routledge.

Stott, T. Lynn
1998   "Symbolic Healing and the Body at Corinth: An Anthropological Analysis of Paul's Rhetoric." Ph.D. diss., Vanderbilt University.

Stratton, Jon
2000   "The Beast of the Apocalypse: The Postcolonial Experience of the United States." Pp. 21–64 in *Postcolonial America,* ed. C. Richard King. Urbana: University of Illinois Press.

Strozier, Charles B.
1994   *Apocalypse: On the Psychology of Fundamentalism in America.* Boston: Beacon.

Sugirtharajah, R. S.
2003   *Postcolonial Reconfigurations: An Alternative Way of Reading the Bible and Doing Theology.* St. Louis, MO: Chalice.

Suh, Sharon A.
2004   *Being Buddhist in a Christian World: Gender and Community in a Korean American Temple.* Seattle: University of Washington Press.

Sui Sin Far
1995   "Leaves from the Mental Portfolio of an Eurasian." Pp. 218–30 in *Mrs. Spring Fragrance and Other Writings,* ed. Amy Ling and Annette White-Parks. Urbana: University of Illinois Press.

Swanson, Tod D.
2002   "To Prepare a Place: Johannine Christianity and the Collapse of Ethnic Territory." Pp. 11–31 in *John and Postcolonialism: Travel, Space and Power,* ed. Musa W. Dube and Jeffrey L. Staley. New York: Sheffield Academic.

Takaki, Ronald
1989   *Strangers from a Different Shore: A History of Asian Americans.* New York: Penguin.

Talbert, Charles H.
1976   "The Myth of a Descending-Ascending Redeemer in Mediterranean Antiquity." *New Testament Studies* 22: 418–40.

2003   *Reading Luke-Acts in its Mediterranean Milieu.* Leiden: Brill.
Tan, Amy
   1995   *The Hundred Secret Senses.* New York: Putnam.
   2003   *The Opposite of Fate: A Book of Musings.* New York: Putnam.
Tan, Yak-hwee
   2006   "The Johannine Community: Caught in 'Two Worlds.'" Pp. 167–82 in
          New Currents through John: A Global Perspective, ed. Francisco Lozada,
          Jr., and Tom Thatcher. Atlanta: Society of Biblical Literature.
Tannehill, Robert C.
   1994   *The Narrative Unity of Luke-Acts: A Literary Interpretation. Volume 2:
          The Acts of the Apostles.* Minneapolis: Fortress.
Tanner, Kathryn
   1997   *Theories of Culture: A New Agenda for Theology.* Minneapolis: Fortress.
Taylor, Mark Lewis
   1998   "Reading from an Indigenous Place." Pp. 117–36 in Segovia and Tolbert,
          eds. 1998.
Theissen, Gerd
   1982   *The Social Setting of Pauline Christianity.* Ed. and trans. John H. Schütz.
          Philadelphia: Fortress.
Tiede, David L.
   1980   *Prophecy and History in Luke-Acts.* Philadelphia: Fortress.
Tolbert, Mary Ann
   1989   *Sowing the Gospel: Mark's World in Literary-Historical Perspective.* Min-
          neapolis: Fortress.
   1995   "Reading for Liberation." Pp. 263–76 in *Reading from this Place: Volume
          1, Social Location and Biblical Interpretation in the United States,* ed. Fer-
          nando F. Segovia and Mary Ann Tolbert. Minneapolis: Fortress.
   1998   "A New Teaching with Authority: A Re-evaluation of the Authority of the
          Bible." Pp. 168–89 in Segovia and Tolbert, eds. 1998.
Torgovnick, Marianna
   1990   *Gone Primitive: Savage Intellects, Modern Lives.* Chicago: University of
          Chicago Press.
Trinh T. Minh-ha
   1989   *Woman, Native, Other: Writing Postcoloniality and Feminism.* Blooming-
          ton: Indiana University Press.
   1999   *Cinema Interval.* New York: Routledge.
Tseng, Timothy
   2002   "Second-Generation Chinese Evangelical Use of the Bible in Identity Dis-
          course in North America." *Semeia* 90/91: 251–67.
Tuan, Mia
   1998   *Forever Foreigners or Honorary Whites? The Asian Ethnic Experience
          Today.* New Brunswick, NJ: Rutgers University Press.

Turner, Jonathan H., and Edna Bonacich

1980 "Toward a Composite Theory of Middleman Minorities." *Ethnicity* 7: 144–58.

Turner, Victor W.

1967 *The Forest of Symbols: Aspects of Ndembu Ritual.* Ithaca, NY: Cornell University Press.

1977 "Death and the Dead in the Pilgrimage Process." Pp. 24–39 in *Religious Encounters with Death,* ed. Frank E. Reynolds and Earle H. Waugh. University Park: Pennsylvania State University Press.

Ty, Eleanor, and Donald C. Goellnicht, eds.

2004 *Asian North American Identities: Beyond the Hyphen.* Bloomington: Indiana University Press.

Tyson, Joseph B.

1992 *Images of Judaism in Luke-Acts.* Columbia: University of South Carolina Press.

1999 *Luke, Judaism, and the Scholars: Critical Approaches to Luke-Acts.* Columbia: University of South Carolina Press.

2003 "From History to Rhetoric and Back: Assessing New Trends in Acts Studies." Pp. 23–42 in Penner and Vander Stichele, eds. 2003.

Utset, Manuel

1995 "Back to School with Coase: The Production of Information and Modes of Knowledge within and across Academic Disciplines." *Boston University Law Review* 75: 1063–96.

Vander Stichele, Caroline

2003 "Gender and Genre: Acts in/of Interpretation." Pp. 311–29 in Penner and Stichele, eds. 2003.

Visweswaran, Kamala

1993 "Predicaments of the Hyphen." Pp. 301–312 in *Our Feet Walk the Sky: Women of the South Asian Diaspora,* ed. Women of South Asian Descent Collective. San Francisco: Aunt Lute.

Waetjen, Herman C.

1989 *A Reordering of Power: A Socio-Political Reading of Mark's Gospel.* Minneapolis: Fortress.

Wald, Gayle

2000 *Crossing the Color Line: Racial Passing in Twentieth-Century U.S. Literature and Culture.* Durham, NC: Duke University Press.

Wald, Priscilla

1993 "Terms of Assimilation: Legislating Subjectivity in the Emerging Nation." Pp. 59–84 in Kaplan and Pease, eds. 1993.

Wallerstein, Immanuel

1998 *Utopistics: Or, Historical Choices of the Twenty-first Century.* New York: New Press.

1999 *The End of the World as We Know It: Social Science for the Twenty-first Century*. Minneapolis: University of Minnesota Press.

Wan, Sze-kar

2000a "Collection for the Saints as Anticolonial Act: Implications of Paul's Ethnic Reconstruction." Pp. 191–215 in Horsley, ed. 2000.

2000b "Does Diaspora Identity Imply Some Sort of Universality? An Asian-American Reading of Galatians." Pp. 107–31 in Segovia, ed. 2000.

2000c *Power in Weakness: Conflict and Rhetoric in Paul's Second Letter to the Corinthians*. Harrisburg: Trinity International.

2006 "Betwixt and Between: Towards a Hermeneutics of Hyphenation." Pp. 137–51 in Foskett and Kuan, eds. 2006.

Wang, David Der-wei

2000 "Three Hungry Women." Pp. 48–77 in *Modern Chinese Literary and Cultural Studies in the Age of Theory: Reimagining a Field*, ed. Rey Chow. Durham, NC: Duke University Press.

Wang, L. Ling-chi

1995 "The Structure of Dual Domination: Toward a Paradigm for the Study of the Chinese Diaspora in the United States." *Amerasia Journal* 21: 149–69.

Warnke, Georgia

1992 *Justice and Interpretation*. Cambridge, MA: MIT.

Weber, Eugen

1999 *Apocalypses: Prophecies, Cults, and Millennial Beliefs through the Ages*. Cambridge, MA: Harvard University Press.

Weeks, Jeffrey

1995 *Invented Moralities: Sexual Values in an Age of Uncertainty*. New York: Columbia University Press.

Wei, William

1993 *The Asian American Movement*. Philadelphia: Temple University Press.

Wiegman, Robyn

1995 *American Anatomies: Theorizing Race and Gender*. Durham, NC: Duke University Press.

Williams, Raymond

1985 *Keywords: A Vocabulary of Culture and Society*. Rev. ed. New York: Oxford University Press.

2001 "Base and Superstructure in Marxist Cultural Theory." Pp. 158–78 in *The Raymond Williams Reader*, ed. John Higgins. Malden, MA: Blackwell.

Wilson, Rob

1995 "Tracking the Pacific Rim, Fast and Loose: Censorships, Diasporas, and the Return of the Cultural Uncanny." *Boundary* 2 22: 275–84.

Wilson, Walter T.

2001 "Urban Legends: Acts 10:1–11:18 and the Strategies of Greco-Roman Foundation Narratives." *Journal of Biblical Literature* 120: 77–99.

Wire, Antoinette Clark
　　1990　*The Corinthian Women Prophets: A Reconstruction through Paul's Rhetoric*. Minneapolis: Fortress.
Wong, Sau-ling Cynthia
　　1988　"Necessity and Extravagance in Maxine Hong Kingston's *The Woman Warrior:* Art and the Ethnic Experience." *MELUS* 15: 3–26.
　　1993　*Reading Asian American Literature: From Necessity to Extravagance*. Princeton, NJ: Princeton University Press.
　　1995a　"Denationalization Reconsidered: Asian American Cultural Criticism at a Theoretical Crossroads." *Amerasia Journal* 21: 1–27.
　　1995b　"'Sugar Sisterhood': Situating the Amy Tan Phenomenon." Pp. 174–210 in *The Ethnic Canon: Histories, Institutions, and Interventions*, ed. David Palumbo-Liu. Minneapolis: University of Minnesota Press.
　　1997　"Chinese American Literature." Pp. 39–61 in Cheung, ed. 1997b.
　　2001　"The Stakes of Textual Border-Crossing: Sinocentric, Asian American, and Feminist Critical Practices on Hualing Nieh's *Mulberry and Peach*." Pp. 130–52 in Chuh and Shimakawa, eds. 2001b.
Wong, Shelley Sunn
　　1994　"Unnaming the Same: Theresa Hak Kyung Cha's *Dictée*." Pp. 103–40 in Elaine Kim and Alarcón, eds. 1994.
Wood, David C.
　　2002　*Thinking after Heidegger*. Cambridge: Polity.
Wordelman, Amy L.
　　2003　"Cultural Divides and Dual Realities: A Greco-Roman Context for Acts 14." Pp. 205–32 in Penner and Stichele, eds. 2003.
Wray, Matthew
　　1997　"White Trash Religion." Pp. 193–210 in *White Trash: Race and Class in America*, ed. Matthew Wray and Annalee Newitz. New York: Routledge.
Wright, Richard
　　1998　*Black Boy*. Perennial ed. San Francisco: Harper Collins.
Yamamoto, Hisaye
　　2001　*Seventeen Syllables and Other Stories*. Rev. and expanded ed. New Brunswick, NJ: Rutgers University Press.
Yamamoto, Traise
　　1999　*Making Selves, Making Subjects: Japanese American Women, Identity, and the Body*. Berkeley: University of California Press.
Yamanaka, Lois-Ann
　　1997　*Blu's Hanging*. New York: Farrar, Straus and Giroux.
Yang, Fenggang
　　1999　*Chinese Christians in America: Conversion, Assimilation, and Adhesive Identities*. University Park: Pennsylvania State University Press.

Yarbro Collins, Adela
  1984   *Crisis and Catharsis: The Power of the Apocalypse.* Philadelphia: Westminster.
Yee, Gale A.
  2006   "Yin/Yang Is Not Me: An Exploration into an Asian American Biblical Hermeneutics." Pp. 152–63 in Foskett and Kuan, eds. 2006.
Yeğenoğlu, Meyda
  1998   *Colonial Fantasies: Towards a Feminist Reading of Orientalism.* New York: Cambridge University Press.
Yeo Khiok-khng
  1995   *Cross-Cultural Rhetorical Hermeneutics.* Hong Kong: Alliance Seminary.
  1998   *What Has Jerusalem to Do with Beijing? Biblical Interpretation from a Chinese Perspective.* Harrisburg: Trinity International.
  2001   *Eschatology and Hope: First and Second Epistles to the Thessalonians.* Hong Kong: Renewal Resources.
Young, Iris Marion
  1990   *Justice and the Politics of Difference.* Princeton, NJ: Princeton University Press.
Young, Robert J. C.
  1995   *Colonial Desire: Hybridity in Theory, Culture and Race.* New York: Routledge.
Yun, Chung-Hei
  1992   "Beyond 'Clay Walls': Korean American Literature." Pp. 79–95 in *Reading the Literature of Asian America,* ed. Shirley Geok-lin and Amy Ling. Philadelphia: Temple University Press.
Žižek, Slavoj
  1989   *The Sublime Object of Ideology.* New York: Verso.

Index

About the Author

TAT-SIONG BENNY LIEW is currently Associate Professor of the New Testament at the Pacific School of Religion in Berkeley, California. He is the author of *Politics of Parousia: Reading Mark Inter(con)textually* and guest editor of the *Semeia* volume on "The Bible in Asian America."

Production Notes for Liew / What Is Asian American Biblical Hermeneutics?

Designed by University of Hawai'i Press production staff with Sabon text and display in Tonneau

Composition by Josie Herr

Printing and binding by Versa Press, Inc.

Printed on 60# Accent Opaque, 435 ppi